From Martin
17.5.'6.

IN THE SHADOW OF NELSON

Admiral Charles Cotton. Painting by James Ramsey. © The British Museum. Reprinted with permission.

IN THE SHADOW OF NELSON

The Naval Leadership of Admiral Sir Charles Cotton, 1753–1812

PAUL C. KRAJESKI

Foreword by N.A.M. Rodger

Contributions in Military Studies, Number 184

Greenwood Press
Westport, Connecticut • London

Library of Congress Cataloging-in-Publication Data

Krajeski, Paul C., 1963–
In the shadow of Nelson : the naval leadership of Admiral Sir Charles Cotton, 1753–1812 / Paul C. Krajeski ; foreword by N.A.M. Rodger.
p. cm.—(Contributions in military studies, ISSN 0883–6884 ; no. 184)
Includes bibliographical references and index.
ISBN 0–313–31039–4 (alk. paper)
1. Cotton, Charles, Sir, 1753–1812. 2. Great Britain. Royal Navy—Officers Biography. 3. Great Britain—History, Naval—18th century. 4. Great Britain—History, Naval—19th century. 5. Admirals—Great Britain Biography. I. Title. II. Series.
DA87.1.C74K73 2000
940.2′745′092—dc21 99–15455
[B]

British Library Cataloguing in Publication Data is available.

Library of Congress Catalog Card Number: 99–15455
ISBN: 0–313–31039–4
ISSN: 0883–6884

First published in 2000

Greenwood Press, 88 Post Road West, Westport, CT 06881
An imprint of Greenwood Publishing Group, Inc.
www.greenwood.com

Printed in the United States of America

The paper used in this book complies with the Permanent Paper Standard issued by the National Information Standards Organization (Z39.48–1984).

10 9 8 7 6 5 4 3 2 1

To my wife, Margaret

Contents

Foreword

Posthumous fame fell very unevenly upon the sea officers of the Great Wars against France. Nelson was always in a class of his own. St.Vincent received two substantial biographies within thirty years of his death. In the course of the nineteenth century "Lives and Letters" of varying quality were published (often by admiring and uncritical relatives) of Duncan, Collingwood, Gambier, Howe, Keith, and Saumarez. Cochrane did it for himself, in still more laudatory terms. Yet other admirals, of equal or greater importance, such as Cornwallis, Hotham and Pellew, had to wait for a biography until the twentieth century. Many were done no justice until the Navy Records Society published their papers. Some, notably Lord Bridport, have been almost completely ignored to this day. At the same time a great number of lesser careers, including such frankly obscure and insignificant names as John Harvey Boteler, Frederick Hoffman, W.S. Lovell, C.V. Penrose, Charles Tyler, Bartholomew James, and William Wolseley, became known to history (and in most cases to the *Dictionary of National Biography*) for no other reason than that they or their relatives had published their lives.

Sir Charles Cotton is certainly one of the unlucky casualties of this process. In his lifetime he complained that fame had eluded him, and posterity has not until now done much to redress the balance. Though he had a full and successful career, and was the only admiral apart from St. Vincent to have commanded both the Channel and Mediterranean Fleets, he never led in a fleet action, which was until recently by far the best way to attract the notice of naval historians. Prudent, reliable, unspectacular service was his hallmark. He never did anything strikingly brilliant, but he never committed any notable blunders. Though some of his actions (notably his participation in the Convention of Cintra) aroused remark at the time, no major historical controversy has gathered around his name. He had the misfortune, moreover, to reach high rank after Trafalgar, when there was hardly any prospect of fleet action. The professional challenges he faced as a commander-in-chief had mainly to do with blockade, diplomacy and cooperation with the army: difficult, technical and unspectacular. Moreover he confined himself to his sea career more closely than many of his brother officers. He had no extended periods on half pay in wartime, and he declined to enter Parliament. Unlike many of his contemporaries, who were politicians as well as (if not as much as) admirals, he had no public life outside the Navy.

It is only in recent years that naval historians have come to appreciate that such a career as Cotton's has an interest which any number of Nelsons cannot supply. Exceptional men are, by definition, exceptional: they tell us about themselves alone. An admiral like Sir Charles Cotton, who rose to the top of his profession and assumed large responsibilities without ever having the chance to display any dazzling talents, is a much more revealing indicator of what a career in the Navy of his day was usually like, of what qualities the officer of human rather than superhuman gifts needed to rise to the top. In this sense it has a particular relevance today. Nelson's career can still inspire us, but Cotton's instructs us. There has never been another Nelson, but there have been, and are, many Cottons. He faced problems of complex logistics, amphibious operations, delicate negotiations with allies and neutrals, which are familiar to many senior officers now. Though the technology of warfare has changed completely in two centuries, these problems are with us still.

Paul Krajeski's admirable study, therefore, does more than simply rescue the life of an important senior officer from unmerited obscurity. It is a valuable contribution to history, but it also presents a career which has many points of interest and relevance for modern officers. Knowledge and judgment of political and diplomatic issues, tact and understanding in working with other services and other nations, administrative skill in managing large and complex forces with precarious lines of communication—all these are qualities which carried Cotton to high command, and which are still much in demand. Cotton suffered in his lifetime, and has suffered since, from the shadow of Nelson. He had neither the opportunity nor the talent to shine in that way; but the talents and opportunities he had, he used well. He deserves to be recalled for posterity, for the sake of his own merits, and for the interest and instruction which we can derive from his career.

N.A.M. Rodger

Preface

Through an examination of the career of Sir Charles Cotton, this book seeks to provide an insight into eighteenth-century British naval leadership and to develop a better understanding of the possibilities of British maritime power and amphibious operations. Cotton served in the Royal Navy over a forty-year period, from 1772 to 1812, actively employed for all but the ten years between 1783 and 1793. His experiences were typical for his generation of British naval officers, who participated in the war for American independence as junior officers and assumed leadership of the Royal Navy during the wars of the French Revolution and Napoleon. The leadership required of officers during this troubled time depended on technical and tactical mastery of their profession developed over a lifetime of naval service. This is by no means a controversial assertion. Cotton's career nonetheless provides a fresh perspective on leadership development and helps us understand why the Royal Navy had so many capable post captains and admirals from 1793 to 1815.

During the Napoleonic period, the British government struggled to find the most effective way to apply its maritime power against the land power of its French adversary. The opposition in parliament often criticized the administration for frittering away scarce resources on the conquest of "sugar islands." Not until British involvement in the Peninsular War (1808–1814) did British maritime power realize its full potential as a weapon in the allied arsenal against France. Thanks to the Royal Navy's force projection capability, Britain was able to project its land power upon the Continent to directly confront the source of Napoleon's strength—his armies. Lest we forget, forty-two days after the Battle of Trafalgar, Napoleon achieved his greatest victory at Austerlitz, which destroyed the Third Coalition and apocryphally hastened the death of the British chief minister, William Pitt. The impact of the Peninsular

War on French military power was not as subject to interpretation. With British maritime resources providing nearly unrestricted support for the war's duration, the allied army operating in Spain and Portugal proved a thorn in Napoleon's side. Because Cotton held three major commands around the Iberian Peninsula from 1808 to 1812, an understanding of his contributions is necessary to fully comprehend how British maritime power and amphibious operations eroded Napoleon's military strength. Furthermore, elaboration on the details of naval and amphibious operations around the peninsula can provide insight into how Britain maintained the superiority at sea she attained at Trafalgar. The French naval threat did not disappear after 1805, and Napoleon's armies remained very active in the littoral environment. It was in this period that Sir Charles Cotton made his most noteworthy and visible contributions to the cause.

This work would not have progressed without the assistance of several institutions and the generosity of many people. Most helpful were the staffs of the United States Military Academy Library, especially Faith Coslett; the Strozier Library at Florida State University; the Cambridgeshire County Record Office, particularly Philip Saunders; the Public Record Office, Kew; and the Special Collections at the University of Southampton. The staffs at the British Library, National Maritime Museum, Library of Congress, New York Public Library, and Yale's Sterling Memorial Library also deserve special recognition for assisting me with their collections.

Several individuals guided and motivated me throughout this project. Foremost among them is Donald Horward of Florida State University, who originally suggested the topic. Brian DeToy proved a wellspring of research advice and generated countless questions that we enthusiastically discussed. William Flayhart of Delaware State University, Linda Frey of the University of Montana, Dennis Showalter of Colorado College, and Jeremy Black of the University of Exeter helped me shape the manuscript with their useful comments. Vincent Tedesco was a godsend for help with my maps, and Versalle Washington generously showed me how to prepare a camera-ready manuscript. Colonels James Johnson and Cole Kingseed of the United States Military Academy facilitated my research by helping me resolve time-management issues. Words inadequately express my deep appreciation to Matt Dawson, Kevin Farrell, and Chris Kolenda for sharing with me the challenges of their research experiences. I must gratefully acknowledge the assistance of the Honorary Archivist of Madingley Hall, Lionel Munby, who patiently answered all of my queries and selflessly provided additional information.

I am indebted to the research grants provided by the Faculty Development Research Fund of the United States Military Academy, funded by the Association of Graduates.

My family has been a source of strength and inspiration during the sometimes seemingly endless progression of this book. I thank my parents, Vernon and Catherine, for constantly "pulling for me" with their prayers. I am especially indebted to my dad for his work on the index. To my children, Elena and Stephen, thank you for your patience. My wife, Margaret, has been a source of strength who has always believed in my ability to finish this work. She deserves much of the credit for its completion.

To benefit the reader, I have adjusted capitalization and punctuation in primary source extracts to reflect modern grammar and writing style. Though many have helped me complete this work, I alone am responsible for any of its shortcomings.

Introduction

> I wish to look at the picture in the most favourable point of view, and have no desire to hunt after defects. But if they are brought before me, if they are pointed out to my understanding, I think it my duty to notice them. . . . Vice and deformity should be held up for execration as well as virtue and good conduct for imitation.
>
> —James Ralfe to Dr. Thomas Morgan, 13 January 1825[1]

Thirteen years after Admiral Sir Charles Cotton's death, James Ralfe began compiling biographical information for what he would publish in 1828 as *The Naval Biography of Great Britain* in four volumes. He intended to present as accurately as possible a picture of each officer's naval career and did not want to misrepresent an officer's overall performance by focusing too narrowly on any specific event. However, if he were to make an incorrect assessment, he wished rather to "err on the side of praise than on that of censure."[2] With this injunction in mind, Ralfe sent an inquiry requesting data on the late admiral to Dr. Thomas Morgan, who had served under Cotton's flag for nine years as a secretary and had furnished papers for the admiral's biographical memoir that appeared in *The Naval Chronicle* in 1812. Morgan had no new additional information about his former employer, and furthermore, he could not authenticate the accuracy of a report brought to Ralfe's attention that shed unfavorable light upon Cotton's career. The report claimed that Cotton had avoided a confrontation with two French warships off the coast of Ireland while commanding the *Mars* in 1795. When a subordinate officer mentioned that the enemy warships were likely to attack, Cotton allegedly replied: "Well, we'll give them as good as they send," thus insinuating cowardice.[3] Ultimately, Ralfe's biographical sketch of Cotton was not notably different from the original memoir; Cotton's legacy was shaped initially by the perceptions of a personal acquaintance and second by an author who wished to "err on the side of praise"—hardly the foundation for an unbiased assessment of this relatively unknown yet important figure in British naval history.

Cotton is one of many British admirals whose contribution to the Royal Navy during the Napoleonic wars was long overshadowed by the Nelsonian mystic and leadership paradigm. With a captivating personality and a heroic career that culminated in death at the Battle of Trafalgar on 21 October 1805 and near deification by the British public, Vice Admiral Lord Horatio Nelson became the standard by which other admirals of the period were measured. There were risk-taking admirals like Nelson who took offensive action with a spirit of aggression and self-confidence whenever opportunity occurred, and there were those who did not. Although many British naval officers wished to emulate Nelson and his "band of brothers," the opportunity for heroism against the enemy did not occur with regularity during the Napoleonic wars, especially after Trafalgar. Instead, officers and men of the Royal Navy most often faced the drudgery of escort and blockade duty. Despite the occasional pursuit of enemy merchantmen or isolated warships, the common experience was that of monotonous routine. It follows that the Nelsonian stereotype of leadership—charismatic, opportunistic aggressiveness—did not represent the leadership style necessary for the average British naval officer to successfully accomplish the typical activities of the Royal Navy during the Napoleonic period.

A broader understanding of British naval leadership during the late eighteenth century can be gained through a balanced assessment of Cotton's career, which spanned thirty-eight years and included a wealth of diverse experiences. He not only blockaded French ports for several years but also participated in a few of the great fleet actions of the era, including Admiral Sir George Rodney's Battle of The Saintes in 1782 and Admiral Lord Richard Howe's Battle of Ushant on "The Glorious First of June" in 1794. Although Cotton participated in other engagements that earned a few lines in subsequent naval histories, due recognition eluded him during his time and for the past two hundred years. For instance, Cotton, along with Vice Admiral Lord Cuthbert Collingwood, was one of the officers not awarded a gold medal for "The Glorious First of June."[4] The light of honor shone brightly on a man decorated by the king with a medal. Of little consolation to Cotton was the fact that Lord Howe did not intend to establish such exclusive reward criteria. Further illustrating Cotton's low historical profile, one British historian proclaimed Cotton to be "one of the most famous admirals of his day."[5] Yet, he disregarded Cotton's command of the Mediterranean and Channel fleets from 1810 to 1812—he asserted that Cotton's command at Lisbon in 1808 "was the last service he was enabled to render his country."

It seems Cotton clearly understood that history would little recognize his contributions. Eleven years after "The Glorious First of June," Collingwood reaped fame at Trafalgar with Nelson while an apparent twist of fate marooned

Cotton to blockade duty off the coast of Brittany. A frustrated man lamented to his wife: "I have gulped the bitter pill again."[6] After two more years with additional disappointments, the unpalatable taste of obscurity subsided when Cotton was appointed commander of a squadron based at Lisbon. This squadron became instrumental in creating the initial crack in Napoleon's veneer of military invincibility—a crack that became a trap from which Napoleon could not escape. Napoleon's loss of nearly 300,000 troops during the Peninsular War from 1808 to 1814 contributed immensely to the collapse of his empire.[7]

Cotton's command influence on the Peninsular War extended along the entire Iberian coastline in three chronologically and geographically distinct increments from 1808 until his death in 1812. Having arrived off Lisbon in January 1808, Cotton used his squadron to shape an environment along the Portuguese coast that ensured the successful landing of a large body of British troops. His squadron's active involvement with the Portuguese promoted a cooperative civil-military relationship that supported the operations of Lieutenant General Sir Arthur Wellesley, the future Duke of Wellington, throughout the campaign that summer. Furthermore, Cotton's squadron conducted diversionary amphibious operations in support of Wellesley's army and directed the deployment of transports as they arrived off the Portuguese coast with reinforcements and supplies. After Wellesley defeated the French army in Portugal, Cotton became involved in the negotiations that culminated with the infamous Convention of Cintra, which repatriated a French army laden with Portuguese loot. Many in that army returned to fight in Iberia. In hindsight, Cotton's experience in Portugal was the high-water mark of his naval career, even though he would still command two more fleets.

Cotton lowered his flag from the Lisbon command in January 1809, but raised it again in April 1810 to assume command of the Mediterranean Fleet, the most important and challenging command in the Royal Navy. This command stretched from Cape St. Vincent in southern Spain to the Dardanelles, well over 2,000 miles. The Mediterranean Fleet commander had more than naval operations to consider because of his geographical separation from Britain and the nature of his fleet's relationship with numerous foreign governments. He also needed diplomatic skills and the ability to anticipate decisions made in London, often several weeks away by packet ship. Among many regions within the jurisdiction of the Mediterranean Fleet, Cotton's decisions particularly affected military operations in the Spanish provinces of Catalonia, Valencia, Murcia, and Andalusia.

After fourteen months on station in the Mediterranean, Cotton assumed command of the prestigious Channel Fleet in August 1811. The Channel Fleet commander's primary responsibilities were home island defense and blockade of the French Atlantic ports. He was also responsible for naval operations along the coast of northern Spain. British interest in naval operations off this portion of the Spanish coast intensified in 1811 as the tide of Wellington's military operations in Spain advanced towards the Pyrenees. The most significant period of this activity occurred after Cotton's death in February 1812 with the operations of Rear Admiral Sir Home Popham and the shift of the British army's supply base from Lisbon to Santander. Notwithstanding the short, six-month duration of his Channel command, the extent to which Cotton influenced affairs in northern Spain merits examination.

Historians have neglected Cotton's aggregate contribution to the Peninsular War and the maritime dimension of that struggle for several reasons, particularly the absence of a major fleet action during the war. After Trafalgar, the Royal Navy settled into the laborious task of maintaining its naval superiority. Blockade and force protection duty did not inspire the imagination nor achieve the immediately quantifiable results of a fleet action. Instead, the Royal Navy's role was defined predominantly in terms of its support to the British army's operations in Spain and Portugal. Although recent works have emphasized the critical nature of this support, most historians still recognize that the Peninsular War was fundamentally a continental war, not a maritime one. An additional factor discouraging a naval account of the war was the geographically dispersed nature of naval operations around the Iberian peninsula, which was not as conducive to cogent historical accounts as were the centralized military operations of Wellington's army. Finally, British naval officers in general did not memorialize their experiences in the Napoleonic wars as prolifically as their counterparts in the army.

However, the decentralized nature of naval operations during the age of sail required commanders to communicate prolifically in writing. Fortunately, the Admiralty kept meticulous records in the late eighteenth century, preserving an abundance of documents and dispatches associated with Cotton's naval career. Few have used them for a meaningful analysis of that career. The best analysis appeared in Dr. Donald D. Horward's "Portugal and the Anglo-Russian Naval Crisis, 1808" in *Naval War College Review* (1981). Horward's article was the only published scholarly account of Cotton's performance in the Royal Navy until this study. Other historians have discussed Cotton's role in Portugal, but with an almost exclusive focus on the Convention of Cintra. Other than Horward's article, historical accounts of Cotton's career have lacked detailed analysis and insight into his character and ability.

Cyril Northcote Parkinson described Cotton as an admiral whose abilities seemed to be "mainly administrative."[8] Parkinson lauds Cotton as an admiral of ability, but the implication is obvious—Cotton lacked the Nelsonian characteristic of inspirational leadership. Parkinson's assessment seems to have merit. Some evidence suggests that Cotton was not merely uninspiring, but incompetent as well. For example, while serving as second-in-command of the Channel Fleet in 1806, Cotton had somehow failed to impress the First Lord of the Admiralty, Thomas Grenville. In scathing remarks to his brother, Grenville stated, "[My] present difficulty is about Cotton whose claims are hourly growing by serving in the Channel Fleet to reach the command of it, for which he is, as I believe, entirely unfit."[9] Still, many of Cotton's contemporaries held him in high esteem. Admiral Collingwood, who is regarded by many historians as Nelson's peer in terms of ability, allegedly responded to a query about the Channel Fleet that "he never would command the Channel Fleet when [Cotton's] flag was flying." This remark was not derogatory, but intended to compliment Cotton's professional abilities.[10] Of course, a few opinions presented with limited context are no foundation upon which to judge Cotton's character and ability. An impartial assessment must span an entire career and not, as Ralfe said, "look too narrowly" into one particular aspect.

The profile of Admiral Sir Charles Cotton developed in this work does more than provide insight into British naval leadership of the eighteenth century. It also contributes to a growing base of knowledge about the Royal Navy's role in the Peninsular War, for which numerous histories of its land campaigns already exist. A better comprehension of how British naval and land forces cooperated enhances the value of studying the Peninsular War as the world enters the twenty-first century, a period of uncertainty in which international prosperity and security likely will be promoted and enforced by the land, sea, and air forces of traditional alliances and hasty coalitions. In other words, it is unlikely that future threats to the stability of the international community will be countered unilaterally by one service component or one nation. As occurred during the Peninsular War, when the British army and navy had to synchronize their operations while cooperating with the armed forces of Portugal and Spain, twentieth-century warfare will present similar challenges requiring joint and combined cooperation. Technologies have changed, but how personalities, interservice rivalry, national will, international rivalry, and geography affect warfare have remained remarkably consistent over the last two hundred years. The naval career of Sir Charles Cotton provides a window through which to catch a glimpse of how these "threads of continuity" have affected and continue to affect the human experience of warfare.

NOTES

1. James Ralfe to Dr. Thomas Morgan, 13 January 1825, National Maritime Museum, Greenwich, MSS, AGC/36/50/MS.0145.

2. Ibid.

3. Ralfe to Morgan, 13 January 1825, Morgan to Ralfe, 5 December 1824, 13 February 1825, National Maritime Museum, AGC/36/50/MS.0145.

4. After filing a protest, Collingwood later received a gold medal.

5. Charles R. Low, *Her Majesty's Navy* (New York, 1892), 3: 205–207.

6. Vice Admiral Sir Charles Cotton to Lady Philadelphia Cotton, 11 November 1805, Cambridgeshire County Record Office, Cambridge, England, MSS, Cotton Naval Papers, 588/c71.

7. Estimates on the number of French casualties during the Peninsular War vary between 200,000 and 300,000. An accurate casualty figure is difficult to assess because of the war's duration and the geographical and organizational fragmentation of the

French army operating in Spain and Portugal. In Donald D. Horward's article "British Seapower and Its Influence upon the Peninisular War, 1808–1814," *Naval War College Review*, 31 (1978): 54–71, the author posits that 300,000 French soldiers died during the war.

8. Cyril Northcote Parkinson, *Britannia Rules: The Classic Age of Naval History, 1793–1815* (London, 1977), 128.

9. Thomas Grenville to George Grenville, Lord Buckingham, 25 November 1806, Huntington Library, San Marino, California, Stowe-Grenville Collection, Box 37.

10. Captain Charles Boyles to Cotton, 25 May 1811, National Maritime Museum, AGC/36/50/MS.0145.

1

A Commissioned Sea Officer: The Formative Years, 1772–1783

> The Navy in the mid-eighteenth century was remarkably effective in advancing men of ability, and, equally important, retarding those without it.
>
> —N.A.M. Rodger[1]

The only American World War II cemetery in Britain is located three miles west of the university city of Cambridge on Highway A–1303. Unofficially called the Madingley American Cemetery, it is the burial place for 3,811 servicemembers and a memorial for 5,216 of others whose bodies were never recovered or identified from the Battle of the Atlantic and the strategic bombing campaign of northwest Europe. This thirty-acre cemetery is located on what was once the southeastern portion of the Cotton family estate, which traces its regional origins from the beginning of the thirteenth century. Sir Charles Cotton, fifth baronet of Madingley, managed the land on which this cemetery lies for many of the years that he lived, from 1753 until 1812. Like the Americans memorialized there today, Cotton's life was best characterized by service and commitment, to both his country and family.[2]

The family's heritage of service to country dated to the seventeenth century, when Sir John Cotton was created a baronet on 14 July 1641. As High Sheriff of Cambridgeshire in the Great Rebellion, he was said to have proclaimed the Earl of Essex a traitor in every market town and to have taken up arms for King Charles. He allegedly delivered the plate of the University of Cambridge to the king at Oxford, despite being challenged by a troop of Cromwell's horse. Sir John Hynde Cotton, third baronet of Madingley, was a prominent member for the town of Cambridge in several parliaments during the reigns of Queen Anne, George I, and George II. As one of the chief supporters of the Tory party, he was a loyal opponent of Sir Robert Walpole's administration. His son,

Charles Cotton's father, continued the family tradition of service as a member of Parliament in 1741 for St. Germains in Cornwall, in 1752 for Marlborough upon Sir John Hynde Cotton's death, and in 1765 and 1774 for the county of Cambridge. Because of the deaths of Charles' two older brothers, he succeeded to the baronetcy upon his father's death on 23 January 1795.[3]

For Britons of Charles Cotton's class, the landed establishment, service to king and country were expected norms, whether under arms or in politics. The strong inclination of this class to serve was motivated as much by the need for self-preservation as it was by selfless patriotism. The strength and durability of this ruling order needed to be demonstrated to convince itself and those being ruled of its right and ability to maintain and exercise power. Other less self-serving forces propelled Britons into the king's service. Without question, the vast economic and territorial power of this class launched many careers in local government and parliament. The forces that propelled the sons of Britain's elite into the army or navy, however, were notably different.[4]

A peer's first-born son inherited his estate, thereby freeing subsequent sons from the responsibilities of administration and maintenance. Less fortunate children within the primogeniture system were more likely to answer the call to military or naval service or a religious vocation. For many, like Charles Cotton, a natural inclination for the sea apparently did more to inspire naval service than did the lack of opportunity at home. Cotton's biographical memoir in the contemporary *Naval Chronicle* claimed that even in boyhood his propensity to "embrace the nautical profession was strongly apparent."[5] He reinforced this notion when he withdrew from membership at Lincoln's Inn, one of four such schools that had existed in London since the fourteenth century for the study of law. After a brief period in London, the allure of naval service proved stronger than his father's desire that he practice law—Charles Cotton went to sea for the first time as an eighteen year old.

Not long after Charles left Lincoln's Inn, which was likely in 1781, Sir John Hynde Cotton sent him on an East Indiaman to India. Perhaps the elder Cotton subsidized this voyage to persuade his son about the sense of a career in law rather than a life at sea. If so, the baronet failed. Charles returned from India with a zeal for naval service. Resigned to his son's wishes, Sir John Hynde resolved to take advantage of his friendship with the First Lord of the Admiralty, John Montagu, Fourth Earl of Sandwich. With support from the controversial yet capable Sandwich, Cotton overcame the only real obstacle for entrance into the naval service—lack of patronage. He joined the 20-gun *Deal Castle* as a midshipman on 24 October 1772.[6]

Patronage, for all its alleged faults, was an effective system in its time. It was process by which someone with power interceded on behalf of a young officer to ensure that he received the necessary assignments for advancement. The modern negative view of patronage is based on the assumption that an organization is best served by merit-based promotions, without the corrupting effect of self-interest. Yet the system of patronage used by the Royal Navy in the eighteenth century, detrimental as it might seem at first, actually helped advance competent officers who might have been overlooked by a modern merit-based promotion system. Admittedly, incompetent officers might also benefit by the patronage system. According to a twentieth century British naval officer, if the applicants for naval service in the eighteenth century were subjected to modern entry requirements, the likes of a Nelson would have been replaced by mediocrities. How then did an apparently inefficient system manage to provide the Royal Navy during Cotton's lifetime with so many capable officers?[7]

An appreciation of the differences between political and naval patronage provides the basis for answering this question. Political patronage might have been the mechanism by which many entered the service and some advanced, but by and large, the mechanism of naval patronage driven by professional concerns determined advancement in the Royal Navy. A senior officer who commanded loyalty and respect had the advantage over a less capable officer. The competent officer could attract subordinates eager to serve with him—an important benefit when highly competent officers were scarce, especially in wartime. Conversely, subordinates who attached themselves to a rising star were likely to reap the benefits of prize money or more rapid advancement. On overseas stations, an admiral often filled key vacancies with officers who served on his flagship. In summation, patronage effectively identified and promoted worthy officers as well as some who were unworthy to command. The system was not always fair or impartial, but British naval success in the eighteenth century attested to its utility. The system clearly benefited Cotton early in his career, especially considering the strong control over naval patronage that Earl Sandwich exercised. Sir John Hynde Cotton's relationship with the First Lord of the Admiralty and his son's appointment on 27 October 1778 to HMS *Ardent*, flagship of Rear Admiral James Gambier, were fortunate circumstances that helped propel Charles rapidly through the lower echelons of rank. Patronage was vital for promotion, but experience in American waters proved the major factor that propelled his career.[8]

Britain was at war for twenty-eight of Cotton's thirty-eight years of naval service. During the war for American independence, he served eight of those years off the waters of North America and in the West Indies. He left the *Deal Castle* and home waters in September 1775 and sailed to North America as an acting lieutenant aboard the 32-gun frigate *Niger*, commanded by Captain George Talbot. Vice Admiral Sir Thomas Graves, commander-in-chief of the fleet on the American station, posted the *Niger* off Cape Cod harbor to support British army operations in and around Boston. Cotton had arrived on the North American coast at the beginning of a very active period for the Royal Navy. The *Niger* participated in the evacuation of the British army from Boston on 17 March 1776. Cotton also served in another major combined operation when the *Niger* supported the Long Island campaign of August 1776. This complex operation succeeded in driving Washington's army out of New York City, but the revolutionaries survived to fight another day.[9]

On 12 July 1776, Vice Admiral Lord Richard Howe assumed command of the fleet on the American station in time to direct naval operations for the Long Island campaign. He remained in this position until tendering his resignation in 1778 because of a disagreement with the government in London. It was Howe who confirmed Cotton in the rank of lieutenant on 29 April 1777. Promotion to lieutenant required a midshipman to pass an examination—the only test of an officer's professional ability regulated by the navy. To qualify for the exam, an officer candidate must have attained the age of twenty and served at least three years as a midshipman and three years at sea in another capacity. The exam was designed to confirm that a midshipman had mastered the rudimentary knowledge of the naval profession. It was normally administered in London, but Cotton probably took his exam in North American waters. Since Cotton's apprenticeship in the navy had not reached six years upon his confirmation as lieutenant, the navy likely recognized the value of his earlier cruise to India.[10]

After Cotton's confirmation, Howe assigned him to the 16-gun sloop *Vigilant*, the former *Empress of Russia* purchased by the Royal Navy that year in North America. The *Empress of Russia*, a "large transport well-armed," recently had spent time off the Boston lighthouse protecting the artificers there. The Royal Navy eventually fitted the vessel with twenty-eight guns as an armed ship under the command of Captain H.C. Christian.[11]

Cotton's first assignment on the *Vigilant* was in a combined operation off the Delaware River and Chesapeake Bay in support of landings that were key to British strategy in 1777. Lieutenant General Sir William Howe, commander-in-chief of the British Army in America and brother of Admiral Lord Richard Howe, recently had decided to shift the main effort of his military operations from New England to the Middle Atlantic colonies. Lieutenant General Sir John Burgoyne's force would advance from Canada to Albany, intending to join a force from New York sent by Howe up the Hudson Valley. To Burgoyne's regret, the supporting force from New York was smaller than he had anticipated because General Howe had a new plan. The British strategy of crushing the rebellion in New England, although not completely abandoned, was now redefined by General Howe as a supporting effort to end the war by capturing Philadelphia and overrunning the Middle Colonies.[12]

A convoy with 14,000 troops destined for Philadelphia via the Delaware River sailed from New York on 23 July 1777. Upon the army's arrival at the mouth of the Delaware, a frigate captain informed General Howe that American defenses and difficult navigation conditions made a landing operation in the Delaware extremely risky. Consequently, Howe decided to proceed through the Chesapeake to disembark at Head of Elk. Twenty-five days later, on 25 August, the army landed. The *Vigilant* was one of six ships appointed to cover the landing. Cotton's *Naval Chronicle* memoir stated that he was involved "in the arduous duty of protecting the landing of troops, and in other services, as occasion required," yet details of his involvement were omitted. Nevertheless, Cotton's participation in this combined operation certainly advanced his education about the nature of military and naval cooperation. The frequency and difficulty of combined operations in the eighteenth century made experience the best teacher for the conscientious naval officer.[13]

As frequent and difficult as combined operations were, eighteenth-century military and naval commanders displayed a surprising professional ambivalence toward this kind of war. This attitude existed because the British army focused predominantly on fighting land battles at the end of a presumed secure line of communication while the Royal Navy focused on securing that line by gaining and maintaining naval superiority. As a result, amphibious warfare in the littoral environment that connected the two services received little theoretical attention. A concerted effort to advance the study of amphibious warfare was launched in the midst of the Seven Years' War with the publication of a treatise that expressed the intent to reduce this "amphibious kind of warfare to some safe, regular system, to leave as little as we can to fortune and her caprices."[14] Despite worthy efforts by eighteenth-century writers to identify and disseminate ideas about amphibious warfare, the school of experience remained the most common teacher for British naval and military officers.[15]

Cotton's schooling continued after he left the *Vigilant* and joined the *Ardent* on 27 October 1778. He served five months on this flagship until Admiral Gambier, who had succeeded Lord Howe as commander-in-chief on the North American station, appointed him to command the 32-gun storeship *Grampus* on 3 April 1779. Cotton's rapid promotion through the ranks continued four months later on 10 August with an appointment to post rank as captain of HMS *Boyne* of 70-guns. At the age of twenty-six and less than seven years after entering the navy, Captain Cotton assumed responsibility for a third rate ship-of-the-line with 520 crewmembers. By comparison, the twenty-year-old Nelson attained post rank on 11 June 1779, also about seven years after becoming a midshipman. Cotton joined the *Boyne* while on service in the Leeward Islands, a station where the Royal Navy waged a war markedly different from the one in North America.[16]

The war for American independence had expanded to the West Indies after Burgoyne's decisive defeat at Saratoga in October 1777. The French sensed Britain's vulnerability and signed treaties of commerce and alliance with the United States on 6 February 1778. This launched France into a maritime and colonial struggle with the high stakes of West Indian trade and American independence hanging in the balance. In the Caribbean, both France and Britain had strong economic interests; both nations were determined to defend their colonies with naval and military reinforcements. Despite Britain's strong military and naval presence in the West Indies, its security was undermined by the geographic disposition of French possessions; with French and British territory in the Lesser Antilles interspersed and in close proximity, naval superiority for either power did not eliminate the threat of invasion from a neighboring island. The British lost Dominica and the French lost St. Lucia in 1778. Furthermore, a squadron's stealthy departure from port also posed a threat to the security of the trade convoys, on which the colonies heavily depended for supplies. The "want of provisions for the necessary supply of the King's ships employed in these seas" was an unrelenting concern for the commander of His Majesty's ships employed in the Caribbean.[17]

The Royal Navy's organization in the West Indies consisted of two separate stations: the Leeward Islands and Jamaica stations. In the summer of 1779, Rear Admiral Sir Hyde Parker temporarily commanded the former and Rear Admiral Peter Parker commanded the latter. That summer Cotton joined the Leeward Islands station to participate in the arduous task of protecting the islands and the trade routes. Initially, Cotton's *Boyne* and the rest of the fleet remained inactive as they waited out the hurricane season. Once the weather improved, Hyde Parker issued orders to Cotton on 29 October 1779 placing him under the command of Captain Alan Gardner of HMS *Sultan*.[18] The next three years would be some of the most eventful of Cotton's career. They were heralded by the arrival at Barbados on 17 March 1780 of Admiral Sir George Rodney, who assumed command of the entire West Indies station.

Rodney had been given the command despite a somewhat dubious reputation. His lavish lifestyle and notoriety for raiding the public till had put him in debt and caused him to lose the trust of many in government and of the West India merchants. Upon his return to England from command at Jamaica from 1771 to 1774, Rodney had to live in Paris to avoid his creditors and, ironically, returned home in 1778 only after receiving a loan from a marshal of France. Although he was self-absorbed and financially reckless, Rodney had earned the reputation as an aggressive naval officer from his exploits at the Second Battle of Finisterre in October 1747 and the capture of Martinique in 1762. One month after arriving at Barbados, he confirmed that reputation and set an example for a young naval officer from Cambridgeshire. Rodney promptly issued orders to Cotton:

> You are in particular "to use your utmost endeavours to take or destroy all ships and vessels belonging to France and French subjects, Spain and Spanish subjects, and to His Majesty's rebellious North American subjects which you may discover and be able to come up with and by every means in your power to annoy and distress His Majesty's said enemys, wherever there may be a probability of success" and for so doing this shall be your order.[19]

The 22 March 1780 arrival at Fort Royal Bay, Martinique, of a convoy from France consisting of sixteen ships-of-the-line and eighty-three transports gave Cotton a superb opportunity to "annoy and distress" the enemy as Rodney had ordered.[20]

Luc-Urbain du Bouexic, Comte de Guichen, now commanded the French fleet in the West Indies. He quickly devised a plan to recapture St. Lucia or take Barbados from the British. Under the guise of convoy escort duty to St. Domingo, Admiral de Guichen planned to use his fleet to entice Rodney's ships to sea and then turn back on the undefended islands. Rodney and de Guichen had twenty-one and twenty-two battleships respectively, but the British ships were sluggish because of their extended time on station—an advantage that de Guichen hoped to exploit with his quicker, more recently refitted ships. The French fleet sailed on the night of 13/14 April, and as expected, Rodney's fleet began the chase at noon on the 16th.

The *Boyne* was second astern of Rodney's flagship, HMS *Sandwich*, in the center division. Rear Admiral Joshua Rowley, Cotton's future father-in-law, commanded the rear division and Hyde Parker commanded the van. What became known as the Battle of Martinique proved indecisive. When the two fleets drew parallel on the morning of 17 April at a distance of four or five leagues, Rodney planned to concentrate his ships to attack the French rear. Through a series of missed signals and a rigid adherence to the Fighting Instructions, Rodney failed to convey fully his intent to the rear and van divisions. Furthermore, de Guichen somehow divined Rodney's intent and changed the direction of his fleet as the British began to bear down. After subsequent maneuvering, the fleets entered a general engagement at 1:30 p.m. Although his fleet failed to concentrate according to instructions, Rodney lived up to his reputation as one of the best tacticians of his day by leading his division directly into the French center. The ensuing battle did not result in the mêlée associated with breaking the enemy's line, but it was nevertheless an intense engagement. Rodney's 98-gun flagship sustained seventy shot in her hull, tottering masts, and sixty-four casualties while discharging 3,260 round-shot, sixty grape, and 100 of langridge, a type of case shot loaded with scrap iron for damaging sails and rigging. Inexplicably, support from the ships astern of the *Sandwich* was inadequate. As noted by Captain John Bazely of the repeater frigate *Pegasus*, "3 ships on to the Sandwich at a time and Verry Ill supported by the Ships in her Division astern."[21]

Why Cotton's ship and the other two astern of Rodney did not engage the enemy cannot be adequately explained. The *Boyne* did sustain four casualties, but that pales in comparison to the thirty-two, twenty, and seventy casualties sustained by each of the three ships ahead of Rodney. If casualty figures are the standard of measurement, then in this situation Cotton appears a cautious, nonaggressive commander. Misunderstandings or ignorance of Rodney's instructions explain some of the blunders committed by other commanders that day, but these excuses did not seem to plausibly explain Cotton's absence from the heat of battle. Rodney's example should have made the course of action to follow clear to the commander of the *Boyne*. Rodney later accused many of his officers of failing to "properly" support the "British flag" at the Battle of Martinique.[22] Cotton certainly was troubled by the blanket accusation, even though there might have been mitigating circumstances that kept the *Boyne* out of the fight. Ultimately, Rodney's attempt to overtake the French failed; his fleet returned to Gros Islet Bay, St. Lucia, on 27 April. Although de Guichen's fleet was not decisively defeated, Rodney had frustrated its attempt to invade Barbados and forced it to find anchorage to the north at Guadaloupe. The Battle of Martinique was a tactical draw, but a British strategic victory. During the fleet's brief time in port, carpenters, shipwrights, and riggers worked furiously to make it seaworthy. After only two weeks in port, Rodney's spirit of aggression gave Cotton the chance to redeem his damaged reputation. On 6 May 1780, Rodney again sent his ships to sea in pursuit of de Guichen, whose fleet the British sighted to windward of Martinique four days later. Rodney's fleet struggled to draw close enough for an engagement because the French had the advantage of being to windward and had better sailing ships. Finally, the fleets drew up, and two engagements followed on 15 and 19 May. Again, Rodney could not win a decisive victory against de Guichen's force, but the British admiral's insistence on strict obedience to his orders helped. The tighter discipline of his officers had significantly improved the fighting ability of the fleet since the Battle of Martinique. Cotton's crew sustained no casualties during these engagements because the opportunity for combat presented itself to only a portion of the fleet. Even Rodney's temporary flagship, the frigate *Venus*, sustained no casualties. Besides lack of aggressiveness or opportunity, another reason that helps explain Cotton's indecisive involvement in the naval engagements of April and May 1780 was the condition of the *Boyne*. While chasing de Guichen's fleet after the action of 19 May, Cotton sent a dispatch to Rodney explaining the poor seaworthiness of his vessel. Rodney's response acknowledged the distress of the *Boyne*, offered words of encouragement to its captain, and subsequently ordered it to Gros Islet Bay while the remainder of the fleet sailed to Barbados.[23]

Rodney's aggressive tactics did not eliminate the threat to British interests in the West Indies. On 6 June 1780, a frigate screen sighted a Spanish convoy of twenty ships-of-the-line and about 100 transports and merchant vessels 150 miles to the windward of Martinique. The prospect of a combined Franco-Spanish fleet of thirty-four ships-of-the-line against now only seventeen British ships-of-the-line posed a renewed threat to Rodney. The French and Spanish fleets did join, but Rodney failed in an attempt to bring them to battle that June. In early July the crisis ended with the arrival of reinforcements from England; the Franco-Spanish fleet sailed west to the Greater Antilles. However, the game of naval cat-and-mouse had already ended for Cotton. Shipwrights condemned the *Boyne* upon its arrival at Gros Islet Bay in late May. It was no longer of use in the West Indies. On 10 June, Rodney dispatched instructions for Cotton to sail to English Harbor, Antigua, and then proceed with the next convoy to England. Rodney also gave the *Boyne* priority for repair from all caulkers available at St. Lucia. Shipwrights thus spent the remainder of June and the better part of July making the *Boyne* seaworthy enough for its passage across the Atlantic.[24]

While he waited for the repair of his ship at Gros Islet Bay, Cotton apparently favorably impressed his future father-in-law, Sir Joshua Rowley, under whose command he then belonged. Whatever the nature of their relationship, their time together was short. In mid-July Rodney ordered Rowley to reinforce the Jamaica station with nine ships-of-the-line. Upon Rowley's departure from St. Lucia, Cotton came under the command of Commodore William Hotham, who supplemented Rodney's instructions for Cotton's voyage to England. Hotham ordered Cotton to proceed in the *Boyne* to collect the homeward-bound trade at Carlisle Bay, Barbados. On the way there he would escort the frigate *Brune*, laden with a large sum of money. From Barbados he was to pick up the trade convoy at Antigua and proceed to St. Kitts with an arrival no later than 30 July. Hotham also ordered Cotton to transport the invalids from Barbados and Antigua to England. Finally, he instructed Cotton to disembark his contingent of marines on one of Rodney's ships in the West Indies before proceeding to England.[25]

When the August trade convoy assembled off St. Kitts, it consisted of seventy-four merchant ships, the *Boyne*, and HMS *Preston* of 50-guns. The *Preston*'s commander, Captain William Truscott, was in charge of the convoy when it departed in early August. At some point on the trans-Atlantic passage, a heavy gale disrupted the convoy, causing the *Boyne* to separate. Eventually, on 13 September, the *Boyne* arrived alone in Plymouth Sound; Cotton immediately dispatched a journal of his activities to the Admiralty, including a report on the state and condition of his ship. The *Boyne*'s fourteen years of active service soon came to an end. The Admiralty ordered Cotton to pay off his ship, a service that he completed on 17 November 1780. The *Boyne* was broken up less than three years later. The ship's condition must have made Cotton's fifteen-month experience as its captain an exercise in frustration. Not only was the ship slow, but it nearly foundered at sea during pursuit of de Guichen's fleet. In summary, a worn-out ship unquestionably hampered Cotton's performance in the West Indies, but it also made him acutely aware of the value of maintenance and quality vessels. The sketchy details of Cotton's experience in the *Boyne* provide limited insight into determining whether he was a naval officer willing to take calculated risks or to err on the side of safety.[26]

Cotton was assigned to a faster ship for his next posting to the West Indies. His new vessel, the 32-gun frigate *Alarm*, was eight years older than the *Boyne*, but it had a distinct qualitative advantage that mitigated the effects of age. Under an experimental process initiated in 1758, the *Alarm* was the first ship in the Royal Navy to receive a copper bottom. From then until 1781, only a few small frigates received copper bottoms. A copper bottom prolonged the life of a wooden vessel by deterring the work of the *teredo navalis*, a marine borer. The copper sheathing also decreased accumulation of barnacles and other marine life, thereby reducing the ship's weight and decreasing drag, which naturally increased speed. After becoming Comptroller of the Royal Navy in August 1781, Charles Middleton persuaded Sandwich and King George to authorize sheathing every ship in the service. Copper was readily available, and it was a relatively inexpensive process that took little time to complete. According to a report from the First Lord of the Admiralty, 313 ships in the navy received a copper bottom by December of that year.[27]

Cotton assumed command of the *Alarm* on 21 April 1781. The strategic situation for the Royal Navy that year had become more precarious in what was a war of global proportions. Unlike all other wars of the eighteenth century, the strength of the French navy from 1776 to 1783 was on par, if not superior, to that of its arch rival on the high seas. For the first time that century, a continental war in Europe did not distract the French from giving adequate support to its navy. The rise of French naval power corresponded with a time when many contemporaries in Britain blamed Sandwich for allowing political patronage to degrade the quality of the Royal Navy, both of its ships and of its leadership. With the balance of naval power temporarily shifted, the French navy was able to command the Chesapeake and isolate the British army at Yorktown. The French navy and a French army under Lieutenant General Comte de Rochambeau allowed the struggling American colonists to achieve their decisive victory in October 1781. In September, a French fleet commanded by Admiral François Joseph Paul, Comte de Grasse, had repelled Admiral Grave's attempt to relieve the beleaguered British troops at Yorktown. Even though the victory at Yorktown effectively ensured American independence, the struggle between the British and French navies continued until the war ended in 1783. Meanwhile, in the spring of 1782, they met again at the Battle of The Saintes, decisive not in its effect on the war for North America, but as a symbol of the Royal Navy's resurgence to naval dominance.[28]

Cotton spent the months preceding the Battle of The Saintes serving in the Channel Fleet under Vice Admiral George Darby. From April 1781 to February 1782, the *Alarm* served Darby's fleet by escorting inbound trade convoys within Channel waters and protecting the home islands from invasion by the combined fleets of France and Spain.[29] The nature of Cotton's duty in the *Alarm* differed from that of his previous command in the West Indies. A ship-of-the-line such as the *Boyne* performed a variety of duties but was designed primarily to oppose enemy ships-of-the-line, whereas the frigate's lack of firepower precluded it from major fleet engagements. Yet the frigate was the most versatile ship in the Royal Navy and popular among the officers and men. Its speed was ideal for reconnaissance and commerce raiding. Although much less heavily armed than a ship-of-the-line, the frigate still had enough firepower for engagements against similar opponents. In addition, frigates served as repeaters during fleet engagements. Often, only the ships immediately ahead and astern of a flagship saw the admiral's signals. To rectify this problem, frigates stationed on the fleet's disengaged side relayed the admiral's signals. Cotton's *Alarm* fulfilled this function when Rodney began his pursuit of de Grasse's fleet in April 1782.[30]

After the Americans no longer needed French naval support, de Grasse planned an expedition to capture Jamaica. Following the Allied victory at Yorktown, he promptly left North American waters for the Leeward Islands, where he supported the easy recapture of St. Eustatius by troops from Martinique in November 1781. In February 1782 St. Kitts fell to the French, despite the retreat of de Grasse's twenty-seven ships-of-the-line upon arrival of twenty-two British ships-of-the-line commanded by Rear Admiral Sir Samuel Hood. Even the presence of the British fleet could not rally the island's defenders against the isolated French invaders. During this tumultuous period, Rodney was on leave in England. His return to the Leeward Islands on 19 February with twelve ships-of-the-line gave the British a numerical edge and set the stage for the end of the French navy's remarkable string of victories.[31]

Cotton arrived in the *Alarm* at Gros Islet Bay, St. Lucia, on or about 21 March with a convoy from Britain that included seven additional warships for Rodney's fleet. Rodney expected the reinforcements to remain at Barbados, their initial port of call, with the exception of two frigates. He dispatched a message to the convoy commander, Captain Benjamin Caldwell of HMS *Agamemnon*, with orders to send the frigates *Alarm* and *Endymion* to join him at the rendezvous; the remaining ships would await further orders at Barbados. Already in Gros Islet Bay with all seven of the warships in his convoy and before receiving Rodney's dispatch, Caldwell sent Cotton to inform Rodney of the convoy's location and to receive further orders.[32]

Cotton apparently did not return to Caldwell's convoy because Rodney ordered the *Alarm* to Barbados. Major General James Cunningham, the governor of the island, had told Rodney about the frequent escape of American prisoners held there. Relocation appeared the best solution to the problem. Therefore, on 29 March Rodney instructed Cotton to embark fifty Americans at Carlisle Bay and transport them to St. Lucia. Rodney placed Cotton under his command and ordered the captain to "lose no time in returning" to join him at Gros Islet Bay because nine days earlier a French convoy with naval reinforcements had arrived at Martinique.[33] As the admiral expected that de Grasse's fleet would embark soon, he needed every available warship, including the *Alarm*.

De Grasse planned to join the Spanish fleet at San Domingo before the invasion of Jamaica. After a failed attempt to sail from Fort Royal Bay on the night of 6/7 April, thirty-three French ships-of-the-line successfully put to sea on the 8th. De Grasse's delay gave Rodney the warning his fleet of thirty-six sail-of-the-line needed to quickly close the forty-mile gap between the two fleets. Meanwhile, Cotton had completed his mission to Barbados with the American prisoners and rejoined the fleet before its departure from Gros Islet Bay. Rodney designated the *Alarm* as a repeating frigate for the central division of the fleet. Cotton incurred a crucial responsibility with this assignment, for a mistake by one repeating-frigate captain could ruin an admiral's battle plan more than the negligent independent action of one ship-of-the-line. Misinterpretation or ignorance of Rodney's signals had been at the core of the problems encountered at the Battle of Martinique. Although the *Alarm* was not expected to fight, Cotton nevertheless assumed an important role during the approaching battle.[34]

The British fleet closed on the French one day after leaving port. On the morning of the 9th, de Grasse decided to attack the van division of Rodney's fleet northwest of Dominica because the center and rear divisions were becalmed to lee of the island and could offer no support. The ensuing engagement did little damage to either fleet. The chase continued until the morning of the 12th, when both fleets were positioned between Dominica and an island group called The Saintes. Rodney's calculation that de Grasse could not avoid battle proved correct. At 6:00 a.m. he ordered the Union flag at the mizzen peak, the signal for line ahead at two cables distance, or about 400 yards, between ships. The van division headed north, and one hour later, by hoisting another flag under the Union, Rodney ordered the ships of the fleet to close within a cable of each other. To prevent miscommunication, he ensured that his order for the divisions to close was repeated continually. The execution of these orders led to an engagement at eight o'clock in the morning in the precise manner that Rodney intended: with his fleet concentrated from about ten miles to five, line ahead. Two hours later, HMS *Formidable*, Rodney's flagship, turned into the French center division and broke the enemy's line. Unlike at the Battle of Martinique, the van and rear divisions followed his example. The battle lasted all day and effectively ended that evening with the capture of de Grasse's flagship. A half-hearted pursuit failed to completely destroy the French fleet, but the invasion threat to Jamaica was eliminated. The Battle of The Saintes conclusively decided the question of naval dominance in the West Indies.[35]

At some point during the battle, the *Alarm* passed through the enemy line. What exactly did Cotton's ship do? With the simple nature of Rodney's signals and the concentration of the fleet before it formed line ahead, superb conditions existed for the efficient relay of signals. As a repeating frigate, the *Alarm* served its most crucial function during the morning hours, when it helped disseminate Rodney's orders throughout the fleet. Regarding shots fired against the enemy, Rodney's order for Cotton to transfer fifty half-barrels of powder to HMS *Monarch* implies that the *Alarm* fired few shots, if any.[36] Cotton's *Naval Chronicle* memoir stated that Rodney commended him for the "promptitude" with which the *Alarm* "rendered assistance to some of the disabled ships of the squadron."[37]

The Battle of The Saintes was another superb learning experience for Cotton. As captain of a repeating frigate, he saw how clear signals effectively communicated were a prerequisite for orderly naval operations. Furthermore, Rodney's example of breaking the enemy line established a precedent for naval combat that certainly made a lasting impression. Cotton experienced first-hand the importance of aggressive tactics at The Saintes in this, the second major fleet battle of his young career.

Assuming that Rodney questioned Cotton's professional ability because of his performance at the Battle of Martinique, then his performance at The Saintes apparently changed the admiral's attitude. Ten days after the battle, Rodney ordered Cotton to proceed to Port Royal Bay, Jamaica, in the *Alarm* to deliver his dispatches and fifty French prisoners of war.[38] Upon completion, Rodney wanted Cotton to join him off Cape Tiberoon, Haiti. Rodney would not have placed dispatches, likely related to The Saintes and the current disposition of the fleet, into the hands of an officer with questionable professional ability. Cotton delivered the dispatches and human cargo without incident and received subsequent assignments from the fleet admiral. On 29 June, Rodney directed the *Preston* to join Cotton's *Alarm* and proceed to Cape François off the north coast of San Domingo. Despite British victory at The Saintes, the French and Spanish navies remained actively opposed in the West Indies. Recent reports indicated that seven enemy ships-of-the-line were to escort a trade convoy from Port-au-Prince to Cape François. Rodney wanted Cotton to conduct a reconnaissance of the combined fleets and obtain as much information about them as possible without risking capture of the *Alarm* or *Preston*. Relying on Cotton's judgment, Rodney instructed him to "lose no time in giving me information" before the flagship embarked from Port Royal on 10 July.[39] At the latest, Rodney wanted Cotton to join him off Navassa Island, between Jamaica and Haiti, shortly thereafter. These responsibilities clearly indicate that Cotton's performance at The Saintes had earned him the trust and confidence of perhaps the most irascible admiral in the Royal Navy.

Cotton's service aboard the *Alarm* continued in the West Indies for the remainder of the war. On orders from the Admiralty, she became one of the warships to remain at Jamaica through the hurricane season of 1782 to the spring of 1783. Cotton served under Sir Joshua Rowley for much of this period, and the admiral kept his future son-in-law busy with a variety of assignments. One notable dispatch on 9 February 1783 instructed Cotton to proceed off the Havannah with another frigate and two sloops under his command for the purpose of gathering intelligence on an enemy squadron in that port. After dispatching a sloop back to Rowley, Cotton was then to proceed with his small force to the Tortuga bank north of Haiti for about six weeks to "capture or destroy the armed force and trade of H.M. enemies."[40]

By February of 1783, however, the strategic issues of the war had been settled. In spite of the Royal Navy's dominance in the West Indies after the Battle of The Saintes, its previous failures in North America, coupled with a few, yet decisive, defeats of the British army in the colonies, decided the fate of American independence. Nevertheless, the war in America provided a valuable training ground for the next generation of senior leadership in the Royal Navy, including Charles Cotton. As he sailed home for Britain in 1783, Cotton could look back with satisfaction on his first eleven years of naval service. For seven of those years the Royal Navy fought a global war. The conflict provided Cotton with a wealth of experience ranging from amphibious landings to convoy escort to fleet battles. In these operations, Cotton proved himself a reliable subordinate and capable of independent command. Whether or not he was a risk-taker still remained to be seen. Upon arrival in England, Cotton paid off the *Alarm* and returned to the family estate in Cambridgeshire, which he had sorely missed since his arrival off North American waters sevens years before.[41] In 1776 he had written, "How I long to be at Madingley. I am heartily sick of this new world."[42] The lieutenant's desire to return home likely subsided with time as the responsibility of command, campaigns against the French in the West Indies, and a love interest with the daughter of Sir Joshua Rowley at Jamaica competed for his attention. Cotton resided peacefully on the family estate from 1783 to 1793, a period when his country's observation of the political and social changes in France turned from curiosity to alarm.

NOTES

1. N.A.M. Rodger, "Patronage and Competence," in *Les Marines de Guerre Européennes XVII–XVIIIe siècles*, ed. Martine Acerra (Paris: Presses de l'Université de Paris-Sorbonne, 1985), 245.

2. Although the official name is "Cambridge American Cemetery and Memorial," it is informally referred to as the "Madingley American Cemetery." For information on the cemetery, see *Cambridge American Cemetery and Memorial* (American Battle Monuments Commission, 1975).

3. "Biographical Memoir of the Late Sir Charles Cotton, Bart. Admiral of the White Squadron," *The Naval Chronicle* 27 (1812): 395–96; Leslie Stephen and Sidney Lee, eds., *Dictionary of National Biography* (Oxford, 1917), 4: 1226.

4. Linda Colley, *Britons: Forging the Nation 1707–1837* (New Haven, 1992), 192–93.

5. "Memoir of Cotton," *Naval Chronicle* 27 (1812): 353.

6. Ibid., 353-54; James Ralfe, *The Naval Biography of Great Britain: Consisting of Historical Memoirs of Those Officers of the British Navy Who Distinguished Themselves during the Reign of His Majesty George III* (London, 1828), 2: 215; for a summary of Sandwich's abilities as First Lord, see Piers Mackesy, *The War for America, 1775–1783* (Cambridge, 1964), 162–65.

7. Commander R.D. Ross, "The Naval Officer, 1793–1815: His Efficiency, Conditions of Service, Prospects and Handicaps," *Army Quarterly and Defence Journal* 78 (July, 1959): 71–72; Rodger, "Patronage and Competence," 237; David Syrett, "The Role of the Royal Navy in the Napoleonic Wars after Trafalgar, 1805–1814," *Naval War College Review* 32 (1979): 72.

8. Rodger, "Patronage and Competence," 239, 240, 245.

9. Robert Beatson, *Naval and Military Memoirs of Great Britain from 1727 to 1783* (London, 1804), 4: 113, 114, 156–83; 6: 43, 53.

10. Vice Admiral Graves turned the fleet over to Rear Admiral Lord Shuldham on 27 January 1776. Howe was appointed to the command in February, but did not join it until

12 July off Staten Island. Beatson, *Naval and Military Memoirs*, 4: 114, 154; Brian Lavery, *Nelson's Navy: The Ships, Men and Organisation, 1793–1815* (London, 1989), 88–93; Ross, "The Naval Officer," 72.

11. J.J. Colledge, *Ships of the Royal Navy: An Historical Index* (London, 1987), 1: 592; Beatson, *Naval and Military Memoirs*, 4: 113; 6: 76, 109.

12. Mackesy, *War for America*, 112.

13. The other five ships that supported the 25 August landing were the *Roebuck* (44), *Apollo* (32), *Sphynx* (20), *Senegal* (16), and *Swift* (14). Beatson, *Naval and Military Memoirs*, 4: 251–52; 6: 74–76; Captain John M. Rose, Royal Marine Artillery, estimated that the British had conducted 120 expeditions of various sizes from 1744 to 1815. Of these, thirty-eight failed to obtain their objective. He made this conclusion based on the writings of nineteenth-century British naval historians and the works of Alfred Thayer Mahan. See the table that accompanies "Landing of Expeditionary Forces," *Journal of the Royal United Service Institution* 39 (1895): 672–720; Mackesy, *War for America*, 125–26.

14. Thomas More Molyneux, *Conjunct Expeditions; Or Expeditions that have been carried on jointly by the Fleet and Army; with a Commentary on a Littoral War* (London, 1759), 2: 1.

15. The British referred to amphibious operations as combined operations during the age of sail. Today, the armed forces of the United States define operations that involve two or more countries as combined and two or more services as joint. See *Field Manual 100-5: Operations* (Headquarters, Department of the Army, 1993), 4-1, 5-1; for more on the nature of eighteenth-century combined operations, see Richard Harding, "Sailors and Gentlemen of Parade: Some Professional and Technical Problems Concerning the Conduct of Combined Operations in the Eighteenth Century," *Historical Journal* 32 (1989): 35–55; and Piers Mackesy, "Problems of an Amphibious Power: Britain against France, 1793–1815," *Naval War College Review* 30 (1978): 16–25.

16. The Admiralty did not confirm Cotton's appointment to captain on 3 April 1779 until 5 May 1781. See Appointment Certificate, 5 May 1781, in Library of Congress, Washington, D.C., Mary Edith Powell Collection, Container 2; Beatson, *Naval and Military Memoirs*, 6: 160.

17. Vice Admiral James Young to Philip Stephens, 7 April 1778, Library of Congress, PRO ADM 1/310; for a succinct account of the British operation at St. Lucia, see John Creswell, *Generals and Admirals: The Story of Amphibious Command* (Westport, Conn., 1976), 85–88; Mackesy, *War for America*, 160, 225–29.

18. Parker to Cotton, 29 October 1779, Cambridgeshire County Record Office, Cotton Naval Papers, 588/032.

19. Ibid., Rodney to Cotton, 16 March 1780.

20. John Creswell, *British Admirals of the Eighteenth Century: Tactics in Battle* (London, 1972), 141-43; David Spinney, *Rodney* (Annapolis, 1969), 317–19; Mackesy, *War for America*, 319–21.

21. Cited in Spinney, *Rodney*, 325; Beatson, *Naval and Military Memoirs*, 5: 55–62; 6: 222.

22. Excerpt from Rodney's public dispatch on the Battle of Martinique cited in Spinney, *Rodney*, 329; William Laird Clowes, *The Royal Navy: A History from the Earliest Times to the Present* (London, 1900), 3: 454–60.

23. Rodney to Cotton, 20 May 1780, Cambridgeshire County Record Office, Cotton Naval Papers, 588/032; Godfrey Mundy, *Life and Correspondence of the Late Admiral*

Lord Rodney (London, 1830), 1: 307–14; Spinney, *Rodney*, 332–38.

24. Rodney to Cotton, 10 June 1780, Cambridgeshire County Record Office, Cotton Naval Papers, 588/032; Spinney, *Rodney*, 338–42.

25. Rowley to Cotton, 22 May 1780, Hotham to Cotton, 17, 18 July 1780, Cambridgeshire County Record Office, Cotton Naval Papers, 588/032; "Memoir of the Public Services of the Late Sir Joshua Rowley," *Naval Chronicle* 24 (1810): 96–97.

26. Admiralty to Cotton, 19 September 1780, 2 October 1780, Cambridgeshire County Record Office, Cotton Naval Papers, 588/032; Spinney, *Rodney*, 342; Colledge, *Ships of the Royal Navy*, 1: 86.

27. Maurer Maurer, "Coppered Bottoms for the Royal Navy: A Factor in the Maritime War of 1778–1783," *Military Affairs* 14 (1950): 57–61; Colledge, *Ships of the Royal Navy*, 1: 30.

28. N.A.M. Rodger, *The Wooden World: An Anatomy of the Georgian Navy* (Annapolis, 1986), 341–42; Mackesy, *War for America*, 10–11.

29. Beatson, *Naval and Military Memoirs*, 5: 392-97; 6: 312-14; Rodney to Captain Balfour, 8 December 1781, George Rodney, *Letter-Books and Order-Book of George, Lord Rodney, Admiral of the White Squadron, 1780–1782* (New York, 1932), 2: 526–27.

30. Spinney, *Rodney*, 321; Lavery, *Nelson's Navy*, 43, 49.

31. Mackesy, *War for America*, 454-57; Spinney, *Rodney*, 389–90.

32. Rodney to Captain Benjamin Caldwell, 20 March 1782, Caldwell to Rodney, 21 March 1782, Caldwell to Rodney, 24 March 1782, *Letter-Books of Lord Rodney*, 1: 310, 316, 317, 321, 322.

33. Ibid., 2: 629, 630, Rodney to Cotton, 28, 29 March 1782; Mackesy, *War for America*, 456.

34. Creswell, *British Admirals*, 165–66; Mackesy, *War for America*, 456-57; Spinney, *Rodney*, 393–94.

35. Rodney to Philip Stephens, 14 April 1782, Mundy, *Life of Rodney*, 254-58; Creswell, *British Admirals*, 167–74; Spinney, *Rodney*, 395–402; the order of battle for The Saintes is in Clowes, *Royal Navy*, 3: 520.

36. Rodney to Cotton, 17 April 1782, *Letter-Books of Lord Rodney*, 2: 664–65.

37. "Memoir of Cotton," *Naval Chronicle* 27 (1812): 355.

38. Rodney to Cotton, 22 April 1782, *Letter-Books of Lord Rodney*, 2: 674.

39. Ibid., 2: 807, Rodney to Cotton, 29 June 1782.

40. Rowley to Cotton, 9 February 1783, Cambridgeshire County Record Office, Cotton Naval Papers, 588/032; Rowley to Rodney, 4 July 1782, "Line of Battle" in Port Royal Harbor, 8 July 1782, "A List of Ships Left at Jamaica," 8 September 1782, *Letter-Books of Lord Rodney*, 1: 482, 511; 2: 817–18.

41. Rowley to Cotton, 21 April 1783, Cambridgeshire County Record Office, Cotton Naval Papers, 588/032.

42. Excerpt from lecture notes by Lionel Munby, archivist of Madingley Hall, in possession of the author.

2

Continuing Education: Service in the Channel Fleet, 1793–1797

> Constant service afloat, cruising and blockading, could hardly fail to inject the basic principles of seamanship into the great majority, and periods of unemployment on half-pay were not considered to affect professional proficiency in an unscientific age when the arts of sailing and gunnery remained at a standstill.
>
> —Commander R.D. Ross, Royal Navy[1]

Before breakfast on 30 July 1781, John, first son of Sir John Hynde Cotton, left the house and went to Madingley Park to hunt rabbits. Not long after his departure, his three sisters, Sarah, Anne, and Lettice, heard the sound of a gunshot. John's body was not found until the next day. Somehow, the gun accidentally discharged, hitting him in the head. With his death and the earlier demise of Sir John Hynde's second son, Humphry, in 1757, Charles Cotton was the next in line of two other brothers to inherit the baronetcy. Thus, Sir John Hynde's eldest surviving son spent a ten-year interlude from naval service on the family estate that he would inherit upon his father's death in 1795. Because of Sir John Hynde's financial difficulties, he transferred control of the estate to Charles in 1791.[2]

Charles also attended to affairs of the heart during the years of peace. On 27 February 1788, he married Philadelphia Rowley, daughter of his former commander in the West Indies and granddaughter of Sir William Rowley, a former Admiral of the Fleet. Charles and Philadelphia immediately started a family that eventually included five children: Maria Susanna (1790–1871), Philadelphia Lætitia (1791–1860), John Hynde (1798–1807), St. Vincent (1801–1863), and Charles (1804–1828). Excerpts from a few letters indicate that Cotton had a very strong passion and concern for his family at Madingley while he was away on naval service. Cotton corresponded frequently with his wife, explaining his service, giving advice and instructions pertaining to the estate, and expressing love for his family. Despite active naval service for seventeen of the first twenty-two years of marriage, Cotton remarked in a letter to his wife in 1810 that he had "never been more than fifteen months absent from his family" before his extended service in the Mediterranean. Prior to the Mediterranean, his twelve years of service in the Channel Fleet facilitated many brief visits to his family at Madingley.[3]

Maria and Philadelphia maintained an active correspondence with their father while he was away from the estate. Their letters described family events, visits, health reports, and even current political events. On the eve of the Treaty of Amiens in March 1802, Maria Susanna, apparently an ardent student of politics, remarked to her father: "I think the government acts perfectly right to be no longer trifled with, especially by an Usurper; this affair ought to have been decided some time since: If Bonaparte breaks off the Treaty I think he will not be long first Consul."[4] In another letter to her father, Maria Susanna credits him for making many efforts to compensate for his prolonged absences. After receiving a gift from her father, she wrote: "Though I should always feel pleasure in wearing so pretty an ornament, be assured my dear Papa, that will be much increased on reflecting to whom I am indebted for it and also by considering it as an additional proof of your constant wish to oblige us."[5] Cotton expressed warmth to his children not only with gifts but with words as well. For example, he wrote to the future sixth baronet of Madingley, his three-year-old son John Hynde: "As mamma and your sisters have left you in command at Madingley, to you I must apply to know how everything goes on; and as I have no doubt you are constantly abroad in fine weather under the care of your excellent nurse, you are able to inform me."[6] In the competition between the Cotton family and the Royal Navy for Charles' time, His Majesty's service was the clear winner. But though he was often at sea, his heart and mind were rooted firmly to his ancestral home and family at Madingley.

Not long after Cotton had married Philadelphia, a member of the House of Lords and lord lieutenant of the town of Cambridge, Philip Yorke, Lord Hardwick, offered to support Cotton as a candidate for the town of Cambridge. In his reply to the offer on 22 May 1788, Cotton asserted,

> My determination has been fixed for some time never to offer myself a candidate for the town of Cambridge, and which your friendly promise of assistance, and the fairest prospect at success can never alter.[7]

Apparently, his attitude on politics remained unchanged throughout his naval career. In fact, no evidence suggests that Cotton ever became involved heavily with political interest, even as a senior admiral. This does not imply that he thought political involvement inappropriate for a naval officer. The patronage that brought many naval officers into the political world was a fundamental aspect of British government in an age when personal loyalties were stronger than party ones. From 1790 to 1820, one hundred naval officers served in parliament. No doubt, Cotton recognized the impossibility of completely withdrawing from the political world since patronage was a necessity for each promotion in rank. The dual responsibilities of naval service and management of the family estate at Madingley seemed enough to satisfy Cotton's ambition.[8]

Cotton's years ashore ended when Britain joined the First Coalition against revolutionary France in 1793. With the political and social equilibrium of Europe shaken by events in France after 1789, Austria and Prussia formed the coalition on 26 June 1792, primarily to preserve the position of the European monarchies. After the execution of Louis XVI on 21 January 1793, the British government, led by William Pitt the Younger, decided that Britain could not stay aloof from continental affairs when they threatened the social and political fabric of England. But on 1 February, France declared war, and that decision was wrenched from the hands of Pitt. Thus began a period of twenty-two nearly uninterrupted years of war between Britain and France; during this period the officer ranks of the Royal Navy swelled from 2,000 to 10,000 within the first four years alone. Cotton was among that group of men who selflessly responded to the country's call to arms. He left half-pay status at Madingley and joined the Channel Fleet at Chatham with an appointment to the 74-gun HMS *Majestic* on 1 March 1793.

Admiral Lord Richard Howe, under whom Cotton had served for three years in North America, commanded the Channel Fleet from February 1793 to May 1797. The sixty-seven-year-old Howe spent the first four months of command preparing his rapidly expanding fleet for the arduous task it faced. The fleet's territorial parameters extended along the European coast from Ferrol, Spain, in the south to Le Havre, France.[9] Its main purpose was home island defense; this was to be accomplished by keeping enemy warships blockaded in port. Two types of blockade existed for Howe to choose from: close and open. The close blockade required a fleet to keep enough ships on station directly before an enemy port to deter any vessels from putting out. Although an effective technique, the wear and tear on ships and crew constantly at sea rapidly decreased efficiency while enemy vessels anchored snugly in port. Furthermore, strong gales often blew a blockading squadron off station, thereby granting an enemy the opportunity for making its escape anyway. The close blockade and the open blockade differed considerably. Proponents of the open blockade conceded that a close blockade could not keep an enemy fleet constantly bottled in port because of inclement weather. Therefore, in an open blockade, the admiral used the fleet as a reaction force. Once the screen of a few warships reported the enemy's departure from port, the main fleet then pursued from its sheltered anchorage, where it did not have to suffer the ravages of constant sea service. In theory, despite the gap with the enemy, the better-conditioned fleet of the open blockade could rapidly close with the enemy and fight more effectively.[10]

Howe implemented an open blockade when his fleet was ready to embark in May 1793. Until December of that year, it remained active in the Channel while attempting to blockade Brest; however, his ships spent much time in the sheltered anchorage at Torbay, the main rendezvous between the home ports of Plymouth and Portsmouth. With the home islands remaining secure, the fleet returned to port for refit and repair through the winter months of 1793–1794.[11]

Although an inauspicious beginning to the war, the unglamorous rigors of blockade duty typified Cotton's experience in the Channel for the next twelve years. Opportunities for major fleet action had become rare because the French navy was less of a threat than it had been from 1778 to 1783. During the war for America, France avoided a European land war. Its alliances strongly benefited naval operations since it did not have to raise a large army. Of course, this favorable condition for the French navy did not exist from 1793 to 1815. The threat to French territorial integrity created the need for a large army, while naval power was largely ignored. In addition, the social upheaval of the French Revolution created turmoil within the navy, further degrading its quality. Insubordination and lack of discipline among the ranks contributed to the majority of *Grand Corps* officers leaving the naval service by 1791; this created a void of experienced leadership. Despite its many problems, the French navy continued to operate offensively throughout the period. Its strength comparative to the Royal Navy had decreased since the American Revolution, but it was still capable of challenging the British fleet at sea.[12]

One challenge came from a grain convoy of 130 ships that departed Chesapeake Bay on 17 April 1794 for a voyage to Brest. Rear Admiral Pierre-Jean Vanstabel, the escort commander, expected the convoy to arrive in France around mid-May. The previous summer's poor harvest had made the food supply in France critically low. To stave off famine, the convoy had to make its voyage across the Atlantic undetected by the Royal Navy. Under pressure from Jeanbon Saint-André, a member of the Committee of Public Safety, the commander of the French fleet at Brest responded to the emergency. Rear Admiral Louis Thomas Villaret de Joyeuse assembled a fleet of twenty-four ships-of-the-line at Brest. Villaret intended to use his fleet to divert British attention away from the inbound convoy and then avoid battle. However, the prospect of the guillotine should the convoy be lost also proved an incentive for Villaret to fight. The French fleet sailed from Brest on 16 May. Meanwhile, the Channel Fleet was already searching for the grain convoy.[13]

Howe had received reports of the convoy's arrival before his fleet put to sea on 2 May. Cotton's *Majestic* was assigned with four other ships-of-the-line to the second division of the rear squadron, commanded by Rear Admiral Sir George Montagu. On the 4th, Howe detached Montagu's flagship with six other ships, excluding the *Majestic*, to escort a West Indian convoy out of the Channel. Howe gave Montagu additional instructions to search the western approach to the southern Bay of Biscay for the grain convoy. With Montagu's departure, Cotton came under the command of Admiral Sir Alexander Hood,

Lord Bridport, and the *Majestic* became third from the end of a twenty-six-ship line of battle. After searching for the French fleet off Ushant and finding it still at Brest, Howe sailed west with the fleet along the convoy's logical approach route. Having searched fruitlessly, the Channel Fleet returned to Ushant on the 19th only to find that the Brest fleet had embarked. A westward pursuit began at once. After ten anxious days, lookout frigates sighted Villaret's fleet 350 miles west of Ushant on Wednesday, 28 May.[14]

A new signal for breaking the enemy's line appeared in Howe's signal book of 1790. Rodney's technique to break the line at The Saintes in 1782 involved severing the enemy line into isolated fragments and then concentrating the fleet upon one of them. Ships would pass successively through the same gap in the line. Rather than follow the technique employed by Rodney, Howe envisioned each ship in the line of battle bearing down abreast toward the enemy line from windward. Upon passing through the line simultaneously, each ship would fire its broadsides as it gained the leeward position. Holding this position could produce a decisive mêlée and made escape by the enemy difficult. This was precisely the strategy that Howe wanted to use as his fleet bore down upon the French fleet.[15]

Cotton's *Majestic*, near the middle of the rear squadron, did not make contact with the enemy that Wednesday. His actions were limited to tacking in succession per signal and observing the weather squadron's partial action with the French rear. At 10:15 p.m. firing ceased and darkness intervened to drape a veil of uncertainty over both fleets. At 4:00 a.m. the next morning, the *Majestic* made sail ahead of the 100-gun *Queen Charlotte*, Howe's flagship, to take station as fifth ship in the van. Cotton's ship had somehow moved ahead from the rear squadron during the night. Howe now wanted to gain the weather gauge by passing through the enemy's line, but Villaret's maneuvers frustrated the attempt. At 10.00 a.m. the vans of both fleets drew up and commenced an ineffectual dual at long range. The *Majestic*, one of eight ships engaged, fired its guns "now and then" for about an hour. Although few of the British or French shot reached their targets, both squadrons sustained some damage.[16]

At about noon Howe signalled for the fleet to tack in succession. This maneuver, although poorly executed, gave the two fleets opposite parallel tacks and sent the British van heading toward the French rear. In the process of executing Howe's order, the *Majestic* followed the example of its van and wore instead of tacked. By 2:30 p.m. Cotton's ship was under the lee of the enemy at an unknown distance behind the flagship. Simultaneously, the *Queen Charlotte* and two other British ships tacked through the rear of the enemy line. A heavy engagement accompanied the British movement to the weather gauge.[17] As Howe's flagship broke through the enemy line, the *Majestic* passed close to the stern of the rearmost enemy ship. The resultant "close and heavy fire" left one man dead and thirteen wounded on the *Majestic* and damaged its main topmast, larboard fore yard arm, and mizzen mast—shot through with a forty-two pounder. The French fleet then wore to cover its disabled ships and ran to leeward of the British. At 5:00 p.m. the fleets disengaged. On this day of indecisive engagements and decisive maneuvers, Cotton received the baptism of fire that eluded him in the West Indies.[18]

For the next two days heavy fog prevented Howe from using the weather gauge to close with the enemy. The British fleet used the time advantageously by restoring its sailing order and making repairs. Meanwhile, the *Majestic* resumed its position in the rear squadron, third from the end of the twenty-five-ship line of battle. Both fleets were nearly equal in strength—the French fleet had twenty-six ships-of-the-line. Its losses from the actions of the 28th and 29th were repaired by the arrival on the 31st of five additional warships. Fortunately for the French, on the 30th or 31st the grain convoy from America slipped by without attracting Howe's attention. Unaware of the grain convoy's passage, Howe prepared his fleet for battle on the morning of 1 June. The haze had cleared, and the enemy fleet was in line of battle three or four miles to leeward under sail to the westward.[19]

Howe hoisted the signal at 5:15 a.m. for the fleet to close up as it maintained a parallel line with the French. At about 8:30 a.m. he ordered each ship to "steer for and engage her opponent in the enemy line" with the intent to "pass through the enemy line for engaging them to leeward."[20] Howe's fleet began sailing in a line abreast formation towards the French. The battle began at 9:30 a.m. as firing commenced and British ships began penetrating the French line. The *Majestic* bore up after the 100-gun *Royal George*, Hood's flagship, while exchanging shot with three French ships in passing. Cotton's ship then followed the *Royal George* through the enemy line to leeward. This maneuver violated Howe's intent. The admiral wanted each ship to pass through the enemy line independently, not in succession. Nevertheless, the *Majestic* became heavily engaged for about an hour with the rearmost ships in the French column, probably the 74-gun *Pelletier* and 80-gun *Scipion.* At 10:30 a.m. the smoke created by the mêlée limited visibility between ships, which resulted in the collision of HMS *Thunderer* of 74-guns into *Majestic*'s larboard quarter. Neither ship sustained significant material damage. When the smoke finally lifted at noon, Cotton wore his ship around to catch up with the *Royal George*, firing at several dismasted enemy ships on the way.[21]

Together, the *Royal George* and *Majestic* fired at two French ships passing them to windward as they attempted to join the remnants of their fleet assembling to the north. The *Majestic* ceased firing at 1:20 p.m. as the two French ships passed out of range and joined Villaret to leeward. Later that afternoon, as the British fleet began reconsolidating, Cotton's ship approached a dismasted enemy vessel, the 80-gun *Sans Pareil.* After the *Majestic* fired, the French warship quickly struck its colors; at 3:20 p.m, Cotton's crew took possession of the *Sans Pareil.* Six other dismasted French vessels were similarly captured by other British warships. Despite the Royal Navy's overwhelming tactical victory, Howe chose not to pursue the remnants of Villaret's fleet. On the day after the battle, the *Majestic*, with the *Sans Pareil* in tow, sailed past the *Queen Charlotte*. Cotton and his crew cheered Howe, who responded in kind.[22]

The Battle of "The Glorious First of June" was over. Even though the French fleet had achieved its strategic goal by ensuring the safe passage of the grain convoy, it suffered a major tactical defeat. The British towed six French vessels to Portsmouth, sank one, and damaged heavily many others, not to mention inflicting 5,000 French casualties, compared to 1,100 British casualties. Like the Battle of The Saintes, "The Glorious First of June" became the standard by which contemporary Britons measured later naval battles. Unfortunately, the battle's aftermath was beset with controversy. Some officers in the fleet believed that a more complete victory was within grasp had Howe elected to pursue the French. Although many British ships were incapable of pursuit, personal fatigue appeared as Howe's only excuse for failing to do so. But Howe's failure to annihilate the French fleet in the wake of his great tactical victory did not attract as much attention as did the distribution of awards. Cotton was one of several captains who did not receive the coveted gold chain and medal, which recognized meritorious service at the Battle of "The Glorious First of June."[23]

Howe's oversight bore much "misery" on Cotton.[24] Although criticized for having had "little share in the action" by one of Howe's biographers, Cotton believed that his performance indeed was worthy of recognition.[25] His friend Collingwood also believed that Cotton deserved commendation.[26] Unfortunately, factors other than performance contributed to Howe's oversight of Cotton's efforts. Foremost among them was the process by which the medals were awarded. Upon arriving at Spithead after the battle, Howe received several letters from the Admiralty that requested details of individual meritorious service. Howe suspected that submission of a limited list of individuals would result in "disagreeable consequences" but nonetheless omitted Cotton, Captain Cuthbert Collingwood, and Rear Admiral Benjamin Caldwell, among others. Howe did not want the selections in the letter to "be construed to the disadvantage of other commanders, who may have been equally deserving of the approbation of the Lord Commissioners of the Admiralty."[27]

The *Majestic*'s limited casualty figures, eight compared to an average of forty for British ships in the battle, might imply that Cotton did not aggressively bring his ship to bear against the enemy. Furthermore, following the *Royal George* through the line instead of independently breaking it suggests a reluctance to initiate an unsupported ship-to-ship action. On the other hand, misunderstanding of a signal might explain the *Majestic*'s method of penetrating the enemy line. Regardless of how the line was crossed, Cotton's ship "kept up an incessant fire," but apparently not at point-blank range. The collision with the *Thunderer* and confusion of combat might explain the *Majestic*'s light casualties more accurately than the ship having a cautious commander. Notwithstanding Howe's oversight of Cotton's performance, Cotton's participation in the Battle of "The Glorious First of June" further acquainted him with the sights and sounds of naval combat. This was Cotton's last major fleet engagement, but not the last time one of his ships would engage a French warship.

The Channel Fleet's June victory proved transitory because the French continued to threaten British maritime security and commercial interests. Before Howe and Villaret de Joyeuse fought their battle, the Committee of Public Safety had proposed an invasion of England. French troops concentrated in Brittany throughout the first three months of 1794, but the expedition never sailed because of several difficulties. On 30 May, Lazare Carnot, an influential member of the Committee, called off the invasion attempt because troops were needed to face emergencies in the Rhine region. The French would make other attempts in 1796 and 1797. Yet, while the threat to the British Isles temporarily subsided, the threat to British commerce rose.[28]

In the aftermath of "The Glorious First of June" and the postponed invasion attempt, the French government resorted to a more indirect manner of waging war on Britain. Unable to challenge the Royal Navy at sea, France increasingly encouraged the *guerre de course* to threaten British commerce in the English Channel. French privateers netted an estimated 5,600 ships and 600,000 tons of shipping between 1793 and 1801. Still, these captures caused more anxiety among the British than actual damage to their economy. French captures represented only a small percentage of the British trade passing through the Channel, and many privateers were themselves captured, about 600 in the same period. Regardless of the reality, the threat of invasion and nuisance of privateering (to include the French fleet in being) demanded that the Channel Fleet remain constantly employed off French ports and in the waters between Scilly and Ushant.[29]

Considering the strategic situation after "The Glorious First of June," the Channel Fleet could not long remain in port. Accordingly, it spent most of the remaining months of 1794 at sea cruising the western entrance to the Channel not only to protect British trade but to molest French trade as well. Conversely, French naval vessels frequently sailed from port to threaten commerce when a gap appeared in the British blockade. This type of warfare continued in the Channel without a significant event until the spring of 1795, when the British government sponsored the landing of 3,600 French émigrés on the Quiberon peninsula in southern Brittany. The British hoped the émigrés would inspire an uprising of Bourbon sympathizers in the Vendée against the revolutionary French government in Paris. Cotton's participation in support of the landing resulted in the next direct naval combat of his career.[30]

Howe organized his fleet into three separate forces for the Quiberon expedition, with one squadron presiding over the landing while the other two provided security and protection. Hood's squadron would watch Brest to the north while Vice Admiral William Cornwallis, under whom Cotton served, led a squadron south of the Quiberon peninsula. Now commanding the 74-gun *Mars*, Cotton embarked from Portsmouth harbor on 26 May 1795 with three other 74s, two frigates, and the 100-gun flagship *Royal Sovereign*. The squadron initially cruised off the waters of Belle-Île, south of Quiberon. Unfortunately for Cornwallis, Hood assumed that the French fleet would remain anchored at Brest. Therefore, he did not embark from Portsmouth with his fourteen ships-of-the-line until 12 June. In fact, Villaret's fleet had departed from Brest on 11 June and five days later joined a force commanded by Rear Admiral Jean Gaspard Vence. On that day the combined French force of nearly thirty sail, including twelve ships-of-the-line, sighted Cornwallis' seven ship squadron near the Penmarks. The chase was on—Villaret's fleet pursued at once.[31]

Cornwallis realized that superior British gunnery and seamanship could not overwhelm the numerically superior French fleet. On the evening of 16 June he began organizing his squadron for a withdrawal while the French fleet slowly approached from windward. Because of the *Mars*' fine sailing qualities, Cornwallis placed it astern of his flagship; consequently, Cotton's ship bore the brunt of the fighting the following day. As a squadron can sail only as fast as its slowest ship, the French came upon both quarters of the British on the morning of the 17th. At 9 a.m. the 74-gun *Zélé* commenced firing on the *Mars*. Throughout the day French ships-of-the-line came up in succession to fire on the British rear, including one frigate to leeward, the *Virginie*, that frequently yawed and fired on the *Mars*. Damage to her rigging and sails caused Cotton's ship to fall behind the squadron to leeward. In the evening the French made a stronger show of force against the *Mars*, but timely support provided by the *Royal Sovereign* put an end to the French attack. At sunset Villaret stood off with his fleet because he incorrectly suspected that Hood's force was on the horizon. Without enemy pressure, Cornwallis then led his bruised, yet intact squadron back to England.[32]

Besides material damage, the *Mars* had twelve men wounded, the only casualties of consequence in the squadron. In his account of the engagement to the Admiralty, Cornwallis lauded Cotton's handling of his ship: "The Mars and Triumph, being the sternmost ships, were of course more exposed to the enemy's fire, and I cannot too much commend the spirited conduct of Sir Charles Cotton and Sir Erasmus Gower, the captains of those ships—the former's conduct was intrepid and he had every disadvantage of a new formed ship's company."[33] By virtue of his ship's sailing quality, Cotton received his last noteworthy opportunity to excel in combat as a captain in the Royal Navy. He conducted himself well. His ship, and the *Triumph*, diverted French warships from attacking other less capable sailing ships in Cornwallis's squadron. It was not an action that required independent thought on behalf of Cotton, but rather one that called upon personal fortitude to remain resolute under fire and superb nautical skills to keep his damaged ship from falling too far behind the van. Perhaps the recognition Cotton received from Cornwallis alleviated the "misery" he felt from not receiving "The Glorious First of June" gold medal.

Cotton remained in the Channel Fleet after Cornwallis' masterful retreat, serving under Howe and Hood in various capacities. The need for competent commanders remained strong as privateers reached the apex of their activity in 1797 and the French sent an expedition to Bantry Bay. However, Cotton's days as captain of the *Mars* were numbered. Once posted a captain, promotion in the Royal Navy to the various grades of admiral depended on seniority. On 20 February 1797, Cotton was promoted to rear admiral of the blue. This promotion inaugurated a frustrating period for him. For the next ten years he served on the periphery of glory, narrowly missing all the prominent naval battles of the period. His name would remain in relative obscurity while the likes of Nelson and Collingwood became recognized names in the British press and parliament.

Nevertheless, Cotton's naval experience between 1793 and 1797 as commander of the *Majestic* and *Mars* proved valuable for his service as a flag officer in the Channel Fleet. Those four years familiarized Cotton with the waters and coastlines within the fleet's jurisdiction, exposed him to the challenge of keeping a vessel on station off the French coast, and helped to establish his professional reputation in the Royal Navy. Whether by merit or by virtue of seniority, Cotton had reached a position of responsibility that demanded an expertise that could have been achieved only by many years of active naval service. Events in the Channel over the next ten years would put Cotton's expertise as a flag officer to the test.

NOTES

1. R.D. Ross, "The Naval Officer, 1793–1815: His Efficiency, Conditions of Service, Prospects and Handicaps," *Army Quarterly and Defence Journal* 78 (1959): 82.

2. Reverend William Cole to Horace Walpole, 5 August 1781, W.S. Lewis and A. Dayle Wallace, eds., *Horace Walpole's Correspondence with the Reverend William Cole* (New Haven, Connecticut, 1970), 2: 280–81; "Memoir of Cotton," *Naval Chronicle* 27 (1812): 396; lecture notes of Lionel Munby, archivist of Madingley Hall, in possession of the author.

3. Charles Cotton to Philadelphia Cotton, 27 August 1810, Cambridgeshire County Record Office, Cotton Naval Papers, 588/c95; the birth and death dates of the Cotton children are based on a genealogical sketch sent to the author by Mr. Philip Saunders from the Cambridgeshire County Record Office.

4. Maria Susanna Cotton to Charles Cotton, 12 March 1802, Cambridgeshire County Record Office, Cotton Naval Papers, 588/c69a.

5. Ibid., 588/c69b, Maria Susanna Cotton to Charles Cotton, 12 May 1808.

6. Ibid., 588/c114, Charles Cotton to his son, 29 March 1801.

7. Cotton to Philip Yorke, Lord Hardwick, 22 May 1788, British Library, London, Correspondence of 3rd Lord Hardwick, Add. MSS 35684.

8. Linda Colley, *Britons: Forging the Nation, 1707–1837* (New Haven, 1992), 184–85; N.A.M. Rodger, *The Wooden World: An Anatomy of the Georgian Navy* (Annapolis,

1986), 328–33; Michael Lewis, *The Navy in Transition, 1814–1864: A Social History* (London, 1965), 22.

9. Leslie Stephen and Sydney Lee, eds., *Dictionary of National Biography*, 10: 97-98; Brain Lavery, *Nelson's Navy: The Ships, Men and Organisation, 1793–1815* (London, 1989), 245.

10. A.N. Ryan, "The Royal Navy and the Blockade of Brest, 1689–1805: Theory and Practice," in *Les Marines de Guerre Européennes XVII–XVIII*[e] *siècles*, ed. Martine Acerra (Paris, 1985), 184–85.

11. Stephen and Lee, *Dictionary of National Biography*, 10: 98; Lavery, *Nelson's Navy*, 246.

12. William S. Cormack, *Revolution and Political Conflict in the French Navy, 1789–1794* (Cambridge, 1995), 1–17, 109.

13. André Delaporte, "Combats de Prairial et Convoi de Vanstabel: le point de vue français," *Revue historique des armées* 4 (1995): 13–15; John Creswell, *British Admirals of the Eighteenth Century: Tactics in Battle (London, 1972)*, 197–99.

14. *Narrative of the Proceedings of His Majesty's Fleet under the Command of Earl Howe, from the Second of May to the Second of June* (London, 1796), 3–9, "Line of Battle" fold-out map; Creswell, *British Admirals*, 198–99.

15. Julian S. Corbett, ed., *Fighting Instructions, 1530–1816* (London, 1905), 255–59.

16. Remarks on board HMS the Majestic at sea, 6 June 1794, British Library, London, "The Original Despatches Communicating the Principal Victories Obtained by the British Navy over the Fleets of France and Her Allies in the Course of the Revolutionary Wars, 1794–1806" (1821), Add. MSS 23207; Log of Andrew Tracey, Master of the Majestic, 28, 29 May 1794, in Thomas S. Jackson, ed., *Logs of the Great Sea Fights, 1794–1805* (London, 1899), 1: 115; John Barrow, *Life of Richard Earl Howe, K.G., Admiral of the Fleet and General of Marines* (London, 1838), 229–30.

17. When a vessel gains the weather gauge, it is in a position to windward of another vessel.

18. Remarks on board HMS the Majestic at sea, 6 June 1794, British Library, London, "The Original Despatches Communicating the Principal Victories Obtained by the British Navy," Add. MSS 23207; Tracey log, 29 May 1794, Jackson, *Logs of the Great Sea Fights*, 115–16; Barrow, *Life of Richard Earl Howe*, 230–31; Creswell, *British Admirals*, 200–204.

19. *Narrative of the Proceedings of His Majesty's Fleet*, 13–15; Barrow, *Life of Richard Earl Howe*, 232–33; Creswell, *British Admirals*, 205.

20. Barrow, *Life of Richard Earl Howe*, 233; Creswell, *British Admirals*, 208.

21. Remarks on board HMS the Majestic at sea, 6 June 1794, British Library, London, "The Original Despatches Communicating the Principal Victories Obtained by the British Navy," Add. MSS 23207; Tracey log, 29 May 1794, Jackson, *Logs of the Great Sea Fights*, 117; *Narrative of the Proceedings of His Majesty's Fleet*, 13-15; Creswell, *British Admirals*, 208–10.

22. Remarks on board HMS the Majestic at sea, 6 June 1794, British Library, London, "The Original Despatches Communicating the Principal Victories Obtained by the British Navy," Add. MSS 23207; Tracey log, 29 May 1794, Jackson, *Logs of the Great Sea Fights*, 117–18.

23. Barrow, *Life of Richard Earl Howe*, 251–52; Cormack, *Revolution and Political Conflict in the French Navy*, 281–86.

24. Richard Knight to Lady Cotton, 1 August 1795, Cambridgeshire County Record Office, Cotton Naval Papers, 588/c83.

25. Barrow, *Life of Richard Earl Howe*, 259.

26. Collingwood to Dr. Alexander Carlyle, 2 July 1795, Edward Hughes, ed., *Private Correspondence of Admiral Lord Collingwood* (London, 1957), 67–69.

27. Howe to Philip Stephens, 20 June 1794, *Narrative of the Proceedings of His Majesty's Fleet*, 35–41.

28. Donald R. Come, "French Threat to British Shores, 1793–1798," *Military Affairs* 16 (1952): 178–79.

29. T.C.W. Blanning, *The French Revolutionary Wars, 1787–1802* (London, 1996), 202-203; Patrick Crowhurst, *French War on Trade: Privateering, 1793–1815* (Aldershot, 1989), 46–50.

30. Guy E. Cooper, "Methods of Blockade and Observation Employed during the Revolutionary and Napoleonic Wars," *Journal of the Royal United Service Institution* 61 (1916): 526–28.

31. Éduoard Chevalier, *Histoire de la Marine Français sous la Première République* (Paris, 1886), 201–3; G. Cornwallis-West, ed., *Life and Letters of Admiral Cornwallis* (London, 1927), 266–67.

32. Cornwallis to the Admiralty, 19 June 1795, Cornwallis-West, *Life of Cornwallis*, 267–70; Chevalier, *Marine Français*, 203–5.

33. Cornwallis to the Admiralty, 19 June 1795, Cornwallis-West, *Life of Cornwallis*, 267–70.

3

Channel Fleet Admiral: A Decade of Understudy, 1797–1806

> Styles of leadership may be very much products of past experience or may arise from a misunderstanding of the past. Battle experience may give confidence in facing a new situation, but it may give no insight into changing conditions of warfare.
>
> —John Horsfield[1]

Napoleon Bonaparte threatened Europe between 1797 and 1807. From the collapse of the First Coalition with the Treaty of Campo Formio to the destruction of the Fourth Coalition at Tilsit, he earned a reputation of martial invincibility unmatched by any contemporary. Military victories against Austria, Russia, and Prussia came in succession, and the map of Europe changed according to Bonaparte's dictates. Yet, victory against the nation that threatened his political legitimacy and power eluded him during these years. Britain used its economic strength, not its military might, to challenge France on the Continent. Financial aid and diplomatic encouragement fueled the fires of Austrian, Prussian, and Russian resistance. As long as this activity continued, Bonaparte believed the vanquished foes could rise again. While most pieces of the emperor's strategic continental puzzle fit neatly into place during the first decade of the nineteenty century, the emperor's attempt to isolate Britain from continental affairs represented a critical error. The Royal Navy was Britain's primary executive arm to frustrate Bonaparte's political and military aims and to keep the British government diplomatically linked to Europe.

Cotton served almost continuously in the Channel Fleet during this period, a period when decisive battles did not adequately measure the navy's contribution to the war effort. Detachments from the Channel did participate in the battles of

Copenhagen (1801) and Trafalgar, but the Channel Fleet never fought battles on this scale after "The Glorious First of June" for the remainder of the Napoleonic period. Rather, blockade duty best characterized the fleet's service. This duty did not lend itself to large naval engagements, but created maritime conditions essential for long-term success in the wars against Napoleonic France. The relative obscurity of Cotton's service during the period 1797 to 1806 belied its actual importance to the British cause.

Admiral Alexander Hood, Lord Bridport, served as the commander of the Channel Fleet during the first three years of Cotton's admiralcy. With Howe's infirmities preventing sea duty, Hood had actually been the de facto commander since 1795. However, for the two years before Hood officially assumed command of the fleet, an awkward arrangement of dual command undermined control of the fleet. While Howe, respected by seamen and officers alike, spent his time on shore, Hood's style of leadership failed to inspire trust and confidence. The Admiralty increasingly became involved in making decisions normally reserved for the fleet commander. Meanwhile, the fleet continued its open blockade. While this form of blockade reduced fair wear and tear on warships, it conversely was detrimental to discipline because idleness encouraged friction and contempt. Poor leadership, too much leisure in port, and legitimate petitions to the authorities combined to provoke the Spithead mutiny of April 1797.[2]

For two months mutinies immobilized the Royal Navy from Spithead to the Nore. At no other time during the wars against revolutionary France were the British Isles more prone to invasion. Yet, the French recognized England's vulnerability too late to exploit it. The mutinies ended in mid-June before the French could mount an expedition. As Britain survived this emergency, so too did Cotton. The mutiny had a negligible effect on his career. Certainly, he was not one of the 100 officers whose dismissal the mutineers at Spithead demanded and received. In fact, evidence suggests that the admiral might have been at Madingley during much of the mutiny and its aftermath. His youngest brother Edward addressed a letter on 5 August 1797 to Charles at Madingley. In the letter, Edward announced his appointment by William Pitt as the customs collector at Grenada and asked Charles if he could "seek a passage for me in a King's Ship, the bigger the better; I have a vast aversion to a French prison."[3] Edward's letter had its humor, but it also proved that his brother was absent from the fleet that summer for more than just a few days—the exact period is unknown. To some extent, Cotton must have avoided any repercussions from or involvement in the mutiny simply by being absent from the fleet.

Having weathered the storm created by the mutiny, Cotton and the fleet returned to the pressing business of controlling the Channel. After his time at Madingley, Cotton hoisted his flag aboard the 98-gun *Prince* at Spithead on 13 March 1799. The *Prince* was a three-deck second rate with a complement of over 700 officers and men. She sailed poorly because of her inefficient design—

some admirals preferred the 80-gun ship of two decks to the 98-gun class. Nevertheless, Cotton had risen to third flag officer of the Channel Fleet, subordinate to Lord Bridport and Vice Admiral Sir Alan Gardner. After heavy gales prevented the *Prince* from putting to sea on 8 April, Cotton finally sailed with Lord Bridport to Ushant to resume the tedious blockade of Brest. Routine duty in the Channel, however, was disrupted on 25 April by the escape from Brest of Vice Admiral Éustache Bruix's fleet with twenty-five ships-of-the-line.[4]

Bruix's flight from Brest was prompted by Nelson's naval victory at Aboukir Bay on 1 August 1798, which had isolated Bonaparte and his army in Egypt. In response to this crisis, the French government dispatched orders in January 1799 to Brest instructing the fleet to begin preparing for a cruise to the Mediterranean. The Brest Fleet reacted expeditiously, as it did in response to the food crisis of 1794. Before its departure, Bruix receieved orders detailing the scope of his operation. He was first to effect a junction with seventeen Spanish ships at Cadiz. Then his combined fleet would proceed into the Mediterranean, embark troops on the Italian peninsula, and provision Corfu, Malta, and Alexandria. Finally, with those tasks completed, the French admiral would seek a decisive battle with the British Mediterranean Fleet.[5]

Meanwhile, Cotton's ship, joined by fifteen other vessels in Bridport's squadron, stood off Brest the evening of Bruix's departure. Unfortunately for the British, fresh gales and cloudy weather gave Bruix the window of opportunity he needed to escape undetected. While the French headed south, Bridport prepared his fleet for action on the 27th and gave chase to the north. To cover Bruix's true intentions, the French government had given the impression of renewed interest in Ireland by allowing fake dispatches to fall into British hands. Acting on this information, Bridport proceeded to Bantry Bay, where he believed the French fleet could do the most harm.[6]

Cotton arrived off the southeastern coast of Ireland in early May with Bridport's fleet and remained on station there, waiting for Bruix for the rest of the month. Cotton commanded the van squadron that cruised actively until the fleet entered Bantry Bay on the 24th. When the news of Bruix's actual destination was learned, Bridport immediately organized a squadron for dispatch to the Mediterranean. He placed Admiral Gardner in command of the squadron's sixteen ships-of-the-line with Cotton and Collingwood leading the van and rear divisions respectively. After saluting Gardner with thirteen guns, the *Prince* eased out of Bantry Bay on 1 June to begin a two-and-a-half-month absence from Channel waters.[7]

After one week's sailing, command of the squadron devolved upon Cotton nineteen leagues off Cape St. Vincent when Gardner returned to the Channel with the Mediterranean trade and prizes from the Battle of Aboukir Bay. Commanding twelve ships-of-the-line, Cotton resumed the cruise on 9 June with orders to report to Admiral John Jervis, Lord St. Vincent, in the Mediterranean. After receiving St. Vincent's written instructions at Gibraltar,

Cotton led his squadron into the Mediterranean on the 13th. As British naval forces concentrated, Bruix's fleet remained at large in the Mediterranean. Having failed to join the Spanish fleet at Cadiz because of the British blockade commanded by Vice Admiral George Elphinestone, Lord Keith, Bruix had sailed for Toulon where his fleet anchored on 14 May. On the 26th it departed for Vado Bay on the Ligurian coast; it managed to elude the British fleet through luck and faulty orders from St. Vincent to Keith. By June, however, Bruix lost his nerve in a sea where he believed the Royal Navy had achieved numerical superiority. In fact, Keith's and Cotton's squadrons had not yet joined. Nonetheless, Bruix sailed for Carthagena to combine with the Spanish fleet that had escaped from Cadiz after Keith's departure.[8]

A judicial action overseen by Cotton during a pause in the search for Bruix illustrates the Royal Navy's emphasis on discipline. On 22 June, the day before Bruix arrived at Carthagena, Cotton authorized the execution of three men aboard Captain Sir Edward Pellew's *Impetueux*. Their offense, conspiring to mutiny, had occurred at Bantry Bay on 30 May. Cotton quickly learned that St. Vincent's brand of discipline was harsher than Bridport's. When Cotton went ashore at Port Mahon, Minorca, on the 18th, no doubt St. Vincent made clear that the rear admiral should convene a court-martial immediately, despite the unknown whereabouts of Bruix's force. Cotton wasted little time. A courts-martial convened two days later and sentenced three conspirators to death, one to receive 200 lashes, and four to receive 100. After administration of the punishment, Cotton returned to the task of joining Lord Keith's squadron.[9]

Cotton's squadron sailed from Port Mahon on 23 June. The following day he received intelligence from the frigate *Caroline* that identified eighteen or nineteen French sail-of-the-line off Cape Palos, north of Carthagena. With this report and its subsequent confirmation, Cotton's squadron remained off the waters of Minorca in anticipation of the arrival of Lord Keith's squadron from Toulon. In addition, Cotton's squadron remained in these waters because the size of the Franco-Spanish fleet made an enemy descent upon one of the Balearic Islands a distinct possibility. While cruising off Corsica on the 29th, Keith received word of Bruix's arrival at Carthagena. His squadron immediately sailed for Minorca. On 7 July, the squadrons of Cotton and Keith combined into a fleet of thirty-one ships-of-the-line. Keith then ordered the fleet into Port Mahon. Previously, sickness had compelled St. Vincent to sail for Gibraltar and relinquish control of the Mediterranean Fleet to Keith. It rested with Keith to interpret the lastest intelligence on the enemy's disposition. Reports of recent naval activity at Barcelona made Keith suspect that the Spanish would attempt to recover Minorca while his fleet chased Bruix through the straits of Gibraltar. Based on this assumption, Keith spent several days after his junction with Cotton making preparations for the defense of Minorca.[10]

The fleet of Keith and Cotton finally departed Port Mahon on 12 July and pursued Bruix's fleet westward through the straits. Having departed Carthagena on 29 June, the Franco-Spanish fleet had a significant lead over the pursuing British. Although the combined fleet appeared to have the advantage in size and initiative, it left the Mediterranean primarily because Bruix and the Spanish commander could not agree on their objective there. They settled instead on a combined movement to the west, with plans to mount an expedition to Ireland. Keith's fleet closed the gap considerably during its pursuit, but it ultimately failed to catch Bruix before the Franco-Spanish fleet arrived at Brest on 11 August. Keith and Cotton arrived off Ushant the following day and then proceeded, without prizes for their effort, to Torbay.[11]

Bruix's cruise to the Mediterranean frustrated both the French and British. The French admiral took the offensive with a superior force in the Mediterranean, but he failed to capitalize on this strength in any significant manner. In hindsight, Bruix's cruise did create a diversion that facilitated Bonaparte's escape from Egypt—he landed on 9 August at Fréjus on France's Mediterranean coast. For Keith, three months of fruitless searching left him empty-handed. Cotton surely felt Keith's frustration, but his venture into the Mediterranean had personal tangible benefits other than the capture of French warships. For the first time, he commanded a large squadron away from the English Channel. This independent flag command introduced him to the Mediterranean Fleet, which he would command in later years. It also introduced him to St. Vincent, who would assume command of the Channel Fleet within the year. The pursuit of Bruix gave Cotton a learning experience not available within the confines of the English Channel.[12]

After a four-month absence from its home port, Cotton's squadron naturally needed time to refit. The *Prince*, having been rebuilt in 1796, finished the cruise "in perfect order," a testimonial to the quality of her crew and perhaps a reflection of Cotton's leadership.[13] The fate of the *Prince*, however, took an unfortunate turn for the worse with an accident in the winter of 1800. Inclement weather had hampered several attempts by Cotton to lead a squadron of six ships-of-the-line and two frigates out of the Channel on a cruise into the Atlantic. In the attempt of 15 January, the second rate *Saturn* and *Prince* collided; Cotton's ship returned to Portsmouth on the 20th. An ensuing court-martial cleared the respective commanders of negligence, but damage to the *Prince* caused the dissolution of the project for which Cotton's squadron was intended.[14]

The accident between the *Prince* and *Saturn* probably did not cause the same consternation with Lord Bridport as it would have with his successor. However, Bridport's tenure as commander of the Channel Fleet had its share of controversy and some doubted the admiral's suitability for high command. He was criticized for his handling of the mutinies in 1797 and the loose standard of blockade he imposed on Brest in April 1799 that facilitated Bruix's escape. Upon hearing of a new commander appointed to the Channel Fleet, Sir Edward Pellew wrote of Bridport: "A more contemptible or more miserable animal does not exist. I believe there never was a man so universally despised by the whole service."[15] Differences certainly existed between Bridport and his replacement, St. Vincent, but most noteworthy was their approach to blockade duty.

When St. Vincent assumed command of the Channel Fleet in April 1800, he imposed a close and continuous blockade upon French ports. This radically altered the fleet's method of operations as practiced under Bridport. The arguments for and against both close and open blockade were strong topics of debate at the time. St. Vincent advocated the close blockade as vociferously as Bridport did the open blockade. However, considering the condition of the British fleet in 1800, the arguments for close and continuous blockade became more convincing. Improved dockyards and more effective administration better supported the fleet, translating into less time spent refitting the average warship. In addition, the health of seamen had improved through better diets and new methods of ventilating and cleaning ships. The Royal Navy was better prepared in 1800 to impose a close and continuous blockade than during the previous seven years of war, and the strategic situation in Europe now provided a more compelling reason for doing so. The War of the Second Coalition continued on account of General André Masséna's victory at Zurich on 26 September 1799. The following November, Bonaparte seized power in France as First Consul. Incidentally, any notions among British leadership of a short war against France dissipated. The Channel Fleet responded to the crisis on the Continent by imposing on French ports a close and continuous blockade.[16]

Cotton retained the position of third flag officer in the Channel Fleet upon St. Vincent's assumption of command in April 1800. He was senior to four other flag officers in the fleet: rear admirals Collingwood, James Whitshed, the Honorable George Berkeley, and Sir John Warren. Sir Alan Gardner retained his position as second-in-command of the fleet, but much to his dissatisfaction. After six years of service in the Channel, he thought himself more suited for its command than St. Vincent, who had spent his last four years in the Mediterranean. With Gardner's August 1800 appointment as commander-in-chief on the coast of Ireland, Cotton moved to second-in-command of the Channel Fleet. Notwithstanding changes in the command structure, the War of the Second Coalition continued, and St. Vincent had to determine how best to employ his fleet.[17]

Cotton served much of the remaining two years of the Second Coalition's existence at sea off Ushant, imposing St. Vincent's stranglehold on Brest. The winter months were not too difficult for St. Vincent as they had been for Bridport—hence a sizable squadron remained off Ushant the entire year. With Brest virtually isolated from the French coastal trade and with fewer opportunities to escape, the quality of the Brest fleet deteriorated substantially.

In addition to the normal duties of blockade, convoy escort, and cruising, the Channel Fleet also cooperated with the army in mounting expeditions. An attempt to seize Belle-Îsle was canceled before the landing and another expedition to Ferrol failed after a desultory effort. Cotton apparently had no direct involvement with these limited operations. As second-in-command, his attention remained focused on the fleet's main effort: the blockade of Brest.[18]

When not on station off Ushant, Cotton's attention was occasionally diverted to matters of personal interest. Prize money was one such interest that he held in common with every other officer. Once an enemy vessel became a prize, the navy turned it over to a prize agent at the nearest port. After adjudication and sale of the prize, the agent then distributed the money according to the rules of the Prize Act. Flag officers received a very high percentage of prize value, normally one-eighth for a commander-in-chief. If subordinate flag officers were in the fleet, the commander-in-chief gave one-sixteenth of his money for equal distribution among them. Because prize money could make an admiral rich very quickly, its distribution was often of great concern. For enemy frigates taken in the Mediterranean during his brief time there in 1799, Cotton received £144. In a letter dated 8 October 1800, he told his wife that he expected to receive £6,000 for prizes taken since he hoisted his flag in the Channel. This was a handsome supplement to the annual pay of a rear admiral, £420.[19]

With the fall of William Pitt and the rise of Henry Addington's ministry, St. Vincent left the Channel in February 1801 to become First Lord of the Admiralty. Cornwallis succeeded him, and Cotton continued as second-in-command of the fleet. The next year brought little opportunity for distinguished service for either man. St. Vincent selected Admiral Sir Hyde Parker to lead an expedition to Copenhagen, where the battle on 2 April 1801 became another accolade on Nelson's professional résumé. The opportunity for distinguished service ended the following year on 25 March 1802, when hostilities ceased between Britain and France with the Treaty of Amiens. The two nations finally took time for recovery after nine continuous years of war. With the Channel Fleet's sudden peacetime status, Cotton lowered his flag and returned again to Madingley, where he enjoyed the "domestic life and agricultural pursuits."[20]

After a month of peace, Cotton received a promotion to vice admiral of the blue on 29 April 1802. Also during the peace, Charles and Philadelphia nurtured their year-old son, whom they had named St. Vincent in honor of the current First Lord. Whatever the status of their professional relationship, Cotton and St. Vincent apparently maintained a warm personal one. Not only did Cotton name his firstborn son after the First Lord, but he also invited St. Vincent to become the boy's godfather, an offer that was gratefully accepted. In a letter to Lady Cotton, St. Vincent expressed pride in his godson and hoped "he may live to be a comfort to your Ladyship and Sir Charles to whom, and every individual in your family, I beg leave to offer the best wishes."[21] However warm this personal relationship, St. Vincent's reputation in the Royal Navy was that of a harsh disciplinarian who spared no one criticism. Even a close personal tie did not shield Cotton from the First Lord's watchful eye over performance in the naval service.

Barely had the ink dried on the Treaty of Amiens when indications arose that war between Britain and France was again imminent. For his war-weary nation, Addington had been willing to make diplomatic concessions that overwhelmingly favored French interests. Yet despite favorable treaty terms, Bonaparte continued with a national and international agenda that the British perceived as threatening, if not directly hostile. Among other issues, France continued territorial aggrandizement in Europe, sent an expeditionary army to San Domingo, and dispatched a mission to the eastern Mediterranean intended more for espionage than diplomacy. If these actions did not violate the letter of the treaty, they certainly violated its spirit. The British ministry delayed implementation of some terms from the treaty, most notably British evacuation from Malta and the Mediterranean. By the spring of 1803, the question became not if but when hostilities would resume between the two nations. Already the Royal Navy had put its press gangs in motion and was preparing warships "laying up in ordinary" for sea. After Addington issued an unacceptable ultimatum on 10 May 1803, France responded six days later with a declaration of war. Cotton's time at Madingley ended abruptly after fourteen months of peace.

Vice Admiral Cotton returned to Portsmouth as second-in-command of the Channel Fleet, and on 11 June he hoisted his flag aboard the 112-gun *San Josef*, a former Spanish ship captured by Nelson at the Battle of St. Vincent in February 1797. Cornwallis also returned as commmander-in-chief, while St. Vincent retained his position as First Lord. Collingwood remained in the fleet with rear admirals Sir Robert Calder and Sir Thomas Graves as additional flag officers. These were the leaders with whom Cornwallis reinstituted the close and continuous blockade of Brest. Adhering to the precedents established by St. Vincent, Cornwallis kept twelve of twenty Channel Fleet ships-of-the-line constantly at sea. Of the twelve, six remained off Ushant, prepared to attack any ships that should escape from Brest, while a couple other vessels joined the frigates of the inshore squadron overlooking the port. The purpose of the inshore squadron was to observe the French fleet and, should it leave Brest, to keep it in check until the offshore squadron could bring it to action. The remaining ships-of-the-line would cruise off Lorient, Rochefort, and Ferrol as necessary.[22]

Besides the usual reasons for blockade, Bonaparte's mobilization of the Army of England and construction of the invasion flotilla in 1803 placed additional importance on the Royal Navy's containment of the Brest Fleet. After the collapse of peace in May 1803, Bonaparte ordered Vice Admiral Denis Decrès, Minister of Marine, to prepare a flotilla of 310 boats by the end of September to be poised along the Strait of Dover from Étaples to Ostend. The number of boats increased at least fivefold by the end of the year to meet the requirement of transporting some 130,000 troops, 15,000 horses, and 500 artillery pieces across the English Channel. This military and naval force, regardless of Bonaparte's strategy, legitimately threatened the Royal Navy. Whether or not Bonaparte really intended to send a flotilla across the Channel has been a subject for debate, but it is now generally agreed that he genuinely was planning an invasion.[23]

Since the jurisdiction of Cornwallis's fleet extended only as far east as Selsey Bill, the North Sea Fleet, commanded by Lord Keith, directly opposed the French flotilla. Thus, the French invasion plan did not materially affect the nature of the Channel Fleet's duty, only its intensity. Cornwallis took station off Ushant in the *Ville de Paris* of 110 guns on 9 July 1803 and remained there until driven away by a gale in December. His presence off Ushant for such an extended period demonstrated the resolve that he wanted his inshore squadron commanders to display. The difficulty of inshore duty was illustrated by Collingwood's comments from October 1803: "It was a station of great anxiety and required so constant a care and look-out, that I have often been a week without having my clothes off."[24] The difficult weather that forced Cornwallis to Plymouth did the same to Cotton's ship, and the strain of sea duty at this time of year wore on the crew of the *San Josef*—thirty were sent ashore with dysentery.[25]

Cornwallis' second long cruise off Ushant lasted from 3 February to 18 July 1804. Although on station for another extended period of time, his grip on Brest weakened because his squadron seldom ventured away from its position northwest of Ushant. Assumption of this position was a tacit admission that the difficulty of operating closer to shore produced diminishing returns. In addition, the offshore squadron could better exert control over all the approaches to the Channel if further off Ushant. St. Vincent's departure as First Lord in May 1804 might further explain the weakened condition of the Brest blockade. As second-in-command to Cornwallis from July 1803 to July 1804, Cotton witnessed the evolution of the Brest blockade and gained experience that prepared him to assume command of the Channel Fleet when Cornwallis went ashore for leave in July 1804.[26]

During the summer of 1804 rumors circulated that the Brest Fleet was preparing to embark with nine or ten ships-of-the-line. The new First Lord, Henry Dundas, Viscount Melville, suspected that the French were planning an expedition to the Cape of Good Hope or the Leeward Islands. He further speculated that this enemy force might attempt to engage the blockading squadrons off Ferrol and Rochefort, thereby allowing the French squadrons there to escape into the Mediterranean. Then, the French fleet in the Mediterranean would gain superiority over Nelson's fleet.[27] Melville communicated these thoughts to Cornwallis, who may have received them before instructing Cotton on how to manage the fleet in his absence.

Should any circumstance or accident occasion the French squadron to escape without being observed by the squadron with you, or the ships cruising closer to the mouth of the harbour, you are not to follow them, unless you can be very sure of the route they have taken, or leave the mouth of the Channel unguarded, as the enemy might in that case take the opportunity to push up the Channel for the purpose of aiding the threatened invasion of his Majesty's dominions, the protecting of which at this particular time being the principal object of the force placed under my command.[28]

These orders clearly summarized the Channel Fleet's primary purpose and demonstrated Cornwallis's sound strategy. He ordered Cotton to avoid reacting speculatively to French naval activity and not to give Bonaparte the opportunity he needed to gain temporary naval superiority in the Channel. Cotton's goal was the security of the home islands, not a seamless blockade or pursuit and destruction of an enemy squadron.[29]

Caution was the guiding principle for Cotton to follow. His command of the Channel Fleet that summer proved suspenseful, but uneventful. A few days after Cornwallis took leave, the commander of the inshore squadron off Brest reported to Cotton that there appeared "every reason to believe that nine sail-of-the-line have an intention to put to sea shortly . . . it being my firm opinion that they will make the attempt the first opportunity."[30] The Brest Fleet never made the attempt, and operations for the inshore and offshore squadrons continued normally. However, a few officers grew impatient with the Channel Fleet's defensive posture and consequently proposed schemes to destroy the Brest Fleet in port. Captain Peter Puget proposed one scheme before Cornwallis departed on leave. The captain believed that fireships could destroy the enemy fleet at anchor. Rear Admiral Sir Thomas Graves proposed another scheme to Cotton on 23 August. Graves wanted to destroy the Brest arsenal by means of an amphibious raid involving several thousand British soldiers who would land north and south of the port. Simultaneously, eight or ten ships-of-the-line would enter the harbor to destroy or capture the enemy fleet. Cotton, of course, did not have the authority to approve this venture.[31]

Cornwallis returned to the fleet in late August and received Cotton's proceedings of the previous month. In preparation for Puget's outlandish scheme, fireships sailed from Portsmouth on 7 September, but Cornwallis never executed the plan. Graves's plan entailed too many risks and was never seriously considered. Notwithstanding the Channel Fleet's defensive posture, not one French squadron escaped from a blockaded port since the resumption of war in 1803. Cornwallis and his admirals had made a remarkable effort to prevent French naval forces from entering the Channel to support Bonaparte's invasion plans. Despite Cornwallis's strong will and perseverance, however, the Royal Navy could not contain the French in port forever because of the weather and Bonaparte's incessant provocation of his admirals. The winter of 1804–1805 saw heavy gales and the initiation of another French plan to concentrate a superior naval force in the Channel.[32]

The essence of Bonaparte's naval plan in December 1804 required Vice Admiral Édouard Missiessy to lead his Rochefort squadron to the West Indies with the intent of wrecking British commercial interests and luring the Channel Fleet away from its post. Meanwhile, the Toulon Fleet, commanded by Vice Admiral Pierre-Charles Villeneuve, would proceed to Cadiz and combine with the Spanish fleet commanded by Admiral Charles Gravina. The combined fleet would then sail to South America, attack British interests, and join Missiessy in the West Indies. Finally, the Franco-Spanish fleet would sail to the English Channel, where it could act in concert with the Brest Fleet, commanded by Vice Admiral Honoré Ganteaume. Throughout the evolution of this plan, Bonaparte modified its details several times, frustrating his admirals and displaying his ignorance of naval affairs.[33]

Missiessy made the first move on 11 January 1805. He embarked from Rochefort in a snowstorm with five ships-of-the-line and two frigates for his passage to the West Indies. While he proceeded across the Atlantic, news of the Rochefort squadron's departure reached Cotton, who at the time was on station off Ushant. Captain Jervis of the *Tonnant* joined the *San Josef* on the 23rd, but intense weather hampered communication between the two ships. Unable to board the *San Josef*, Cotton received Jervis's signalled report that six French ships-of-the-line and two frigates had sailed from Rochefort. Deteriorating weather conditions prevented further communication. After three days, Jervis decided that he could no longer delay a conversation with Cotton. Jervis launched in a boat from the *Tonnant*, but drowned before reaching the *San Josef*. The winter weather not only caused this unfortunate death, but left Cotton assuming that Missiessy's squadron had entered Brest.[34]

Meanwhile, during the spring of 1805, Ganteaume's fleet remained within the confines of Brest harbor. Napoleon's initial orders were for Ganteaume to fight Cornwallis' squadrons in order to break the blockade. Just when Ganteaume believed his fleet was prepared for battle, Napoleon changed his orders: the twenty-one ships-of-the-line at Brest would avoid battle with the Channel Fleet and escape to the West Indies via Ferrol to participate in the larger scheme involving the combined fleets of Villenueve, Missiessy, and Gravina. Ganteaume would lead the combined fleet back to Boulogne to support the invasion sometime between 10 June and 10 July 1805.[35]

When Ganteaume made his attempt to execute Napoleon's order in March, Cotton was on station off Ushant, again in temporary command of the Channel Fleet while Cornwallis took another leave of absence to recover his health. However, the Admiralty did not entrust the fleet to Cotton's care for the duration of the commander-in-chief's absence. Lord Melville had made an arrangement the previous fall for Gardner to assume command of the Channel Fleet whenever Cornwallis went ashore. Gardner, still commanding the Irish station at Cork, was readily available to transfer between the two commands. Correspondence provides no indication that Melville did not trust Cotton's ability to temporarily command the fleet. Melville's arrangement with Gardner appeared a matter of seniority rather than merit. As the First Lord told Cornwallis:

> You need not be informed of the importance which the public naturally attaches to the command of the Channel Fleet. Under that impression my wish is that the command

> should belong either to you or to Lord Gardner. . . . [T]he Channel Fleet will at all times be under the immediate command of an officer of such distinction and rank as will secure the confidence of the public.[36]

If not yet an officer of distinction, Cotton certainly did not have the proper rank. Regardless, Gardner was in England when the Brest Fleet challenged the Channel Fleet under Cotton's temporary command.

On 27 March, Ganteaume moved twenty-one ships-of-the-line to the Bertheaume and Camaret anchorages at the entrance to the port of Brest. Having received specific instructions from Napoleon to avoid an engagement with the British squadron, Ganteaume waited for the right conditions to make his escape. Cotton, informed of the French disposition, stood offshore about five miles from the French fleet. Cotton's total force off Brest of fifteen ships-of-the-line was decidedly inferior to the French force. The French advantage of coastal batteries provided additional firepower for Ganteaume's force as he awaited the right moment to escape from the British. Cotton chose not to risk battle with an enemy fleet anchored close to shore—he did not replicate Nelson's Battle of Aboukir Bay. That evening Cotton stood off with his squadron while Rear Admiral Graves remained inshore with four ships-of-the-line and other vessels to observe Ganteaume's next move. The weather was not in Ganteaume's favor, so he withdrew his fleet into Brest harbor on the 29th.[37]

Cotton missed a superb opportunity for a decisive engagement with the Brest Fleet, but the odds were distinctly against him. The French were superior in numbers and had the advantage of a familiar anchorage within range of coastal batteries. By standing offshore with his squadron on the night of 27 March, Cotton sought to entice the French out—he had not abandoned hope for a decisive battle. Despite numerical inferiority, Cotton wanted to intercept the French fleet should it proceed to sea. There the British fleet could bring its superior seamanship and gunnery to bear more effectively. When Gardner arrived off Ushant on 3 April to assume command, he found Ganteaume's fleet nestled securely within the port of Brest.[38]

During 1805, a unique command relationship developed in the Channel Fleet between Cornwallis, Gardner, and Cotton. Cornwallis's fragile health led to frequent furloughs. Consequently, his command often fell to his second-in-command. This provided Cotton with several opportunities to temporarily lead the fleet during his ten years as a Channel admiral. However, he was not the most senior admiral available for this role. Gardner, now an admiral of the blue, was still commander-in-chief of the squadron off the coast of Ireland. The question arose over the possibility of Gardner and Cornwallis sharing command of the Channel Fleet, relieving each other but never acting together. The success of such an arrangement, however, depended heavily upon personalities and relationships. Although George III among others believed that Gardner was unsuitable for command of the Channel Fleet, the Admiralty still considered him worthy. Gardner commanded the fleet from 3 April 1805 until

Cornwallis's resumption of command on 6 July. Evidently, Gardner's relationship with Cornwallis and Cotton was not conducive to such a solution. Gardner expressed his anxiety about the proposal to Melville's replacement as First Lord, Charles Middleton, Lord Barham.

> I am sure you must be aware of the very unpleasant situation in which I have been placed, both with respect to Admiral Cornwallis and Vice Admiral Sir Charles Cotton, which I can assure your lordship has occasioned a great deal of anxiety and uneasiness in my mind not easily to be described, and which has affected my health and depressed my spirits so much, that I find myself unequal to the discharge of my duty in the manner I could wish, nor have I any hope of my being able to do so, until my mind is more at ease.[39]

Gardner subsequently requested a two-month leave of absence for recovery. Cotton must have felt slighted by the admiral's presence in the fleet. After so many years in the Channel, Cotton surely believed himself qualified for command. In addition, Cotton might have viewed Gardner's selection as a vote of no confidence from the Admiralty. It was a situation that seems to have caused Cotton to consider lowering his flag. According to Collingwood in a letter to Nelson: "[Sir Robert Calder] tells me, that Cotton, dissatisfied with something, is likely to leave the Fleet."[40] In a letter to his wife, Cotton spoke of the "Question," which could have been an allusion to the matter concerning Gardner. If not the matter of Channel Fleet command, then another controversial issue caused him to remark: "Had I gone ashore in resentment what bitter reflections might have been formed on the supposition that I might have been there [Trafalgar]."[41] Whatever the case, the chain of naval events unleashed by Napoleon required the Admiralty's undivided attention and left little time for reflection on the matter of Channel Fleet command.

Cornwallis returned in July to a situation very different from the one he had left in March. Having missed Napoleon's order to join the combined fleet in the West Indies, Missiessy led his squadron back to Rochefort, arriving there on 20 May. Villeneuve and Gravina had sailed with their combined fleet from Cadiz on 10 April, arrived in Martinique on 16 May, and embarked for Europe on 11 June. The unknown status of the Franco-Spanish Fleet and heightened apprehensions concerning the enemy squadrons in Rochefort, El Ferrol, and Cadiz placed additional stress on the Channel Fleet. It became more dispersed when the Admiralty detached a squadron under Collingwood's command. After several changes in orders, Collingwood received instructions to establish a watch over the harbor of Cadiz.

Villeneuve's combined fleet arrived off El Ferrol on 22 July and clashed with a squadron commanded by Vice Admiral Sir Robert Calder. In the aftermath of this indecisive battle, Villeneuve withdrew to Vigo and then to El Ferrol, while Calder sailed to Cape Finisterre in hope of joining Nelson. Failing to join Nelson, Calder sailed back to El Ferrol, where he arrived on 9 August.

With only nine sail-of-the-line, Calder could not hope to blockade the combined fleet's twenty-nine sail. Therefore, he abandoned the blockade and sailed for Ushant to meet with Cornwallis. On 16 August, two days after Calder's arrival, Cornwallis appointed him to command a fleet of nineteen sail-of-the-line for the purpose of preventing the combined fleet's departure from El Ferrol or intercepting it if already at sea. Cornwallis had thus anticipated similar orders from the Admiralty. On 19 August, Barham directed Cornwallis to dispatch Cotton with two junior flag officers and twenty ships-of-the-line to El Ferrol, the mission that Cornwallis had already given Calder. Cotton had barely missed a superb opportunity to serve as commander of a sizable detached squadron because he likely had taken leave of absence at Madingley after Cornwallis returned to the fleet in early July. This much was implied by a letter from Calder to Cotton on 24 September: "I have just heard you are returned to the Fleet."[42]

Before Calder's squadron departed Ushant on 17 August, the Franco-Spanish fleet had sailed from El Ferrol; it arrived at Cadiz on the 21st. Calder's fleet pursued and arrived off Cadiz on 21 September, much to the relief of Collingwood, who had only eight ships-of-the-line facing an estimated thirty-six enemy line of battleships. Thus, the stage was set for the Battle of Trafalgar. Nelson assumed command of the reorganized Mediterranean Fleet on 25 September and promptly sent Calder back to Britain, where he would stand trial for his performance during the battle of 22 July—he was reprimanded and not employed again on naval service. Collingwood became the second-in-command. Had the timing been different, Cotton might have been in command of the squadron that Cornwallis detached from the Channel, a squadron that formed the bulk of Nelson's fleet at Trafalgar. Cotton, senior to Collingwood, also might have commanded the lee column that smashed the combined fleet's rear on 21 October. Cotton's reflection on this lost opportunity caused him no small amount of mental anguish, as painfully articulated to his wife two weeks after Trafalgar: "I have thought, and still can hardly think of anything else. Collingwood's present situation in the service might have been mine, what short sighted mortals we are. . . . Such an event as his succeeding to such high honors makes me feel my degradation here, but I have gulped the bitter pill again."[43] The Battle of Trafalgar, the seminal naval event of the Napoleonic period, profoundly shaped the contemporary reputation and legacy of every participant. Yet, decisive battles normally do not occur in a strategic vacuum. Nelson certainly displayed tactical genius, but the road to Trafalgar was paved by the strategic vision of leaders like Cornwallis and by the unassuming, steady professionalism of leaders like Cotton. Cotton felt cheated by his absence from Trafalgar, but the work he did in the Channel was also important.

From Napoleon's perspective, the Battle of Trafalgar was anticlimactic. While the French navy attempted to support the Boulogne flotilla's cross-Channel invasion, the Third Coalition of Britain, Austria, Russia, and Sweden solidified. By mid-August 1805, Napoleon recognized that the armies mobilizing east of France posed more of a threat than the shopkeepers of Britain. Therefore, on 26 August, he issued definitive orders that sent the *Grande Armée* marching east to victories at Ulm and Austerlitz. Meanwhile, Cornwallis continued to command in the Channel. After Napoleon shattered the Russian and Austrian armies at Austerlitz on 2 December 1805, the Third Coalition collapsed, as well as the health of the British prime minister. In the wake of Pitt's death in January 1806, the Ministry of All the Talents was organized and led by William Wyndham, Lord Grenville. The change also shuffled leadership in the Royal Navy. Charles Grey, Viscount Howick, became First Lord of the Admiralty, and St. Vincent was recalled from retirement to replace Cornwallis in the Channel. Cotton experienced his fourth change of senior commander while serving in the Channel when St. Vincent hoisted his flag on HMS *Hibernia* on 22 February 1806.

St. Vincent immediately reimposed his stern form of discipline and arduous method of blockade upon the Channel Fleet; he believed that standards had dropped dramatically since his departure from the fleet five years earlier. For the third consecutive year Cotton watched the Brest Fleet, rotating between Ushant and Portsmouth for refitting. Soon after taking station again off Brest, St. Vincent's negative first impression of the fleet became more positive. St. Vincent's second-in-command received some of the credit for his renewed confidence in the Channel Fleet: "I think the system [of blockade] is now established on such principles it cannot be departed from; the more especially as Sir Charles Cotton has been witness to the certainty of keeping hold of Ushant in any wind or weather, by taking shelter under that island in an easterly gale, and profiting of the tides."[44] St. Vincent relied heavily on Cotton, for of all the admirals on active service in the Royal Navy, none had Cotton's experience and consequent understanding of the waters off the port of Brest.

St. Vincent held the noose around Brest harbor tight enough to prevent any ship-of-the-line from leaving during the remainder of 1806. While the sense of crisis in the Channel Fleet had diminished after Trafalgar, the British government perceived a new crisis developing in Portugal. With his continental victories, Napoleon controlled all the major European ports between the Adriatic and the Baltic except one. In the summer of 1806, the British government believed that Lisbon had become another military objective for Napoleon. One indication of this intention came from intelligence received by St. Vincent that a French army was assembling at Bayonne with instructions to march on Lisbon. Reports of French intrigue within the Portuguese House of Braganza further increased British anxiety over the fate of its traditional ally. St. Vincent urged the First Lord to send him to Lisbon with a squadron to assist the Portuguese by whatever means possible. If necessary, St. Vincent would secure the Portuguese fleet and help the royal family escape to Brazil.[45]

St. Vincent spent about two months on station off Lisbon while Cotton commanded the main body of the Channel Fleet off Ushant from mid-August to mid-October 1806. During St. Vincent's absence, the French navy increased its activity in the Channel Fleet's waters—unquestioned British naval superiority after the Battle of Trafalgar had not completely paralyzed the enemy fleet. In late September, an expedition of five frigates and two brigs with 1,600 soldiers embarked from Rochefort for Martinique. On the 25th, the blockading squadron off Rochefort captured four of the frigates in an action that was "attended with much slaughter."[46] Among the casualties, Captain Sir Samuel Hood, commander of the blockading squadon, lost his right arm. Cotton's report of this action to the Admiralty might have contributed to the subsequent erosion of the First Lord's confidence in him.[47]

Thomas Grenville became First Lord of the Admiralty on 29 September 1806 while St. Vincent was posted off Lisbon. The new First Lord's impression of Cotton's leadership of the Channel Fleet in St. Vincent's absence was extremely unfavorable, soon proving the cliché that "first impressions are lasting impressions." Grenville received a report that at least three ships-of-the-line had escaped from Brest under Cotton's watch, and he wanted to know if the report was accurate upon St. Vincent's return to Plymouth. St. Vincent expressed doubt that any ships had escaped while Cotton commanded off Brest and additionally stated to Grenville: "There certainly is no difficulty in the blockade, with an easterly wind, if it does not overblow; but this can only be done by tacking in the night, so as to be close in with Ushant at daylight; which I have always practiced, and it is natural to suppose that in my absence the practice was not discontinued."[48]

St. Vincent's remarks did not diminish Grenville's concerns about Cotton. The First Lord continued his investigation of Cotton's performance. He asked St. Vincent to send him a copy of the instructions that were left to guide Cotton's "mode of cruising." In addition to satisfying this request, St. Vincent forwarded a copy of Cotton's journal so that the First Lord could judge how well Cotton had complied with the instructions.[49]

Grenville's faith in Cotton continued eroding as a result of the investigation. In a letter dated 17 November 1806 to his brother, the Marquis of Buckingham, Grenville stated that he did no "hold [Cotton] high" and was "in distress for a tolerable second" to St. Vincent in the Channel Fleet.[50] The First Lord continued a week later:

> My chief present difficulty is about Cotton, whose *claims* are hourly growing by serving in the Channel fleet to reach command of it, for which he is, as I believe entirely unfit. My present views for replacing Lord St. Vincent whenever he goes, rest with Collingwood and Duckworth, the first of whom must, I suppose, have the Channel, and the second the Mediterranean; but this is inconsistent with keeping Cotton; and yet it is not easy to remove him.[51]

The Admiralty had promoted Cotton to vice admiral of the red on 9 November 1805, the last gradation before full admiral—the traditional rank for commander-in-chief of the Channel Fleet. Grenville's "difficulty" with Cotton prompted him to initiate a search for a new second-in-command senior to Cotton. One candidate, Vice Admiral Sir Charles Pole, turned down the offer of second-in-command because Grenville would not promise command of the Channel Fleet to him after St. Vincent's retirement. Grenville, with only two months as First Lord, sought advice about available candidates from St. Vincent, who had no alternative choices to recommend: "I do not know one flag-officer upon half-pay, senior to Sir Charles Cotton, whom, if I filled the station you do, I could confide in to guard the port of Brest. There is such a deficiency of nerve under responsibility, that I see officers of the greatest promise and acquired character sink beneath its weight."[52] With no suitable replacement for Cotton, Grenville resorted to another means of ensuring that he would not rise to command the Channel Fleet: assignment to another station.

In late November 1806, Grenville sought St. Vincent's advice on sending Cotton to the Jamaica station. St. Vincent replied that he would "sound [Cotton's] inclinations by this post," adding that their relationship was on the "very best footing."[53] St. Vincent penned his response on 30 November: Cotton had no desire to command at Jamaica because of the climate, but he expressed interest in the Newfoundland station. This news came as a surprise to Grenville because the First Sea Lord, Rear Admiral John Markham, had stated that Cotton had already declined Newfoundland. Cotton likely reconsidered when approached with the offer by his mentor, St. Vincent. Be it as it may, the principal purpose of this station was to protect both British trade sailing to and from the St. Lawrence and fishing interests off the Grand Banks. The squadron was small. It escorted trans-Atlantic convoys and challenged French *guerre de course* off Newfoundland. Perhaps Grenville believed that Cotton could do less harm to British interests in North America than in the English Channel. Or maybe the Admiralty simply reserved the Channel command for senior admirals who had successfully held an independent command elsewhere.[54]

Grenville offered command of the Newfoundland station to Cotton on 2 December 1806, expecting him to assume the post in February 1807. The First Lord concluded in his offer: "I have only to add that it will give me great pleasure to hear that this arrangement which the public service and your rank in the Navy seems to prescribe, is likewise agreeable to your views and wishes."[55] Cotton accepted the offer, no doubt much to the First Lord's relief and satisfaction. Grenville granted his request for "some weeks leisure" before proceeding to Newfoundland.[56]

After nearly continuous service in the Channel Fleet since 1793, Cotton resigned his post as second-in-command in December 1806. His service in the Channel, if not distinguished, had been noteworthy for its longevity, consistent reliability, and unwavering loyalty to the successive commanders-in-chief. By virtue of circumstances through no fault of his own, he had missed a few opportunities to distinguish himself in combat and personally felt the sting of obscurity among his peers. Ironically, Cotton spent the majority of his time in the Channel conducting a mission in which success was measured by preventing an engagement with the enemy. With few exceptions, the Brest Fleet rarely challenged the blockading squadron off Ushant. Although Cotton's abilities were questioned by some, he earned enough respect and interest to continue advancing professionally during a period of national crisis. He had served honorably in the Channel Fleet. Upon resignation, he returned to Madingley and began preparation for his new command. Opportunity awaited on the other side of the Atlantic.

NOTES

1. John Horsfield, *Art of Leadership in War: The Royal Navy from the Age of Nelson to the End of World War II* (Westport, Conn., 1980), 8.

2. Cyril Northcote Parkinson, *Britannia Rules: The Classic Age of Naval History, 1793–1815* (London, 1977), 42–44; Conrad Gill, *Naval Mutinies of 1797* (Manchester, 1913), 16–28; Richard Saxby, "Lord Bridport and the Spithead Mutiny," *Mariner's Mirror* 79 (1993): 170–73.

3. Edward Cotton to Charles Cotton, 5 August 1797, Cambridgeshire County Record Office, Cotton Naval Papers, 588/c66.

4. Logbook of HMS *Prince*, 8–14 April, Cambridgeshire County Record Office, Cotton Naval Papers, 588/035; Parkinson, *Britannia Rules*, 45, 67; "Memoir of Cotton," *The Naval Chronicle* 27 (1812): 358.

5. A. Thomazi, *Napoléon et ses Marins* (Paris, 1950), 62–67; Édouard Chevalier, *Histoire de la Marine Français sous la Première République* (Paris, 1886), 408–09.

6. Logbook of HMS *Prince*, 25–27 April; Alexander Allardyce, *Memoir of the Honourable George Keith Elphinestone, K.B., Viscount Keith, Admiral of the Red* (London, 1882), 158–59; Parkinson, *Britannia Rules*, 67.

7. Logbook of HMS *Prince*, 8 May-1 June 1799.

8. Ibid., 8–12 June 1799; Chevalier, *Marine Français*, 411–13; Thomazi, *Napoléon et ses Marins*, 68.

9. Logbook of HMS *Prince*, 18–22 June 1799; Cyril Northcote Parkinson, *Edward Pellew, Viscount Exmouth, Admiral of the Red* (London, 1934), 218–21.

10. Logbook of HMS *Prince*, 22 June–7 July 1799; Keith to his sister, Mary Elphinstone, 29 June 1799, Intelligence of Spanish Fleet, 8 July 1799, Christopher Lloyd, ed., *The Keith Papers* (London, 1950), 2: 40, 49; Georges Douin, *La Campagne de Bruix en Méditerranée, Mars–Août 1799* (Paris, 1923), 182–83, 203.

11. Georges Douin, *Campagne de Bruix*, 189–95; Allardyce, *Memoir of Viscount Keith*, 168–69.

12. For a summary of Bruix's cruise, see Chapter 11, "The Bruix Cruise (April 25–August 13, 1799) and Its Consequences" in Charles B. Arthur, *The Remaking of the English Navy by Admiral St. Vincent: Key to the Victory over Napoleon* (New York, 1986), 133–42.

13. "General State and Condition of H.M. Ships employed on the Mediterranean Station," 7 August 1799, Lloyd, *Keith Papers*, 2: 55–57.

14. The purpose of Cotton's cruise was not specified by *The Times* of London or Cotton's *Naval Chronicle* memoir. *The Times* of London, 22, 25 January 1800.

15. Excerpt from letter of Sir Edward Pellew, undated, cited in Parkinson, *Britannia Rules*, 44.

16. A.N. Ryan, "The Royal Navy and the Blockade of Brest, 1689–1805: Theory and Practice," in *Les Marines de Guerre Européennes XVII–XVIIIe siècles,* ed. Martine Acerra (Paris, 1985), 186–87.

17. Herbert W. Richmond, ed., *Private Papers of George, second Earl Spencer, First Lord of the Admiralty, 1794–1801* (London, 1924), 3: 295; Parkinson, *Britannia Rules*, 79–80.

18. Richmond, *Papers of Earl Spencer*, 3: 296–301.

19. Cotton to Philadelphia Cotton, 8 October 1800, Cambridgeshire County Record Office, Cotton Naval Papers, 588/c85; Tony Gutridge, "Aspects of Naval Prize Agency, 1793–1815," *Mariner's Mirror* 80 (1994): 45–48; N.A.M. Rodger, *The Wooden World: An Anatomy of the Georgian Navy* (Annapolis, 1986), 128–29; The basic pay of a rear admiral was £1.15.0 per day. Brian Lavery, *Nelson's Navy: The Ships, Men and Organisation, 1793–1815* (London, 1989), 252.

20. "Memoir of Cotton," *Naval Chronicle* 27 (1812): 360.

21. St. Vincent to Philadelphia Cotton, 26 August 1802, Cambridgeshire County Record Office, Charles Cotton Naval Papers, 588/c90.

22. Cotton to Sir Evan Nepean, 11 June 1803, John Leyland, ed., *Dispatches and Letters Relating to the Blockade of Brest, 1803–1805* (London, 1899), 1: xxx, xl, 32; admirals serving in the Channel Fleet in spring 1803 listed in note 1, David B. Smith, ed., *Letters of Admiral of the Fleet the Earl of St. Vincent whilst First Lord of the Admiralty, 1801–1804* (London, 1927), 2: 305.

23. Bonaparte to Decrès, 30 May 1803, in Édouard Desbrière, *Projets et Tentatives de Débarquement aux Iles Britanniques, 1793–1805* (Paris, 1902), 3: 84; Maurice DuPont, *L'Amiral Decrès et Napoleon, ou la fidélité orageuse d'un ministre* (Paris, 1991), 111–14; Lloyd, *Keith Papers*, 3: 5; Harold Deutsch concluded that Napoleon's cross-channel invasion was not a bluff: "The ingenuity and vastness of conception which characterize the evolution of the project are in fact the best arguments for the sincerity of Bonaparte's intentions." Harold C. Deutsch, *The Genesis of Napoleonic Imperialism* (Cambridge, 1938), 175.

24. Cited in H.F.B. Wheeler and A.M. Broadley, *Napoleon and the Invasion of England: The Story of the Great Terror* (London, 1908), 162; Guy E. Cooper, "The Methods of Blockade and Observation Employed during the Revolutionary and Napoleonic Wars," *Journal of the Royal United Service Institution* 61 (1916): 545–46.

25. Cornwallis to Nepean, 31 December 1803, 1 January 1804, Leyland, *Blockade of Brest*, 1: 231–33.

26. Cooper, "Methods of Blockade and Observation," 545–46.

27. Melville to Cornwallis, 14 July 1804, Leyland, *Blockade of Brest*, 1: 366–68.

28. Ibid., 1: 368–69, Cornwallis to Cotton, 17 July 1804.

29. Julian S. Corbett, *Some Principles of Maritime Strategy* (London, 1911; reprint, Annapolis, 1988), 181.

30. Sir Thomas Graves to Cotton, 21 July 1804, Leyland, *Blockade of Brest*, 2: 36.

31. Graves to Cotton, 23 August 1804, G. Cornwallis-West, ed., *Life and Letters of Admiral Cornwallis* (London, 1927), 429–36.

32. Ibid., 433–34.

33. DuPont, *L'Amiral Decrès*, 134–38, 142; Ernest H. Jenkins, *A History of the French Navy* (London, 1973), 248.

34. Cotton to Admiral Alan Gardner, 25 January 1805, British Library, Hardwicke Papers, Add. MSS 35755; Unknown correspondent to Rear Admiral Sir Home Popham, 19 February 1805, Hugh Popham, *A Damned Cunning Fellow: The Eventful Life of Rear-Admiral Sir Home Popham* (Tywardreath, Cornwall, 1991), 127.

35. DuPont, *L'Amiral Decrès*, 149–53; Jenkins, *French Navy*, 251.

36. Melville to Cornwallis, 15 November 1804, Library of Congress, Washington, D.C., Melville Papers; Cornwallis to Mr. Marsden, 14, 18 March 1805, Cornwallis to Cotton, 18 March 1805, Cotton to Mr. Marsden, 19 March 1805, Leyland, *Blockade of Brest*, 2: 210–14.

37. Cotton to Mr. Marsden, 28 March 1805, Leyland, *Blockade of Brest*, 2: 216; Geoffrey Bennett, *Battle of Trafalgar* (Annapolis, 1977), 105–106; Oliver Warner, *Nelson's Battles* (New York, 1965), 157–58.

38. Gardner to Mr. Marsden, 3 April 1805, Leyland, *Blockade of Brest*, 2: 219–20.

39. Gardner to Barham, 25 June 1805, John K. Laughton, ed., *Letters and Papers of Charles, Lord Barham, Admiral of the Red Squadron, 1758–1813* (London, 1911), 3: 253–54; Parkinson, *Britannia Rules*, 79–80.

40. Collingwood to Nelson, 18 July 1805, Sir Nicholas Harris Nicolas, ed., *The Dispatches and Letters of Vice Admiral Lord Viscount Nelson* (London, 1846), 6: 472.

41. Cotton to Lady Cotton, 11 November 1805, Cambridgeshire County Record Office, Cotton Naval Papers, 588/c71.

42. Calder to Cotton, 24 September 1805, Cambridgeshire County Record Office, Cotton Naval Papers, 588/c70; Barham to Cornwallis, 19 August 1805, Laughton, *Letters of Lord Barham*, 3: 250.

43. Cotton to Lady Cotton, 5 November 1805, Cambridgeshire County Record Office, Cotton Naval Papers, 588/c71.

44. St. Vincent to Rear Admiral Markham, 17 May 1806, Edward P. Brenton, *Life and Correspondence of John, Earl of St. Vincent, G.C.B., Admiral of the Fleet* (London, 1838), 2: 283–84.

45. St. Vincent to Viscount Howick, 27 July 1806, 1, 2 August 1806, Brenton, *Life of St. Vincent* 2: 294–97; Geoffrey Marcus, *The Age of Nelson: the Royal Navy, 1793–1815* (New York, 1971), 306; James Ralfe, *The Naval Biography of Great Britain* (1828; reprint, Boston, 1972), 1: 314–15.

46. Captain Sir Samuel Hood to Cotton, 26 September 1806, *Naval Chronicle* 16 (1806): 346–47; DuPont, *L'Amiral Decrès*, 238.

47. Cotton to Marsden, 30 September 1806, *Naval Chronicle* 16 (1806): 346.

48. St. Vincent to Thomas Grenville, 22 October 1806, Brenton, *Life of St. Vincent*, 2: 318–19.

49. Ibid., 2: 321–22, Vincent to Grenville, 26 October 1806.

50. Thomas Grenville to George Grenville, Lord Buckingham, 17 November 1806, Duke of Buckingham and Chandos, K.G., ed., *Memoirs of the Court and Cabinets of George the Third* (London, 1855), 4: 95–97.

51. Ibid., 99–101, Thomas Grenville to George Grenville, Lord Buckingham, 25 November 1806. See also Huntington Library, Stowe-Grenville Collection, Box 37.

52. St. Vincent to Grenville, 16 November 1806, Brenton, *Life of St. Vincent*, 2:327–28.

53. Ibid., 2: 330–31, St. Vincent to Grenville, 28 November 1806.

54. Ibid., 2: 331–32, St. Vincent to Grenville, 30 November 1806.

55. Grenville to Cotton, 2 December 1806, Cambridgeshire County Record Office, Cotton Naval Papers, 588/036.

56. Grenville to the Marquis of Buckingham, 6 December 1806, Buckingham and Chandos, *Memoirs of the Court and Cabinets of George the Third*, 4: 103.

An Admiral's Flag at Lisbon: Squadron Command off the Tagus, January–May 1808

> Buonaparte has placed us, as it were, under the ban of the Continent—he has endeavoured to set all of the Continent against us, and we are justified in taking such measures, as our safety may render necessary, against all those nations which he can controul.
>
> —"Retrospective on Naval History of the Present Year,"
> *The Naval Chronicle,* 1807[1]

> These are times in which you cannot reasonably expect to remain long in quiet. They are times such as no nation ever experienced before. . . . So many extraordinary things happen in this vile world—for you may depend on it.
>
> —Collingwood to Cotton, 20 November 1807[2]

Unforeseen events forced Cotton to change his mind about accepting appointment to the Newfoundland station. According to Cotton's memoir in the *Naval Chronicle*, he resigned the appointment because of an "impaired state" of health, which appeared to be rheumatism, and a "domestic affliction." The "domestic affliction" might have been a euphemism for the death in late March 1807 of his oldest son, nine-year-old John Hynde.[3] The memoir mentioned another explanation for Cotton's decision: "The command of the Newfoundland station, however, notwithstanding its respectability, can never lead to distinguished service."[4] Notwithstanding a desire to serve king and country, assignment to an insignificant station while Napoleon was at the height of power in Europe did not appeal to the vice admiral. In addition, the demands of managing his estate, a desire to spend more time with his family, and magisterial duties in the county seemed to produce within Cotton an ambivalence about naval service on a distant station. An undated letter from

Cotton to his wife indicates how the admiral must have been torn between the service and his responsibilities at Madingley:

> Dear Maria advises me of a letter to come tomorrow from Mr. Phipps with a full account of the farm. I wish I had wrote to you about a successor for him. . . . I do hope that I shall be at home to arrange all that business this summer. . . . I trust there is some preparation made about goslings, turkey, and pea chicks. Must I come home to regulate that business? If there is no better look out this year than the last, what a miserable return there will be of produce of all my cackling friends. . . . Rest assured that soon I shall be home to administer to all your wants.[5]

Although management of the estate occupied Cotton in 1807, he nevertheless kept himself available should the First Lord call again. He suspected that the winds of change were about to produce a new ministry in London and a replacement for Grenville.

The Portland ministry was formed in March 1807 to replace the ministry of "All the Talents." Henry Phipps, Lord Mulgrave, succeeded Grenville as First Lord on 4 April 1807. With Grenville's departure from the Admiralty, Cotton expected to receive better support from the new First Lord, a friend in the past. Mulgrave was an army officer during the war in America and was stationed for twelve months in Jamaica during Cotton's time there in 1782–1783.[6]

Mulgrave offered several commands to Cotton in 1807. He declined the offer of a seat on the Admiralty Board as well as command of the North American squadron at Halifax.[7] Of particular interest was Mulgrave's offer of the command of an expedition to the Baltic. After the Treaty of Tilsit, George Canning, the Secretary of State for Foreign Affairs, became convinced that Napoleon had enticed Emperor Alexander I of Russia to collaborate in forcing Denmark to place her fleet at the disposal of France for employment against Britain. Canning's subsequent demand that the Danish government temporarily surrender its fleet was not surprisingly rejected. The British government then resorted to the use of force to seize the Danish fleet at Copenhagen.[8]

On 26 July 1807, an expedition of twenty-five ships-of-the-line, forty smaller vessels, and about 377 transports carrying 27,000 troops embarked from Yarmouth for Copenhagen. Mulgrave offered naval command of the expedition to Admiral Sir James Gambier, who held a seat on the Admiralty Board. The First Lord offered the command to Cotton if the first choice, Gambier, did not accept.

> I have in the first instance felt it right to offer this command to an officer who stands higher on the List than you do, but in the event of his not accepting the command, I shall be very happy to commit this service to you perfectly persuaded that it cannot be in better hands. The ships are now collecting and the necessity of an immediate decision with respect to the command has induced me cordially to tell you the actual state of the affair that I may have my arrangement ready, in case (as it is probable) the officer to

whom I have already committed myself should from circumstances feel obliged to decline the command.[9]

Cotton accepted the provisional offer, although his health was still fragile. Mulgrave's strong belief that Gambier would decline the offer caused him to submit Cotton's candidacy prematurely to King George. The First Lord also requested a promotion to full admiral for Cotton in case he received the command.[10]

Gambier unexpectedly accepted the command, which left Mulgrave the uncomfortable task of dashing Cotton's expectations. Mulgrave thanked Cotton for accepting the provisional offer and attempted to mitigate his friend's disappointment by accentuating the positive: "I trust that a further respite will further restore your health and leave no obstacle in the way of your future success."[11] While Cotton continued recuperating at Madingley, Gambier led the expedition to Copenhagen. In conjunction with the British army, the Royal Navy bombarded the city from 2 September to 5 September. Two days later, the surrender of Copenhagen and the Danish fleet were formally concluded. The British force was far superior to its opponent, and the mission required little genius on behalf of Gambier and his army counterpart, Lieutenant General William Schaw, Lord Cathcart. Nevertheless, the expedition secured its strategic goals, and a grateful British government raised several admirals and generals to the peerage, including Gambier. Not long after Gambier returned to England in late October 1807 with the Danish warships, Mulgrave called upon Cotton with another offer of command. This time Cotton accepted and King George approved. In early December 1807, Cotton was named commander of a naval squadron destined for the Iberian peninsula.[12]

Mulgrave appointed Cotton commander of His Majesty's ships off the Tagus, a squadron of seven ships-of-the-line and two frigates presently commanded by Rear Admiral Sir William Sidney Smith. The Admiralty had appointed Smith to this command off Lisbon on 27 October 1807 in response to a French threat to Portuguese sovereignty. That threat had emerged after conclusion of the Treaty of Tilsit between France and Russia. Napoleon's 25 June meeting with Tsar Alexander on a raft in the Niemen River was the symbolic event that shaped the Continental System, that is, Napoleon's effort to wage economic warfare against Britain. The Continental System as refined at Tilsit was the culmination of several measures already taken by the emperor to destroy the British economy. In response to the British maritime blockade of 16 May 1806, Napoleon issued the Berlin Decrees on 21 November 1806. These decrees dictated that all trade between Britain and the continent would cease immediately and ordered the confiscation of all British goods in French occupied territory. Subsequent decrees extended the restrictions to neutral nations. The British responded by issuing a series of Orders in Council that also affected neutrals trading with France by mandating their submission to search and subjection to customs duties.[13]

While the British and French governments implemented economic measures and countermeasures against each other, Portuguese trade continued unabated with Britain, an ancient trading partner. Britain was the largest importer of Portuguese goods, and the Portuguese relied heavily on British exports, especially gunpowder and muskets for her army. From 1801 to 1807, geographic isolation had permitted the House of Braganza to maintain political neutrality, despite the polarizing efforts of British and French diplomats. However, the terms of Tilsit effectively forced the hand of the Portuguese ruler, Prince Regent João. On 12 August 1807, a French representative delivered an ultimatum to João that demanded that the Portuguese government close its ports to British trade and confiscate all British goods, arrest all British subjects in Portugal, join its fleet to the allied powers, recall its ambassador from London, and declare war on Britain by 1 September 1807. If these demands were not met, the French army would invade Portugal, with assistance from Spain. The timid João did not comply fully with Napoleon's demands. Therefore, the emperor unleashed his forces against the small kingdom; on 18 October 1807 25,000 soldiers of the "1st Corps of Observation of the Gironde" crossed the Bidassoa River into Spain en route to Portugal.[14]

General Jean-Andoche Junot commanded the French army destined for Portugal. He had earned a reputation not only as a brave battlefield commander but also as one who lacked the qualities required for independent command. Napoleon recognized the shortcomings of his old comrade in arms; nevertheless, he was appointed to lead the expedition. On 12 November, the same day that Junot's army arrived at Salamanca and Rear Admiral Smith sailed from Britain on the *Hibernia*, Napoleon wrote a letter to Junot with specific instructions for the occupation of Lisbon. The emperor instructed his general to seize the Portuguese fleet; disarm the Portuguese army and send much of it to France; convince the Prince Regent to go to France "willingly"; and collect taxes, confiscate English goods, and arrest individual Englishmen. As though honesty and fair dealing might make the Portuguese people less alarmed by the violation of their country's sovereignty, Napoleon also instructed Junot to "set an example of absolute incorruptibility."[15]

Meanwhile, events in Lisbon contributed to a mounting sense of crisis within the House of Braganza as Junot's French and Spanish armies approached the Portuguese frontier. In an attempt to appease Napoleon on 20 October, João declared war on Britain while simultaneously conveying his regrets to His Majesty's plenipotentiary at the court of Lisbon, Viscount Sir Percy Strangford. João supplemented the declaration of war on 8 November with an order to seize all British property and detain all British subjects in Portugal. A disgruntled Strangford demanded his passport and prepared to leave Portugal, but inclement weather prevented an immediate departure.

The situation at Lisbon became more complicated with the arrival of over 5,000 Russians. While Strangford waited for calmer seas and before Smith's squadron from Britain arrived, a Russian squadron of nine sail-of-the-line and two frigates, commanded by Vice Admiral Dmitri Seniavin, was forced into the Tagus River by heavy gales on 10 November. Seniavin's ships were sailing from the Mediterranean to the Baltic. Because they were in poor condition after an active campaign against the Turks and French before the Treaty of Tilsit, Seniavin had little choice but to stay in Lisbon harbor until the next spring. João welcomed the Russians and promised them support from the port facilities of Lisbon. Then, a few days after the Russian's appearance in the Tagus, Smith's squadron arrived off Lisbon. On the 17th, Strangford joined Smith aboard the *Hibernia* and proceeded to assess the very complex situation unfolding in Portugal. In accordance with the Admiralty's guidance and Strangford's recommendation, Smith instituted a blockade of Lisbon harbor on the 20th "so long as the present state of misunderstanding exists."[16]

João's attempts to appease Napoleon failed. The entrance of Junot's army into Portugal on 21 November presented the Prince Regent with two unenviable options. He could either submit to French rule or relocate the House of Braganza in the Portuguese colony of Brazil. The British government had anticipated the latter option and had given Smith instructions to assist members of the House of Braganza in their flight to South America (or to seize the Portuguese fleet if the Prince Regent chose to remain in Lisbon). João decided on the day the French army entered Portugal to make the trans-Atlantic voyage to Rio de Janeiro. The Regent prepared for departure by loading fifteen warships and more than twenty merchant vessels with his family, state papers and treasure, and several members of his court. Bearing a flag of truce, Strangford proceeded to Lisbon on 27 November on board the frigate *Confiance* to assure João of the British government's intention to assist the House of Braganza's passage to Brazil.[17]

The Portuguese fleet sailed from Lisbon on the morning of 29 November. The next day, after the Portuguese and British fleets in passing exchanged twenty-one-gun salutes, Smith observed that the "scene impress[ed] every beholder, except the French army on the hills."[18] The exhausted van of Junot's army entered Lisbon on the 30th, while an anxious population awaited its fate and the officers and men of Seniavin's squadron observed the drama in bewilderment.[19]

Notified of the Russian squadron's arrival in the Tagus on 27 November, yet still unaware of the House of Braganza's departure from Lisbon, the Admiralty issued orders to Cotton on 9 December. If the Portuguese government wanted to proceed to Brazil and the Russian fleet tried to prevent it, Cotton should "demand possession of the principal forts upon the Tagus . . . and having obtained it, to proceed up the river for the purpose of attacking the Russian squadron, and conveying the Portuguese fleet out of the Tagus."[20] The British government wanted not only to safeguard the House of Braganza but also to prevent the Russian squadron from falling under French control. Perhaps Cotton could accomplish in Lisbon with the Russian squadron what Gambier had accomplished the previous September in Copenhagen. Although word of the Russian declaration of war against Britain had not yet reached the Admiralty, a de facto state of war already existed between the two countries after Russia had renounced all intercourse with England in October 1807.

To assist Cotton, Lord Hawkesbury, one of His Majesty's principal Secretaries of State, ordered Major General Sir Brent Spencer's corps of 7,000 troops to proceed with the admiral to Lisbon before continuing to Sicily. In addition, Hawkesbury expected Lieutenant General Sir John Moore's force of 8,000 troops, en route from Sicily to England, to lead military operations against the forts on the Tagus in order to facilitate capitulation of the Russian fleet. In the event that the combined force could not attack the Russian ships in the Tagus, Moore's and Spencer's forces would proceed to Sicily while Cotton imposed a strict blockade of the Tagus "so as to prevent the entrance of any supplies whatever, even of provisions."[21] If the Portuguese government surrendered the Portuguese and Russian fleets, the Admiralty instructed Cotton to relax the blockade only as it related to provisions for the inhabitants of Portugal.

The fleet that embarked from Portsmouth on 20 December was the largest force Cotton had ever commanded. It consisted of sixty-two transports conveying the troops and stores of Spencer's corps, as well as the 50-gun *Antelope*, *Nymphe* frigate, *Nautilus* and *Milbrook* sloops, and the 74-gun *Minotaur*, Cotton's flagship. With an easterly wind upon departure, the fleet sailed southwesterly into the Bay of Biscay until the 24th, when the winds began blowing hard from the southwest. Deteriorating weather carried away the bowsprit and foremast of the *Milbrook* and separated the convoy on the night of the 28th. Cotton's instructions in case of separation and a westerly gale mandated a return to Falmouth if the convoy was beyond the Lizard or to a rendezvous twelve leagues southwest of Cape Finisterre if far advanced into the Bay of Biscay. The fleet was on the border between these two positions, and the rendezvous decision depended on the judgment of each ship's captain. Cotton decided on the 29th to bear up for Falmouth and was accompanied by fifteen transports and the *Antelope*, Spencer's ship. With much of his fleet scattered across the Bay of Biscay and Channel waters, Cotton entered Falmouth harbor in the *Minotaur* on the last day of 1807. Those transports and victuallers that did not return to a British port after separation in the storm of 29 December arrived safely at Gibraltar on 23 January 1808. The separation of the fleet was an inauspicious beginning for the most important enterprise of Cotton's naval career.[22]

While Cotton consolidated his fleet at Falmouth, the Royal Navy maintained its presence off the Tagus. Sir William Sidney Smith had detached four warships, under the command of Captain Graham Moore, to accompany the Portuguese fleet to South America while he continued in command off the coast of Portugal. Smith soon found himself concerned with more than the environs of Lisbon. On 4 December, the British subjects on the island of St. Michael in the Western Islands addressed a letter to the admiral.[23] On their behalf, Captain

H. Curzon of the 74-gun *Elizabeth* requested that Smith send a small naval force to the island for its protection: "two frigates and a sloop or two would be quite sufficient." In the wake of Junot's occupation of Lisbon, the British inhabitants believed that Napoleon had plans to occupy the Western Islands: "Sir, if we not prevent it, France will make them a depot for Spanish cargoes, and Spanish treasure, and a harbour for privateers to annoy the British outer and homeward bound trade."[24] In a letter to the governor of the Azores, Smith did not mention sending a naval force, but he did apply as a "faithful subject and servant of our ally the Prince Regent of Portugal for leave to procure supplies of wood, water and other refreshments" from the Azores.[25] The governor agreed to all of Smith's proposals.[26]

The island of Madeira, as well as the Azores, was Portuguese territory that would provision the Royal Navy during the Peninsular War. The terms of a secret treaty signed in London on 22 October 1807 between British and Portuguese ministers stipulated that should Prince João depart for Brazil, British troops would not occupy Madeira until His Royal Highness had passed the island. Brigadier General William Beresford arrived off Madeira on 24 December with an expedition of 3,600 troops. British troops occupied the island without force after Beresford guaranteed that the British government would return it to Portugal after the war. The general established a garrison of two battalions on the island and remained as its governor until chosen in 1808 by the Portuguese regency to command the Portuguese army. Smith's letter of instruction to the governor of Madeira for the British occupation of the island arrived after the fact. Both the Azores and Madeira fell within the jurisdiction of Cotton's command off the Tagus, which extended from these islands to northwestern Spain at Cape Finisterre and southern Spain at Cape St. Vincent.[27]

While Smith presided over the establishment of British authority in the Azores, Madeira, and the waters off the coast of Portugal, Junot attempted to consolidate his power by issuing several edicts to the inhabitants of Lisbon. As he entered the city, Junot asked its citizens to reflect upon their abandonment by the Prince Regent into "the arms of his enemies." Furthermore, the general ordered the people of Lisbon to remain quietly within their homes and not to fear his army because "We are only frightful to our enemies, and to villains."[28] With the peaceful French occupation of Lisbon, the effort to win the voluntary support of the Portuguese now became critical for the French. Despite their aversion to the occupation of their city by a foreign army, the people of Lisbon did not resist, nor did the provisional government. An absence of leadership partially explains this passiveness. Illustrative of Portuguese submission to French authority was an address by the Patriarch of Lisbon:

Fear not, beloved children. . . . Remember, that this army is of his Majesty the Emperor of the French and Kingdom of Italy. Napoleon the Great, whom God has destined to support, and protect religion, and make mankind happy. You know it, the world knows it. Confide with unalterable security in this prodigious man, unequaled in all ages. He will pour upon us the blessings of peace.[29]

Not surprisingly, some of the inhabitants of Lisbon objected to the "blessings" bestowed by the French. A riot occurred on 13 December when the French tricolor replaced the Portuguese flag on public buildings of the city and, according to Junot, French troops were fired upon. Junot responded the following day with several restrictive measures, including prohibiting the right to assemble and threatening the instigators of revolt with death. Despite an intention to conciliate the people, Junot tightened the grip of French control over Lisbon with additional restrictions. One of the measures most injurious to Franco-Portuguese relations consisted of Napoleon's order of 23 December for Junot to levy a tax of 100,000,000 francs upon the kingdom. Notwithstanding such financial exactions, Junot continued the battle to win popular support.[30]

Junot also attempted to earn the support of Admiral Seniavin, because the Russian squadron was capable of challenging the blockading squadron. Immediately after the French occupation of Lisbon, Junot and Seniavin made an agreement by proxy regarding supply of the Russian squadron. They finally met on 10 December when Seniavin travelled to Junot's headquarters. Junot returned the visit the following day. Junot's chief of staff, General Paul Thiébault, described his chief's visit to the Russian fleet. He claimed that Seniavin ordered a cannon salute by the entire squadron to the health of Napoleon and Alexander. The salute, outwardly intended to honor Napoleon, actually belied the admiral's true sentiment toward the French. Only five months before, Seniavin had directed operations against French forces in Dalmatia. The realignment of alliances at Tilsit could not erase the aristocratic hatred that Seniavin felt for the French regicides. Furthermore, the close relationship between the Russian and British navies in the eighteenth century profoundly shaped Seniavin's attitude. He had many British friends, including Admiral Collingwood, and in fact several British officers currently served in his squadron. Collingwood said of Seniavin: "[He] is a good kind of man—perhaps not very brilliant and as obstinate as a Russian can be. He hates the French and never yet was near them without dispute and quarrel. At Corfu they were bickering all the time."[31] Therefore, it was unlikely that Junot could persuade Seniavin to commit a hostile act against the Royal Navy. In addition, Junot and Seniavin developed a mutual dislike of one another. Though allied with France, Seniavin's squadron assumed a position of neutrality while anchored in the Tagus. The admiral wished to prevent its misuse by Junot as well as its capture by the British navy.[32]

Meanwhile, Cotton had yet to influence affairs in Portugal. From 31 December to 10 January, he supervised the reunification of his fleet at Falmouth harbor for the vessels that did not proceed to Gibraltar. Those transports that did not sail to the rendezvous off Cape Finisterre trickled into Falmouth and Plymouth during this period. The fleet was irrevocably divided.

Fortunately, Cotton's return to England gave him the opportunity to receive updated guidance from the Admiralty and intelligence relating to the Peninsula. A report from Lord Strangford suggested that the British blockade of the Tagus was reducing the Russian squadron to a "state of the utmost distress." In a letter to Castlereagh, George Canning responded to Strangford's report by recommending a scheme to secure the surrender of the Russian squadron. Canning wanted Cotton to "convey to the Russian admiral a proposal for the surrender of the fleet to His Majesty, offering as a condition, that the officers and men shall not be considered as prisoners of war, but shall be conveyed to Russia by the earliest opportunity, at the expence of Great Britain."[33] The Admiralty endorsed Canning's suggestion and sent it to Cotton along with new instructions.[34]

The Admiralty directed Cotton to seize or destroy all ships and vessels belonging to Russia, with few exceptions; to initiate a strict blockade of Oporto and Setúbal; to seize and garrison the Burling Islands off Peniche; and to send all transports that originally sailed with the convoy directly to Gibraltar. Evidently, the Admiralty believed that French occupation of the forts protecting the port of Lisbon rendered an amphibious operation in the Tagus too risky. According to the intelligence from Strangford, the blockade alone would force the Russian squadron to capitulate. Demonstrating impatience, the Admiralty exhorted Cotton to depart Falmouth harbor at once to execute his orders.[35]

After several days of calm, hazy weather, the *Minotaur* picked up a light breeze on 10 January and weighed anchor from Falmouth with the sloop *Talbot* and the cutter *Cheerful*. Spencer remained at Falmouth to reorganize his force and did not sail for Lisbon until 21 February 1808. Cotton's passage to Portugal was rapid—it took only four days to cover the 700 statute miles between Falmouth and Oporto. As the *Minotaur* passed abreast of Oporto on the 14th, Cotton dispatched the *Cheerful* with an order for Captain Grant, commander of the 16-gun *Raven*, to institute a blockade of that port. Proceeding southward, the *Minotaur* joined Sir Sidney Smith off the Tagus the next day, and Cotton immediately received the latest information regarding affairs on station. Smith informed his replacement about the Prince Regent's departure and the arrival of twenty-two sail of transport that had dispersed from Cotton's convoy on 29 December. In addition, Smith believed that the Russian squadron was ready for sea because it was reported lying at single anchor. The possibility of a Russian escape attempt influenced Cotton's first crucial command decision off the Tagus: He decided not to dispatch the 80-gun *Foudroyant*, 74-gun *Conqueror*, and 74-gun *Plantagenet* to Cadiz as directed by the Admiralty.[36]

Smith did not depart the squadron immediately after Cotton's arrival off the Tagus. Ignoring orders, as often suited Smith's purposes, he remained off the coast of Portugal for another month rather than escort the Portuguese royal family to Brazil. Considering the "peculiar circumstances" off the Tagus, the Admiralty approved Smith's decision, but did not provide him with orders to follow the royal family after being relieved by Cotton.[37] Therefore, Cotton needed to accommodate Smith until his receipt of further orders from the Admiralty.

The ensuing friction regarding the condition of a number of ships created outright disagreement between the two admirals. When Cotton superseded Smith off the Tagus, he shifted his flag to the *Hibernia*, and Smith took the *Minotaur*. The *Minotaur* was a ship in need of repair and one that Smith soon discovered was not worthy of being a flagship. Cotton later admitted to Smith that the *Minotaur* "has certainly some good qualities, but she was hurried out of dock, from Chatham, without justice done to her."[38] Furthermore, the perception that the Russian squadron was preparing to sail provided Smith with another reason to request a better ship. Only two days after they exchanged ships, inclement weather temporarily decided the flagship controversy. On 18 January, a heavy gale carried away the *Minotaur*'s main top mast and the ship began taking on water. Smith had no choice but to shift his flag to the *Foudroyant*. The final justification for Smith to leave the *Minotaur* was the unknown whereabouts of a French squadron that had escaped from Rochefort on 17 January and was last reported heading west. Smith said of the *Minotaur* before he shifted his flag: "She is the last ship in this squadron on board which I should chuse [*sic*] to have my flag."[39]

Cotton initially acceded to Smith's request to remain on the *Foudroyant*, but an Admiralty dispatch dated 25 January 1808 and received in mid-February specified that Smith not be given that ship. Moreover, the dispatch ordered Smith to proceed with two ships-of-the-line and the *Confiance* to Brazil to join the British squadron that accompanied the House of Braganza. Cotton then recommended that Smith shift his flag to the 74-gun *Hercules*. However, a thorough survey ordered by a wary Smith found that it too was not seaworthy. Cotton subsequently recommended the *Agamemnon* of 64 guns, but its small size was unacceptable for the pretentious Smith. He considered the third rate *Conqueror* a suitable vessel, but it had recently lost an anchor and two cables and was separated from the fleet. After discussing the flagship issue for several days, Cotton finally authorized Smith to remain on the *Foudroyant* and to depart the Tagus in accordance with directions from the Admiralty. On 20 February, Smith sailed from Portugal to the Gibraltar dockyard to refurbish his ship before proceeding across the Atlantic.[40]

The *Foudroyant*'s departure must have been an immense relief to both admirals. Smith was a self-confident, competent leader, but he was also self-serving. Some of his actions while off Portugal implied that he wanted to reap the credit for what had transpired there since November. Though Cotton outranked Smith and their correspondence seemed convivial, Smith probably disdained serving under Cotton because it constrained his freedom of action and left him out of the limelight. Cotton certainly would have preferred that Smith departed Portugal immediately upon the change of command, but circumstances did not permit this. The cursory efforts to find a proper flagship for Smith were unfortunate but unavoidable, considering the state of the available ships in the squadron and the explicit orders from the Admiralty not to give Smith the *Foudroyant*. Regarding this ship, Cotton admitted to Smith that "the repetition of their Lordships' order is too strong a push to parry."[41] However, by ultimately allowing Smith to take the *Foudroyant* anyway, Cotton did what the Admiralty expected of its commanders on foreign station. He dismissed an order because adherence would not have been in the best interest of the service.

Cotton's month-long confrontation with Smith was inconvenient but did not significantly distract his attention from the object of capturing the Russian squadron. Soon after arriving off the Tagus, Cotton attempted to establish a dialogue with Seniavin. Unfortunately, Cotton soon discovered that there was "no direct means of communication with Vice Admiral Seniavin[,] all intercourse with the squadron under my command being entirely forbidden by the most rigorous decrees, imposing fine, imprisonment, and corporal punishment on any breach of such restrictions."[42] He therefore devised a simple scheme to communicate with Seniavin. Cotton had several dispatches from the Russian minister in London addressed to Seniavin and for the Russian minister in Lisbon. As a pretext for opening communication, Cotton requested that Seniavin send a trusted officer to the *Hibernia* to collect these dispatches. Using conciliatory language in his letter to Seniavin, Cotton regretted "most sincerely that the correspondence between two nations like ours, which have so long been in amity with each other . . . should for a moment be subjected to any difficulty."[43]

On 20 January, Cotton gave his dispatch for Seniavin to Captain C. Ekins of the *Defence* and ordered him to deliver some Spanish prisoners to St. Ubes. In the process of delivering the prisoners to Spanish authorities, Cotton hoped that either a Spanish or Portuguese officer would accept the dispatch from Ekins and convey it to the Russian squadron. Ekins failed to complete this mission because he reacted to a report from Captain Jones of the *Talbot*. Jones reported sighting an enemy squadron consisting of six ships-of-the-line sailing westward of southern Portugal. This might have been the squadron of Rear Admiral Sir John Duckworth, which was in pursuit of a French squadron that had escaped from Rochefort on 17 January. On the 23rd, the *Defence* began pursuing the alleged enemy squadron toward the West Indies. Before departing the coast of Portugal, however, Ekins transferred his prisoners and Cotton's letter to the *Talbot*—contact was not made with the Russian admiral.[44]

Meanwhile, Cotton attended to the needs of his squadron. The same storm that battered the *Minotaur* also damaged the *Hibernia*, carrying away its fore yard. In addition to damaged ships, the squadron that Cotton inherited from Smith suffered from a shortage of provisions and water. As Cotton estimated that his squadron could not remain at sea for more than five weeks, he urged the Admiralty to send him enough provisions to furnish his squadron for five months. To emphasize the seriousness of the shortage, Cotton informed the Admiralty that Portuguese detainees within the squadron were being released in order to reduce consumption of provisions and water. A state of emergency did not exist for Cotton, but the poor condition of his squadron, the unknown whereabouts of the Rochefort squadron, and the mystery shrouding the Russian squadron created a tense environment that made him reluctant to individually detach any ships to replenish their supplies.[45]

According to one account, Cotton's squadron could not have prevented the Rochefort squadron, should it have appeared off the Rock of Lisbon, from entering the Tagus to join Seniavin's fleet. Captain Charles Paget of the *Cambrian* observed:

> We reached the Rock of Lisbon . . . and looked into the Tagus, where we saw the Russian Squadron in the offing and a long way to Leeward was Sir Charles Cotton. It immediately occurred to me that, had the Rochefort Squadron been in our situation, with what perfect ease might they in defiance of Sir Charles have got into the Tagus, and thus have formed a force which would have been infinitely superior to his own."[46]

Cotton was aware that the Rochefort squadron was at large and perhaps deserves some criticism for not keeping a tighter blockade of Lisbon, despite the poor condition of his vessels and the weather. Considering his experience with blockades, however, he most likely decided that the risk of losing his vessels against a hazardous shore was more dangerous than a junction between the Russian and French fleets.

On 31 January, Cotton learned that Ekins had not, in all probability, delivered Seniavin's letter as instructed. Consequently, he sent a second copy of the letter by a more reliable means. This time Seniavin received the letter, but after the French intercepted and copied it. Seniavin agreed to send a confidante to the *Hibernia* to receive all letters for himself and André Dubatchersky, the Russian consul in Lisbon. Echoing Cotton's lament, Seniavin was no "less afflicted at the actual state of the relations between our two august courts."[47]

On 7 February, Seniavin sent two officers accompanied by a French officer out of the Tagus under a flag of truce to the *Hibernia*. Finally, Cotton received reliable information about the Russian squadron. While one Russian distracted the French officer, the other told a British officer that his countrymen were "extremely dissatisfied with their situation," especially since the French had occupied all the batteries on the banks of the Tagus and were currently building new ones. Contrary to previous reports, Cotton learned that Seniavin's squadron was not short of provisions but was supplied for at least ten months. These revelations made capitulation of the Russian squadron unrealistic without the use of force. A blockade alone would not force Seniavin's hand. As the shroud of uncertainty regarding the Russian squadron lifted from British eyes, so too did the shroud that obscured the situation in Lisbon.[48]

Two British merchants, John Carpenter and William Ford, left Lisbon on 27 January and presented themselves aboard the *Hibernia* a few days later. They had remained in Lisbon to collect debts, but pressure from the French authorities compelled them to leave. Carpenter and Ford reported the arrest of several fellow English merchants and the presence of some English families on the Russian ships. They also reported that the Portuguese were "extremely dissatisfied" with the French occupation and that the wheat supply in Lisbon was expected to last only until mid-March. The French imposition of heavy general contributions and large individual exactions on the Portuguese had created more tension. Furthermore, Cotton learned that the Russian naval officers had little rapport with the French and that English officers serving on the Russian ships would quit this service once Seniavin formally notified them of the war between their countries. If the reports of Carpenter and Ford were accurate, then conditions in Lisbon were ripe for British military and naval intervention. Yet, with the poor condition of his squadron and its limited resources, there was little that Cotton could do to expel the French army from Portugal or capture the Russian squadron other than attempt to boost Portuguese morale and negotiate with Seniavin.[49]

By its strategic nature, Cotton's blockade of Portugal was defensive. The blockade succeeded if the Royal Navy controlled the passage of ships into and out of Portuguese ports, but the mere presence of British warships often deterred enemy naval and maritime activity. Yet, Cotton's squadron could not deter all French naval activity in the Tagus. Junot was determined to challenge the Royal Navy by mustering all available vessels in the Tagus under French colors. His goal was to have eleven ships-of-the-line by May to challenge the British blockade.[50] Of course Junot wanted to co-opt Seniavin's squadron, but he also pressed into French service Portuguese vessels that were in the Tagus. Junot's aggressive naval plans practically ensured that Cotton's blockade of Portugal would not go unchallenged. The British would have to employ aggressive naval tactics to contain Junot and maintain the blockade's viability. It became clear to Cotton by mid-February that the Rochefort squadron posed no threat to his command, but by then he also believed that his squadron needed more ships to properly fulfill its duties.[51] Cotton made the Lords of the Admiralty "aware of the utter impossibility effectually to carry their instructions for blockading the kingdom of Portugal into execution with line of battle ships only."[52] Because of damaged ships, the need for provisioning and watering, peripheral missions, and the requirement to blockade the entire Portuguese coast, Cotton's flagship and the *Confiance* were the only ships-of-the-line available off the Tagus in early February—an unsatisfactory situation for Cotton.

Cotton continued fulfilling his orders, despite his squadron's numerous limitations. The Admiralty had instructed Cotton to seize the Burling Islands, a small island group located fifty miles north of Lisbon, about ten miles off the coast near Peniche. The fort of St. John the Baptist protected the largest of these islands and was occupied by a small Portuguese contingent at the time Cotton dispatched a vessel to capture it. Even though the island's garrison posed no threat to British naval operations, the Burlings were important because of their potential value as a watering site. Considerably further from Lisbon than the Burlings, the islands of Bayonne and Ons off Vigo were presently the nearest watering site. The round trip between Lisbon and Vigo for warships completing with water took two to three weeks. Cotton later learned that the water sources at the Bayonne and Ons islands were not "so favourable with respect to procuring a supply as [he] expected."[53] Furthermore, he heard reports that an estimated 2,000 French at Vigo were planning to seize and fortify these islands. The harsh weather of late January had caused Cotton to postpone attacking the Burlings until the first week of February. He selected Captain George McKinley of the *Lively* frigate to lead the attack. McKinley was a very capable officer who possessed an intimate knowledge of the Portuguese coast. His report to the Admiralty in December 1807 had described in detail his concept of how naval operations ought to be conducted on the Lisbon station. McKinley's recent return to the Tagus gave Cotton an invaluable asset that was immediately put to use.

After conducting reconnaissance in the Tagus on 8 February, the *Lively* and the *Viper* schooner proceeded north to the Burlings. After they arrived off the fort of St. John the Baptist on the 12th, McKinley sent a flag of truce with a request for the garrison to surrender. The garrison was overmatched. It consisted of only a sergeant and twelve soldiers to operate six cannons, but Portuguese honor required a refusal to surrender. A symbolic exchange of fire between the fort and the *Lively* quickly satisfied this requirement. McKinley sent a contingent of Royal Marines to accept the surrender and occupy the fort while he proceeded to survey the Burlings for fresh water. His failure to discover a sufficient water source disappointed Cotton. In fact, McKinley observed that the Burlings were of little value for the British navy: "I do not think it a safe anchorage for any of His Majesty's Ships; and the island within itself produces nothing."[54] Nonetheless, McKinley erected a signal post on the height of Vigie to communicate with passing ships, and he made a sketch of the island with soundings. Unfortunately, the Burlings provided no material benefit for Cotton's squadron, but at least British occupation of them made the passage between England and Lisbon marginally safer. Cotton secured the Burlings by posting a detachment of Royal Marines from the *Hibernia* at the fort and by stationing there the gun-brig *Rapid*.[55]

Another explicit order required Cotton to issue a series of proclamations to the Portuguese. Cotton arrived off the Tagus with a proclamation written by the Admiralty that promised safe passage to Brazil aboard British transports for those Portuguese subjects formerly enlisted in the army or navy who wished to join their monarch. The Admiralty proclamation also promised that Portuguese subjects could stay on board British warships while waiting for a transport. Cotton was grateful when few Portuguese responded to the offer. He did not want the Portuguese burdening his poorly provisioned squadron. However, within a couple of months, the flow of Portuguese refugees to Cotton's squadron would increase dramatically because of Junot's indiscretions.[56]

Despite the diplomatic standoff between the British, Russians, and French, the mouth of the Tagus was the scene of much naval and maritime activity. Life went on for Portuguese fishermen, and increasing numbers of Portuguese made their way to British warships. Junot continued refitting and exercising ex-Portuguese vessels; Seniavin's squadron remained restlessly at anchor off Belem; and British boats patrolled each night to observe this activity.

Inevitably, British and French forces clashed. On the night of 13 February, when two boats from the *Confiance* were patrolling the mouth of the Tagus, Robert Trist, masters mate in charge of the patrol, sighted a French gunboat at anchor between the forts of Belem and São Julião. He immediately led his force of sixteen men toward the enemy vessel and, despite receiving fire, boarded it. French resistance was light, and Trist's force quickly captured the vessel, *La Cannonier No.1*. The absence of any British casualties in this attack was remarkable considering that a twelve-pound cannon, two six-pound cannons, one hundred muskets, and fifty men were on the enemy gunboat. As a reward for Trist's gallant performance, Cotton appointed him acting lieutenant of the *Alfred*.[57]

Though British naval raids against small enemy targets in the Tagus had a fair chance of success, Cotton knew that a major attack there would fail. The fortifications around Lisbon harbor housed an estimated 382 pieces of artillery that protected the Russian squadron and French vessels at anchor. In addition, the ships of Seniavin's squadron reportedly had 756 guns.[58]

Reinforcements finally reached Cotton when Major General Sir Brent Spencer arrived off the Tagus in the *Antelope* on 26 February with sixty-four transports. Cotton deemed it impossible "from the existing state of things to employ the force under Major General Spencer with any effect in offensive operations in the Tagus."[59] Therefore, he recommended that Spencer carry out his specified orders from the government by continuing to Gibraltar or Sicily. Spencer's corps immediately left the Tagus for Gibraltar; it would return that summer when offensive operations became possible.

In late February, Cotton, who still considered his squadron unfit to blockade the coast of Portugal, repeatedly asked the Admiralty to send more ships, provisions, and water. Reports about the enemy's intention to sail made him more reluctant to detach any of his eight ships-of-the-line for victualling. Although Cotton believed his squadron barely capable of executing its primary mission, the Admiralty appeared ambivalent about his concerns. The Admiralty directed that should the Brest Fleet escape undetected, Cotton was to detach a squadron of equal number in pursuit. It was to pursue as needed to Madeira, Barbados, Martinique, Jamaica, or even the Chesapeake before returning to Cawsand Bay. Cotton received these orders on 27 February and promptly informed the Lords of the Admiralty how compliance with this contingency would impair his blockade of Portugal. The Admiralty later responded to Cotton's concern by repeating the original instructions.[60]

Despite Cotton's pessimism, the condition of his squadron was improving. The late February arrivals of the *Blossom* sloop and frigates *Africaine* and *Comus* augmented his squadron's ability to cruise the coastline and communicate with the Portuguese, although it hardly added firepower to strengthen his command. Furthermore, eight victuallers arrived off the Tagus on 1 March and supplied Cotton's vessels with enough provisions to last five months. The water shortage problem remained until the 30th when four water-laden transports joined the squadron. In addition, the Admiralty directed that these transports remain with Cotton for continuous employment watering his squadron. The British naval presence off Lisbon would no longer be weakened by warships watering at the Bayonne and Ons islands. The Admiralty finally had listened to their admiral's urgent requests; now Cotton could pursue negotiations with Seniavin with a little less anxiety.[61]

Since capturing the Russian squadron was out of the question for the foreseeable future, Cotton became more concerned about the fate of British officers serving under Seniavin. Several British officers had served honorably under the Russian flag in the Mediterranean—notably, Rear Admiral Alexander Greig, whose ship the *Ratvisan* captured two Ottoman frigates and one other vessel after the battle off Tenedos on 18 July 1807. Cotton had heard that Seniavin's British officers had "resigned their employments" because of the "relative situation" between Russia and Britain. In a 29 February letter to Seniavin, Cotton requested that the Russian admiral send all British officers to his squadron "in order that they may be sent to England." To be more persuasive, he informed Seniavin that those Russians serving in the Royal Navy had already been "forwarded from England to their native land."[62] Before receiving this letter, Seniavin had received instructions from St. Petersburg to "withdraw those [British] officers from their respective commands or employments, and to send them to Russia."[63] Seniavin could not fulfill Cotton's request without disobeying a direct order. The Russian admiral informed Cotton that the seven British officers still serving under his flag would soon be sent to Russia, "furnished with every necessary for their safe conveyance."

Given the urgency of Cotton's request and his proximity to Seniavin, it seems surprising that this exchange between the two admirals took one month to complete. Cotton did not receive Seniavin's reply until 28 March because of Junot's intensified measures to disrupt all communication between the Royal Navy and the port of Lisbon. Initially, the French general prohibited using flags of truce. According to a 4 March letter from Cotton to the Admiralty, Junot even threatened to sink a boat "conveying his wounded countrymen on shore from the gun vessel captured by the boats of the *Confiance*."[64] To communicate with the Russians, Cotton had to rely on an unreliable means—Portuguese fishing boats. On 5 April, Junot made this method more unreliable by publishing an edict prohibiting any communication with the British squadron. He decreed that all officers commanding batteries or forts would fire on any English vessel approaching the Portuguese coast. Failure to do so would result in a court-martial. In addition, the edict threatened with imprisonment or death any individual who attempted to board an English vessel and anyone who abetted such an escape. Junot's edict was clearly aimed at preventing any desertions from the ranks of the Portuguese or French armies. The edict also encouraged Portuguese citizens to report individuals engaged in this activity by offering a reward of up to 200 *cruzados*. To enforce his edict, Junot required all boats to carry a copy of it. The French would seize and sell any boat found without one. Junot's edict did not stop all communication between shore and the British squadron, but it did disrupt significantly Cotton's attempts to communicate with the Russians and gather intelligence from Lisbon.[65]

On the day Cotton received Seniavin's reply regarding the disposition of British officers in the Russian squadron, a boat bearing Portuguese colors and a Mr. Setaro approached the squadron. After boarding the *Hibernia*, Setaro presented his credentials as a former supply agent for the British and presently a commissary for the French army. The purpose of his visit was to obtain Cotton's permission for the "importation of flour to support the native inhabitants of Portugal." Setaro told Cotton that the British blockade of Portugal would soon cause famine because only two to three weeks of grain remained for the people while the French army was supplied for up to six months. Cotton refused to grant this request. Setaro then suggested that Cotton allow fifteen merchant vessels laden with cargo and passengers to sail for Brazil. Cotton assented to this request because it was within the spirit of the British proclamation guaranteeing safe passage to Brazil for those Portuguese who wished to join their sovereign. Cotton stipulated, however, that these vessels were subject to British examination. Setaro volunteered additional information with an estimate of 15,000 troops in Lisbon; he also reported the 17 March fall from power in Spain of Don Manuel Godoy, the so-called Prince of Peace. The threat of famine concerned Cotton, but not enough for him to lift the blockade. Instead, he forwarded Setaro's request to London and then awaited guidance from the Admiralty.[66]

While Cotton awaited the Admiralty's reply during the month of April, the possibility of conflict in the Tagus increased. On 1 April, Cotton understood the Russian squadron to be at single anchor and ready to leave the Tagus, a condition allegedly caused by a dispute with the French. Furthermore, he had recently received reports from Sir Sidney Smith and Rear Admiral Sir John Child Purvis at Gibraltar that three Russian ships-of-the-line were likely to enter the Tagus to augment Seniavin. Smith surmised that Seniavin's reinforced squadron would then escape from the Tagus and sail to join the French naval force at Cadiz. As Cotton prepared for this possibility, many Portuguese decided that the time was right to leave their country. They flooded to the inshore squadron. Cotton had to immediately send the refugees to Britain before passage to Brazil because of their consumption of the squadron's provisions and water and to make room for more refugees. Having sent 173 refugees aboard the storeship *Hindostan* on the 5th, two days later Cotton sent another 210 aboard the *Caledonia* transport.[67]

The flow of refugees almost stopped with the dissemination of Junot's edict of 5 April forbidding contact with the British fleet. However, the papal nuncio in Lisbon managed to escape on the 21st in a neutral vessel, despite repeated assurances to Junot that he would not. Before proceeding to Rio de Janeiro aboard the *Strella del Norte* under convoy of the frigate *Mediator*, the papal nuncio gave Cotton more information with which to assess the situation on the peninsula. He confirmed much of what Setaro had reported about the Spanish royal family, specifically the abdication of Charles IV and the assumption of the throne by his son, Ferdinand VII. Moreover, he had heard that Ferdinand was to marry one of Napoleon's nieces. Cotton received other alarming reports about the situation in Spain from other sources. He had recently received a dispatch from Lieutenant General Sir Hew Dalrymple, governor of Gibraltar, that reported the approach to Madrid of 50,000 French troops led by Joachim Murat, Grand Duke of Berg. Dalrymple believed that Murat's troops were destined for Cadiz. As the month of April progressed and additional reports arrived, Cotton viewed the situation in Spain as increasingly unstable.[68]

An unfortunate event happened on the night of 22/23 April that made the news from Spain seem bleaker. In what was the last significant naval engagement in the Tagus between the two adversaries, five British longboats with 150 men from the *Nymphe* and *Blossom* attacked the French sloop *Gaivota*. The attack failed with heavy British casualties. On the third attempt to board the French vessel, the British were "received with so warm and well directed a fire, that they only thought of saving themselves by leaving to their fate such of their men as got entangled in the ropes, and who were then thrown into the sea."[69] The British raiders had an estimated forty casualties and lost their commander, Captain Shipley, who was killed by the French sloop commander. With the death of Shipley and the Tagus forts firing upon the boats, Captain Pigott of the *Blossom* canceled the attack. Despite this setback, the British continued their nightly patrols of the Tagus.[70]

At a time when events on the peninsula seemed to be reaching a crescendo, Cotton received the Admiralty's response regarding Setaro's request for a provisional relaxation of the Tagus blockade. Lord Castlereagh had seen Cotton's letter of 29 March and subsequently drafted a detailed memo for the admiral. Essentially, Castlereagh used Setaro's request as a catalyst for negotiating the surrender of Seniavin's squadron. Without making any contextual changes to Castlereagh's instructions, the Lords Commissioners forwarded them to the Tagus. Cotton was ordered "to open a communication by a flag of truce with the existing government at Lisbon," as well as with the Portuguese military commander, Seniavin, and Junot. Once communications were open, Cotton had to accomplish several specified tasks. First, he was to declare that the blockade was a "necessary operation of war" and to express the British government's sincere regret that it was causing famine among the inhabitants of Portugal. Unfortunately, the blockade of Lisbon was "an indispensable measure of self-defence" because its occupation by the enemy made it a "port of equipment for the invasion of His Majesty's dominions." Blame for any suffering rested on "those who exercise the powers of government in Lisbon." The Admiralty instructed Cotton to remove the pressure of the blockade only if the French accepted the British government's "most liberal terms of maritime capitulation." If the proposed terms were rejected, Cotton was to "continue the blockade with the utmost rigour."[71]

The terms, framed into six articles, called for the immediate surrender of Seniavin's squadron to Cotton for sequestration in a British port. The British would return the surrendered vessels within six months of the conclusion of peace between King George and Tsar Alexander. Seniavin and all those under his command would be returned to Russia "without any condition or stipulation respecting their future services." In addition, the French were to transfer to Cotton all Portuguese warships and merchant vessels with their attendant stores, sails, and equipment; the Royal Navy would hold all enemy merchant vessels in deposit until the conclusion of peace; and all neutral vessels in the Tagus would leave according to a specified schedule. With the acceptance of these terms, Cotton would "suffer the free entry of provisions, not being enemy property, into the several ports of Portugal, and shall relax the strict military blockade of such ports."[72]

The *Cheerly* gun-brig delivered these instructions to Cotton on 27 April. Although he had misgivings about his ability to communicate with the mainland because of Junot's draconian measures, Cotton planned to do so through the crews of Portuguese fishing boats. He immediately drafted a proclamation for distribution to the inhabitants of Portugal between St. Ubes and Oporto. The proclamation explained why the British blockade existed and that His Majesty's government was concerned about the welfare of the Portuguese people. The proclamation concluded: "On the decision of those that exercise the powers of government in Lisbon, therefore, depends the relief of the suffering inhabitants; it is with them, by acceding to terms most liberal, at once to throw open the ports of Portugal for the admission of grain, or by rejecting those terms, to increase the rigour of the blockade to its utmost possible extent."[73] Cotton hoped that the proclamation would incite the people to pressure the Lisbon authorities to establish communication with him and eventually accept the British terms of maritime capitulation.[74]

With all his vessels provisioned for six months and all the water they could hold, Cotton patiently waited for a response to his proclamation. A response from Junot came on 18 May, again delivered by Setaro. He told Cotton that Junot had received the admiral's proclamation on the 12th and had forwarded it to Napoleon. While awaiting the emperor's reply, Setaro suggested that Cotton explain to him the terms of the maritime capitulation in order to expedite the negotiation process. Cotton balked at the request and reminded Setaro that officers of rank under a flag of truce usually act as representatives between two opposing commanders-in-chief. Only under such circumstances would Cotton communicate the terms of the maritime capitulation. However, his insistence on this formality proved immaterial with the arrival in Lisbon of Napoleon's 23 May guidance to Junot about the proclamation: "Regarding the maritime capitulation, I do not know what the admiral wishes to say. A capitulation is a dishonorable act in military terms. It is only necessary to respond with cannon fire."[75] Junot's reaction on 3 June was predictable. He told Napoleon: "I am so disposed to receive the dishonorable provisions by cannon fire, that I have announced in Lisbon . . . that I will fire on any parliamentarian if he refuses to take to the open sea, and I will have nothing to do with the commander of the enemy squadron."[76] This attitude eliminated negotiation as a means for Cotton to secure Seniavin's squadron.

Cotton's conversation with Setaro extended beyond the topic of maritime capitulation to a discussion about the Russian squadron and the revolt in Spain. Setaro intimated that in the event of the French army's defeat by Spanish and Portuguese forces, Seniavin would "not act in any manner hostile to either of those countries" because the Russian government was not at war with them. Setaro claimed to know Seniavin's response should a British naval force enter the Tagus: "Unless a very commanding and superior force rendered such a measure improper—fight them." Regarding affairs in Spain, he stated that Junot was worried that the Spanish revolt would spread to Portugal. In that event, Setaro mentioned, the people would probably arm themselves if they had either "sword, pike or even knives within their reach." He also suggested that "a transport or two loaded with arms might be highly beneficial." Although Setaro was likely sympathetic to the plight of the Portuguese, Cotton had to assume that his comments were designed to ascertain any British plans of support for the Portuguese. Cotton divulged nothing to Setaro until the end of their discussion. The admiral proposed sending to Junot the Captain of the Fleet, Captain Sir Lawrence William Halsted, with a draft of the articles of maritime capitulation, but only if an officer from Junot first intimated that a flag of truce would be received.[77]

A deadlock existed over the fate of maritime activity in the Tagus. Yet, both Cotton and Junot knew that the impasse would not last much longer because of the revolution breaking out in Spain. As it became increasingly probable that the Spanish revolt would isolate the French army in Portugal, Junot placed more emphasis on gaining naval support from the Russian squadron. Napoleon also recognized the danger and ordered Junot to prepare three ships-of-the-line, three frigates, and three corvettes for an expedition by 1 July. Despite Napoleon's assurance of support and Junot's efforts, the French squadron was never properly fitted to sail. Cotton and Junot did what they could to prepare for an uprising before the Spanish revolution spread to Portugal.[78]

Before the impact of the Spanish revolt hit Portugal, Cotton perceived one last problem affecting his squadron. His vessels were complete with water and provisions, and Portuguese refugees no longer burdened them. However, he still needed more small vessels to cruise the coast; he had lost the gun-brig *Rapid* and earlier the sloops *Milbrook* and *Raven*. While cruising off Cape St. Vincent on 18 May, the *Rapid* and *Primrose* sloop began chasing two Spanish feluccas. The feluccas retired into Segares Bay under the protective cover of a "very strong fortification." That evening Lieutenant Henry Baugh, commander of the *Rapid*, prepared his boats to capture them. Unfortunately for Baugh, two well-placed shots from the fortification struck the *Rapid* below the water line before he embarked on the raid. The carpenter from the *Primrose* could not plug the holes, and Baugh had no choice but to abandon ship so quickly that the crew had no time to gather their belongings. The *Rapid* sunk within minutes of its evacuation. Cotton regretted the loss but approved of Baugh's aggressiveness.[79]

News of the Spanish revolt trickled into Portugal from early May to early June; it created an atmosphere of tension among the Spanish soldiers serving with the French in Portugal and gave the Portuguese people cause for hope that the French army would soon leave their nation, willingly or by force. Although Cotton received several reports about current events on the peninsula, he received no direct personal communication from anyone on shore between the day of Setaro's last visit on 18 May and 7 June. This period was the calm before the storm. Cotton used it to analyze various reports and plan his next active measure in the Tagus. From an agent in Oporto, Cotton learned that Napoleon had detained the King of Spain and Ferdinand VII as hostages. From a report by the Marquis Solano, commander of Spanish troops at Badajoz, the admiral learned of the 2 May conflict between the citizens of Madrid and French soldiers, later known as "*Dos de Mayo*." Rear Admiral John Purvis at Cadiz also kept Cotton informed of the events in Spain and of his attempt, in conjunction with Spencer's corps, to capture French vessels at anchor in Cadiz harbor. Cotton analyzed the implications of these events, and he soon realized that capturing the Russian squadron had become subordinate to the more important matter of supporting rebellion against the French.[80]

Cotton had arrived off Portugal expecting to capture the Russian squadron, perhaps in a manner reminiscent of Gambier's attack at Copenhagen. Cotton quickly realized the futility of such an attack in the Tagus and settled into a blockade, hoping that this defensive measure would provoke Seniavin to surrender his squadron. Because Seniavin received Junot's support, the British blockade failed to significantly weaken the Russians. Nonetheless, the blockade persisted while the condition of Cotton's squadron gradually improved from its degraded state under Sir Sidney Smith. Because of the Admiralty's support and Cotton's initiative, by June 1808 the squadron off the Tagus was fully provisioned for operations through the summer; as a result, every vessel could operate without logistical constraints beyond the routine. Furthermore, the Admiralty had rescinded its order for Cotton to dispatch a pursuit squadron should the Brest Fleet escape. With the *Lively* cruising the Azores, the *Africaine* protecting Madeira, small vessels along the coast from Cape St. Vincent to El Ferrol, and his ships-of-the-line off the Tagus, Cotton had managed the stage upon which Britain would soon assume the leading role in the expulsion of the French from the Iberian peninsula. Cotton's 28 April 1808 appointment to admiral of the blue came at a time, as future events would tell, when the commander-in-chief of His Majesty's squadron stationed off the Tagus needed all the prestige and authority befitting this rank.[81]

NOTES

1. "Naval History of the Present Year," 1807, *The Naval Chronicle* 18 (1807): 148–49.

2. Collingwood to Cotton, 20 November 1807, Cambridgeshire County Record Office, Cotton Naval Papers, 588/c74.

3. Sir Joshua Rowley sent his condolences for the death of Cotton's son. Rowley to Cotton, 28 March 1807, ibid., 588/c72.

4. "Memoir of Cotton," *Naval Chronicle* 27 (1812): 361.

5. Cotton to his wife, undated, Cambridgeshire County Record Office, Cotton Naval Papers, 588/c79.

6. Leslie Stephen and Sydney Lee, eds., *Dictionary of National Biography* (London, 1885–1901), 15: 1119; for a biographical sketch of Mulgrave, see Percy M. Thornton, *Foreign Secretaries of the XIX Century to 1834* (London, 1881), 1: 105–46.

7. Captain Thomas Fremantle to the Marquis of Buckingham, 4 April 1807, Duke of Buckingham and Chandos, K.G., ed., *Memoirs of the Court and Cabinets of George the Third* (London, 1855), 4: 157–58.

8. A.N. Ryan, "The Causes of the British Attack upon Copenhagen in 1807," *English Historical Review* 68 (1953): 37.

9. Mulgrave to Cotton, 11 July 1807, Cambridgeshire County Record Office, Cotton Naval Papers, 588/c72(a).

10. Mulgrave to the King, 16 July 1807, A. Aspinall, ed., *Later Correspondence of George III* (Cambridge, 1968), 4: 605.

11. Mulgrave to Cotton, 16 July 1807, Cambridgeshire County Record Office, Cotton Naval Papers, 588/c73(b).

12. Mulgrave to the King, 3 December 1807, The King's reply, 4 December 1807, Aspinall, *Correspondence of George III*, 4; 654; Georgiana, Lady Chatterton, *Memorials, Personal and Historical of Admiral Lord Gambier, G.C.B.* (London, Hurst and Blackett, 1861), 2: 10–94; Cyril Northcote Parkinson, *Britannia Rules: The Classic Age of Naval History, 1793–1815* (London, 1977), 132–33.

13. Admiralty to Cotton, 9 December 1807, England, House of Commons, *Papers, Presented to the House of Commons, Relative to the Russian Fleet in the Tagus, and to the Convention concluded with the Russian Admiral* (London: House of Commons, 9, 10 February 1809), 1: 3 (hereafter cited as *Papers*); Mulgrave to Smith, 27 October 1807, "Memoir of Cotton," *Naval Chronicle* 27 (1812): 368.

14. Alphonse Louis Grasset, *La Guerre d'Espagne, 1807–1813* (Paris, 1914), 1: 94–121; Donald D. Horward, "Portugal and the Anglo-Russian Naval Crisis, 1808," *Naval War College Review* 34 (1981): 49.

15. Napoleon to Junot, 12 November 1807, Napoleon Bonaparte, *Correspondence de Napoléon Ier publiée par ordre de l'Emperor Napoléon III* (Paris, 1864), no. 13351, 16: 156–58; Baron Thiébault, *The Memoirs of Baron Thiébault* (London, 1896), 2: 190–94;

Lord Russell of Liverpool, *Knight of the Sword: The Life and Letters of Admiral Sir William Sidney Smith, G.C.B.* (London, 1964), 162; Charles William Chadwick Oman, *A History of the Peninsular War* (Oxford, 1902–1930), 1: 26. For a more detailed account of Junot's character and why Napoleon appointed him to command the army destined for Portugal, see Charles MacKay, "The Tempest: The Life and Career of Jean-Andoche Junot, 1771–1813," Ph.D. dissertation, Florida State University, 1995.

16. Extract from "Official Declaration of the Blockade of the mouth of the Tagus," cited in Horward, "Portugal and the Anglo-Russian Naval Crisis," 49, 50; John Barrow, *Life and Correspondence of Admiral Sir William Sidney Smith, G.C.B.* (London, 1848), 2: 259–60; I.U. Davydov, *Seniavin* (Moscow, 1972), 194; N.W. Emmott and J.N. Portney, "*The Seniavin Saga,*" *Litton Avionics Newsletter* (undated): 91–92; André Fugier, *Napoléon et l'Espagne* (Paris, 1930), 2: 337–38.

17. Admiralty to Smith (Most Secret), 30 October 1807, Cambridgeshire County Record Office, Cotton Naval Papers, 588/041/a1; Strangford to George Canning, 29 November 1807, Barrow, *Life of Sir William Sidney Smith*, 261–65; Oman, *Peninsular War*, 1: 30; Horward, "Portugal and the Anglo-Russian Naval Crisis," 50.

18. Smith to William Wellesley Pole, 1 December 1807, Barrow, *Life of Sir William Sidney Smith*, 266–69. Several unserviceable Portuguese ships remained at Lisbon and would later be a subject of dispute with the French. They were the *San Sebastian* (64), *Maria Prima* (74), *Vasco de Gama* (74), *Princesa da Beira* (64), *Fenix* (48), *Amazona* (44), *Perola* (44), *Tritao* (40), and *Veney* (30). See "List of the Portuguese Ships that remained in Lisbon," *Naval Chronicle* 18 (1807): 509.

19. Grasset, *La Guerre d'Espagne*, 1: 179-80; Oman, *Peninsular War*, 1: 30, 31; Horward, "Portugal and the Anglo-Russian Naval Crisis," 50.

20. Admiralty to Cotton, 9 December 1807, *Papers*, 1: 3. According to the "Chronological Sketch of the Most Remarkable Naval Events of the Year 1807," London received intelligence on 27 November of the Russian fleet's arrival in the Tagus. See *Naval Chronicle* 19 (1808): 129.

21. Admiralty to Cotton, 9 December 1807, *Papers*, 1: 3; Lord Hawkesbury to Lieutenant General Sir John Moore, 4 December 1807, Cambridgeshire County Record Office, Cotton Naval Papers, 588/041/a1; Lord Russsell, *Knight of the Sword*, 168.

22. Rendezvous Instructions, 18 December 1807, Cotton to W.W. Pole, 19, 31 December 1807, Great Britain, Public Record Office, Kew, MSS (hereafter PRO), Admiralty (hereafter ADM), 1/339; Castlereagh to the King, 3 March 1808, Aspinall, *Later Correspondence of George III*, 5: 36.

23. The Azores were often referred to as the Western Islands during the nineteenth century.

24. Honorable Captain H. Curzon to Smith, 4 December 1807, PRO ADM 1/339; Smith detached the *Marlborough* (74), *London* (90), *Monarch* (74), and *Bedford* (74) to accompany the Portuguese fleet to South America. Smith to W.W. Pole, 1, 6 December 1807, *Naval Chronicle* 18 (1807): 508–10; Graham Moore was the brother of Lieutenant General Sir John Moore. For Smith's instructions for Moore's voyage to South America, see Smith to Commodore Graham Moore, 5 December 1807, in Gerald S. Graham and R.A. Humphreys, eds., *The Navy and South America, 1807–1823* (London, 1962), 3, 4.

25. Smith to the Governor of the Azores, 6 January 1808, PRO ADM 1/339.

26. Curzon to Smith, 19 January 1808, Cambridgeshire County Record Office, Cotton Naval Papers, 588/041/a18.

27. Extract of a Secret Convention signed in London on 22 October 1807 by the Plenipotentiaries of the Prince Regent of Portugal, Article 2, Smith to the Governor of Madeira, 5 January 1808, PRO ADM, 1/339; Russell, *Knight of the Sword*, 169; W.W. Pole to Cotton, 8 February 1808, Cambridgeshire County Record Office, Cotton Naval Papers, 588/041/a14.

28. Junot's edict to the Inhabitants of Lisbon, published without date in French and Portuguese, PRO ADM 1/339; Fugier, *Napoléon et l'Espagne*, 2: 352–54.

29. Excerpt from a declaration by Josephus II, Cardinalis, Patriarcha, Lisbonensis, 8 December 1807, PRO ADM 1/339.

30. Ibid., decrees by Junot to the Inhabitants of Lisbon, 14, 19, 21, 22 December 1807, 5 January 1808, 1 February 1808; Napoleon to Junot, 23 December 1807, *Correspondence de Napoléon Ier*, no. 13416, 16: 214–16.

31. Collingwood to Cotton, 1 February 1808, Cambridgeshire County Record Office, Cotton Naval Papers, 588/042.

32. Thiébault, *Memoirs*, 2: 200; Horward, "Portugal and the Anglo-Russian Naval Crisis," 50–53; Robert W. Daly, "Operations of the Russian Navy during the Reign of Napoleon I," *Mariner's Mirror* 34 (1948): 176–79; M.S. Anderson, "Great Britain and the Growth of the Russian Navy in the Eighteenth Century," *Mariner's Mirror* 42 (1956): 132–46.

33. Extract of a letter from Mr. Secretary Canning to Lord Castlereagh, 25 December 1808, Admiralty to Cotton, 28 December 1808, Cambridgeshire County Record Office, Cotton Naval Papers, 588/041/a7.

34. Cotton to W.W. Pole, 7 January 1808, PRO ADM 1/339.

35. Ibid., Cotton to W.W. Pole, 7, 9, Nos. 1 (Secret) and 2, 10 January 1808; Admiralty to Cotton, 1 January 1808, PRO ADM 2/153; Admiralty to Cotton, 29 December 1807, 6 January 1808, Cambridgeshire County Record Office, Cotton Naval Papers, 588/041/a11.

36. Cotton to W.W. Pole, 9, 10, 16 January 1808, PRO ADM 1/339. The ships Cotton joined off the Tagus were the *Hibernia* (110), *Alfred* (74), *Agamemnon* (64), *Defence* (74), *Ganges* (74), *Foudroyant* (80), *Conqueror* (74), *Plantagenet* (74), *Ruby* (64), and *Nymphe* (36); John W. Fortescue, *A History of the British Army* (London, 1910), 6: 113–14.

37. W.W. Pole to Smith, 30 October 1807, Cambridgeshire County Record Office, Cotton Naval Papers, 588/041/a1; letter from an unknown officer, 2 June 1808. See note in "Memoir of Cotton," *Naval Chronicle* 27 (1812): 363–64.

38. Excerpt of letter from Cotton to Smith, undated, in "Memoir of Cotton," *Naval Chronicle* 27 (1812): 370.

39. Ibid., 366, Smith to Cotton, 24 January 1808; Vice Admiral Sir John Duckworth to Cotton, 22 January 1808, Cotton to W.W. Pole, PRO ADM 1/339.

40. See the letter from an unknown officer, 2 June 1808, Cotton to Smith, 15, 20 February 1808, Smith to Cotton, 15, 20 February 1808, in "Memoir of Cotton," *Naval Chronicle* 27 (1812): 363–70; Barrow, *Life of Sir William Sidney Smith*, 2: 280.

41. Excerpt of a private letter from Cotton to Smith, in "Memoir of Cotton," *Naval Chronicle* 27 (1812): 371; Lord Russell, *Knight of the Sword*, 172.

42. Cotton to W.W. Pole, 25 January 1808, PRO ADM 1/339.

43. Ibid., Cotton to Seniavin, 18 January 1808.

44. Ibid., Duckworth to Cotton, 22 January 1808, Cotton to W.W. Pole, 25 January 1808, 2 February 1808, Ekins to Cotton, 23 January 1808. As on 22 January,

Duckworth's *Royal George* was eighteen leagues west northwest from the Rock of Lisbon, what Captain Jones likely saw was a British, not French, squadron. The fact that both British and French squadrons were reported to consist of six ships each adds to the uncertainty of Jones's report. Cotton was of the opinion that Jones had sighted the British squadron.

45. Ibid., Cotton to W.W. Pole, 24 January 1808, Captain James Grant to Cotton, 24 January 1808.

46. Captain Charles Paget to Arthur Paget, 7 February 1808, Arthur Paget, ed., *The Paget Brothers, 1790–1840* (London, 1918), 79-80.

47. Seniavin to Cotton, 6 February 1808, Cambridgeshire County Record Office, Cotton Naval Papers, 588/041/a52; Cotton to W.W. Pole, 31 January 1808, PRO ADM 1/339; Horward, "Portugal and the Anglo-Russian Naval Crisis," 52.

48. Cotton to W.W. Pole, 8 February 1808, PRO ADM 1/339.

49. Ibid., Cotton to W.W. Pole, 1 February 1808, "Intelligence obtained from Mr. Carpenter and Mr. Ford, two persons that left Lisbon on the 27th January 1808."

50. Junot to Napoleon, 22 April 1808, in Grasset, *Guerre d'Espagne*, 2: 69.

51. On 6 February, the squadron of Rear Admiral Sir Richard Strachan passed off the rock of Lisbon on the way to Cadiz in pursuit of the Rochefort squadron. He had a conference with Cotton on the *Hibernia* that evening before proceeding. Once at Cadiz, Strachan's squadron sailed into the Mediterranean upon the recommendation of Rear Admiral John Child Purvis. Strachan to Cotton, 6 February 1808, Cotton to W.W. Pole, 7 February 1808, PRO ADM 1/339; Purvis to Cotton, 26 February 1808, Cambridgeshire County Record Office, Cotton Naval Papers, 588/041/a20.

52. Cotton to W.W. Pole, 2 February 1808, PRO ADM 1/339; Horward, "Portugal and the Anglo-Russian Naval Crisis," 53.

53. McKinley to W.W. Pole, 7 December 1807, Cambridgeshire County Record Office, Cotton Naval Papers, 588/041/a5.

54. Ibid., 588/041/a19, McKinley to Cotton, 15, 26 February 1808, "A Return of Ordnance, Stores, and Provisions left in charge of Lieutenant G. Huskisson of the Royal Marines, Commanding the Fort of St. John the Baptiste on the Burlings, 24 February 1808." The wreck of the *Milbrook* schooner on 25 March 1808 after being driven from its anchorage off the Burling Islands underscored McKinley's assessment. Cotton to W.W. Pole, 8 April 1808, PRO ADM 1/339.

55. Cotton to W.W. Pole, 16 February 1808, PRO ADM 1/339; The *Rapid* was sunk on 18 May 1808 by French batteries in the Tagus. J.J. Colledge, *Ships of the Royal Navy* (London, 1987), 451.

56. "Project of the Proclamation to be signed by the British Naval Commander," Admiralty to Cotton, 29 December 1807, Cambridgeshire County Record Office, Cotton Naval Papers, 588/041/a8; Cotton to W.W. Pole, 8 February 1808, PRO ADM 1/339.

57. The French suffered three killed and nine wounded in Trist's attack. Captain Yeo to Cotton, 14 February 1808, Cotton to W.W. Pole, 17 February 1808, PRO ADM 1/339; Horward, "Portugal and the Anglo-Russian Naval Crisis," 53.

58. The harbor was protected by forts São Julião, Cascais, Belem, and Bugio as well as many smaller works. See Horward, "Portugal and the Anglo-Russian Naval Crisis," 52. The ships of Seniavin's squadron consisted of *Tverdoi* (80), *Silnoi* (80), *Raphael* (80), *Motstnoi* (74), *Elene* (74), *Yaroslav* (74), *Selaphael* (74), *Ratvisan* (64), *Skoroi* (80), *Venus* (44), and the transport *Kildnine* (32). See "List of the Russian Squadron

now at anchor in the River Tagus, from a most authentic source," 17 November 1807, PRO ADM 1/339.

59. Ibid., Cotton to W.W. Pole, 26 February 1808; Fortescue, *History of the British Army*, 6: 114–15.

60. Admiralty to Cotton, 18 February 1808, Cambridgeshire County Record Office, Cotton Naval Papers, 588/041/a15; Cotton to Admiralty, 21, 27 February 1808, 19 April 1808, PRO ADM 1/339.

61. Cotton to W.W. Pole, 22, 27 February 1808, 5, 30 March 1808, PRO ADM 1/339.

62. Ibid., Cotton to Seniavin, 29 February 1808; Emmott, *Seniavin Saga*, 89–90.

63. Seniavin to Cotton, 7 March 1808, Cambridgeshire County Record Office, Cotton Naval Papers, 588/041/a53.

64. Cotton to Admiralty, 4, 28 March 1808, PRO ADM 1/339.

65. Ibid., Edict to the Inhabitants of Portugal from the General in Chief of the Army of Portugal, 5 April 1808.

66. Ibid., Cotton to W.W. Pole, 29 March 1808.

67. The source for Smith's conjecture was a French deserter who had arrived at Gibraltar before the admiral departed for Brazil. Smith to Cotton, 9 March 1808, Purvis to Cotton, 17 March 1808, Cambridgeshire County Record Office, Cotton Naval Papers, 588/041/a21, a23; Cotton to W.W. Pole, 1, 5, 7 April 1808, PRO ADM 1/339.

68. Dalrymple to Cotton, 31 March 1808, "Edict and Information obtained from His Excellency the Pope's Nuncio off Lisbon," 21 April 1808, Archbishop of Nisibi to Cotton 18 April 1808, Cambridgeshire County Record Office, Cotton Naval Papers, 588/041/a92,a93; Cotton to W.W. Pole, 22 April 1808, PRO ADM 1/339.

69. "Order of the Day of the 24th of April," Maximilien Foy, *History of the War in the Peninsula* (London, 1827), 2: 563.

70. Cotton to W.W. Pole, 23 April 1808, PRO ADM 1/339; Horward, "Portugal and the Anglo-Russian Naval Crisis," 53–54.

71. Castlereagh to the Admiralty, 16 April 1808, Admiralty to Cotton, 16 April 1808, PRO ADM 1/339. See also *Papers*, 1: 7–9.

72. Ibid.

73. "Proclamation by Sir Charles Cotton, Baronet, Commander in chief of his Britannic Majesty's Ships and Vessels, blockading the Ports of the Kingdom of Portugal," 28 April 1808, *Papers*, 1: 11.

74. Cotton to W.W. Pole, 27, 28 April 1808, PRO ADM 1/339. See also *Papers*, 1: 10–11.

75. Napoleon to Junot, 23 May 1808, *Correspondence of Napoleon Ier*, no. 13968, 17: 188; Cotton to W.W. Pole, 27 April 1808, 18 May 1808, PRO ADM 1/339. See also *Papers*, 1: 11–12.

76. Horward, "Portugal and the Anglo-Russian Naval Crisis," 56.

77. Cotton to W.W. Pole, 18 May 1808, PRO ADM 1/339. See also *Papers*, 1: 11–12.

78. Horward, "Portugal and the Anglo-Russian Naval Crisis," 56–57.

79. Captain James Mein to Cotton, 25 May 1808, Lieutenant Henry Baugh to W.W. Pole, 25 May 1808, Cotton to W.W. Pole, 16, 26 May 1808, PRO ADM 1/339.

80. Ibid., Matthew Smith to Cotton, 1 May 1808, Letters from Marquis Solano at Badajoz, 5, 6 May 1808, Cotton to W.W. Pole, 16 May 1808, 7 June 1808, Purvis to Cotton, 29 May 1808.

81. Ibid., Cotton received word of his appointment to admiral of the blue on 30 May 1808. Cotton to W.W. Pole, 30 May 1808, 4, 6 June 1808.

5

Portugal Takes Center Stage: Preparation for the British Army, June–July 1808

> Yesterday we had a popular commotion that lasted four hours, in which several inhabitants and Frenchmen lost their lives. . . . The devil knows what the consequences will be because the populace are in a bad humour.
>
> —Marquis Solano, commander of Spanish troops at Badajoz, 3 May 1808[1]

> I hope Sir Arthur Wellesley will not be a teaser. I have seen so much of it . . . that indeed I would never let a soldier out of England—they are deadweights on the necks of those who have to care for them. And as for Expeditions, I wonder how the word got squeezed into the line of service. I would as soon send a tortoise on Expedition.
>
> —Collingwood to Cotton, 22 July 1808[2]

A Mr. Wilson, formerly a British merchant at Lisbon, boarded the *Hibernia* on 8 June, thus becoming the first person from shore with whom Cotton had direct personal contact since 18 May. Now Cotton had an opportunity to validate an intelligence report from Wilson that had reached him a week earlier. From their discussion, the admiral regarded Wilson an "intelligent man" and therefore considered his reports reliable. Based on requirements for baked bread, Wilson reported that between 3,000 and 4,000 French troops were in the forts and environs of Lisbon. It had been observed that Junot was in the process of fortifying the castle of St. George in the center of Lisbon in anticipation of a popular uprising. Furthermore, Wilson reported that Seniavin's squadron appeared to be making preparations to sail. The Russians had recently purchased large quantities of pitch and tar, and Setaro was busy baking bread and salting and barreling beef for them. Based on the limited number of French troops around Lisbon and the "expressions of detestation at the French" by the Portuguese, Wilson suggested:

From 5,000 to 10,000 British troops should land below Fort St. Julian, march direct for the city, seize the army ovens at Alcantara, shoot on the forts by possessing the high ground that surround them all nearly. [French] bellies would soon capitulate, [and] no risk of hot shot need be run by the fleet—they may enter in holiday triumph. The first shot would produce an acclamation and rising among the Portuguese and not a Frenchman would be able to appear.[3]

Although Wilson was a merchant with no military credentials, his suggestion piqued Cotton's interest because of particular Admiralty guidance he had received on 4 June. In light of the existing circumstances in Spain, the Admiralty had instructed Cotton to act in any way he deemed expedient. Before Cotton could respond to Wilson's intelligence, however, news came on 9 June from Captain Creyke of the sloop *Eclipse* that the revolt in Spain had finally spread to Portugal. Three days earlier Spanish troops in Oporto had captured General François Jean Quesnel and his personal escort of thirty French dragoons. Before marching his troops to Galicia with the prisoners, the Spanish commander encouraged the leaders of Oporto to raise the Portuguese colors in the forts around their city and organize resistance against the French. After the forts exchanged a salute with the *Eclipse*, the Deputy Governor of Oporto informed Creyke that "all persons who held authority under the Prince Regent had been restored to their commands." The Portuguese representative also told Creyke that he expected the adoption of similar measures in Lisbon.[4]

Cotton reacted to this news immediately by distributing a notice to the inhabitants of Lisbon. Cotton hoped that the promise of British support would entice them to follow the example at Oporto: "All the assistance His Britannic Majesty's Fleet can afford, shall be readily given to you, and your generous allies the Spaniards, in the noble attempt to emancipate your capital from the severe oppressions it has suffered since the French army marched into it."[5] Had the 7,000 Spanish soldiers stationed on the Tagus followed the example of their countrymen at Oporto, Cotton's notice might have triggered a revolt among the people of Lisbon against Junot's army. However, on the morning that Cotton wrote his notice, the French army disarmed almost all of the Spanish troops in Lisbon. Junot had issued movement orders that sent the Spanish units marching unsuspectingly into a square lined with French artillery and troops. After the Spanish surrendered, Junot sent them to unserviceable hulks in the Tagus, where they remained for ten weeks until rescued by the British. Without a sizable military force to support them, the people of Lisbon remained passive under the watchful eye of the anxious French army.[6]

Cotton recognized that the insurrections in Spain and Portugal were creating opportunities for the Royal Navy to exploit. On 11 June he received aboard the *Hibernia* Don Sebastiani Solis, a Spanish officer who had been sent by the Supreme Council of Seville to entice the Spanish troops at Lisbon to revolt. Unfortunately, Solis arrived there too late for that—nevertheless, his understanding of the situation in Spain and Portugal proved valuable to Cotton.

Solis reinforced Wilson's claim that 4,000 French troops were in Lisbon, and he described the entire Spanish nation as up in arms, from Andalusia to Galicia. Solis also reported that all Spanish ports were open to Britain; consequently, the Royal Navy entered Cadiz harbor on 1 June to assist in the capture of six French warships.[7] Finally, the Spanish officer requested that Cotton help spread the word to the Spanish troops dispersed in garrisons along the Portuguese coast about the danger of being disarmed. Cotton obliged Solis by writing another proclamation for distribution by British cruisers. Before leaving the *Hibernia*, Solis received from Cotton a certificate for presentation to the Supreme Council of Seville. The certificate verified Solis's visit and expressed the desire of Britain to help the Spaniards in any way possible "for restoring the independence of the Spanish monarchy and ultimately the independence of Europe."[8]

With the latest reports from Spain and Portugal, Cotton believed that now was the time to send British troops back to Lisbon. On 12 June, the day after Solis's departure, Cotton wrote to the Admiralty with the opinion "that five or six thousand British troops might effect a landing, gain possession of the forts on the banks of the Tagus, and by cooperating with His Majesty's Fleet give to our possession the whole of the maritime means now collected in the Tagus."[9] The estimate of 5,000 or 6,000 British troops was based on the reports Cotton had received of about 4,000 French troops in Lisbon. There were in fact 26,500 French troops in Portugal, of whom about 15,000 were in and around Lisbon. After cruising five months off French-occupied Portugal, it seems that Cotton should have been more skeptical of the low enemy troop strength estimate received from Wilson and Solis. Furthermore, the admiral's estimate of the number of British troops required reveals a measure of naiveté about landing operations. Given the enemy situation around Lisbon, several thousand more British soldiers would be needed to land successfully against a hostile shore. Nevertheless, Cotton conveyed the estimated requirement for British troops to General Dalrymple at Gibraltar and suggested that Spencer's corps proceed immediately to Lisbon. Should Dalrymple decide to send the number of troops requested, Cotton urged Admiral Purvis to "aid their progress by every possible means . . . furnishing any escort that may be necessary." Although Cotton's scheme appeared destined for a military debacle, it had a favorable long-term impact because it supported the British government's decision to send an expedition to Portugal instead of Spain.[10]

The revolution in Spain had captured the imagination of the British press, people, and politicians well before any news of the revolt in Portugal reached London. Having received a Spanish deputation from Asturias on 4 June that sought British assistance, the Duke of Portland's government immediately suspended hostilities with Spain and pledged its support to help defeat the common foe. The British government finally had an opportunity to abandon its policy of "filching sugar islands"[11] by sending a sizable body of troops to a region on the European continent where a reasonable chance for success existed. The most readily available body was a corps of 9,000 troops assembled at Cork for an expedition to South America to support revolution against Spain among her colonies. With the sudden change in alliances, this British force became a friend rather than foe to the Spaniards. On 14 June, ten days after the Spanish deputation arrived in London, the Duke of York appointed Lieutenant General Sir Arthur Wellesley, on the recommendation of Lord Castlereagh, to command the corps assembled at Cork, "to be employed upon a particular service." While the corps prepared to sail, the British cabinet deliberated over its precise destination on the Iberian peninsula because the Portuguese had also appealed for aid.[12]

Initially, the northern Spanish provinces of Galicia and Asturias seemed the logical regions to send Wellesley's expedition. However, the Spaniards did not want British soldiers employed on their soil, but rather wanted them to conduct a "powerful diversion in their favor" in Portugal.[13] Sudden common purpose could not completely overcome traditional rivalry. Portland's cabinet accepted the suggestion, without Portuguese consent; Castlereagh ordered Wellesley to direct his attention "to the expulsion of the enemy from Portugal. . . . The entire and absolute evacuation of the Peninsula, by the troops of France, being . . . the only security for Spanish independence." As a means to this end, Castlereagh instructed Wellesley to consider an attack on the Tagus in conjunction with Spencer's corps, which was ordered to proceed to the Tagus from its station off the coast of southern Spain. In addition, the secretary ordered 10,000 more troops to prepare for service in Portugal. Despite public sentiment to land the British army in Spain, the decision to focus on Portugal made sense because Lisbon offered perhaps the best harbor on the Iberian peninsula in which to establish a base for military operations and because the English had been allied to the Portuguese for 500 years. Furthermore, Seniavin's squadron remained a coveted prize. Castlereagh clearly articulated the strategic objective of the expedition, but its details were left much to Wellesley's "judgment and decision on the spot."[14]

Cotton's letter of 12 June arrived in London on the 30th, within hours after Castlereagh instructed Wellesley to consider operations on the Tagus. Although the decision to send the expedition to Portugal already had been made, the admiral's suggestion to send 5,000 or 6,000 troops to the Tagus proved an important catalyst and changed Castlereagh's guidance to Wellesley in terms of emphasizing the urgency of proceeding toward Lisbon as expeditiously as possible. That day Castlereagh dispatched a second letter to Wellesley that urged the general to proceed off the Tagus "with the least possible delay" instead of first going to Coruña as originally instructed.[15]

Wellesley prepared his detachment for the expedition while the cabinet continued deliberating over strategy in Iberia. Besides organizing his military force, Wellesley paid particular attention to naval matters. Captain Pulteney Malcolm, captain of the 76-gun *Donegal*, was the senior naval officer of transports for the expedition. He was responsible for organizing the seventy-five transports that eventually arrived at the disembarkation site in Portugal. Before embarking from Cork, Wellesley expressed his concern in a long letter to Malcolm about the landing operation. The letter addressed the "arrangements of transports into divisions, a code of signals for the army, and return of transports and flat bottomed boats." Though Wellesley was the junior lieutenant general in the British army, his years of campaign experience, especially in India, prepared him well for the vicissitudes of conjunct operations. Cotton would soon cooperate with the British army's most capable general.[16]

On 13 July, Wellesley sailed from Cork ahead of the main flotilla on the frigate *Crocodile*. Contrary to Castlereagh's recommendation to proceed directly to the Tagus, Wellesley still believed that he should first stop at Coruña to gather the latest intelligence. He reasonably thought that his presence with the fleet during the voyage was unnecessary and that he could trust no one but himself with the decision on where to send the expedition. Shortly after the main flotilla had sailed, the cabinet decided to strengthen the expeditionary force and alter its command structure. From Wellesley's initial force of 9,505 troops and 4,793 under Spencer, the cabinet increased it to an estimated 30,129 by ordering to Portugal a corps of 11,253 under Lieutenant General Sir John Moore, which was returning from an expedition in the Baltic. In addition, 4,803 more soldiers were preparing to embark from Ramsgate and Harwich. Command of the enlarged force passed to Sir Hew Dalrymple, who was senior to Wellesley and whose recent involvement with the Spanish army in southern Spain had helped to advance the common cause. Also based on seniority, the cabinet placed Lieutenant General Sir Harry Burrard as second-in-command. Wellesley learned of these changes on 1 August, but he remained in command until after the Battle of Vimeiro, three weeks later. Slow communication and transport, usually considered a liability, now preserved the British expedition to Portugal under the leadership of Wellesley.

Before word of the government's decision to send British troops to the peninsula had reached the Tagus, Cotton was busy responding to requests for aid from delegations representing several Portuguese and Spanish cities, including Badajos, Coimbra, Sines, Oporto, Lagos, Faro, and Figueira da Foz. A proclamation to the "Inhabitants of Portugal" on 4 July typified Cotton's response to their solicitations:

> Deputations have reached me from all parts of your kingdom, soliciting aid, succour, and assistance, and stating to me the loyal, brave, and manly determination of the people of Portugal, to establish the government of their lawful Prince, and emancipate their country from French oppression. I send agreeably to your repeated requests, ships, troops, arms, and ammunition; and have directed the standard of his Royal Highness the Prince Regent of Portugal to be reared, round which every loyal Portuguese is hereby invited immediately to rally, and to take up arms in so just and glorious a cause.[17]

To support his rhetoric, Cotton sent 200 stand of arms to Oporto, 100 to Lagos, and 500 to Figueira da Foz. In Cotton's dispatches to the Admiralty about these contributions and others, he described a situation in Portugal that looked progressively dismal for Junot's army. The Portuguese allegedly could field nearly 20,000 troops near Oporto; their leaders believed that a force of 3,000 British troops would be sufficient to enable the Portuguese army to advance upon Lisbon. It was believed that Junot's force of 11,000, an underestimation of the 26,500 French troops actually in Portugal, could not withstand the sheer mass of Portuguese arms.[18]

Cotton understood that the arms and ammunition distributed by the Royal Navy improved Portuguese morale, as well as having a material benefit. He also realized that the presence of British troops on Portuguese soil could further encourage Portuguese resistance against the French. An opportunity to land British troops arose on 4 July when Cotton learned that the inhabitants of Figueira da Foz had captured the seventy-eight French soldiers garrisoned at Fort Santa Catarina on the north bank of the Mondego River, about 110 miles north of the Tagus. Cotton immediately sent 220 Royal Marines from the fleet—a hasty decision that he believed was fully warranted by the situation:

> I have thought it my duty, in order to manifest a disposition of rendering something more than promise in support of a course so extremely interesting, to dispatch a party of 200 Royal Marines . . . to garrison the forts at that place and I entertain the most sanguine hope that however trifling their numbers the effect may be highly beneficial from the spirit that the presence of British soldiers must at this moment create.[19]

Figueira da Foz was a logical site for the marines because it could be defended with a small garrison and was only seventy miles from Oporto. Mondego Bay also represented the closest anchorage to Lisbon that was safe for a fleet, although Cotton did not use this reason to justify his decision to commit the marines. Unwittingly, Cotton had ordered the establishment of the beachhead upon which Wellesley's troops would land in less than a month.

Cotton assigned Captain John Bligh of the 74-gun *Alfred* to convey the marines to Figueira da Foz. The *Alfred* arrived off the Mondego on 6 July; after a brief survey, the marines landed under the leadership of Captain George Lewis. Bligh estimated that it would take at least 600 French troops to dislodge them from the heights that they occupied on the north side of the river. Should a British retreat from this position be necessary, the marines had easy access to Fort Santa Catarina from which they could safely embark. With respect to the waters off Figueira da Foz as a port facility, Bligh estimated that sixty transports could enter the Mondego, while there was safe anchorage for an unlimited number outside the bar. Believing that the French also recognized the naval value of the Mondego, Bligh suggested to Cotton: "I should not be surprised if the French were to think Figueira an object, as if it is taken there is no place on the coast where troops can be landed nearer than Oporto. This may be a consideration. The men we have are not sufficient to make a stand, but 500 I am confident could keep it."[20] Besides the Mondego's potential as a landing site, Bligh made clear the region's suitability for military operations. Having withdrawn from their garrisons in northern Portugal, the French had established the fort at Peniche as their most northern outpost. With this garrison of 650 French troops situated sixty miles south of Figueira da Foz, the Mondego offered a site that would take a French column several days to interrupt after commencement of a landing operation. If French troops attempted to return to the region before the arrival of a British reinforcement, Bligh believed that the Portuguese would offer more than token resistance: "All the roads [approaching Figueira da Foz from the south] are rendered impassable for artillery or cavalry, and our being here has given so much confidence, that if they perform but half what they promise, it is impossible for the French to advance."

The focal point of Portuguese resistance was at the major city of Coimbra, twenty miles upriver from Figueira da Foz, where Portuguese general Bernandino Freire was attempting to form an army of 10,000 to advance on Peniche and then Lisbon. What the army lacked in arms, ammunition, organization, and training, it made up for with spirit, fostered by hatred of the French. Yet, an army needs more than *esprit de corps* to fight, so Bligh sent 40 barrels of powder and 300 muskets to Coimbra with the hope that the Portuguese would then begin their march southward. Unlike the Spaniards, who wanted only material support from the British, the Portuguese wanted both British material and troops to aid their cause. In response Bligh promised to assist to the best of his ability, even if it meant sending only one British officer to supervise offensive and defensive preparations. To increase the anxiety of both the French and the Portuguese, rumors spread throughout Portugal that a British army would soon land on the coast, even though news of Wellesley's expedition had yet to officially arrive. Moreover, it was rumored that a French force was on the march to Coimbra and Figueira da Foz to prevent such a landing. Bligh and Lewis, therefore, issued a proclamation to the inhabitants of Figueira da Foz and its vicinity for the purpose of repulsing the impending French attack. The officers extended words of encouragement by explaining how the Portuguese could take advantage of their rugged geography to halt the French advance. In addition, Bligh and Lewis offered to train in British tactics a cadre of "200 of your most active young men" for the subsequent purpose of training their fellow citizens. Without foreknowledge of Wellesley's expedition, Cotton had selected officers whose initiative helped prepare for the introduction of British troops into Portugal.[21]

While Bligh and Lewis were busy at Figueira da Foz, the frigate *Hyperion* passed through the fleet off the Tagus with information about the pending arrival of Wellesley's expeditionary force. Even before receiving Bligh's reports from Figueira da Foz, Cotton sensed that the Mondego, not the Tagus, was the best place to land British troops. He at once dispatched the *Lively* to intercept the British expeditionary force north of Oporto. He instructed Captain McKinley to inform Wellesley about the current state of affairs in Portugal and to convey a recommendation to land the army at Figueira da Foz or possibly Peniche. Cotton addressed a letter to Wellesley that concluded: "It will give me great pleasure to confer with you upon the best means for achieving the important object in view; and should you think a conference necessary while arrangements are making for debarking, it may be advisable to direct the convoy to an eligible situation and repair hither."[22] In case the *Lively* should miss Wellesley, Cotton dispatched the *Hercules* of 74-guns to cruise six leagues windward of the Burling Islands. Accounting for the prevailing northerly wind, Cotton did not want Wellesley's transports to proceed too far to leeward of the landing site and then waste precious time regaining the winds to retrace their route to the north. To spread the news about Wellesley's impending arrival, Cotton dispatched the *Blossom* sloop north of Lisbon with instructions to Captain George Pigott to communicate his "strongest expectation that troops, arms, and ammunition may be hourly expected" in support of the Portuguese cause. With the *Blossom* heading north on 10 July, Bligh's *Alfred* off Figueira da Foz, Captain Edward Galway's sloop *Antelope* and the sloops *Talbot* and *Eclipse* off Oporto, Captain Matthew Smith's frigate *Comus* off Sines, and several ships-of-the-line still blockading the Tagus, Cotton awaited Wellesley's arrival.[23]

On 13 July, the *Plover* sloop delivered to Cotton Lord Castlereagh's formal notification of Wellesley's expedition. The secretary explicitly stated that Wellesley's force was "ordered to proceed off the Tagus for the purpose of cooperating with you in the reduction of the enemy's force in that port."[24] Furthermore, Castlereagh enclosed orders for Spencer's corps to join Wellesley's force off Lisbon, unless it could achieve more advantageous results for the common cause elsewhere along the Spanish coast. Castlereagh relied on Cotton to forward the latest information from Lisbon to help Spencer decide where best to employ his corps. In addition to delivering Castlereagh's instructions, the *Plover* brought to the *Hibernia* the military agent Nicholas Trant, a lieutenant in the Royal Service Corps who had been given the rank of lieutenant colonel while on duty in Portugal. Based on reports from Bligh about the situation at Coimbra, Cotton advised Trant that his services would be "most advantageously employed in [that] quarter incommunicado." This recommendation suited the eccentric, hard-drinking Trant, who would later lead a Portuguese force of 200 cavalry and 1,400 light infantry in conjunction with the British army. While sailing to Figueira da Foz on the *Plover* after his brief meeting with Cotton, Trant recorded his observations for Wellesley's benefit of the coast's unsuitability for a landing from the Rock of Lisbon to Peniche. His notes conformed with Cotton's opinion of the coast and stated, "The surf is such as to render a landing almost impracticable." Trant arrived in Coimbra on the evening of 18 July and began organizing Portuguese resistance.[25]

On the day after Trant left the *Hibernia*, another British army officer on a special mission to Portugal joined Cotton. Under orders from Lord Castlereagh to assist the Portuguese, Lieutenant Colonel Samuel Brown had arrived on 7 July at Oporto in the *Peacock* brig. After conferring with Captain Galway off the coast, Brown learned that the Portuguese had driven the French from Oporto and that the Bishop of Oporto now governed the town. Brown also learned that the *Eclipse* was moored in the Douro River to protect a bridge of boats that was the only link between Oporto and central Portugal. After landing in Oporto, Brown met with the bishop, who assured him that the people of Portugal were taking up arms in defense of their country and religion against French forces. Brown stated the intention of his visit and asked for the best information concerning the enemy's force in Portugal The bishop estimated that 14,000 or 15,000 French troops were in Portugal, with 5,000 at Almeida and the remainder at Peniche and near Lisbon. Regarding Portuguese forces, the bishop stated that a total force of 19,127 regulars and militia were mobilizing in the area of the Minho River. To divert French attention from this mobilization, the bishop asked Brown to "impress upon the mind of Sir Charles Cotton the advantages to be derived from any threat on Lisbon." Another of the bishop's concerns was the conveyance of stolen church plate by French vessels. Consequently, Brown sailed in the *Peacock* and joined Cotton on the 14th with the Bishop of Oporto's intelligence and his special request for a naval diversion.[26]

The Bishop of Oporto's intelligence was not entirely correct, but close to the truth when it reached Cotton. The French indeed had garrisons at Almeida and Peniche, but Junot was trying to concentrate his forces in the vicinity of Lisbon. However, he had also ordered the establishment of garrisons at Elvas and Setúbal and had reduced the garrison at Almeida from 5,000 to 1,200. Brown expressed concern to Cotton about the enemy force that began its withdrawal from Almeida to Abrantes on 4 July. He thought that this column, commanded by General Louis Henri Loison, would join with an expedition of 3,000 troops under General Pierre Margaron that had marched from Lisbon with orders to ascertain the status of the insurrection in northern Portugal. Margaron occupied Leiria and Tomar on the 5th. If the junction between Margaron and Loison occurred, so Brown reported, this force of approximately 9,000 troops would pose a serious threat to Figueira da Foz and Coimbra. According to Bligh, Captain Lewis did not believe his marines could resist this large a force. Cotton forwarded Brown's report to the Admiralty, but personally doubted that the French would dare muster so large a force at the expense of defending Lisbon. Although the stream of intelligence was not entirely accurate, by mid-July Cotton did recognize that Junot was trying to consolidate his troops around Lisbon. This left the outlying provinces free to organize the insurrection. In anticipation of Wellesley's arrival, Brown returned to Oporto and continued monitoring the insurrection.[27]

Cotton's understanding of the situation in Portugal was limited mainly to events in and north of Lisbon until the arrival on 14 July of Captain Matthew Smith's report from Sines, located on the coast sixty miles south of Lisbon. Smith sent his dispatch with two prominent Portuguese citizens because he was "so strongly and earnestly supplicated" by the government at Sines "to remain in order to give confidence" that he felt it would be an "abandonment" of Cotton's orders to convey the message in the *Comus* himself. Smith had arrived on 2 July at Sines to the cheers of its inhabitants, who were grateful for the Royal Navy's "prompt and immediate attention shown to their application for assistance." He immediately distributed Cotton's proclamation of 1 July before traveling overland about ten miles to St. Iago do Cacémio, where he further advertised the Royal Navy's willingness to support the Portuguese cause. In case the region should become an object for French military operations, Smith took meticulous notes on matters of operational and logistical significance. The road from Sines to St. Iago consisted of loose sand, but it was capable of supporting heavy cannon; the ruins of an extensive Moorish castle commanded the whole country around St. Iago, and it could easily become "a place of strong defence"; draft animals in the region were plentiful, but water was scarce, especially at Sines; and 800 men offered to take up arms at the town of Odemira and a potential force of 10,000 to 15,000 men could be mobilized in the southern provinces. In addition, Smith reported how 250 to 300 peasants had thwarted a French attempt to seize Sines while commenting that the contribution of the upper class did not extend beyond saber rattling. Before leaving on the 11th to visit Odemira, Smith helped establish the defense of Sines by contributing arms and ammunition and adjusting the displacement of cannons in a castle that commanded the landward approach to the town. Although a landing by Wellesley's force south of the Tagus was an unsound maneuver by which to gain the expulsion of the French army from Portugal, Smith's report gave Cotton useful information about the southern Portuguese provinces, should British troops need to land there for unforeseen circumstances.[28]

While waiting in July for the British army to converge on Portugal, Cotton had time to reflect upon a conference on 24 June aboard the *Hibernia* with General Spencer concerning operations in Lisbon. Spencer's corps was in transports off Ayamonte when he received Cotton's request for troops in Lisbon. Since the beginning of the insurrection in Spain, Spencer had sought to support the Spanish cause by landing his troops somewhere on the southern coast. However, like their brethren in the northern provinces, the Spaniards were suspicious of his intentions and were content with only material support from the British. Lord Collingwood, who left the Toulon blockade and arrived off Cadiz on 11 June, had received Cotton's request for Spencer's corps on the 16th. Despite Collingwood's belief that military operations in Spain should be the British government's priority, he realized that there did not appear to be any service for British troops at present in southern Spain. He therefore authorized Spencer to proceed to Lisbon; the general did so, but without his corps, which remained south of Cape St. Vincent because of adverse northerly winds. When Spencer arrived off the Tagus, Cotton's assessment of the situation in Lisbon had changed from his 12 June suggestion that 5,000 or 6,000 British troops could "gain possession of the forts on the banks of the Tagus." Junot's concentration of force in the vicinity of Lisbon since then had rendered Cotton's original estimate invalid. Since Cotton and Spencer believed that 5,000 troops had no reasonable chance of landing successfully near Lisbon and that the government would likely consider Spain the primary theater of operations, they decided that Spencer's corps should secure the Spanish-Portuguese border near Ayamonte and then return to Cadiz to await further instructions.[29]

As Cotton did not learn of Wellesley's expedition until two weeks after meeting with Spencer, the decision to keep Spencer's corps active off southern Spain rather than passive before Lisbon seemed logical at the time. Had Spencer's corps been off Lisbon when word of Wellesley's expedition arrived, Cotton might have directed Spencer to disembark his corps at Figeuira da Foz to assist the Royal Marines. The junction of Wellesley's and Spencer's forces would have occurred sooner and without the usual anxiety that characterized operations so dependent on the weather. Accordingly, Spencer's corps sailed to Puerto de Santa Maria near Cadiz, where three battalions and four light companies landed to join Spanish forces led by General Don François Xavier Castaños at Xeres. For two weeks the bulk of the British corps remained in transports while Spencer awaited orders from his government. The wait ended on 15 July, when he received an indication that an expedition from Cork was proceeding to Portugal and that he should await Wellesley's orders at Cadiz, but not to the detriment of any ongoing operation. At the time, General Castaños was pursuing the French army of General Comte Dupont de l'Etang along the road from Seville to Madrid. Surrounded by 32,000 Spanish troops near the town of Bailen, Dupont stopped fighting on 19 July and surrendered a force of 17,635 unwounded men four days later. Despite Dupont's defeat and pronouncements from the Junta of Seville and Castaños that the British army was not needed in Andalusia, Spencer hesitated about proceeding to Lisbon. He wrote a long letter on the subject to Collingwood, who answered with a short one in which he urged Spencer to lose no time in joining Wellesley. Spencer withdrew his units from Xeres and sailed for the Tagus on the 22nd without waiting for Wellesley's orders. Spencer's departure from southern Spain brought great relief to Collingwood, who told Cotton: "I am truly glad that General Spencer's army is gone from here. They were never wanted and from the beginning, the Spaniards were determined they should never enter any place of strength." Spencer's force burdened Collingwood's psyche as well: "I am weary, and if [in] war I have to act with soldiers, I shall be worn out and go home an invalid. Whenever we have to act with them there is a jealousy that must always be detrimental to the service." Unlike his good friend Collingwood, Cotton would not experience angst with Spencer's corps.[30]

Collingwood's letters to Cotton were more than a medium to vent frustration. He also kept his friend informed about recent activities in the southern and eastern Spanish provinces, offered sound advice, and expressed prescient opinions about future events on the peninsula. For example, Collingwood thought that Cotton could improve communications with Seniavin by better understanding the Russian's character:

> As far as my observation went in the short acquaintance I had with him, he appears well disposed to, and rather likes the English. He abhors the French. . . . I am told he has good judgment, but stubborn when he has once formed an opinion. He may be led by gentle and conciliatory manners, but resentful if any attempt to force him. I managed him by making him believe that whatever I proposed was suggested by something he had said or done.[31]

Collingwood proposed that Cotton should inform Seniavin about an alleged clamor in St. Petersburg for peace with Britain and that he should exchange signals with the Russian fleet in order to increase Junot's suspicion of Seniavin—Collingwood claimed that Seniavin already had the Royal Navy signal book. No amount of denial by Seniavin that he was not communicating with the British fleet would alleviate Junot's suspicions. Collingwood's advice prompted Cotton to write a note to the Russians suggesting that he was "in possession of certain particulars regarding the relative situation of our respective nations." Seniavin responded on 30 July by sending two representatives to the fleet, a Mr. Mackeren, his flag lieutenant, and a Mr. Sass, "a diplomatic character in the Russian service." Cotton shared with them intelligence from Collingwood about the French seizure of two Russian ships at Livorno and the seizure of two more at Elba that were moved to the inner harbor at Toulon and unrigged. The meeting ended with a discussion about peace rumors and the establishment of a signal by which communication could be maintained between the British and Russian fleets.[32]

In addition to helpful advice, Collingwood offered Cotton insightful predictions. Collingwood's initial reaction to Wellesley's expedition to Portugal was tempered by his forgettable experience with Spencer's corps. After Spencer proceeded to Lisbon, Collingwood had a more positive outlook on expeditions and the likely outcome of affairs in Portugal. He told Cotton: "I am very glad the army is arrived in Portugal, and as Sir Arthur Wellesley is said to be an able general, I do not think he will find much to do. Junot has not more than 20,000 men and they expect to be beaten, or rather I believe they only want a respectable force to justify their surrender. A good arrangement will finish soon."[33] No doubt, Collingwood's ideas and comments influenced Cotton's decisions during the crucial month of August 1808.

Although not privy to decisions made in London, Cotton had spent the first three weeks of July reacting to events and anticipating the needs of a British military force should one be sent to Portugal. Besides attempting to strengthen Portuguese resolve through proclamations of British support and material succor in the form of arms and ammunition, Cotton had established a British military presence at Figueira da Foz with an understanding of its utility as an advance party for the landing of a large body of troops. However, the Royal Marines at Figueira da Foz were in an extremely vulnerable position, situated as they were within a short marching distance from thousands of French troops. Fortunately for Captain Lewis's marines, the Portuguese insurrection made a French sortie too far beyond the vicinity of Lisbon a risky venture. Before Wellesley's arrival off Portugal, Cotton received reassuring news from Captain Bligh that the threat to Figueira da Foz and Coimbra from Margaron's and Loison's forces had passed. At Bligh's request, Cotton sent an additional 100 Royal Marines to augment the 220 already at Figueira da Foz. Bligh was confident that the marines could hold their position until the arrival of Wellesley's force.[34]

While the insurrection gained momentum in Portugal, Cotton remained off the Tagus collecting, processing, and distributing information in a manner that prepared for the coming land campaign. Cotton's knowledge about affairs in Portugal was incomplete, but no other British officer understood the entire situation there better. Wellesley would soon find the admiral an invaluable source of information and material support.

NOTES

1. Marquis Solano, "Letter from Badajoz the 6th of May," PRO ADM 1/339.

2. Collingwood to Cotton, 22 July 1808, Cambridgeshire County Record Office, Cotton Naval Papers, 588/c74.

3. Mr. Wilson to Captain George Pigott, 31 May 1808, Captain Jocelin Percy to Cotton, 2 June 1808, Cotton to W.W. Pole, 3 June 1808, PRO ADM 1/339.

4. Ibid., Cotton to W.W. Pole, 4, 9 June 1808.

5. Notice to the Inhabitants of Lisbon, 9 June 1808, PRO ADM 1/339. See also Donald D. Horward, "Portugal and the Anglo-Russian Naval Crisis, 1808," *Naval War College Review* 34 (1981): 58.

6. Cotton to W.W. Pole, 11 June 1808, PRO ADM 1/339; Charles William Chadwick Oman, *A History of the Peninsular War* (Oxford, 1902–1930), 1: 208–09.

7. Rear Admiral François Rosily commanded a French squadron of six vessels that had taken refuge in Cadiz harbor after the Battle of Trafalgar. With the change of alliance in May 1808, Rosily's squadron was anchored between the Royal Navy and Spanish artillery. While British warships blockaded Cadiz harbor, Spanish artillery commenced firing on 9 June and forced Rosily to capitulate. Although the British did not capture the French squadron, this incident was the first French loss in the peninsula to result from a combined Anglo-Spanish effort. Extract from the Seville Gazette, 14 June 1808, Rosily to Captain General [Morla], 14 June 1808, *Naval Chronicle* 20

(1808): 57–58; John Marshall, "John Child Purvis, Esq.," *Royal Navy Biography* (London, 1823), 1: 238; "Intelligence obtained from Don Sebastian Solis, a Spanish officer," 11 June 1808, Cambridgeshire County Record Office, Cotton Naval Papers, 588/041/a55.

8. Cotton to W.W. Pole, 11 June 1808, Proclamation for "Brave Spaniards," 11 June 1808, Certification to the Supreme Council of Seville, 11 June 1808, PRO ADM 1/339.

9. Ibid., Cotton to W.W. Pole, 12 June 1808 [two letters]. See also *Papers, Presented to the House of Commons, Relative to the Russian Fleet in the Tagus, and to the Convention concluded with the Russian Admiral* [hereafter cited as *Papers*] (London: House of Commons, 9, 10 February 1809), 1: 13.

10. Cotton to Purvis, 12 June 1808, British Library, Sir J.W. Gordon Papers, ADD MSS 49489; Michael Glover, *Britannia Sickens: Sir Arthur Wellesley and the Convention of Cintra* (London, 1970), 41; Oman, *Peninsular War*, 1: 209, 213.

11. Excerpt of speech by Richard Brinsley Sheridan, June 1808, cited in Oman, *Peninsular War*, 1:222.

12. H.R.H the Commander in Chief to Wellesley, 14 June 1808, Arthur Wellesley, Duke of Wellington, *The Dispatches of Field Marshal the Duke of Wellington, during His Various Campaigns in India, Denmark, Portugal, Spain, the Low Countries, and France, from 1799 to 1818* [hereafter cited as *Wellington's Dispatches*], ed. John Gurwood (London, 1852), 3: 16.

13. Castlereagh to Wellesley, 30 June 1808, No. 1, *Wellington's Dispatches*, 3: 19, 20.

14. Ibid.

15. Ibid., 3: 21, Castlereagh to Wellesley, 30 June 1808, no. 2; Mulgrave to the King, 30 June 1808, in Arthur Aspinall, ed., *The Later Correspondence of George III* (Cambridge, 1962–1970), 5: 93.

16. Wellesley to Major General Rowland Hill, 3 July 1808, *Wellington's Dispatches*, 3: 22; Henry N. Shore, "The Navy in the Peninsular War: Naval Operations during Sir A. Wellesley's First Campaign, 1808," *United Service Magazine* 165 (1913): 153.

17. "Proclamation to the Inhabitants of Portugal," 4 July 1808 in "Memoir of Cotton," *Naval Chronicle* 27 (1812): 378.

18. Cotton to W.W. Pole, 3, 5, 7 July 1808, PRO ADM 7/41; Creyke to Cotton, 20 June 1808, Cambridgeshire County Record Office, Cotton Naval Papers, 588/041/a32.

19. Cotton to W.W. Pole, 4 July 1808, PRO ADM 7/41; Cotton to the constituted government at Figueira da Foz, 4 July 1808, PRO ADM 1/340; In a letter to Spencer on 13 July 1808, Cotton indicated that 220 marines, not 200, initially landed at Figueira da Foz. Cambridgeshire County Record Office, Cotton Naval Papers, 588/041/a59.

20. Ibid., 588/041/a36, Bligh to Cotton, 9, 12 July 1808.

21. Ibid., 588/041/a36, Proclamation to "Inhabitants of Figueira and its Vicinity," 12 July 1808, Bligh to Cotton, 9, 12 July 1808.

22. Cotton to Wellesley, 9 July 1808, Hartley Library, University of Southampton, Wellington Papers, 1/207 (folder 2).

23. The *Blossom* had arrived off the Tagus on 10 July with a letter from Captain Creyke that explained the situation in Oporto. Creyke also ordered the *Eclipse* across the bar of the Duoro River "with a view of inspiring the people with greater confidence." Creyke to Cotton, 6 July 1808, Cambridgeshire County Record Office, Cotton Naval Papers, 588/041/a34; Cotton to W.W. Pole, 8, 10, 15 July 1808, PRO ADM 7/41; Horward, "Portugal and the Anglo-Russian Naval Crisis," 59–60.

24. Castlereagh to Cotton, 2 July 1808, Southampton, Wellington Papers, 1/207 (folder 1).

25. Cotton to W.W. Pole, 13 July 1808, PRO ADM 7/41, Trant's "Remarks upon the Coast N. of the Rock of Lisbon," 14, 15, 16 July 1808, Trant to Wellesley, 19 July 1808, Southampton, Wellington Papers, 1/207 (folders 2 & 3); Leslie Stephen and Sydney Lee, eds., *Dictionary of National Biography* (London, 1885–1901), 19: 1081.

26. Castlereagh to Brown, 1 July 1808, Brown to Wellington, 9, 10 July 1808, Southampton, Wellington Papers, 1/207 (folder 2); Cotton to W.W. Pole, 14 July 1808, PRO ADM 7/41.

27. Cotton to W.W. Pole, 14 July 1808, PRO ADM 7/41; Maximilien Sébastian Foy, *History of the War in the Peninsula* (London, 1827), 2: 460–62.

28. Captain Matthew Smith to Cotton, 11 July 1808, Cambridgeshire County Record Office, Cotton Naval Papers, 588/041/a37; Cotton to W.W. Pole, 15 July 1808, PRO ADM 7/41.

29. Spencer to Colonel Sir James Willoughby Gordon, 17, 24 June 1808, British Library, Gordon Papers, ADD MSS 49489; Collingwood to Cotton, 16, 26 June 1808, 2 July 1808, Cambridgeshire County Record Office, Cotton Naval Papers, 588/041/a31, 588/042, 588/c74.

30. Spencer's willingness to accept General Tomas Morla's offer of twenty Spanish gunboats from Gibraltar to assist Cotton's naval operations off Portugal is an example of why Collingwood was frustrated with the army. Spencer to Cotton, 27 July 1808, Collingwood to Cotton, 12, 29, 30 July 1808, Cambridgeshire County Record Office, Cotton Naval Papers, 588/042, 588/c74; Spencer to Wellesley, 16 July 1808, Southampton, Wellington Papers, 1/207 (folder 1); Fortescue, *British Army*, 6: 185–86.

31. Collingwood to Cotton, 15 July 1808, Cambridgeshire County Record Office, Cotton Naval Papers, 588/041/a40.

32. Ibid., 588/042, Collingwood to Cotton, 2, 12 July 1808; Cotton to W.W. Pole, 30 July 1808, PRO ADM 7/41.

33. Collingwood to Cotton, 29 July 1808, Cambridgeshire County Record Office, Cotton Naval Papers, 588/042, 588/c74.

34. Ibid., 588/041/a59, Cotton to Spencer, 13, 18 July 1808; Cotton to W.W. Pole, 14 July 1808, PRO ADM 7/41.

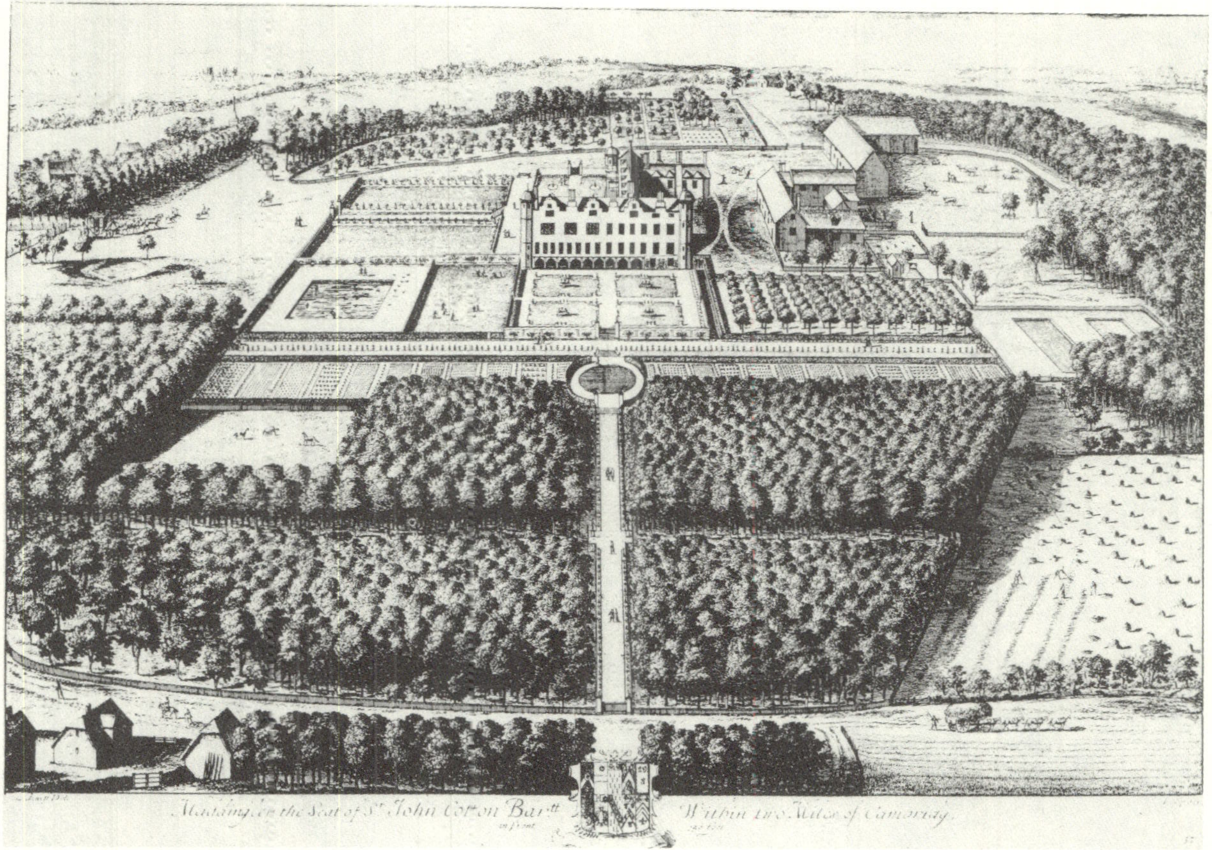

Kip's engraving of Madingley Hall (Cotton's estate). From *Madingley Hall: A Guide to the Interior and Exterior of the House* (Cambridge: University of Cambridge Board of Continuing Education, 1986). Reproduced with thanks to the University of Cambridge Board of Continuing Education.

The North Wing. From *Madingley Hall: A Guide to the Interior and Exterior of the House* (Cambridge: University of Cambridge Board of Continuing Education, 1986). Reproduced with thanks to the University of Cambridge Board of Continuing Education.

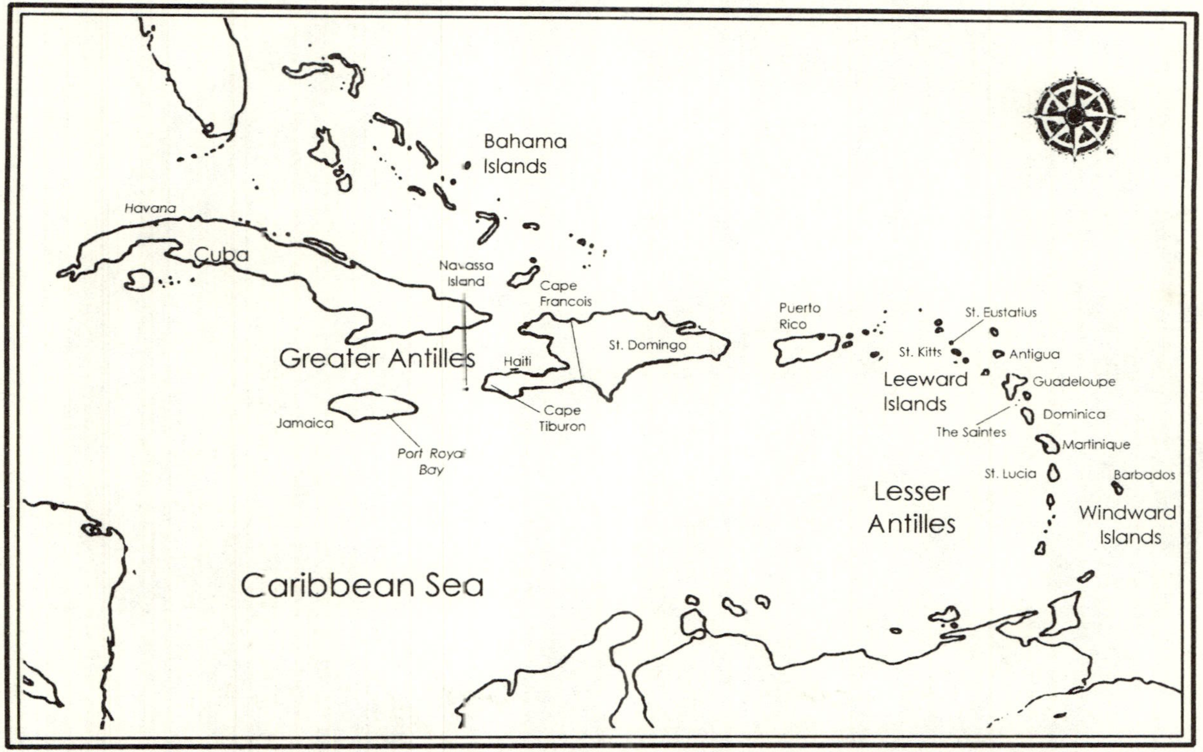

The West Indies. Map by V.J. Tedesco III.

Philadelphia Cotton. Miniature by George Engleheart, 1794. Reproduced with thanks to the University of Cambridge Board of Continuing Education.

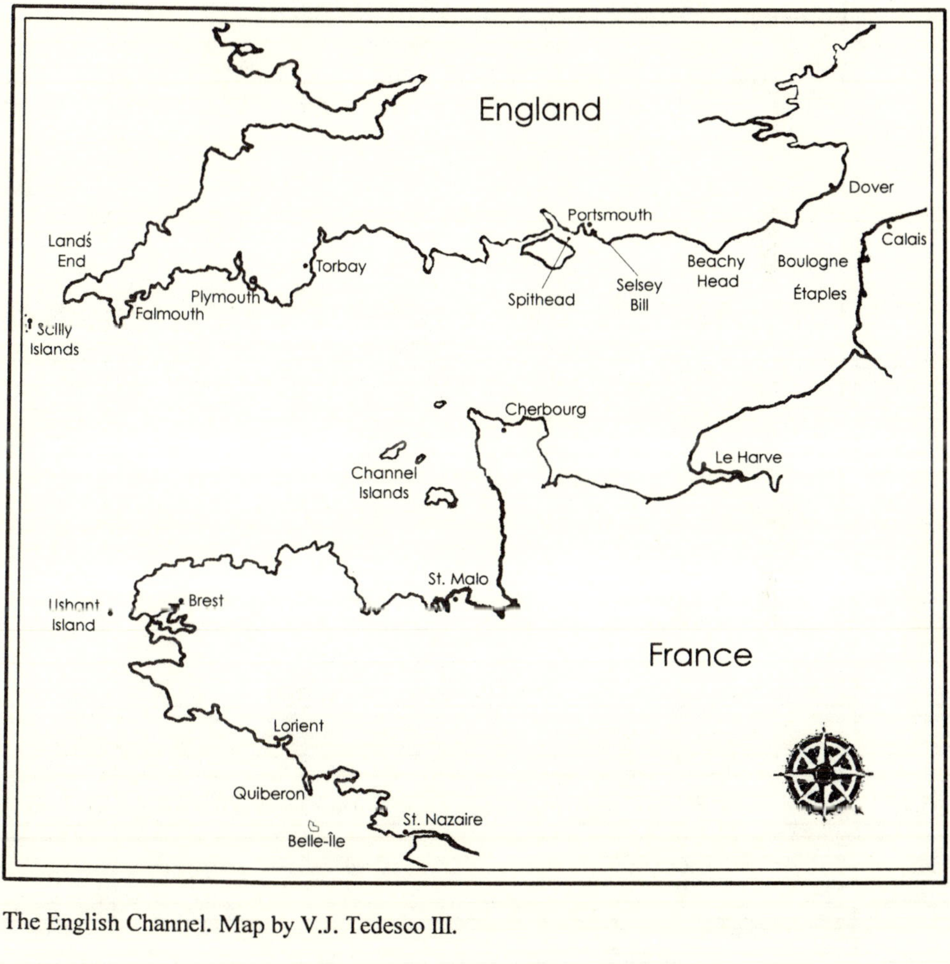

The English Channel. Map by V.J. Tedesco III.

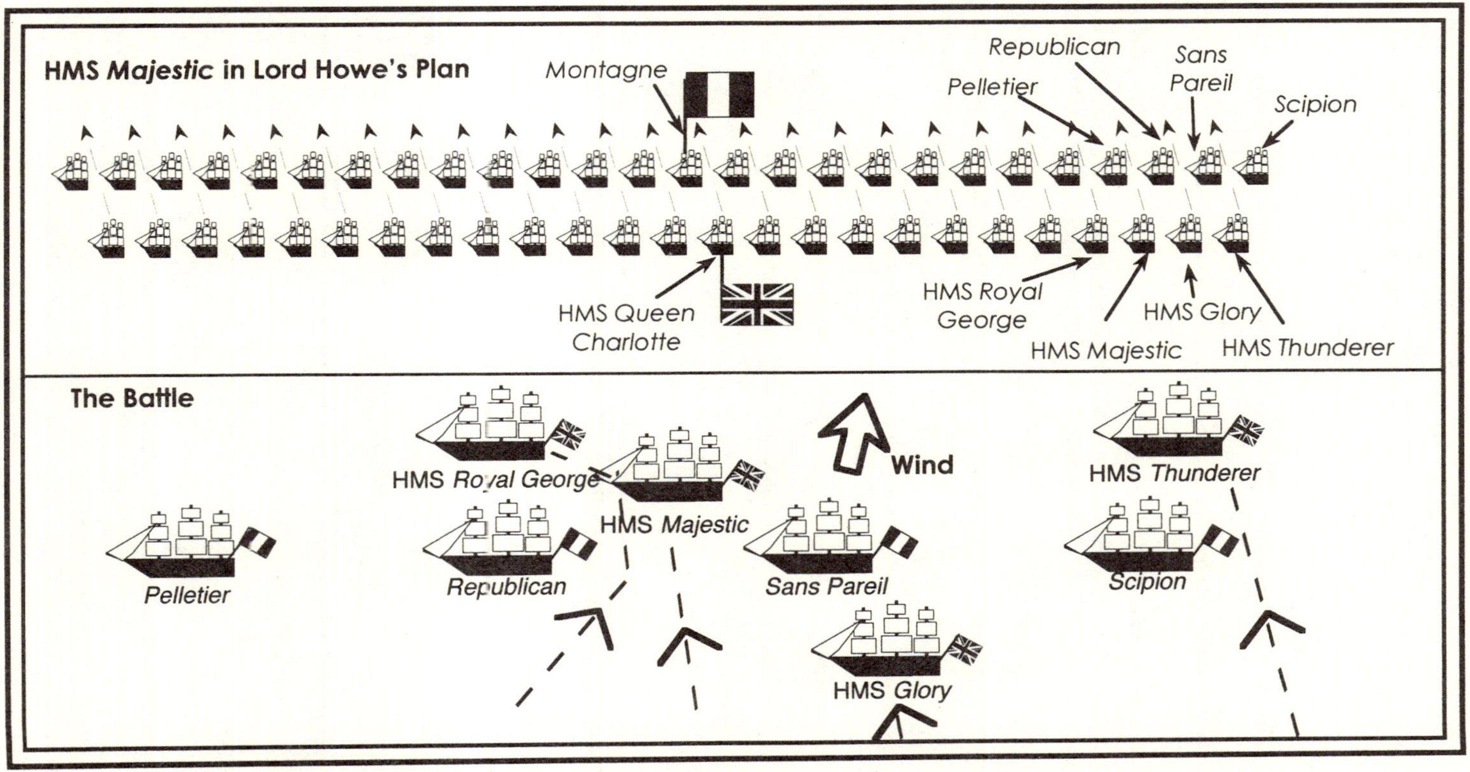

Cotton's *Majestic* at the Battle of "The Glorious First of June," 1794. Map by V.J. Tedesco III.

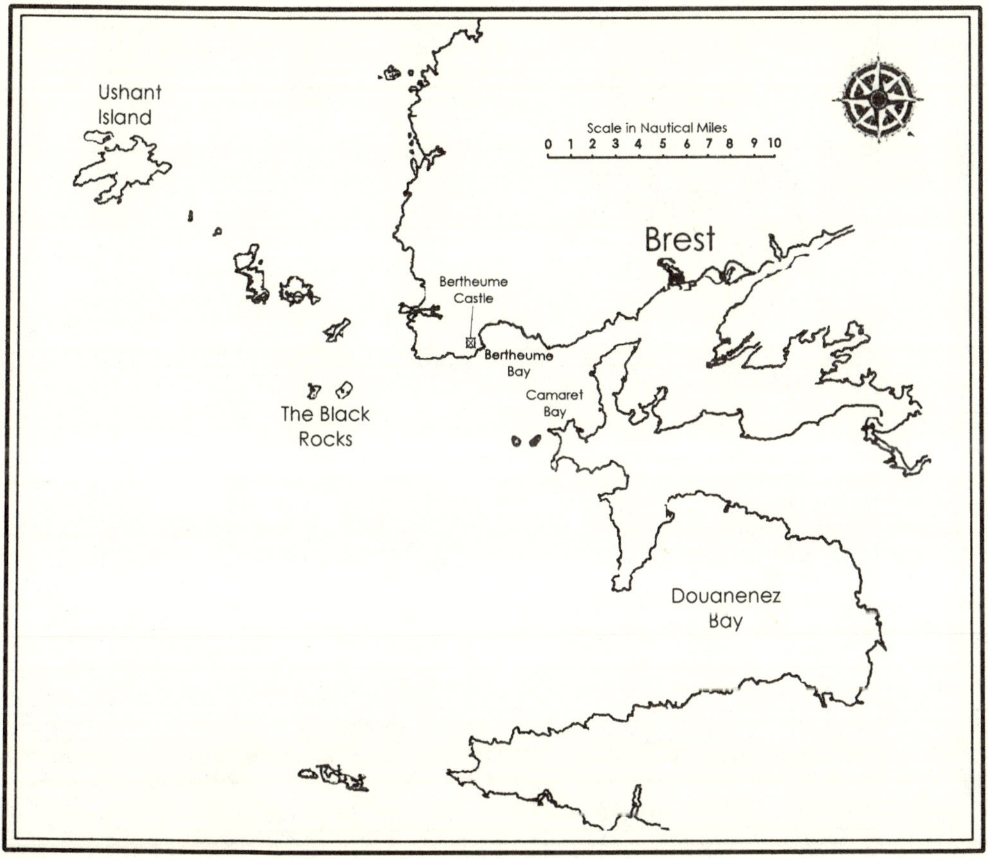

Port of Brest. Map by V.J. Tedesco III.

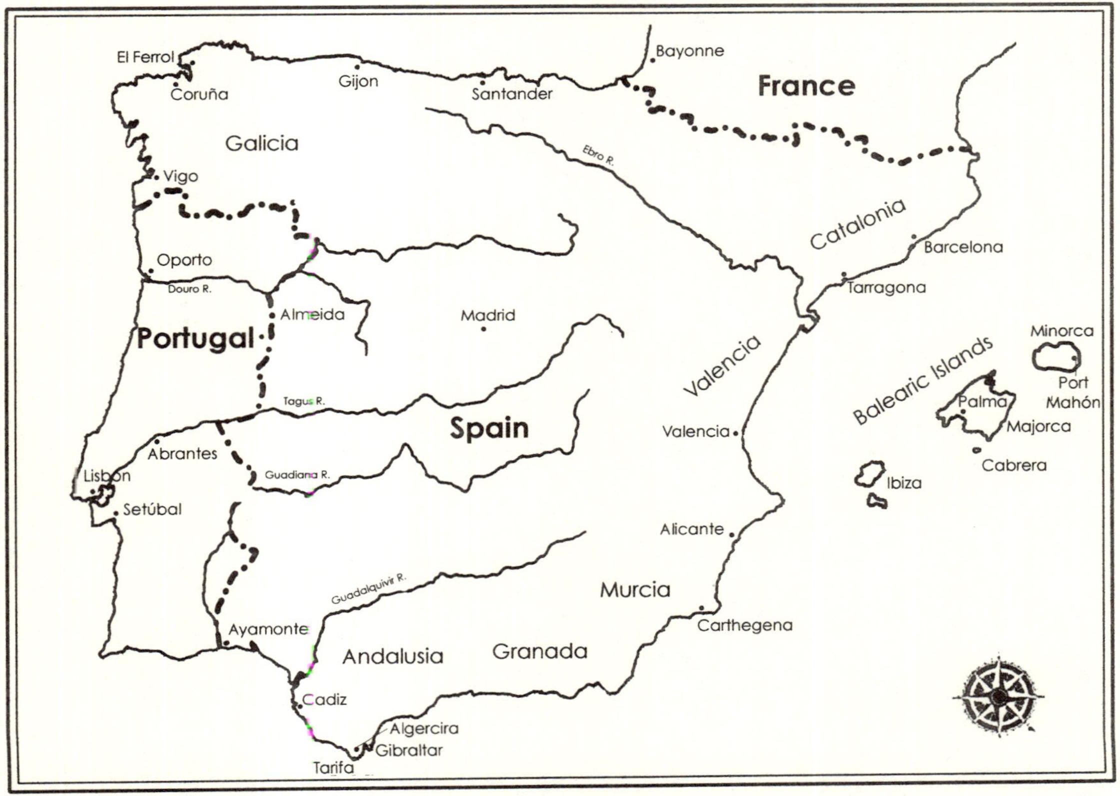

Iberian Peninsula, 1808. Map by V.J. Tedesco III.

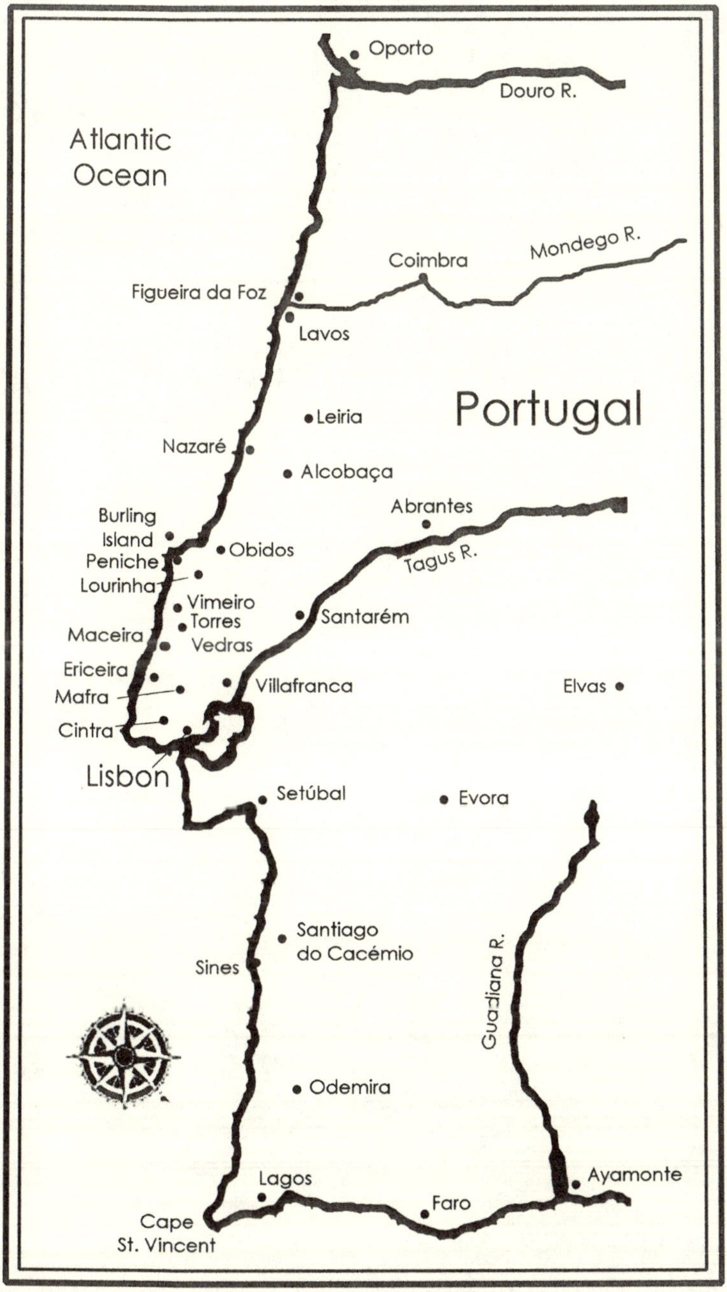

Southern Portuguese Coast. Map by V.J. Tedesco III.

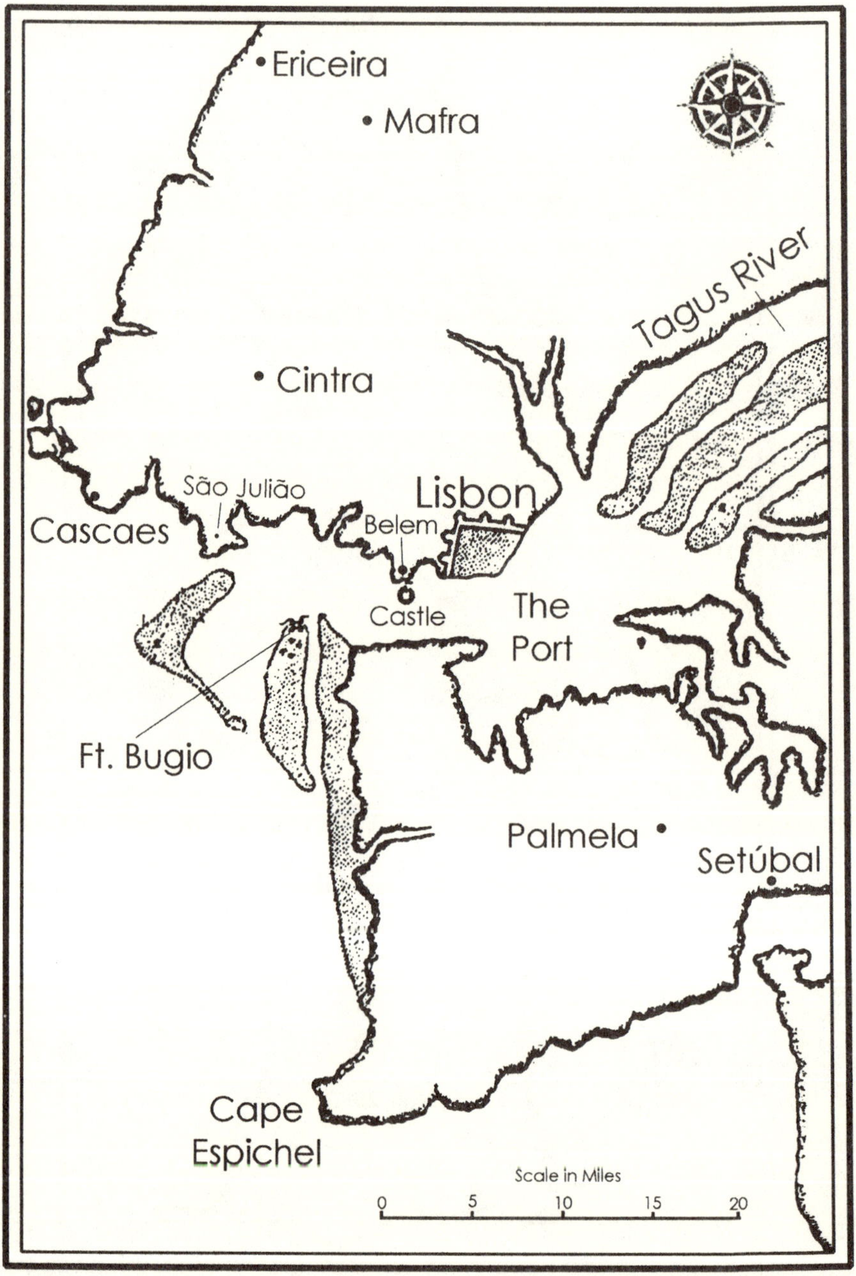

Port of Lisbon. Adapted by V.J. Tedesco III from map printed in London by Joyce Gold in 1808.

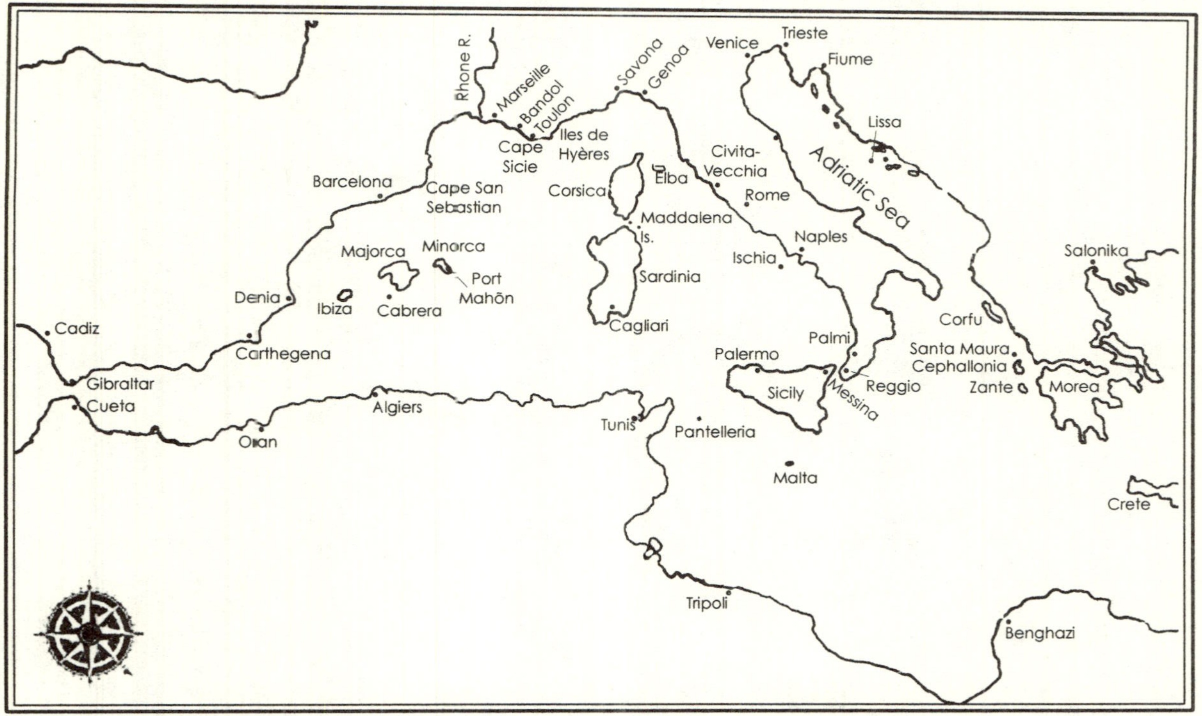

Central Mediterranean. Map by V.J. Tedesco III.

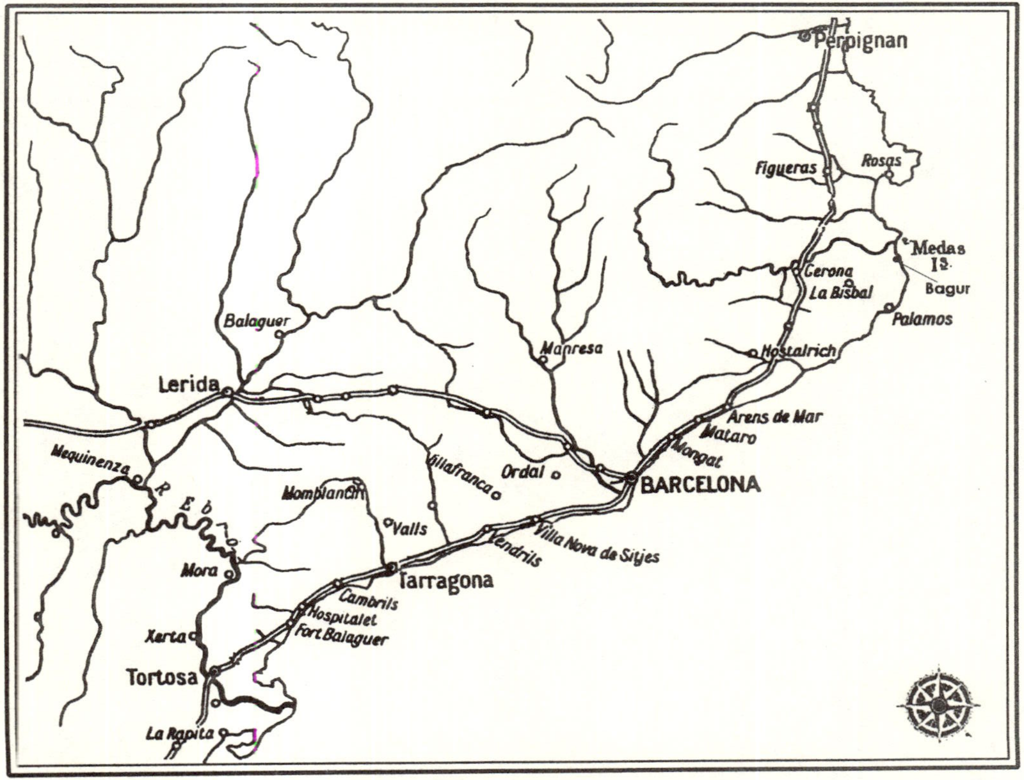

Catalonian Coast. Adapted from Charles William Chadwick Oman, *A History of the Peninsular War* (Oxford, 1911), 4: 538, by V.J. Tedesco III.

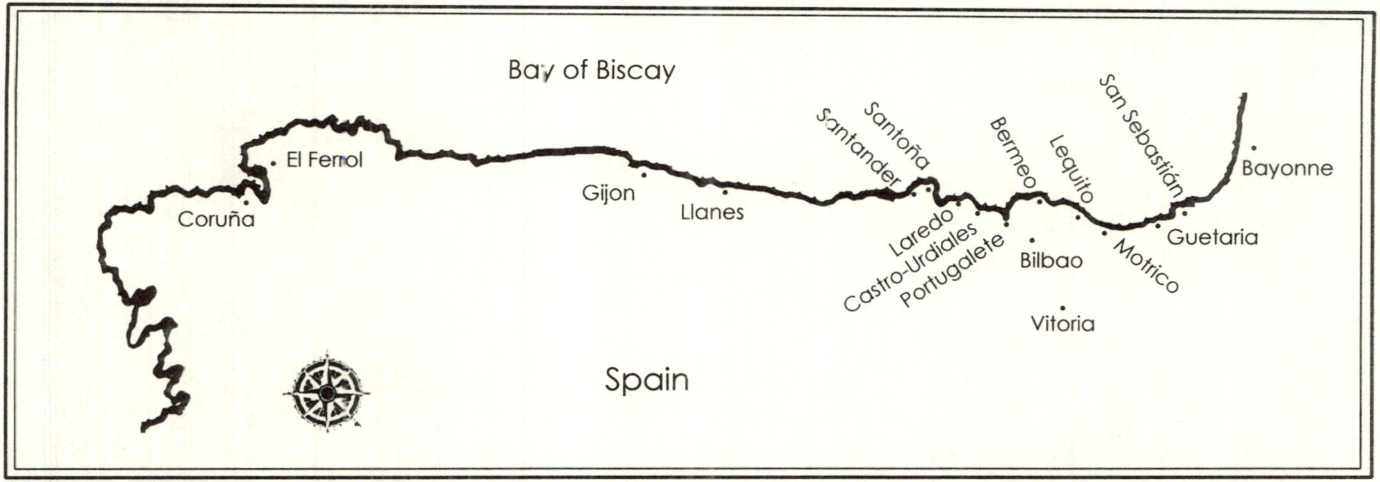

Northern Spanish Coast. Map by V.J. Tedesco III.

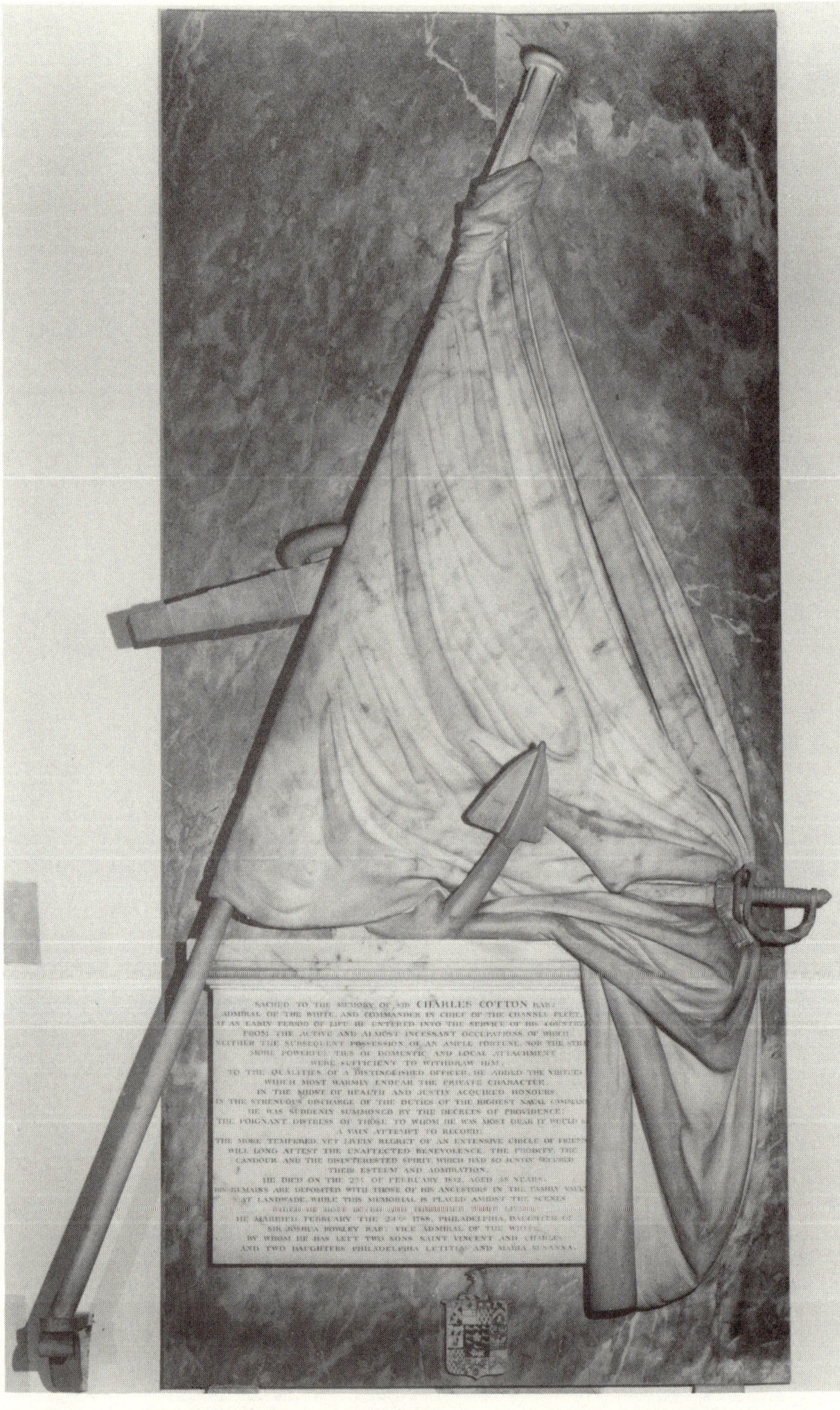

Cotton Memorial in Madingley Church. Photo by Frank Bird in possession of author.

6

Cotton and Wellesley's Amphibious Campaign in Portugal, August 1808

> When the communication is kept open between the fleet and army; when the latter receives their whole subsistence and ammunition from the former; wherefore though they advance fifty miles up the country, in those circumstances, it is still littoral; in those circumstances with regard to their provisions, the two contending armies are nearly upon an equality; a whole country is a magazine to the one, and a whole navy the other.
>
> —Thomas More Molyneux, 1759[1]

Britain's first military campaign of the Peninsular War was amphibious in nature according to Molyneux's definition. The classic example of amphibious warfare is that of an opposed landing, which Wellesley avoided in Portugal. Yet, as stated by Molyneux, how an army was supplied determined whether a campaign was amphibious or continental in nature. It was only when an army developed an organized system of supply and transport independent of coastal shipping that warfare transitioned from amphibious to continental. Given this definition, British military operations in Portugal retained their amphibious nature until Wellesley repulsed the third French invasion of Portugal in 1811 at the Lines of Torres Vedras. Although the British army depended on supplies from the Royal Navy for the entire war, restraints on its operational mobility decreased dramatically after the French no longer threatened to drive Wellesley's force into the sea. Until that time, decisions by the commander of the squadron off the Tagus would influence not only the provisioning of the British army but also how it maneuvered. Cotton's interaction with Wellesley during the Portuguese campaign of August 1808 established an environment of interservice cooperation that would contribute to military victory against Junot and would benefit Cotton's successor off Lisbon.

Eight days after embarking from Cork, Wellesley arrived in the *Crocodile* on 20 July off Coruña, where he conferred with the Junta of Galicia and met Charles Stuart, Lord Stuart de Rothesay, a British minister already employed as a liaison in Spain. The junta briefed Wellesley and Stuart on current affairs in Spain and Portugal and included an outdated, vague report about the disposition of Spencer's corps. The report led Wellesley to doubt that Spencer's force would be available during the upcoming campaign. After providing the latest intelligence to Wellesley, the junta urged him to avoid landing near the French at Lisbon and to disembark instead at Vigo or Oporto, where Portuguese and Spanish forces were better situated to join the British on a march to Lisbon. Consequently, Wellesley became "inclined to land at a distance from Lisbon," thus avoiding a "difficult" landing in front of the enemy. Still Wellesley, understanding that much needed to be learned about the situation on the Peninsula, proceeded in the *Crocodile* to Oporto, where he hoped "to decide upon the measures . . . [to] adopt."[2]

Wellesley arrived at Oporto on 24 July and received a briefing that evening from the British military agent Lieutenant Colonel Brown and the Junta of Oporto. They explained that 5,000 Portuguese troops were assembled at Coimbra and a corps of 1,500 Portuguese and 300 Spanish infantry were present at Oporto, in addition to many peasants willing to fight. Wellesley expected that these forces could not legitimately challenge the French army until they were better armed and equipped. Nearly 1,000 muskets from Cotton's fleet were helpful but not sufficient. Wellesley heard nothing definite about the location of Spencer's corps, but based on Spencer's earlier meeting with Cotton, he believed that the corps would be off the Tagus. While at Oporto, Wellesley was joined by his fleet of transports under Captain Malcolm and by Captain McKinley, who delivered Cotton's letter of 9 July, which recommended a landing at Figueira da Foz or Peniche. The recommendation strengthened Wellesley's inclination to land at a distance from Lisbon. Before proceeding to the Tagus for a conference with Cotton, Wellesley ordered Malcolm to anchor the transports at Mondego Bay. On the 26th, seventy-three transports with 11,112 troops, 562 horses, 817 women, and 666 children arrived off the Mondego. Also on that day, Cotton and Wellesley met for the first and only time.[3]

Cotton and Wellesley confirmed Mondego Bay as the landing site during their conference. Probably neither gave much credence to a paper of suggestion provided earlier by Castlereagh that described a plan of debarkation for troops in the Tagus. Cotton made clear the extreme risk of conducting any landing in the vicinity of Lisbon. Wellesley later summarized the essence of the conference to General Burrard:

> Having consulted with Sir Charles Cotton, it appeared to him and me, that the attack proposed upon Cascaes Bay was impracticable, because the bay is well defended by the Fort of Cascaes, and the other works constructed for its defence, and the ships of war

could not approach sufficiently near to silence them. The landing in the Paço d'Arcos in the Tagus could not be effected without silencing Fort St. Julian, which appeared to be impracticable to those who were to carry that operation into execution. . . . There are small bays within, and others to the northward of the Rock of Lisbon, which might admit of landing troops; but they are all defended by works which must first have been silenced: they are of small extent, and but few men could have landed at the same time: there is always a surf on them, which affects the facility of landing at different times so materially, as to render it very doubtful whether the troops first landed could be supported in sufficient time by the others; and whether the horses for artillery and cavalry, and the necessary stores and provisions could be landed at all. These inconveniences attending a landing in any of the bays near the Rock of Lisbon would have been aggravated by the neighbourhood of the enemy to the landing place, and by the exhausted state of the country in which the troops would have been landed.[4]

In addition, Wellesley eliminated Peniche as a landing site because of its occupation by French troops. Cotton's and Wellesley's analysis of terrain and understanding of the French defense of Lisbon confirmed Mondego Bay as the best landing site. Before departing the Tagus and still ignorant of Spencer's progress towards Portugal, Wellesley sent the major general a letter urging him to proceed with haste to the Tagus, where Cotton would provide further guidance. In deference to Spencer's possible attachment to operations in southern Spain, Wellesley commented: "I am convinced that the most effectual mode in which Great Britain can serve the Spanish cause is by driving the French out of Portugal, and thus to make that Kingdom the point of communication between the northern and southern parts of Spain itself."[5]

On 27 July, Wellesley left the Tagus and returned three days later to Mondego Bay where the *Donegal* and *Resistance* were poised to superintend the landing. The difficulty of disembarking on the Mondego confirmed the wisdom of Wellesley's decision not to conduct an "attack upon the Tagus." Even without enemy opposition, the landing of over 9,000 troops with accompanying horses and artillery still required five days, from 1 August to 5 August. The surf of this "iron coast," as Wellesley described it, made even an unopposed landing a life-threatening endeavor.[6] As a foreboding prelude to the landing, Malcolm's transports experienced great turbulence while anchored off the Mondego. One army officer, with campaign experience in the West Indies, described the wait for Wellesley's return from the Tagus:

Although the weather was perfectly calm, I never remembered to have experienced more motion in a gale of wind, than we felt during the six days spent at this anchorage. The long and heavy swell made the yards of the ship at times almost touch the water, as she rolled from side to side, which caused some awful breakages amongst our wine-glasses and crockery-ware.[7]

As the ocean swell approached the two landing sites designated within Mondego Bay, it became a heavy surf that even the local inhabitants negotiated with difficulty. Wellesley told Cotton that the disembarkation was "very difficult on account of the surf on the bar of the river and on the shore."[8] Some historians claim that a few soldiers drowned during the landing, but this issue is shrouded in uncertainty.[9] Wellesley makes no mention of casualties in his dispatches, and one British officer thanked God that "the whole army landed without any loss but a horse or two."[10] Another army officer's colorful description of his landing illustrates why Wellesley's troops took five days to disembark: "Wave succeeded wave, mountains high, and when it approaches the boat the crew abandon their oars and threw [sic] themselves flat in the bottom of the boat, invoking the Blessed Virgin and all the Saints in the calendar. After a complete ducking and a terrible fright we got on shore."[11] To assist in negotiating the surf, the British resorted to using crescent bow Portuguese boats. From the commencement of the landing, Wellesley recognized its difficulty and quickly heaped praise on the Royal Navy and the local inhabitants: "The landing is attended with some difficulties even here, and would be quite impossible if we had not the cordial assistance of the country, notwithstanding the zeal and abilities of the officers of the navy."[12]

On 1 August, Wellesley's attention was divided between the landing, anticipation of reinforcements from England, the impending arrival of Spencer's corps, and the news received that day of Sir Hew Dalrymple's appointment to command the entire army. To Wellesley's credit, news of his imminent relief as commander and the arrival of several senior officers did not intimidate him nor force him to alter his strategy; on the contrary, it created a heightened sense of urgency. As he told the Duke of Richmond, "I only hope that I shall beat Junot before any of them shall arrive, and then they will do as they please with me."[13] Nevertheless, he did not intend to advance toward Lisbon until the arrival of either the corps from England or Spencer's force. The wait was brief.

Having battled contrary winds since 22 July, when he left Cadiz, Spencer finally arrived in the *Nautilus* sloop off the Tagus on 1 August. After receiving Wellesley's instructions from Cotton, the general proceeded to Figueira da Foz while his main convoy worked to the windward under charge of the *Bulwark* and *Lively*. Spencer joined Wellesley on 4 August at Lavos, three miles south of Figueira da Foz, and his corps arrived shortly thereafter. Spencer's 4,500 troops landed on the 7th and 8th and joined Wellesley's force at Lavos to create a combined force of nearly 15,000 British, who were joined by 5,000 Portuguese soldiers under General Friere.[14]

The late July meeting between Cotton and Wellesley contributed to a successful landing and the British army's concentration at Lavos. However, the general and admiral had their misunderstandings. Apparently, when Wellesley departed the Tagus on 27 July, his instructions to Cotton directed Spencer to wait with his corps off the Tagus for further orders. Not until the 30th did Wellesley resolve that Cotton should send Spencer's corps directly to Figueira da Foz. Meanwhile, Cotton's letter of the 31st to Wellesley reported that

Spencer's corps was proceeding to Lisbon and that DuPont's army had surrendered to the Spanish. Furthermore, Cotton developed his own idea regarding what to do with Spencer's corps. He told Wellesley: "It is my intention to detain MG Spencer, now supposed to be in sight, at this anchorage; presuming that your purposed arrangements may render his landing in this bay or on the south shore [of the Tagus] more desirable. Nothing of course, will however be attempted, until your wishes are signified upon the subject."[15] Fortunately, Cotton had decided in his conversation with Spencer on 1 August that the general should proceed immediately to Figueira da Foz, despite what he had written to Wellesley the day before. Cotton fortuitously arrived at this crucial decision independently—he had not yet received Wellesley's instructions to send Spencer's corps north from the Tagus.[16]

When Wellesley received Cotton's dispatch on 4 August, he was unaware that Spencer was about to join him at Lavos and thought that Cotton had "detained" Spencer's corps off the Tagus. Therefore, Wellesley immediately sent Cotton a letter repeating his request to send Spencer's corps to Figueira da Foz. It explained why the concentration of British forces at the Mondego was the only viable course of action. Reading between the lines of the letter, it appears that Wellesley was somewhat annoyed, because he reminded Cotton that they had already discussed some of the strategic issues that Cotton had again raised. Cotton must not have understood Wellesley's resolution to land British forces north of Lisbon. The general reiterated that any landing in the vicinity of Lisbon was considered a "very hazardous undertaking" and that landing in the country south of the Tagus was operationally unsound and "likely to be attended with bad consequences." Wellesley seemed to state impatiently: "I am fully aware of the advantage to be derived by diverting the enemy's attention to the Bay of Lisbon, during my advance towards that city; and, accordingly, I propose to send a battalion to the fleet . . . to make a very seasonable diversion in my favor." If Wellesley indeed was worried about Cotton's interpretation of their discussion about British strategy in Portugal, then his concern lasted less than a day. The *Scout* departed the Mondego with Wellesley's dispatch a matter of hours before Spencer's arrival. Wellesley must have been relieved, and his estimation of Cotton must have improved dramatically. Although the exigencies of communication during the age of sail best explain Wellesley's misunderstanding with Cotton, this episode had the potential of damaging their command relationship.[17]

Notwithstanding any doubts Wellesley might have temporarily had about Cotton's judgment, the two men cooperated with a professionalism born from decades of service as British military operations progressed in Portugal. For instance, despite having already issued several proclamations promising British support of the Portuguese cause, Cotton recognized the need to issue one with both his and Wellesley's signature. Cotton drafted the joint proclamation and sent it to Figueira da Foz with the opinion that it "might do some good" if distributed before commencement of the British army's march toward Lisbon.[18]

The time is arrived to rescue your country and restore the government of your lawful prince. His Britannic Majesty . . . in compliance with the earnest entreaties and ardent supplications for succour from all parts of Portugal, sent to your aid a British army, directed to cooperate with his fleet already on your coast. . . . The English soldiers that land upon your shore do so with every sentiment of friendship, faith, and honour. The glorious struggle in which you are embarked is for all that is dear to man. For the preservation of your Holy Religion, for the restoration of your lawful prince, the protection of your wives and children, and the independence, nay, very existence of your kingdom.[19]

Making only a minor verbal alteration and a better Portuguese translation of the draft, Wellesley concurred entirely with Cotton's opinion and promised to publish the proclamation at Coimbra and have it circulated in the country. Whether or not they were allies, foreign troops on home soil had an unsettling effect on the inhabitants of the country. In the spirit of leaving no stone unturned to increase the prospect of allied success, the joint proclamation was a simple measure crafted to lessen any Portuguese doubts that might hinder Wellesley's operations. The proclamation apparently had its desired effect because, according to a French general, it was "widely distributed" and "read with avidity."[20]

Wellesley prepared to set his army in motion towards Lisbon when his and Spencer's troops completed disembarkation on 8 August. Despite the establishment of a secure foothold in Portugal, cooperation between the British army and navy remained an indispensable ingredient for success because Wellesley needed the fleet for the timely delivery of supplies, "to make a very seasonable diversion" as his army approached Lisbon, and to control reinforcements converging on Portugal. Wellesley summarized how he hoped to achieve these goals in a letter to Cotton on 8 August. That morning the general met with Captain Malcolm to discuss the scheme of operations for the fleet of transports once the British army began its march. Wellesley ordered Captain Bligh of the *Alfred* to lead a convoy of eight vessels down the Portuguese coast adjacent to the army's advance and endeavor to maintain communication between them. These vessels contained enough provisions, military stores, oats, hay, heavy ordnance, and ammunition to supply the army adequately and support an attack on Peniche if necessary. He also ordered Bligh not to arrive with the convoy off Nazaré earlier than the evening of the 13th; an earlier arrival would alert the French to his route of march. Meanwhile, Wellesley wanted Malcolm's *Donegal* and the *Resistance* to stay off the Mondego to protect those transports unable to negotiate the bars of Oporto because of their draft. When the army neared Lisbon, Malcolm would concentrate the transports from the Mondego with Bligh's convoy and lead the flotilla down the coast.[21]

Wellesley also made arrangements for an amphibious diversion near the Rock of Lisbon. He ordered the 4th Veteran Battalion, consisting of 840 soldiers in seven transports, to join the squadron off the Tagus. These soldiers were too infirm for the march to Lisbon and were eventually destined for the garrison of Gibraltar. By staying as close to the coast as possible on the way to Lisbon, the convoy was intended to attract Junot's attention and make him believe that an amphibious attack on the Tagus was imminent. In fact, Wellesley intended to use such an attack as a diversionary tactic. When the army later reached Mafra and Cintra, Wellesley wanted Cotton to lead an attack with the Veteran Battalion and the marines of the fleet somewhere in the vicinity of the Rock of Lisbon. With an estimated 600 effective marines, Cotton would have a total of 1,440 troops for the operation. This force was too small to establish a permanent foothold against determined opposition, but large enough to pose a legitimate threat to Junot if he chose to ignore it.[22]

The landing of reinforcements from England was another matter of concern. Wellesley left instructions with Malcolm that directed Brigadier General Wroth Acland to proceed from the Mondego with his 5,000 troops and communicate with Captain Bligh, who would have updated guidance. Wellesley originally intended Acland's force to attack Peniche if necessary, and if not, then to join Cotton's fleet off the Tagus to participate with the Veteran Battalion and fleet marines in the contemplated diversion. Wellesley wanted Sir John Moore's force of 10,000 soldiers to land at Figueira da Foz and proceed towards the Tagus by way of Santarém, located forty miles northeast of Lisbon. This maneuver would put Moore's force in a position to cut off the enemy's retreat from Lisbon and prevent French reinforcements from striking the unprotected rear of Wellesley's main body. However, Moore's movement towards Santarém created a risky division of the British army before an enemy army that was not significantly inferior in total numbers: 26,000 French against 30,500 British and 5,000 Portuguese soldiers. Nevertheless, this division of force appeared less risky to Wellesley because he expected active Portuguese resistance outside of Lisbon to hinder Junot's operations. Moreover, Wellesley believed that the current French strength in Portugal was between 16,000 and 18,000 troops, well below the actual numbers.[23]

Wellesley's instructions to Cotton, Malcolm, and Bligh completed naval arrangements for his campaign before the army's advanced guard marched on 9 August from Lavos towards Leiria. Cotton had only one minor request. He wanted the *Donegal*, *Alfred*, *Resistance*, and *Crocodile* sent to the Tagus when their services were no longer deemed necessary by the army.[24] Otherwise, the Royal Navy prepared to do Wellesley's bidding without restraint. Meanwhile, Junot had anticipated the British invasion and was busy preparing for it. As early as June, a colonel of engineers in Junot's army had written a "Plan of Defensive Operations for the French Army in Portugal."[25] The plan proposed contingencies that addressed the possibility of British amphibious attacks between Peniche and Setúbal or attacks by land from beyond these locations, and it suggested that should a retreat from Portugal be necessary, the French army should evacuate upon the frontier fortress of Elvas. Perhaps complying with recommendations from this defensive plan, Junot ordered General Louis Henri Loison, who had been suppressing insurrection in the province of Alemtejo with his division of 6,000 men, to move with haste to Abrantes. Loison's division arrived there on 9 August, ready to move against the flank of the British army. To delay the British army's advance on Lisbon, Junot ordered Delaborde's division of 5,000 troops northward. The delay would buy time for the French army to complete its concentration and defensive preparations of Lisbon. Delaborde departed Lisbon on the 6th and arrived at Alcabaça on the 10th, the day Wellesley's main body began its march to Leiria. The remainder of the French Army of Portugal occupied the forts guarding the Tagus and fortifications within Lisbon: A depôt battalion of 1,200 soldiers garrisoned the castle of São Jorge and nearly 6,000 manned the fortresses of Bugio, Tafaria, Cascaes, São Julião, Belem, Bom Succèso, and Ericeira. Clearly, Junot still anticipated a British amphibious attack near Lisbon. Cotton's squadron had heightened this expectation on 1 August by sending a "large number of launches" to attack "French barges placed at the mouth of the Tagus."[26]

With the British squadron off the coast, a British army advancing on Lisbon, and his own army isolated in Portugal because of events in Spain, Junot understood only too well his precarious strategic situation. In fact, Cotton received indications that Junot wanted to negotiate terms for capitulation of his army. On 5 August, Cotton received aboard the *Hibernia* a Dr. Powell, an American who professed to be on intimate terms with Monsieur Combis, one of Junot's secretaries. Powell had previously earned Cotton's confidence by providing intelligence that proved "bearably correct." In this instance, he claimed that Combis believed Junot was "very likely" in the near future to send proposals for capitulation to the British. Furthermore, Powell described "the French to be in great dread from the avowed vengeance of the Portuguese and that various private meetings have been held in Lisbon to concert the means of revolt against the French." On 10 August, Powell again joined Cotton on the *Hibernia*. This time, the doctor requested a passport to enable him to proceed to Wellesley with a message supposedly from Junot, but given to him by Combis. The message queried if Wellesley would receive a flag of truce, which Cotton interpreted as a French attempt to ascertain the British army's numbers, position, or intentions. Cotton did not grant the passport to Powell, but stated that Wellesley probably would receive a flag of truce if sent by an officer of rank with the usual formalities. Cotton forwarded Powell's intelligence to Wellesley, but the rapid pace of events rendered it of little if any consequence. Although Junot might have felt that his army's position was helpless, there is no reliable evidence to suggest that he entertained a serious thought of surrendering without first giving battle. According to Foy, any proposal to evacuate Portugal without a fight would have been met with derision by the French army, and Junot felt personally responsible to Napoleon for the security of Lisbon and the Russian fleet.[27]

As the British army marched south, Junot intensified his effort to persuade Seniavin to support the French defense of Lisbon and the Tagus. Junot reminded Seniavin of the alliance between the two emperors and emphasized that the British approach to Lisbon posed more of a threat to the Russian squadron than Cotton's fleet. Seniavin remained intransigent. He insisted that his vessels had a neutral status in a neutral port and that he would fight only if the British navy forced the entrance of the Tagus. He balked at Junot's proposal that the Russian squadron make a demonstration to leave the Tagus—Junot wanted a Russian escape attempt to cause a concentration of the Royal Navy on the Tagus, thus leaving the remainder of the Portuguese coast unprotected. In addition, Seniavin refused Junot's request that he disembark Russian troops to occupy the forts protecting the Tagus, which would have freed French troops to oppose the British advance. Junot's frustration with Seniavin was probably increased by the Russian daily consumption of 10,000 French rations. Despite Junot's gracious offers of material support and kind platitudes, Seniavin was unlikely to change his mind because of a deep mistrust of the French and the bonds of friendship already forged with officers in the Royal Navy. Junot failed to use the Russian reliance on French rations to gain any leverage over Seniavin.[28]

Having departed Lavos on 10 August, Wellesley's army marched through Leiria and reached Alcobaça four days later. According to plan, Bligh's convoy lay at anchor off Nazaré awaiting the army's arrival. Communication between the fleet and the army was opened on the 14th, and bread, oats, and other necessities were sent from the fleet to Alcobaça on 120 carts provided by Wellesley's commissaries. The general informed Bligh of the French army's current disposition and made arrangements for the convoy to proceed. Wellesley wanted the convoy to appear off Peniche on the 16th, but was uncertain if his line of operations would be close enough to conveniently open communication. If not at Peniche, Wellesley speculated that communication between the fleet and army would next open at Ericeira, twenty-five miles farther south. Whatever the case, Wellesley promised to keep Bligh informed of his intentions and asked him to keep Cotton and Malcolm acquainted with the army's disposition.[29]

As the fleet unloaded supplies at Nazaré, the British advance guard skirmished on 15 August with French troops at Obidos, about twenty miles south of Alcobaça. On the same day, Junot arrived at Villafranca while his army was concentrating in the vicinity of Torres Vedras. As he marched to join the army, Junot hesitated upon receipt of a report on 17 August of a British landing at Cascaes, near Lisbon. Although the report proved false, it underscored the diversionary value of Cotton's fleet maneuvers off the Rock of Lisbon. While Junot hesitated near Villafranca, Wellesley fought his first battle in Portugal at Roliça. Wellesley won the field of battle with 14,000 British and 1,600 Portuguese soldiers against about 4,000 Frenchmen of Delaborde's rear guard. However, the French retired in good order and gained more time for

Junot to concentrate his forces. Instead of pursuing Delaborde along the road to Torres Vedras, however, Wellesley turned his army toward Vimeiro, where he hoped to again open direct communication with the fleet and "favor Anstruther's landing and junction."[30]

Brigadier General Robert Anstruther's 2,700 troops from Britain arrived off the Burling Islands on 17 August under convoy of the 64-gun *St. Albans*. Bligh directed the convoy five miles south of Peniche to Paymogo, where the troops landed on the evening of the 19th and joined Wellesley's force the next day at Vimeiro. Wellesley had decided to bypass Peniche since it was still occupied by French forces and because he recognized the importance of covering the landings of his reinforcements.[31]

Meanwhile, Cotton had been adhering as closely as possible to the intent of Wellesley's instructions. By 14 August the Veteran Battalion had arrived off the Tagus, and Cotton ordered his transports close to the coast to make the French more anxious about a landing. Apparently, the sight of the additional transports off the Rock of Lisbon prompted the report of a landing that had delayed Junot at Villafranca on the 17th. Moreover, as reinforcements arrived off the Tagus, Cotton directed them toward their point of debarkation. Under convoy of the *Amiable*, Acland's convoy of ten transports with 1,682 troops joined Cotton on the 17th. Having received Wellesley's letter to Bligh that suggested Ericeira as the next point of communication between the army and fleet, Cotton directed Acland's convoy there. It left Cotton on the 18th, but actually proceeded ten miles north of Ericeira to make its landing at Maceira Bay. Before Acland's convoy was in sight, Bligh sought guidance from Wellesley for a suitable landing place: "I think it probable that [Acland's brigade] will join me very soon. . . . In that case, where do you purpose that they be landed? I know of no place this side of Ericeira, near Mafra, unless the weather continues very fine and the water smooth." Fortunately, the weather remained calm, and Wellesley made known his desire for a landing at Maceira. Acland's brigade landed there on the evening of the 20th and joined Wellesley's army in time for commencement of the Battle of Vimeiro on the morning of the next day.[32]

Generals Burrard and Dalrymple arrived off Maceira almost simultaneously with Acland's brigade. After first stopping at Figueira da Foz on 18 August to receive Wellesley's instructions from Malcolm, Burrard continued southward to join Bligh's detachment. On the evening of the 20th, Burrard arrived off Maceira in the frigate *Brazen*; Wellesley went aboard for a conference. Meanwhile, Dalrymple had embarked from Gibraltar in the frigate *Phoebe* on the 13th and joined Cotton off the Tagus six days later. Cotton, who had not yet received word of the battle at Roliça, told Dalrymple that Wellesley was not likely to meet much French resistance on his march from the Mondego. In addition, Cotton told the general about the arrival of Spencer's corps and Acland's brigade. According to Cotton, Dalrymple then sailed north on the 19th in the *Phoebe* to join Wellesley at his headquarters. But according to

Dalrymple, he sailed for the Mondego with the intent of joining generals Burrard and Moore. Only on the 21st, when Bligh's fleet was sighted inshore, did Dalrymple decide to proceed to Maceira Bay. Clear visibility alone prevented Dalrymple from bypassing the army. Considering the aftermath of the battle at Vimeiro, this was not the good fortune for Dalrymple that it initially seemed.[33]

On 21 August, the British army defeated the Army of Portugal in two and one-half hours at Vimeiro. In summary, Wellesley's force of 18,000 British and 2,000 Portuguese troops maintained a mobile defense while Junot committed his 13,000 troops in piecemeal attacks. After the French army sustained 1,800 casualties, it withdrew toward Lisbon. Wellesley did not pursue Junot's army because of Burrard, who landed at 9:30 that morning. Burrard wisely chose not to assume command of the army until after the battle, but upon assumption of command, he overestimated the strength of the retreating French army and unwisely rejected Wellesley's proposal to pursue. Nevertheless, Junot's army was in a difficult position. Isolated from France by the insurrection in Spain and by the Royal Navy and outnumbered by Anglo-Portuguese forces, Junot had a choice between losing his army in another battle or negotiating with the British for its return to France. Junot would choose the latter option.[34]

On the day of the Battle of Vimeiro, Cotton received Wellesley's dispatch telling of the action at Roliça. The general also stated that he expected to be in Cotton's "neighbourhood before long" and requested that Cotton not conduct any landing operation until further notice. On the evening of the same day, Cotton received an emissary aboard the *Hibernia* who represented a "secret congress" assembled in Lisbon. Detecting a weakened French garrison in Lisbon and the approach of the British army, some of Lisbon's inhabitants wanted arms and ammunition immediately from the fleet to stage an uprising. According to the emissary, it was becoming increasingly difficult to restrain the populace. Cotton, who had received reports of French depredations against the Portuguese at Leiria, Evora, and other places, offered prudent advice. If the people of Lisbon initially were successful at taking control of their city, the risk still remained that Junot's army would fall back, reoccupy Lisbon, and subject the people to various cruelties. Therefore, he recommended that the people "had much better wait the approach of the English army than run the risk of subjecting the city to pillage by an ineffectual struggle." Had Cotton supported an uprising in Lisbon, there was an increased likelihood that it would have occurred because, after eight continuous months off the Tagus, the admiral's reputation was well-established as a friend of Portugal. According to Cotton's memoir in the *Naval Chronicle*, Cotton's "ready smile of cordial kindness, and his unceasing attentions" to the Portuguese refugees who had joined the fleet had "rendered the name of the British naval commander venerated throughout the kingdom." In this particular instance, Cotton's judgment was sound in the presence of the emotional pleas of a people seeking to throw off the yoke of foreign oppression.[35]

On the day that Cotton sent his congratulations to Wellesley for the Battle of Roliça, Junot decided to propose a suspension of hostilities with the British before settling on a definitive convention. Junot sent General François Étienne Kellermann to British army headquarters at Vimeiro, where generals Wellesley, Burrard, and Dalrymple were uncomfortably adjusting to the rapid succession of command that had occurred within the previous twenty-four hours. Kellermann, whose English skills and military experience since 1785 made him a superb choice as the chief French negotiator, arrived at British headquarters soon after 1:00 p.m. on 22 August. A lengthy discussion followed between Kellermann and the three British generals. Erroneously convinced that the French army had established a strong defense between Lisbon and the British army and that the British could not prevent a French retreat from Portugal, Dalrymple accepted Wellesley's advice and agreed to Kellermann's proposals. The generals then drafted an armistice, but Dalrymple refused to conclude it without Cotton's concurrence. On the morning of the next day, Dalrymple sent Lieutenant Colonel George Murray, the army's Quartermaster-General, to the fleet with a copy of the treaty for Cotton.[36]

Thus began Cotton's involvement with the Convention of Cintra, one of the most contentious treaties in British military history. Until this moment, Cotton had commanded his squadron without controversy and, arguably, in a manner worthy of his government's approbation. Cotton had done everything possible within the guidelines established by his government to force the capitulation of Seniavin's fleet, albeit without taking any undue risks. In June, he had taken the initiative and used British warships to encourage and support uprisings all along the Portuguese coast. In July, he ordered the landing of marines at Figueira da Foz, which further encouraged the Portuguese and established a secure landing site for Wellesley's army. Had Cotton not ordered the occupation of Figueira da Foz, General Margaron's force might have occupied it and denied Wellesley the best landing site south of Oporto, thereby nearly doubling the length of the army's march to Lisbon. Finally, Cotton provided Wellesley with sound advice during their 26 July conference, and he seconded his requests promptly throughout August with a cooperative spirit in support of the general's wishes as the Anglo-Portuguese army advanced towards Lisbon. Had Sir Sidney Smith retained command off the Tagus, it is unlikely that he would have subordinated personal and parochial interests in the manner that Cotton had during his joint operations with the British army that summer. Notwithstanding past performance, perhaps Cotton's greatest test as commander of His Majesty's squadron off the Tagus loomed ahead in the form of an unratified treaty designed to resolve the crisis in Portugal. Both Cotton and the British generals would discover that victory at the negotiating table could be as difficult to achieve as victory on the battlefield.

NOTES

1. Thomas More Molyneux, *Conjunct Expeditions; or Expeditions that have been carried on jointly by the Fleet and Army; with a Commentary on a Littoral War* (London, 1759), Part III, 48–49.

2. Wellesley to Castlereagh, 21 July 1808, Arthur Wellesley, Duke of Wellington, *The Dispatches of Field Marshal the Duke of Wellington, during His Various Campaigns in India, Denmark, Portugal, Spain, the Low Countries, and France, from 1799 to 1818* [hereafter cited as *Wellington's Dispatches*], ed. John Gurwood (London, 1852), 3: 31–34.

3. Ibid., 3: 36-39, Wellesley to Castlereagh, 25, 26 July 1808; Cotton to W.W. Pole, 26 July 1808, PRO ADM 7/41; Cotton to Wellesley, 9 July 1808, Southampton, Wellington Papers, 1/207 (folder 2); Lieutenant Gerard Fleetwood to Cotton with "A List of Transports in charge of Lieutenant Fleetwood," 26 July 1808, Cambridgeshire County Record Office, Cotton Naval Papers, 588/041/a43.

4. Wellesley to Burrard, 8 August 1808, *Wellington's Dispatches*, 3: 57–61; Cotton's report to the Admiralty about his meeting with Wellesley contained little detail of their conversation. Cotton to W.W. Pole, 3 August 1808, PRO ADM 1/340.

5. Wellesley to Spencer, 26 July 1808, *Wellington's Dispatches*, 3: 37–40. Wellesley addressed four letters to Spencer on this day.

6. Ibid., 3: 46, Wellesley to the Duke of Richmond, 1 August 1808.

7. Jonathon Leach, *Rough Sketches of the Life of an Old Soldier* (London, 1831), 41.

8. Wellesley to Cotton [unpublished], 1 August 1808, Cambridgeshire County Record Office, Cotton Naval Papers, 588/041/a64; John William Fortescue, *A History of the British Army* (London, 1910–1930), 6: 203; Maximilien Sébastian Foy, *History of the War in the Peninsula* (London, 1827), 2: 494.

9. Fortescue claims that there was "some loss of life" during the landing; Oman claims that there were "a few lives lost." Fortescue, *British Army*, 6: 203; Charles William Chadwick Oman, *A History of the Peninsular War* (Oxford, 1902–1930), 1: 229.

10. Sir William Warre to his mother, 8 August 1808, Sir William Warre, *Letters from the Peninsula, 1808–1812*, ed. Edmond Warre (London, 1909), 21, 22.

11. William Gavin, *The Diary of William Gavin, Ensign and Quarter-master, 71st Highland Regiment, 1806–1815* (1921), 11.

12. Wellesley to Castlereagh, 1 August 1808, *Wellington's Dispatches*, 3: 42–46; Henry N. Shore, "Naval Operations during Sir A. Wellesley's First Campaign, 1808," *United Service Magazine* 168 (1913): 152–53.

13. Wellesley to the Duke of Richmond, 1 August 1808, *Wellington's Dispatches*, 3: 46.

14. Wellesley to Cotton, 6 (No. 1) August 1808, *Wellington's Dispatches*, 3: 54–55; Fortescue, *British Army*, 6: 203–205. With the exception of Wellesley's dispatch of 1 August 1808 to Cotton, all others from Wellesley to Cotton in the Cotton Naval Papers are in either *Wellington's Dispatches* or *Wellington's Supplementary Dispatches*. Wellesley's dispatches of 6 (No. 1) and 8 August 1808 are not in the Cotton Naval Papers.

15. Cotton to Wellesley, 31 July 1808, Southampton, Wellington Papers, 1/207 (folder 3).

16. Cotton to W.W. Pole, 2 August 1808, PRO ADM 7/41.

17. Wellesley to Cotton, 4, 6 (No. 1) August 1808, *Wellington's Dispatches*, 3: 51, 52, 54.

18. Cotton to Wellesley, 1 August 1808, Southampton, Wellington Papers, 1/210 (folder 1).

19. Proclamation to the People of Portugal, "Memoir of Cotton," *The Naval Chronicle* 27 (1812): 381. See also Donald D. Horward, "Portugal and the Anglo-Russian Naval Crisis, 1808," *Naval War College Review* 34 (1981): 61.

20. Foy, *War in the Peninsula*, 2: 496.

21. Wellesley to Cotton, 8 August 1808, Arthur Wellesley, Duke of Wellington, *Supplementary Despatches, Correspondence, and Memoranda of Field Marshal Arthur Duke of Wellington, K.G.* [hereafter cited as *Wellington's Supplementary Despatches*], ed. by his son (London, 1860), 6: 102-104; Wellesley to Malcolm, 8 August 1808, Wellesley to Bligh, 9 August 1808, *Wellington's Dispatches*, 3: 61, 62, 66.

22. Cotton to Wellesley, 9 August 1808, Southampton, Wellington Papers, 1/210 (folder 2); Wellesley to Cotton, 8 August 1808, Wellesley to Malcolm, 8 August 1808, Cambridgeshire County Record Office, Cotton Naval Papers, 588/041/a67; Cotton to W.W. Pole, 14 August 1808, PRO ADM 1/340.

23. Wellesley to Cotton, 8 August 1808, Cambridgeshire County Record Office, Cotton Naval Papers, 588/041/a67; Wellesley to Burrard, 8 August 1808, *Wellington's Dispatches*, 3: 57–61.

24. Cotton to Wellesley, 10 August 1808, Southampton, Wellington Papers, 1/210 (folder 3).

25. "Translation of the Plan of Defensive Operations for the French Army in Portugal," 28 June 1808, Robert Stewart Castlereagh, *Memoirs and Correspondence of Viscount Castlereagh, second Marquess of Londonderry* (London, 1851), 6: 376–81.

26. Paul Charles Thiébault, *Relation de l'expedition du Portugal, faite en 1807 et 1808, par le 1er corps d'observation de la Gironde, devenu armée de Portugal* (Paris, 1817), 171–72; Foy, *War in the Peninsula*, 2: 500.

27. "Intelligence from Dr. Powell," 5 August 1808, Cotton to Wellesley, 10 August 1808, Southampton, Wellington Papers, 1/210 (folders 3 and 4); Foy, *War in the Peninsula*, 2: 497. In a letter from Cotton to W.W. Pole on 17 November 1808, Cotton claimed that Powell was an American resident of Lisbon. PRO ADM 7/41.

28. Foy, *War in the Peninsula*, 2: 499-500; Horward, "Anglo-Russian Naval Crisis," 61–62.

29. Wellesley to Bligh, 14 August 1808, *Wellington's Dispatches*, 3: 76.

30. Ibid., 3: 86, Wellesley to the Duke of Richmond, 18 August 1808; Fortescue, *British Army*, 6: 209–14; Thiébault claims that Delaborde had 1,900 troops at Roliça while Foy accounts for 2,500 at the battle. Fortescue accepts Oman's estimate of 4,000 French troops at Roliça. Paul Charles Thiébault, *The Memoirs of Baron Thiébault* (London, 1896), 2: 204; Foy, *War in the Peninsula*, 2: 505; Fortescue, *British Army*, 6: 209; Charles McKay, "The Tempest: The Life and Career of Jean-Andoche Junot, 1771–1813," Ph.D. dissertation (Florida State University, 1995), 248–49.

31. Bligh to Wellesley, 19 August 1808, Southampton, Wellington Papers, 1/210 (folder 3); Cotton to W.W. Pole, 19, 21 August 1808, PRO ADM 7/41.

32. Cotton to W.W. Pole, 19, 21 August 1808, PRO ADM 7/41; Bligh to Cotton, Report on proceedings from 26 July to 21 August 1808, undated, Cambridgeshire County Record Office, Cotton Naval Papers, 588/041/a46.

33. Cotton to W.W. Pole, 21 August 1808, PRO ADM 7/41; Lieutenant General Sir Hew Dalrymple, *Memoir of His Proceedings as Connected with the Affairs of Spain and the Commencement of the Peninsular War* (London, 1830), 58–61.

34. Wellesley to Burrard, 21 August 1808, Burrard to Castlereagh, 21 August 1808, *Wellington's Dispatches*, 3: 90, 91; Fortescue, *British Army*, 6: 218–34.

35. Cotton to Wellesley, 22 August 1808, Southampton, Wellington Papers, 1/210 (folder 3); Cotton to W.W. Pole, 22 August 1808, PRO ADM 7/41; Wellesley to Cotton, 18 August 1808, Cambridgeshire County Record Office, Cotton Naval Papers, 588/048/a68; "Memoir of Cotton," *Naval Chronicle* 27 (1812): 382.

36. Dalrymple, *Memoirs*, 63–67; Horward, "Anglo-Russian Naval Crisis," 63; Foy, *War in the Peninsula*, 2: 525–29.

7

Aftermath of Vimeiro: The Convention of Cintra and a Permanent Continental Foothold, August–December 1808

> Never has a victorious army with every advantage in its hands signed an agreement which gave so much to its defeated enemies with so little to itself.
>
> —Michael Glover[1]

> I am sorry for Sir Hew Dalrymple because though I do not pretend to judge of his military ability or political sagacity, I believe him to be an honest and honorable man who has the interest of the country truly at heart and would exercise his best judgment to promote it. But it is so easy to fight battles and give law to an enemy in a coffee house, and so many who consider themselves competent to decide, that an officer whatever his devotion may be, stands in a painful predicament if anything adverse happens.
>
> —Collingwood to Cotton, 30 December 1808[2]

Church bells pealed and cannons thundered in London on 2 September 1808 when news of the British victory at Vimeiro was first published. The country celebrated Wellesley's achievement for the next two weeks as it awaited details of the treaty of surrender. When the Convention of Cintra was published in England on the 17th, the sense of euphoria changed to one of disbelief. After such a successful military operation, the British public and most politicians could not understand why Sir Hew Dalrymple ratified a treaty that allowed a defeated French army with its Portuguese loot to return to France aboard British vessels at no expense. In addition, the British believed that the terms resolving the disposition of Seniavin's fleet were too lenient. Consequently, the British government recalled Wellesley, Burrard, and Dalrymple from Portugal to attend a Board of Inquiry relative to the Convention of Cintra that convened in November 1808. Although Cotton was not recalled and was spared much of the public scrutiny (and ridicule) endured by the generals, he nevertheless had a profound role in shaping the treaty as concluded on 30 August. The treaty need not have been ratified with terms so unfavorable to British and Portuguese honor.[3]

On 23 August, the *Amiable* delivered a letter to Cotton from Captain Bligh that announced the results of the battle at Vimeiro. Bligh's report left no doubt that the British army had clearly won the battle: "[Junot] met with such a reception, as will I have no doubt, prevent his ever rallying again in this country." Bligh believed that the lack of British cavalry for a pursuit after the battle was the only thing that prevented complete destruction of the French army as it retreated towards Lisbon. He also reported that Wellesley's army had proportionally far fewer casualties than the French, captured twenty of twenty-five French artillery pieces, and took about 600 prisoners, including a general officer. A matter of immediate concern was the disposition of these prisoners. Wellesley wanted Bligh to "distribute them among the ships of war," but Bligh decided to place them on board four light transports before seeking Cotton's guidance on the issue. Cotton approved of Bligh's decision and suggested that the prisoners be taken under convoy to England by the *St. Albans*. Considering Bligh's report on the favorable results of the battle, Cotton was mildly shocked when Lieutenant Colonel Murray arrived with the preliminary articles of convention on *Hibernia* the next day.[4]

The agreement as negotiated and signed by Wellesley and Kellermann on 22 August consisted of nine articles. It established terms for an immediate cease-fire and stipulated that the generals of the opposing armies and Cotton would meet to conclude a final convention. Furthermore, the agreement sought to protect from reprisals those Portuguese who had cooperated with the French, and it arranged for the return of all French artillery and horses to France. Two of the more controversial articles were the fifth and seventh.

> Article V. It is provisionally agreed that in no case will the French army be considered as prisoners of war, that all members of it will be transported to France with their arms and baggage, with their personal property of every kind, nothing having been abstracted from it.
>
> Article VII. The port of Lisbon will be recognized as neutral as regards the Russian fleet; that is to say that while the town and port are in possession of the English, the said Russian fleet will not be molested during its stay, nor will it be stopped when it wishes to leave, nor will it be pursued after it has left until after the delay recognized by Maritime Law.[5]

The debate between Kellermann and the British generals over the Russian fleet was long and contentious. Wellesley believed that the French had no right to negotiate on behalf of the Russian fleet. Nevertheless, Kellermann, on Junot's instructions, initially proposed that the British allow Seniavin's vessels to sail unmolested to the Baltic. After Dalrymple rejected the proposal, Kellermann suggested the terms as they appeared in the agreed-upon seventh article. In an ensuing private conversation, Wellesley related to Burrard some insight from his conversation with Cotton during their conference in the Tagus on 26 and 27 July. Cotton believed that the Russians would remain neutral in the event of a clash between British and French forces, and he wanted to know Wellesley's opinion about this issue. Wellesley replied that the best way to ensure that the Russians could not legitimately claim the status of a neutral power in a neutral port was for the British army "to be so quick in [its] operations" that the Portuguese would not have time to make the claim of neutrality before Cotton's squadron could attack the Russians.[6] Regardless of Wellesley's opinion, Dalrymple allowed article seven to remain unchanged because he believed that the Russian fleet was a matter for Cotton to resolve: "I never doubted that the Admiral was the best, if not the only judge of this question, and the event proved that he alone was at that time provided with instructions that bore upon the subject."[7] In fact, Dalrymple wished to involve Cotton with every aspect of any agreement with the French: "I was quite determined to conclude no definitive treaty with the French Commander-in-Chief, to which the British Admiral should not be a party as well as myself."[8]

According to Wellesley, he would have been the officer who conveyed the preliminary articles to Cotton had it not been for Kellermann's objection—the French general well understood Wellesley's strong opposition to the arrangement.[9] Instead, Murray arrived aboard the *Hibernia* early on 24 August as Dalrymple's representative and presented a letter from the general to Cotton. Dalrymple established Murray's credentials: "I send Lcol[sic] Murray, Quarter Master General to this Army, an officer entirely in my confidence to state the motives in question, and to arrange with you such further proceedings as may be deemed necessary."[10] Considering the relative disadvantageous position of the French army, Cotton strongly opposed many articles within the proposed convention. He wrote Dalrymple the day after Murray left the *Hibernia*: "The Preliminary Articles I read yesterday can never be acceded to, so as to form a Definitive Treaty so much in favour of the French army twice beaten, and 30,000 British troops in Portugal. Without great alteration of those Articles, I can never accede to such a Treaty."[11] Cotton especially opposed the article respecting the Russian squadron and insisted that it be struck from the convention. Murray understood Cotton's desire to strike the seventh article but did not understand Cotton's objection to the whole of the preliminary articles. Had Cotton not waited until after Murray's departure to express more vehemently his opposition to the proposed convention, the final convention probably would have been very different.

When Murray returned to British army headquarters at night on the 24th, he informed Wellesley that Cotton would not assent to the terms proposed for the Russians. Cotton's response delighted Wellesley, who claimed to be a reluctant signatory of the proposed convention. Wellesley wrote to Cotton:

I agree entirely with you respecting the Russian fleet. We ought not to allow the French to interfere in any manner between us and the Russians; and although I signed the agreement for the suspension of hostilities at the desire of the Commander-in-Chief, I consider it most fortunate that by your interference that article in it has been struck out; and that if the Convention is to be made, it will be upon a new basis.[12]

However, their rationales for this agreement differed. The Admiralty had sent Cotton to the Tagus to capture the Russian fleet; he had no intention of abandoning this quest, especially since the British army was on the verge of capturing the forts protecting the port of Lisbon. Wellesley was concerned with preventing Seniavin's vessels from returning to the Baltic; he was willing to grant the Russians neutral status within a neutral port as long as the French "should have nothing to do with the negociations[sic] affecting" the Russian fleet.[13] Therefore, Wellesley recommended that Dalrymple use Cotton's sentiments toward the article respecting the Russian fleet as a pretext to end the armistice in forty-eight hours and, without stating the details of Cotton's opposition, allow Junot the opportunity to renegotiate evacuation terms that would presumably be more reasonable considering the balance of power in the region.[14]

Dalrymple ignored Wellesley's recommendation. He decided to inform Junot of Cotton's opposition because of what Dalrymple deemed a binding comment made by Murray to Junot's aide de camp while on the *Hibernia.* When asked by the aide if Cotton had said anything that would prompt an end to negotiation, Murray replied that he had not. Feeling honor bound, Dalrymple thus sent Murray to French headquarters on 25 August with orders to proceed with negotiations for a definitive treaty based on the provisions of the original armistice, excluding the article relating to the Russian squadron. If the French refused to accept elimination of Article VII, then the armistice would end at noon on the 28th.[15] In a letter for Junot that accompanied Murray to Lisbon, Dalrymple explained why Cotton objected so vehemently to the seventh article. However, offering more information than necessary, Dalrymple stated, "The objection on the part of the British Admiral does not proceed from any desire to push to the utmost the advantages which the actual state of War in this quarter might present the British forces." His explanation continued:

Admiral Sir Charles Cotton was put in possession of instructions from the British Government, respecting the line of conduct to be observed towards the Russian Fleet in the Tagus, at a period when circumstances of a nature different from those now existing, induced the expectations that the British Fleet might be under the necessity of leaving the Port of Lisbon, and the British Admiral is ready now to enter on a direct discussion of the subject with Admiral Seniavin on the same grounds. The intimate connection, which so very lately existed between the British Government and that of Russia, as well as the personal regard which the British Admiral entertains for Admiral Seniavin, leaves little reason to doubt of an understanding acceptable to both being the result of a communication between them.[16]

Dalrymple's comments made it very clear that Junot should abandon any attempt to negotiate on behalf of the Russian fleet. However, by divulging Cotton's sentiments, Dalrymple assured Junot that he could likely expect little or no opposition to the remaining articles from the admiral. On 26 August, Junot agreed to let Cotton negotiate the fate of the Russian fleet and then entered into negotiations with Murray for the definitive treaty.[17]

Murray addressed letters to Cotton and Dalrymple with information "respecting the grounds on which [he was] about to enter upon negotiating a convention with the French general."[18] Murray informed Cotton that he would:

> Communicate to you direct from hence with as little delay as possible the steps of the negociation and shall be particularly anxious to be favoured with such communications on the subject as you may be pleased to direct to be transmitted to me in regard to any points connected with the naval part of the arrangement to be entered into. . . . In doing so I believe I shall be acting in the manner which seemed to meet your approbation when I had the honour of seeing you on board the *Hibernia* on the 24th instant.[19]

The "manner which seemed to meet [Cotton's] approbation" on the 24th no longer represented his attitude about all the preliminary articles. After receiving Murray's letter at 8:30 p.m. on the 26th, Cotton hastily replied that he thought many of the articles were as "objectionable as the 7th"; the letter also included an extract of the letter he had written to Dalrymple the day prior expressing his unwillingness to accede to the articles without "great alteration." The letter to Murray concluded with what Cotton assumed would be the logical course of events after the French army's losses at Roliça and Vimeiro: "I was in hopes that hearing nothing yesterday, and not till late this evening, all suspension of hostilities was over, and our Army in full march towards Lisbon."[20] Thus, Cotton missed his best opportunity to influence the final convention because he failed to emphasize to Murray on the 24th his strong negative sentiments about all the preliminary articles. When Dalrymple acknowledged Cotton's sentiments on the 28th, Murray and Kellermann had completed the draft of the final convention.[21]

Shortly before receiving Murray's letter on the evening of the 26th, Cotton received a proposal from Junot for a cessation of hostilities:

> At the moment that a cessation of arms has been concluded with . . . Dalrymple for the purpose of treating of the evacuation of Portugal by the French army, and that this treaty ought to be approved of by yourself. I suppose it is likewise essential to conclude a cessation of hostilities between the squadron which your excellency commands, and the land forces which I have the honour to command; as to the forts and batteries along the coast, and to any movements which might be in the power of either of the parties to put in execution.[22]

A record of Cotton's reply does not exist, but he did send Captain Halkett to negotiate with Junot.

Indicative of Cotton's belief that the British army would continue military operations against the French was his suggestion to Dalrymple on the 25th to detach at least one-half of Sir John Moore's army from Maceira for a landing at Setúbal. Cotton believed that with assistance from the local Portuguese, Moore's army could prevent a French retreat from Lisbon to Elvas. As a precaution, Cotton almost sent the 42nd Foot to Setúbal on the 26th, but was thwarted by contrary winds and news of an extension of the armistice until the 30th. Obviously, Cotton's assessment of the military situation was vastly different from that of the British commanding general.[23]

Murray sent a copy of the convention draft to Cotton, who likely received it sometime on 27 August. From the nine preliminary articles, the draft of the "Definitive Convention for the Evacuation of Portugal by the French Army" had expanded into twenty-three articles with five provisions. Having been "told from correspondents in Lisbon that the French expected nothing less than unconditional surrender and to return as prisoners of war to France," Cotton considered negotiation on the basis of the preliminary articles a mistake. Nevertheless, after reviewing the draft, he seemed resigned to accept it as a *fait accompli* and recommended several alterations rather than make a strong denouncement. Article XII addressed British occupation of Lisbon and the fortresses at Elvas, Almeida, Peniche, and Palmella, as well as those that protected the Tagus. The article stipulated that the forts west of São Julião would be handed over to the British upon ratification of the convention, while the forts of São Julião and the Bugio would not be given up until embarkation of the second division of the French army. Cotton considered this unacceptable since São Julião and the Bugio controlled access to the port of Lisbon. His recommendation that "the Forts of St. Julien and the Bugio, as well as those to the right of St. Julien, are to be given up and garrisoned by British Troops at the ratification of the present Treaty" was incorporated into the final convention.[24]

Another of Cotton's recommendations incorporated into the final convention addressed the collection of "contributions and requisitions" by the French. Article XVI of the draft directed that French collections would cease upon ratification of the treaty but did not cancel those payments in arrears prior to ratification. With Cotton's input, the final article mandated the cancellation of all payments still owed by the Portuguese to the French government. Yet another change to the final convention influenced by Cotton concerned an additional article that would have allowed foreign vessels in the port of Lisbon to assist in the conveyance of French troops to France as necessary. The article was struck in accordance with Cotton's recommendation.[25]

Not all of Cotton's recommendations, however, were incorporated into the final convention. Perceptively, he wanted to add the following to the seventeenth article, which addressed protection of French subjects and allies and their property.

No property belonging to any Portuguese, or the subjects of any Power in alliance with Portugal, at the time of the entry of the French Army into that kingdom, that has been confiscated on account of political opinions, or under any other pretext, shall be removed, but restored to the proper owners. It is also to be clearly understood, that the stipulations in favour of persons carrying away their private property, is not to be made the ground-work of any commercial speculations.[26]

Had this wise recommendation been incorporated into the final convention, Britain might have avoided the embarrassing appearance of having abetted the theft of Portuguese property during the French evacuation. As mentioned in a letter to Dalrymple on 28 August, Cotton understood the negative repercussions of allowing the French to evacuate Portugal without thoroughly inspecting their baggage.

The conveyance of the plunder to France, which may be greatly covered by the unqualified allowance to respect all nominal private property . . . may have the worst consequences both to us and those loyal Portuguese whom we are come to assist. To us, as the means of adding some millions perhaps to Buonaparte's treasury, at a time when all his former resources from Spain are cut off; and a perpetual source of discord with the Portuguese, for suffering their property to be carried away.[27]

The matter of French and Portuguese naval vessels was also of grave concern to Cotton. Since the issue was not mentioned in the draft convention, he wanted to add an additional article directing "the French ships of war, and all other vessels, to be delivered over with all their stores, sails, and equipments," subject to arrangements between the Prince Regent and the British government. On 28 August, Dalrymple learned of Cotton's dissatisfaction with the whole of the preliminary articles in addition to receiving Cotton's recommended changes to the draft of the final convention. The general responded by explaining that he thought elimination of the preliminary article respecting the Russian fleet would have induced Junot to recommence hostilities. Since Murray did not believe that Cotton objected to the remaining preliminary articles, Dalrymple gave the quartermaster authority to use them as the basis for continued negotiations should Junot cooperate. Mindful of Cotton's anxiety over the impending treaty, Dalrymple reassured him that the fate of the Russian fleet was strictly a naval affair to be negotiated between the two admirals. Regarding Cotton's concern about French and Portuguese naval vessels, Dalrymple did not think the inclusion of Cotton's additional article was necessary since the issue of "French ships" did not "come under consideration, as [Kellermann] did not include them in his demand of the things to be retained; they are to be left of course; but I believe there are no French ships, as the *Vasco de Gama* and other Portuguese ships seem no more French property than the church plate." Dalrymple concluded his comments by reminding Cotton: "Upon the whole, the Treaty, when made, is subject to your ratification as well as mine; and if its conclusion cannot be justified by the terms of the basis on which it commenced, that may be objected to, but I confess I think it is now too late to object to any part of the basis itself, which was at first acquiesced in."[28]

While Dalrymple pronounced that the final convention was subject to Cotton's approval, he also stated his belief that the British were bound to the preliminary articles. In essence, Dalrymple told Cotton that it was too late for the British to go back on their word. Considering the stakes involved, however, this was a situation in which the notion of honor should have been subordinated to the pursuit of military and national interests.

The treaty signed by Murray and Kellermann on 28 August arrived at British army headquarters near Ramalhal the next morning at 6:00 a.m. Dalrymple immediately assembled his available lieutenant generals so they could state their "objections and proposed alterations" to each article. Later that day, the treaty was sent back to Lisbon with alterations. Murray renegotiated the disputed items, and the final treaty was sent back to Dalrymple for ratification. Since Dalrymple believed the "season for negotiation was past," he again convened his lieutenant generals to witness ratification of the treaty.[29] With headquarters now at Torres Vedras, Dalrymple signed the treaty early on the morning of 31 August. What became known as the Convention of Cintra now needed Cotton's ratification. However, he was not immediately available because threatening weather that day had forced the entire British fleet to sea. Cotton returned inshore the next day and, without affixing his signature, approved the treaty.[30] As Dalrymple considered naval affairs a matter for the admirals, so too did Cotton likely consider the Convention of Cintra a matter for the generals as he became absorbed in dialogue with Seniavin over the fate of the Russian fleet.

On 29 August, Cotton received a letter from Seniavin seeking clarification of his intentions, since it became clear that British soldiers would soon occupy the forts protecting the Tagus. Having again refused to give any support to Junot,[31] Seniavin wanted to know if the British commanders would "consider Lisbon as a neutral port, in taking possession of it and its forts in the name of the Prince Regent of Portugal, or if they are to consider it as a place making part of the British dominions; and whether the British or Portuguese flag is to be hoisted in Lisbon?"[32] If Portuguese colors were hoisted, Seniavin assumed, then the British commanders would have to treat his fleet as neutral in a neutral port. While marching to Cintra on 1 September, Dalrymple was confronted by two Russian officers who posed the same questions. Dalrymple "did not think [himself] at liberty to interfere in a matter which [Cotton] had reserved to himself," but later admitted that he would have hoisted the Portuguese flag in the forts on the Tagus so as not to offend the Portuguese.[33] Offending the Portuguese, however, was of less concern to Cotton than immediately gaining control of the Russian fleet. In addition, Cotton preferred not to haggle over national colors because his fleet needed immediate access to the harbor as the season of heavy gales approached. Furthermore, the army needed provisions that only British vessels could provide.[34]

Cotton framed his response to Seniavin's questions according to guidance sent by the Admiralty in April when Lisbon was allegedly facing starvation. Besides, he reasoned that Lisbon could not be declared a neutral port because it had been "publicly declared a part of France governed in the name of the French emperor and the government left by the Prince Regent totally abolished."[35] Not only was the neutrality of Lisbon unacceptable, but Cotton wanted Seniavin to ratify two articles.

> Article I. The ships of war of the Emperor of Russia now in the Tagus . . . shall be delivered up to Admiral Sir Charles Cotton immediately with all their stores as they now are; to be sent to England and there held as a deposit . . . to be restored to His Imperial Majesty within six months after the conclusion of a peace between His Britannic Majesty and . . . the Emperor of all the Russias.
>
> Article II. Vice Admiral Seniavin, with the officers, sailors, and marines under his command to return to Russia without any condition or stipulation respecting their future services; to be conveyed there in men of war or proper vessels at the expence of His Britannic Majesty.[36]

Cotton considered these articles relevant to the situation in August even though they were initially drafted by Castlereagh for the situation at Lisbon the previous April. The Admiralty later objected to Cotton's assumption.

Designated as Cotton's representative, Captain Halsted joined Seniavin aboard the *Tverdoi* on 1 September. Without hope of reinforcements or support, Seniavin reluctantly agreed to ratify the proposed convention. However, ratification depended on one condition: "That this convention cannot and shall not be valid, without the English flag is hoisted on the forts and the port of Lisbon is acknowledged as a port belonging to his Britannic Majesty." In an appeal to Russian honor, Seniavin also insisted that the Russian flag on each ship "remain unmolested and untouched" until the ships had been evacuated by their officers and crew.[37]

Disappointed by Cotton's refusal to grant neutrality, Seniavin felt obliged to explain in another letter why the Russian fleet deserved this status. The Russian fleet had entered Lisbon harbor only because of a violent storm and was thereafter granted by the Prince Regent every assistance the harbor could offer. Occupation of Portugal by the French, according to Seniavin, did not change the nature of the alliance between Portugal and Russia. Regardless of the state of negotiations between the governments of Britain and Russia and regardless of Cotton's instructions to prevent the Russian fleet's return to the Baltic, Seniavin concluded that "it does not follow that [the Russian fleet] should be disturbed in the port of a prince the ally of his sovereign." Furthermore, during his ten months in Lisbon, Seniavin had consistently refused to abet the French in their Portuguese campaign, with the most recent example on 24 August, when he dismissed Junot's request for Russian sailors and marines to land and assist in the defense of Lisbon. Seniavin's appeal to Cotton fell upon deaf ears.[38]

Meanwhile, British troops from the 3rd and 42nd Foot landed on 2 September to occupy the forts of Cascaes, St. Antonio, São Julião, and the Bugio under terms of the Convention of Cintra.[39] Junot had promised to evacuate the forts that day at 10:00 a.m, but he did so reluctantly. Captain Halsted, Cotton's representative, had to call Junot's bluff during negotiations for the forts. After Junot proved "insolent, Captain Halsted clapped on his hat, and put his hands aside, and told him he was there on a perfect footing of equality with him, and that if he did not agree to their immediate surrender, he would call for his barge, and he would answer for it, Admiral Cotton would soon bring him to reason."[40] With the negotiation battle won, Dalrymple had authorized Cotton to land the regiments with the fleet.[41] These regiments were given instructions from Cotton to hoist the Union Jack when the French tricolor was lowered. Had Portuguese colors gone up instead, Seniavin would have refused to ratify Cotton's proposed convention. Upon learning that British colors were flying, Dalrymple wrote to Cotton:

> I am doubtful of the propriety of hoisting the British colours in the Portuguese forts, and I know that on another occasion, that measure produced great jealousy and discontent. I shall therefore take it as a favour if you will acquiesce in a measure of which I feel the importance, namely, the immediately hoisting Portuguese colors in lieu of the British: for which purpose I shall order the necessary orders to be immediately given.[42]

By then, however, Cotton knew that Seniavin would consider a convention valid only if British flags flew around Lisbon Harbor. Cotton remained inflexible in his response to Dalrymple: "I am well assured that if the Portuguese flag should be hoisted instead of the English, it may prevent the final conclusion of a convention which, I trust, when settled will be acceptable to our government. I have therefore to request that the English flag may remain hoisted on the forts till it is so."[43] Apparently, Cotton's request was not honored, because Dalrymple stated in his memoir that this "error" was "soon rectified."[44] Yet, British colors flew long enough for Cotton to conclude and implement the convention with Seniavin.

Mr. James Kennedy, Cotton's secretary, met with Mr. Sass, Seniavin's representative, aboard the *Tverdoi* on 3 September to sign a copy of the naval convention; it consisted of the two articles originally proposed by Cotton, without alteration. They then took the convention to the *Hibernia* for Cotton's signature. Availing himself of the opportunity to answer Seniavin's letters of 2 September, Cotton explained to Sass his views on the neutrality issue and British colors flying around the Tagus. Seniavin remained unsatisfied after hearing his representative's interpretation of Cotton's explanation. The Russian admiral vowed not to sign a copy of the convention until Cotton responded to the neutrality question in writing. Cotton responded, in writing, that the subject was fully discussed with Sass and that since British colors were flying in the forts on the banks of the Tagus, Seniavin was obliged to sign the convention. Apparently, the admirals held a conference on 6 September that settled their disagreements.[45]

The ceremonial aspect of surrender became another obstacle created by Seniavin. He thought that a ceremonial act of surrender "would be most proper to be observed on the occasion of the surrender of the squadron of his Imperial Majesty . . . to his Britannic Majesty." Seniavin did not wish for the ceremonial surrender to occur until his ships were evacuated at Spithead. Cotton considered this delay unacceptable and insisted that "some act of surrender is absolutely necessary" before departure from the Tagus. Still, Cotton realized the sensitivity of this subject and did not want to wound Seniavin's pride any further:

> It has since yesterday occurred to me as likely to be more congenial to your feelings, that any act of surrender (the mode still left for your adoption) should be made in presence of an officer of superior rank to Lieutenant [John] Bellamy, and for that purpose I send to your excellency Rear Admiral [Sir Charles] Tyler, the second officer in the command of this fleet.[46]

Tyler later arrived aboard the *Tverdoi* and conducted a detailed discussion of the convention, after which Seniavin signed the second copy to make the agreement final. By 6 September the formalities were concluded; after nine months of tedious blockade, Cotton must have felt deeply satisfied now that Seniavin was about to deliver his fleet to the Royal Navy.[47]

Cotton charged Captain Halsted with delivering news of the convention to London because he had participated in the negotiation and could "explain every particular" to the Admiralty. No sooner had Halsted departed when word reached Cotton that Seniavin wished to alter the convention. In the form of two articles that would be considered part of the convention signed on 3 September, Seniavin proposed:

> The colours of his Imperial Majesty on board the flag-ship, or on board any of the others, are not to be struck until the Admiral quits the ship, or until the respective captains do the same.
>
> At the conclusion of a peace, the ships and the frigate will be restored to his Majesty the Emperor of all the Russias in the same state in which they are actually delivered up.[48]

Cotton considered these articles "of so unimportant a nature" that he acceded to them "without hesitation." After all, the Russian ships would be in British possession anyway and would not pose any threat to British naval operations for the duration of hostilities. Cotton further justified acceptance of these additional articles by informing the Admiralty that the Russians had "committed no act of hostility against Portugal" nor "joined the French in opposing us." Like the Convention of Cintra, Cotton's convention with the Russians seemed militarily logical. By both conventions, the British had gained the "expulsion" of the French from Portugal and, in essence, captured the Russian fleet. However, neither Dalrymple nor Cotton appreciated the political ramifications of their respective conventions until later.

Having resolved the Anglo-Russian naval crisis, Cotton now recognized that efficient administration of port activity had become imperative if the Royal Navy was to sustain itself while supporting the British army and evacuating the French army. Therefore, on 6 September Cotton appointed Mr. Kennedy, his secretary, as "Agent Victualler and Naval Officer for British Ships of War at the Port of Lisbon," with orders to "keep a corrected and particular account of any stores which it may be absolutely necessary to require for the service of His Majesty's Ships here."[49] He sent Captain McKinley into port the next day to take inventory of the stores remaining in the naval arsenals. McKinley was replaced on the 8th by Mr. Henry Andrews, master of the *Hibernia*, whom Cotton appointed as "Master Attendant" of the naval arsenal in the port of Lisbon. The Admiralty later disapproved Andrews' appointment. Cotton nevertheless stood firm with his decision: "As a naval force will now be kept in this quarter, in my humble opinion the service would be greatly benefitted by the establishment here of a person in the capacity of Master Attendant to superintend the refitment of His Majesty's Ships employed on the station, or others that may occasionally put in here for that purpose. . . . An appointment for which I beg leave to repeat my recommendation in favor of Mr. Andrews."[50] The Admiralty remained unconvinced, and Cotton subsequently ordered Mr. Andrews to return to duty aboard the *Hibernia*. Considering the scope of British naval activity in Lisbon harbor for the next several years, Cotton's attempt to establish a permanent "Master Attendant" demonstrated prudent foresight.[51]

Meanwhile, the British army and navy rapidly implemented the provisions of the conventions. On 7 September, British naval officers took possession of twenty-one Portuguese vessels in Lisbon harbor, raising the Union Jack upon their mainmasts. The British occupied them because the French Commandant of Marine, who was in possession of the ships, would not turn them over to the Portuguese. Cotton consulted with the Portuguese Board of Admiralty and suggested that British occupation of the vessels might deter the possibility of French depredations and would serve only as a temporary measure until the Portuguese could make decisive arrangements for occupation. The Portuguese "cheerfully" acquiesced. As promised, the British vacated the vessels within a month, when the new Portuguese government was sufficiently organized.[52]

As the Royal Navy assumed responsibility for administration of the Port of Lisbon, the Russian fleet completed preparations for its passage to Britain. Seniavin had received permission from Cotton, however, to leave the *Raphael* and *Yaroslav* in the Tagus because they were not deemed seaworthy. A subsequent inspection by the *Hibernia*'s carpenter validated Seniavin's assessment of the *Yaroslav* but found the *Raphael* nearly seaworthy. Of the 1,213 officers and crew aboard these ships, all but seventy-six were distributed aboard the other Russian vessels. Those remaining worked to make the *Yaroslav* and *Raphael* seaworthy; Cotton hoped they could make the passage to England by the next spring.[53] He designated Rear Admiral Tyler to escort the seven Russian ships-of-the-line and one frigate to Spithead with a convoy that included the ships-of-the-line *Barfluer*, *Hercule*, *Conqueror*, *Elizabeth*, *Donegal*, *Alfred*, *Ruby*, and the frigate *Crocodile*. The British convoy was matched ship-for-ship with the Russians and had only a slight quantitative advantage in the number of cannons; Cotton was not concerned about a Russian escape because he trusted Seniavin and the superiority of British seamanship and gunnery. Just in case of a problem, however, Cotton instructed Tyler, "Use every exertion to prevent separation, and in event of any decisive act, as a disposition to proceed in a contrary direction to the course you may prescribe, you are to use every means in your power by signal, remonstrance, or if absolutely necessary by actual force to compel their proceeding agreeably to the articles of the Convention entered into."[54]

Seniavin's vessels joined Tyler's convoy off the Tagus on 12 September and proceeded to Spithead, where the Russians arrived on 7 October with music and flags flying; Seniavin allegedly declared that he was in no sense an English prisoner. Regardless of Seniavin's blustering, Tyler ordered him to lower the Russian colors from each vessel because Lord Castlereagh considered invalid the additional article that allowed the colors to fly while the Russians remained on board. The Admiralty informed Tyler that the two additional articles could not be admitted as forming part of the original convention because they were not explanatory articles but had the character of a "distinct and supplementary" convention, "which the parties contracting were not at liberty to negociate and conclude." His Majesty could not accept the "flag of an hostile power to be displayed in the ports and harbors of his dominions." Hence, Tyler followed Admiralty orders to "cause the flag of his Imperial Majesty to be removed from the mast-heads and flag-staves of the said ships as soon as they shall have come to an anchor." In a measure meant to soothe the aches of Seniavin's wounded pride, the Admiralty directed that no other colors would fly aboard the Russian vessels and each commander was allowed to land and remain on shore until his return to Russia. Tyler conveyed the Admiralty's decision to Seniavin, who "consented and [gave] directions that his flag and the colours of the Russian ships shall be hauled down at sun-set this day, and not to be hoisted again."[55]

Seniavin's disappointment was quickly followed by the physical decline of his fleet. A British naval surgeon who had served aboard the *Salafael* observed a week after the colors were lowered that the Russian fleet had its "lower yards down, neither pennants nor colours flying, but lying in dirty neglected state, forming a forcible contrast between their former proud, and present degraded state." Seniavin's officers and men gradually returned to Russia while their vessels awaited the restoration of peace between Britain and Russia, which came in 1812. In 1813 only two of Seniavin's vessels sailed for Russia, the rest having deteriorated and been sold as scrap-wood by the British government; the money was given to the Russians.[56]

The exodus of vessels from Lisbon Harbor continued immediately after Tyler's and Seniavin's departures. Cotton did not want to delay departures because the strong gales expected during September would affect a large fleet of transports along the Portuguese coast. On the 14th, the first division of transports with French troops sailed from the Tagus aboard forty-three British transports. Cotton ordered Captain Lord George Stuart to assume command of the frigates *Amiable*, *Nymphe*, and *Fylla* and escort the transports to "Basque Road or Quiberon Bay according to the state of the weather causing the said transports to enter under flags of truce as cartels, and directing their respective masters to use every possible exertion towards disembarking the French troops; which being done his Lordship is to proceed with the transports to Spithead."[57] Under similar instructions, the frigate *Resistance* and sloop *Trompeuse* escorted fifty-one transports with the second division on the 15th; the frigate *Africaine* and *Zebra* bomb both departed on the 25th with forty-nine transports carrying the third division, making a total of 24,735 French soldiers evacuated from Portugal.

Junot requested that Cotton allow four Danish transports to convey his horses, aides, and staff "in order that they might be more comfortable than on board the [British] transports." He flattered Cotton for his "civility" and explained that much time and expense had gone into fitting the Danish vessels; Junot promised to send the vessels to Britain after disembarkation in France. Cotton refused to support the request, arguing that use of the Danish vessels for the transport of anything other than horses violated article six of the convention. A disappointed Junot departed Portugal aboard the *Nymphe* with the first division of transports.[58]

Regarding the issue of plunder, Cotton reported that seventy-one cases and trunks of indigo and 148 bales of cotton had been intercepted by British officers superintending the embarkation of the French army. Since the indigo and cotton went unclaimed, Cotton sent it to Britain for adjudication as prize of war to British land and naval forces at Lisbon.[59] In at least one case, the interception of plunder turned to violence. French troops from Almeida were attacked in Oporto on 10 October by a mob that suspected plunder within their baggage. After finding some church ornaments, the Portuguese, some 12,000 under arms with artillery, threatened to sink the British transports on board which the French had embarked. To resolve the crisis, the mob was allowed to board and plunder the transports.[60]

Not all of the transports reached France. The transport *Three Brothers* from the first division foundered in a storm with the loss of 273 Frenchmen from the 86th Line, including four women, two children, and six members of the crew.

In addition, General Kellermann returned to Lisbon on the *Africaine* after the frigate had sprung its bowsprit. Kellermann and the nearly 3,000 French troops who remained in Portugal became pawns in a diplomatic struggle between France and Britain.[61]

Lord Castlereagh believed that the British transports of the first and second divisions might be detained in French ports because of the French government's "accustomed disregard to treaties."[62] He thus ordered the third division of transports to remain in Portugal until confirmation of departure from French ports of transports from the first two divisions. Cotton received this guidance after the third division departed, but retroactively applied it to Kellermann and the remaining French troops, many of whom were extremely ill. Kellermann protested his detention and demanded immediate passage to France "in order to communicate with his [superiors] as to his conduct in Portugal." If the British could not grant this request, then Kellermann wished to proceed to an English port from whence he would sooner receive word about the departure of British transports from French ports. Since this latter request adhered to the spirit of Castlereagh's instructions, Cotton and Sir Harry Burrard, then commanding general at Lisbon, allowed Kellermann on or about 10 October to proceed in the *Africaine* to Portsmouth. Cotton mused: "The peculiar circumstance under which [Kellermann] has a second time been at our disposal, gives him a claim to the usual place which he would otherwise have, and consequently justify the arrangement determined on."[63] The *Africaine* arrived at Portsmouth on 22 October, although it is uncertain if Kellermann remained on board. Thiébault claimed in his memoirs that Kellermann was present when French troops disembarked at Quiberon Bay on 16 October.

The French troops remaining in Portugal experienced a fate very different from Kellermann's. Cotton was obligated to detain them according to Castlereagh's instructions. While awaiting confirmation of the departure of British transports from French ports, the physical and moral condition of the French troops deteriorated rapidly. Cotton was "sorry to say these troops are very sickly, occasioned by the want of execution on the part of their officers in enforcing discipline and cleanliness." Despite dreading "spreading of the fever" among the French, Cotton nonetheless could not justify permitting their departure.[64] In the meantime, bad weather impeded the passage of the three divisions of transports to French ports. Thiébault provides a detailed description of the turbulence encountered. One instance was a storm on 24 September that scattered the first and second divisions. HMS *Iris* met ten transports and a frigate about 200 miles west of Oporto on 10 October that "had been a month at sea with French troops on board." Finally, about eighty transports, likely containing transports from all three divisions, approached Quiberon Bay on 14 October; disembarkation of about 15,000 troops was completed two days later. On 8 November, two frigates and a sloop with about twenty transports arrived at Falmouth after disembarking troops in France.[65]

The ugly matter of repatriation officially closed on 18 November, when the Admiralty ordered Cotton to send the remaining French troops in Portugal to Quiberon Bay; he received the order on 14 December. Yet, in the intervening period between late October and receipt of this order, Cotton was left to his own devices with the French troops still in Portugal—dire circumstances forced him to make an decision independent of Admiralty guidance. Efforts on behalf of the British army's medical staff failed to prevent the spread of fever among the French troops; in early December the disease began spreading to British transport crews. In addition, a sense of urgency prevailed when news reached Lisbon of the total defeat of the Spanish armies and the possible withdrawal of Sir John Moore's army to Portugal for embarkation to England. Not wishing sick Frenchmen to interfere with the embarkation of 30,000 British troops from Lisbon and adhering to the "dictates of humanity," Cotton consulted with Major General John Randoll Mackenzie, the new commanding British officer in Lisbon. They decided on 5 December to allow the French troops to embark. Cotton realized this measure was "incompatible" with his instructions, but he hoped that "under the peculiar existing circumstances" the government would approve. The French finally departed the Tagus on 9 December under convoy of the *Myrtle* sloop.[66]

In hindsight, Cotton had little cause to worry about the British government's reaction to his decision. The grave situation of Moore's army, which actually embarked from Coruña in January 1809 after a month-long flight from the French army, served to distract the ministers from technicalities. Furthermore, British public opinion was inflamed by the Convention of Cintra; the government reacted accordingly. Wellesley, Burrard, and Dalrymple were recalled to attend an inquiry, which convened on 14 November 1808 and lasted until 27 December. Although not recalled to attend the inquiry, Cotton did not escape scrutiny of his role in the formulation of the Convention of Cintra and the separate convention with Seniavin. In general, praise for Cotton's rejection of Article VII of the 22 August armistice and the subsequent capture of the Russian fleet overshadowed criticism of the details by which he concluded the convention with Seniavin. Comments from *The Times* of London aptly illustrate the varied assessments of Cotton's performance in the Tagus. The articles of convention with the Russian admiral prompted a sardonic response from the editor:

> We can hardly refrain from shedding tears. . . . Are then the Russian Officers and seamen to be indeed sent home by us—or, in other words, to be conveyed to attack the King of Sweden, our most faithful Ally? If so . . . , the common cause has suffered most grievously by this expedition to the Tagus: it has been cruelly detrimental to our affairs, and, above all, to our character: it has let loose more enemies upon an oppressed and deserted ally.[67]

However, a comment in the next day's edition placed Cotton's proceedings in context: "But this article, bad as it is, is really honourable when compared to the one [Article VII] signed by Sir A. Wellesley in the first Convention."[68]

The Admiralty responded on 17 September with a letter to Cotton that approved of his refusal to grant neutrality to the Russian fleet, yet observed with "regret, in the Convention which you have concluded with the Russian Admiral, the adoption of a new principle of Maritime surrender, by the qualified detention and eventual restoration of the ships of war of the enemy." The Admiralty reasoned that Cotton had acted under "misapprehension of the nature of their temporary instructions of the 16th April last," when a famine allegedly existed in Lisbon. Cotton was "much grieved" by the Admiralty's response and hoped that further explanation of why he granted "such favorable terms with regard to the Russian squadron" would justify his actions.[69]

Although legitimately concerned about his reputation in London, Cotton was unaware of the First Lord's willingness to support his decisions. Likely in response to press reports, Lady Cotton wrote the Admiralty to determine the fate of her husband. Lord Mulgrave instructed Sir Richard Bickerton, the First Naval Lord, to tell her: "Nothing that has occurred has induced his Lordship to alter the high opinion he has ever entertained of Sir Charles, whose conduct during the tedious service he has been engaged in has met with great approbation from all the departments of government, and we all know, that had it not been for Sir Charles the terms granted to the French would have been much more favourable than they were."[70] For instance, George Canning, the Foreign Secretary, gave Cotton credit for having "saved us from the unmeasurable ridicule of neutralizing the Russian fleet in the port of Lisbon." Yet he still had reservations about how it was done.[71] Canning especially deplored letting loose "8,000 Russians" upon the King of Sweden. Despite such a consequence, Lord Mulgrave believed that extension of the government's support to Cotton would be "good policy." More than likely, however, Mulgrave wanted the navy to avoid the scrutiny that the army would undergo in the upcoming Convention of Cintra inquiry. The First Lord explained to Henry Bathurst, President of the Board of Trade: "I have delayed removing Sir Charles Cotton first because I do not wish to confound him in the public impression with those who are called home to explain and answer for their conduct." Furthermore, Mulgrave delayed appointing a successor to Cotton because that too "might rouse an expectation that would create a call for examination of his conduct, and render it unavoidable."[72]

Mulgrave unabashedly protected the interests of a friend and the naval service at the expense of a thorough inquiry into the Convention of Cintra. Indeed, the government would have been justified in recalling Cotton because Dalrymple had made clear to him that the convention with the French was subject to his ratification. The fact remains that Cotton could have rejected the articles of convention, despite its acceptance by the three army generals, and insisted on renegotiating a treaty on terms more favorable for a victorious army.

However, in that case, what would the reactions of Wellesley, Burrard, and Dalrymple have been? After all, they had actually engaged and defeated the French army, and they might have felt that Cotton did not have the right to override their decision. Several other reasons suggest why he did not reject the convention: preoccupation with the Russian fleet, concern for the approaching season of heavy gales, and resignation that the convention was a *fait accompli* when he received it. Regardless, Cotton shared some degree of responsibility for the Convention of Cintra with Dalrymple, who, hoping to spread the guilt, wrote in his memoir: "I was not more responsible than Admiral Sir Charles Cotton for that treaty, or any of its provisions; a circumstance which Ministers seemed to forget, or wish to have forgotten by the public."[73] While the Board of Inquiry exonerated the three lieutenant generals from blame for what had occurred in Portugal, Dalrymple became the *de facto* scapegoat for the convention. His military service was abruptly halted while Wellesley and Burrard continued serving the King. Without doubt, Dalrymple sought vindication by writing so strongly about Cotton's responsibility for the convention. Whether or not his comments were the apologia of a bitter man, they are worthy of consideration in the final assessment of Cotton's part in the Convention of Cintra.

As the Board of Inquiry concluded its proceedings in December 1808, Cotton was concluding his duty in the Tagus with a flourish of activity. With the fate of Seniavin's fleet and Junot's army determined, Cotton expected orders "with regard to returning to England" according to the instructions contained in the Admiralty's order dated 9 December 1807.[74] In addition to shielding Cotton from the Board of Inquiry, Lord Mulgrave delayed his return to Britain pending a decision by Lord Collingwood. On account of declining health, Collingwood had requested relief from command of the Mediterranean Fleet. Mulgrave urged him to retain command, but if he declined, then command as the port admiral at Plymouth was available; Cotton would receive whatever command Collingwood declined. Collingwood reluctantly chose to remain in the Mediterranean. However, Mulgrave did not immediately offer Cotton command at Plymouth. Consequently, Cotton remained unclear about why he had not yet received further guidance. When the Admiralty did write the order on 23 November recalling Cotton to Britain, it might have been with ambivalence towards Collingwood's reply, since Cotton would return home after conclusion of the inquiry and be spared the embarrassing inquiry.[75] Besides, Public indignation over the affair in Portugal had peaked by November. Thomas Grenville remarked: "I incline to think that people are tired of the discussion, and are more ready than they were to suppose that the convention may be vindicated."[76] However, he believed that Cotton should have been recalled for the additional articles to the convention with the Russians.

While awaiting recall, Cotton spent November and much of December managing Lisbon's port facilities, superintending the remaining French prisoners, and monitoring the situation of Sir John Moore's army. Intending to cooperate with the Spanish armies confronting Napoleon's invasion, Moore's army of 33,234 troops departed Lisbon on 26 October. At first it appeared to Moore that he would have to retreat upon Lisbon, so Cotton decided on 4 November to withhold in the Tagus twenty-nine empty army and victualling transports that were almost sent that day to Spithead. Still believing a month later that Lisbon was Moore's preferred place of embarkation, Cotton requested that the Admiralty send more light transports to the Tagus because not enough were there to embark Moore's entire army. In addition, the urgency of moving more transports to Lisbon prompted Cotton to amend the orders for those vessels that had departed on 9 December with the remaining French troops. Instead of proceeding to Spithead after disembarkation in France, Cotton ordered the transports back to Lisbon as long as they could return within five weeks and the fever among the French troops had not spread to the crews. As another precaution, Cotton ordered Captain Smith of the *Comus* to survey the harbor of Setúbal in case Moore's army would have to embark south of the Tagus. Smith included a detailed sketch in his report and concluded: "The position of St. Ubes [Setúbal] is in my opinion very strong and quite capable of protecting the embarkation of a retreating army; but all the points of strength must be occupied; and to give every possible facility great precaution used."[77]

However, an isolated French force north of Madrid, which invited defeat in detail, enticed Moore to lead his army farther north into Spain. After Napoleon captured Madrid on 4 December, a British retreat to Lisbon became untenable; Moore then decided to retreat through northwest Spain to either Vigo or Coruña, where superb anchorage made a rapid embarkation possible. Cotton learned of this decision as he was about to return to Britain, and he promptly ordered the 5,000 ton of transport detained in the Tagus "to proceed to Vigo under convoy of the *Peacock* sloop."[78] Transports varied between 140 and 600 tons each, so Cotton likely ordered about twenty to thirty transports to Vigo. Unfortunately, the *Peacock* and transports remained wind bound in the Tagus until 26 December.[79] In summary, Cotton's determination to collect transports in the Tagus proved valuable when Sir John Moore's army hastily crammed aboard over 250 transports after fighting the Battle of Coruña on 16 January 1809.[80]

As Moore's army advanced deeper into Spain, Lieutenant General Sir John Cradock assumed command of British troops remaining in Lisbon. He arrived in the port of Lisbon aboard the *Lavinia* on 13 December and conferred with General MacKenzie before landing. Although not explicitly stated, Cotton's and Cradock's correspondence implied that they conferred as well. Cradock almost decided not to land in Lisbon for fear of mixing his command with Moore's during a withdrawal. However, after weighing the risks, he decided to assume command and landed in Lisbon on the 14th. The next day Cotton dispatched the *Lavinia* back to Britain with Cradock's dispatches and the most recent account of affairs in Spain.[81]

A day after the *Lavinia*'s departure, the frigate *Niobe* brought orders from the Admiralty for Cotton to "immediately return to Spithead in His Majesty's Ship *Hibernia*" and to place his squadron "under the command of the officer next in seniority to yourself, transferring to him all orders and instructions, either in part, or in the whole unexecuted, and directing him to carry the same into execution."[82] Cotton originally chose Captain William Bradley of the *Plantagenet*, but this was precluded by Admiralty orders received on 18 November to send the *Plantagenet*, *Resolution*, and *Audacious* to Vigo. Captain Peter Halkett, commander of the 74-gun *Ganges*, was the most senior naval officer remaining in the Tagus; Cotton ordered him to hoist a commodore's broad pendant while he held temporary command. Halkett proved a superb officer for the transition between commanders. After assuming command in the Tagus on 14 January 1809 and assessing the bleak situation of Moore's army, Admiral Berkeley remarked: "I have taken every precaution, and indeed found the most of them ready done by Captain Halkett, whose indefatigable zeal, after Sir [Charles] Cotton left the Tagus, has left me little to complete."[83]

On 29 December, Berkeley left Portsmouth and sailed for Portugal aboard HMS *Conqueror,* eight days after Cotton departed the Tagus. Unlike the *Conqueror* and *Hibernia,* which at some point on their passages simultaneously crossed the same line of latitude, the concerns of each admiral as they approached their destinations likely never converged on a similar thought. However, both of their fates were full of uncertainty. Berkeley was approaching a theater of war where the British army appeared on the brink of disaster and the Royal Navy might be its only hope of salvation. Cotton was returning home to an uncertain reception. Would the government and public praise him for capturing the Russian fleet or rebuke him for accepting Seniavin's capitulation under less than honorable conditions? Or worse yet, would they hold him equally responsible with the generals for the Convention of Cintra? On 9 January 1809, one year after leaving Britain, Cotton arrived at Spithead. He remained aboard the *Hibernia* for two more days and prepared several dispatches for the Admiralty that summarized the situation in the port of Lisbon upon his departure, requested reimbursement for expenses incurred as commander-in-chief, explained Sir John Moore's intention to retreat through Galicia rather than Lisbon, and addressed many other administrative issues. After receiving the order to strike his flag and come on shore, Cotton disembarked the *Hibernia* on the 11th for the last time.[84]

Cotton concluded his year of service as commander-in-chief on the Lisbon station with more positive achievements than misfortunes. Upon realization in January 1808 that a British force could not enter the Tagus to capture the Russian fleet, he established a blockade of Portugal that centered around Lisbon. For this he drew on years of experience in the Channel Fleet. Although strong gales and supply shortages threatened, ships of the Royal Navy remained vigilant off the Portuguese coast, thanks in large measure to Cotton's perseverance and management skills. When insurrection spread from Spain to Portugal in May and June, Cotton's fleet became a conduit through which British arms, ammunition, and equipment flowed to the Iberian Peninsula. Any other admiral likely would have recognized the expediency of supporting the insurrectionists, but not all may have acted as decisively, yet with Cotton's prudence and forethought. In several proclamations he boosted Portuguese morale and made no promises that the British government could not keep. Of utmost importance was his decision to establish a garrison of Royal Marines at Figueira da Foz, a beachhead that over time expanded to the Pyrenees.

Wellesley could not have received better naval support during the campaign that culminated with the Battle of Vimeiro. Although a decentralized command structure dictated that Cotton had little control over direct support of the army as it marched from Lavos, his evaluation of the military situation prompted him to keep the fleet off the Tagus properly poised for an amphibious attack; Cotton also served as a superb liaison for those army units converging on Portugal. However, his performance during the twelve days from his first glimpse of the preliminary articles to the acceptance of Seniavin's additional articles has long eclipsed his previous achievements in 1808. Any praise that Cotton receives for rejecting Russian neutrality in the port of Lisbon must be tempered by the knowledge that he could have objected to the Convention of Cintra; of course, such an objection might have been ignored. Criticism of Cotton for the way in which Britain gained control of the Russian fleet was inconsequential compared to what would have been said had the Russian fleet remained untouched in the Tagus. Though some of Cotton's decisions regarding the conventions with the French and Russians might be considered questionable, they were rational considering the circumstances involved. Cotton's absence from a public inquiry and subsequent assignment to the Royal Navy's most challenging command were tacit signs that the British government approved of his overall performance as commander of His Majesty's ships and vessels on the Lisbon station.

NOTES

1. Michael Glover, *Britannia Sickens: Sir Arthur Wellesley and the Convention of Cintra* (London, 1970), 139.

2. Collingwood to Cotton, 30 December 1808, Cambridgeshire County Record Office, Cotton Naval Papers, 588/042.

3. *The Times* of London, 2, 17 September 1808; Richard M. Schneer, "Arthur Wellesley and the Cintra Convention: A New Look at an Old Puzzle," *Journal of British Studies* 19 (1980): 93–95; W.W. Pole to Cotton, 3 September 1808, PRO ADM 7/41.

4. Bligh to Cotton, 22 August 1808, Wellesley to Bligh, 22 August 1808, Cotton to Bligh, 23 August 1808, Cambridgeshire County Record Office, Cotton Naval Papers, 588/041/a48; Cotton to W.W. Pole, 23 August 1808, PRO ADM 7/41.

5. Cease Fire negotiated between Sir Arthur Wellesley and Lieutenant General Kellermann, 22 August 1808, in *Proceedings upon the Inquiry relative to the Armistice*

and Convention, &c. made and concluded in Portugal, in August 1808, between the Commanders of the British and French Armies [hereafter cited as *Proceedings*](London: House of Commons, 1809), 245.

6. Ibid., 57–58.

7. Ibid., 41.

8. Lieutenant General Hew Dalrymple, *Memoir of His Proceedings as Connected with the Affairs of Spain and the Commencement of the Peninsular War* (London, 1830), 65.

9. Wellesley to Castlereagh, 23 August 1808, Arthur Wellesley, Duke of Wellington, *The Dispatches of Field Marshal the Duke of Wellington, during His Various Campaigns in India, Denmark, Portugal, Spain, the Low Countries, and France, from 1799 to 1818* [hereafter cited as *Wellington's Dispatches*] (London, 1852), 3: 122–24.

10. Dalrymple to Cotton, 22 August 1808, Cambridgeshire County Record Office, Cotton Naval Papers, 588/041/a69.

11. Cotton to Dalrymple, 25 August 1808, *Papers, Presented to the House of Commons, Relative to the Russian Fleet in the Tagus, and to the Convention concluded with the Russian Admiral* [hereafter cited as *Papers*] (London, 1809), 2: 4.

12. Wellesley to Cotton, 25 August 1808, Arthur Wellesley, Duke of Wellington, *Supplementary Despatches, Correspondence, and Memoranda of Field Marshal Arthur Duke of Wellington, K.G.* [hereafter *Wellington's Supplementary Dispatches*] (London, 1858–1872), 6: 125–26.

13. Wellesley testimony, *Proceedings*, 60.

14. Ibid., 61.

15. Ibid.; Dalrymple to Murray, 25 August 1808, *Papers*, 2: 3.

16. Dalrymple to Junot, undated, *Papers*, 2: 4.

17. Wellesley testimony, *Proceedings*, 61; Dalrymple, *Memoir*, 67–68.

18. Murray to Cotton, 26 August 1808, Murray to Dalrymple, 26 August 1808, Cambridgeshire County Record Office, Cotton Naval Papers, 588/041/a70.

19. Ibid., Murray to Cotton, 26 August 1808.

20. Cotton to Murray, 26 August 1808, *Papers*, 2: 4–5.

21. Ibid., 2: 6, Dalrymple to Cotton, 28 August 1808.

22. Junot to Cotton, 26 August 1808, Cambridgeshire County Record Office, Cotton Naval Papers, 588/041/a78.

23. Cotton to Dalrymple, 25, 27 August, *Papers*, 2: 4–5.

24. Ibid., 2: 5, 6, Cotton to Dalrymple, 27 August 1808; Conventions of 28 and 30 August for the Evacuation of Portugal by the French Army, *Proceedings*, 7–10, 245–48.

25. Cotton to Dalrymple, 27 August 1808, *Papers*, 2: 5–6.

26. Ibid.

27. Ibid., 2: 6–7, Cotton to Dalrymple, 28 August 1808.

28. Ibid., 2: 6, Dalrymple to Cotton, 28 August 1808.

29. Dalrymple, *Memoir*, 69, 70.

30. Ibid., 71; Dalrymple testimony, *Proceedings*, 45.

31. Maximilien Sébastian Foy, *History of the War in the Peninsula* (London, 1827), 2: 533. According to Shapiro, Seniavin received instructions from the tsar in May 1808 to put his fleet at the disposition of the French. Junot threatened Seniavin with the anger of two emperors if he continued to ignore the Franco-Russian alliance. Seniavin desisted because he did not want to fight Portuguese and Spanish soldiers, with whom his

country was not at war. A. Shapiro, *Admiral Dmitri N. Seniavin* (Moscow, 1958), 265–68.

32. Seniavin to Cotton, 29 August 1808, *Papers*, 2: 7–8.

33. Dalrymple, *Memoir*, 71, 72; Dalrymple testimony, *Proceedings*, 45.

34. Ibid.

35. Cotton to Halsted, 29 August 1808, Cambridgeshire County Record Office, Cotton Naval Papers, 588/041/a71.

36. "Articles of a Convention entered into between Vice Admiral Seniavin Knight of the Order of St. Alexander and other Russian orders and Admiral Sir Charles Cotton, Baronet, for the Surrender of the Russian Fleet now Anchored in the River Tagus," Cambridgeshire County Record Office, Cotton Naval Papers, 588/041/a74-77. See also *Papers*, 1: 14.

37. Seniavin to Cotton, 2 September 1808, Papers, 2: 9.

38. Ibid, 2: 10, Seniavin to Cotton, 2 September 1808. On 22 August, the Supreme Governor of Oporto wrote a declaration for Seniavin that expressed a desire to reestablish "that good faith and harmony which subsisted between the two courts before the departure of His Royal Highness for Brazil." Seniavin probably used this declaration to justify his appeal for neutrality. "Declaration sent to the admiral of the Russian squadron in the port of Lisbon by the Supreme Governor at Oporto," 22 August 1808, PRO ADM 7/41.

39. Cotton to W.W. Pole, 3 September 1808, PRO ADM 7/41.

40. A Confidential Correspondent to the Marquis of Buckingham, undated, Duke of Buckingham and Chandos, ed., *Memoirs of the Court and Cabinets of George the Third* (London, 1855), 4: 255–57.

41. Junot to Cotton, 31 August 1808, Dalrymple to Cotton, 1 September 1808, Cotton to Junot, 1 September 1808, Cotton to Dalrymple, 1 September 1808, Cambridgeshire County Record Office, Cotton Naval Papers, 588/041/a72–73. No longer needing the Veteran Battalion's service in the Tagus, on 31 August Cotton sent it to Gibraltar by convoy with the *Scout*.

42. Dalrymple to Cotton, 4 September 1808, *Papers*, 2: 11.

43. Cotton to Dalrymple, 4 September 1808, Cambridgeshire County Record Office, Cotton Naval Papers, 588/041/a74-77. See also *Papers*, 2: 11.

44. Dalrymple, *Memoir*, 73.

45. Seniavin to Cotton, 4 September 1808, Cotton to Seniavin, 4, 6 September 1808, *Papers*, 2: 11–13. Cotton's remarks in his 6 September letter to Seniavin imply that a meeting took place between the admirals aboard the Tverdoi that day: "I much wish an officer may remain on board your ship, the reason for which I shall have the pleasure to explain when honoured with an interview; an honour I trust your health may be sufficiently renovated to permit this day."

46. Cotton to Seniavin, 4 September 1808, *Papers*, 2: 11–12. The Admiralty appointed Tyler as Cotton's second-in-command on 18 June 1808. Tyler replaced Rear Admiral William Albany Otway, who had served in this position since 4 February 1808. Cotton to W.W. Pole, 4 February 1808, PRO ADM 1/339; Admiralty to Cotton, 18 June 1808, Cotton to W.W. Pole, 5 July 1808, PRO ADM 7/41.

47. Donald D. Horward, "Portugal and the Anglo-Russian Naval Crisis, 1808," *Naval War College Review* 34 (1981): 67.

48. Cotton to W.W. Pole, 4 September 1808, PRO ADM 7/41. See also *Papers*, 1: 14–15.

49. Cotton to W.W. Pole, 8, 25 September 1808, PRO ADM 7/41.

50. Ibid., Cotton to W.W. Pole, 6 November 1808; Cotton to James Kennedy, 6 September 1808, PRO ADM 1/340.

51. Cotton to W.W. Pole, 12 December 1808, PRO ADM 1/340.

52. The Admiralty disapproved Cotton's decision to place British officers aboard the Portuguese vessels and ordered their immediate removal. However, the Admiralty was not fully aware of the conditions that prompted Cotton's decision. W.W. Pole to Cotton, 30 September 1808, Cotton to W.W. Pole, 7, 13, 29 September 1808, 11 October 1808, PRO ADM 7/41; Horward, "Anglo-Russian Naval Crisis," 67.

53. Cotton to W.W. Pole, 12 October 1808, PRO ADM 7/41.

54. Cotton to Tyler, 7 September 1808, PRO ADM 1/340.

55. W.W. Pole to Cotton, 30 September 1808, W.W. Pole to Tyler, 30 September 1808, Tyler to W.W. Pole, 7 October 1808, Cotton to W.W. Pole, 12 September 1808, PRO ADM 7/41; *The Times* of London, 11 October 1808; Louise King-Hall, ed., *Sea Saga, being the Naval Diaries of Four Generations of the King-Hall Family* (London, 1935), 31. As of a 30 October report by the *The Times* of London, Seniavin remained on his ship: "he does not mean to come on shore."

56. King-Hall, *Sea Saga*, 31-32; the British government also rejected the stipulation that promised to restore the Russian ships in the same state in which they arrived at Spithead. Lord Mulgrave to the King, 29 September 1808, Arthur Aspinall, ed., *The Later Correspondence of George III* (Cambridge, 1962–1970), 5: 137.

57. Cotton to W.W. Pole, 8 September 1808, PRO ADM 7/41; Charles William Chadwick Oman, *A History of the Peninsular War* (Oxford, 1902-1930), 1: 280.

58. Junot to Cotton, 8 September 1808, Cotton to Junot, 8[?]September 1808, Cambridgeshire County Record Office, Cotton Naval Papers, 588/041/a79; Paul Charles Thiébault, *The Memoirs of Baron Thiébault*, trans. Arthur John Butler (London, 1896), 2: 216.

59. Cotton to W.W. Pole, 16, 25 September 1808, 16 October 1808, PRO ADM 7/41; Return of French Troops on board the First, Second, and Third Division of Transports, *Proceedings*, 239–41.

60. Lieutenant Dickens to Lieutenant Garrett, 12 October 1808, received aboard the *Hibernia* 14 October 1808, Cambridgeshire County Record Office, Cotton Naval Papers, 588/041/a50.

61. Cotton to W.W. Pole, 29 September 1808, 10 October 1808, PRO ADM 7/41; Captain Richard Raggett of the *Africaine* to Captain T.R. Toker of the *Zebra*, 27 September 1808, PRO ADM 1/340; Thiébault, *Memoirs*, 2: 218; Oman, *Peninsular War*, 1: 284.

62. Castlereagh to Dalrymple, 17 September 1808, Robert Stewart Castlereagh, *Memoirs and Correspondence of Viscount Castlereagh, second Marquess of Londonderry*, ed. by his brother (London, 1848–1853), 6: 437–38.

63. Cotton to W.W. Pole, 10 October 1808, 5 November 1808, PRO ADM 7/41. Thiébault, *Memoirs*, 2: 230; *The Times* of London, 25 October 1808.

64. Cotton to W.W. Pole, 5 November 1808, PRO ADM 7/41.

65. Thiébault, *Memoirs*, 2: 217–30; *The Times* of London, 22 October 1808, 10 November 1808; Cotton to W.W. Pole, 14 December 1808, PRO ADM 7/41.

66. Cotton to W.W. Pole, 19 October 1808, 5, 12 December 1808, Cotton to Mulgrave, 5 December 1808, PRO ADM 7/41; four transports with part of the last remnant of the French army that sailed from the Tagus on 9 December returned

damaged later that month. Captain Peter Halkett to W.W. Pole, 26 December 1808, PRO ADM 1/340.

67. *The Times* of London, 16 September 1808.

68. Ibid., 17 September 1808.

69. W.W. Pole to Cotton, 17 September 1808, *Papers*, 1: 16; Cotton to W.W. Pole, 27 September 1808, PRO ADM 7/41.

70. Bickerton to Lady Cotton, 24 September 1808, Cambridgeshire County Record Office, Cotton Naval Papers, 588/c94.

71. George Canning to Henry Bathurst, Third Earl Bathurst, 16 September 1808, Henry Bathurst, Historical Manuscripts Commission, *Report on the Manuscripts of Earl Bathurst* (London, 1923), 75–76.

72. Ibid., 78-79, Mulgrave to Bathurst, undated, October [1808].

73. Dalrymple claimed that the Admiralty attempted to present to the House of Lords a "spurious" enclosure to Cotton's letter of 27 August 1808 addressed to himself; this paper made it appear that Cotton opposed the Convention. Dalrymple quickly produced the true enclosure, with Cotton's signature, which was published by the House on 9 February 1809. See Dalrymple, *Memoir*, 132–34.

74. Cotton to W.W. Pole, 18 November 1808, PRO ADM 7/41.

75. Collingwood to W.W. Pole, 26 August 1808, Mulgrave to Collingwood, 25 September 1808, G.L. Newnham Collingwood, ed., *Public and Private Correspondence of Vice-Admiral Lord Collingwood* (New York, 1829), 329–330, 335–36; Mulgrave to Bathurst, undated, October [1808], Bathurst, *Manuscripts of Earl Bathurst*, 78–79; Admiralty to Cotton, 23 November 1808, PRO ADM 2/155.

76. Thomas Grenville to William Wyndham, Lord Grenville, 8 November 1808, J.B. Fortescue, *Historical Manuscripts Commission, Report on the Manuscripts of J.B. Fortescue, Esq*. (London, 1915), 9: 239–41.

77. Captain Matthew Smith to Cotton, 15 December 1808, Cambridgeshire County Record Office, Cotton Naval Papers, 588/041/a51; Cotton to W.W. Pole, 4 November 1808, 12 December 1808, Cotton to Mulgrave, 5 December 1808, PRO ADM 7/41; Return of Disposable Transports in the River Tagus, 12 November 1808, PRO ADM 1/340; Oman, *Peninsular War*, 1: 500, 647.

78. Cotton to W.W. Pole, 9 January 1809, PRO ADM 7/41.

79. Halkett to W.W. Pole, 26, 27 December 1808, PRO ADM 1/340.

80. Henry N. Shore, "The Navy in the Peninsular War: The Battle of Corruna," *United Service Magazine* 168 (1913): 485–98; Donald D. Horward, "British Seapower and Its Influence upon the Peninsular War, 1808–1814," *Naval War College Review* 34 (1981): 57.

81. Cotton to W.W. Pole, 13, 15 December 1808, PRO ADM 7/41; Cradock to Castlereagh, 14 December 1808, British Library, J.W. Gordon Papers, ADD MSS 49487.

82. Admiralty to Cotton, 23 November 1808, PRO ADM 2/155; Cotton to W.W. Pole, 16 December 1808, PRO ADM 7/41.

83. Berkeley to Bathurst, 16 January 1808, Bathurst, *Historical Manuscripts Commission*, Earl Bathurst, 82–83; Cotton to W.W. Pole, 18, 19 December 1808, 9 January 1809, "Schedule of standing and unexecuted orders, letters, papers, &c delivered over by Admiral Sir Charles Cotton to Captain Peter Halkett of His Majesty's Ship Ganges, upon his being left in command of the Naval Force in the River Tagus," 20 December 1808, W.W. Pole to Cotton, 10 January 1809, PRO ADM 7/41; Cotton to

Halkett, 20 December 1808, PRO ADM 1/341. The Admiralty approved Cotton's order for Captain Halkett to wear a broad pendant until Berkeley's arrival in the Tagus.

84. Cotton to W.W. Pole, 9 January 1809 [six letters], 11 January 1809, W.W. Pole to Cotton, 10 January 1809, PRO ADM 7/41; *The Times* of London, 31 December 1808.

8

Succeeding Lord Collingwood: Cotton Takes Command of the Mediterranean Fleet, April–August 1810

> We are supporting all the weak and sickly states labouring under centuries of disease, and if we do not catch infection from some of them it will be well. Turkey is ricketty; Sicily is corrupt and has an inflammation in its bowels; Sardinia has lost the use of its limbs and Spain, though strong limbed and athletic in body, has a nervous head, which paralyzes the whole system. To this hospital of states we have to find crutches and plasters, anodynes and restorations; and I am afraid after all we shall get little credit for our cure.
>
> Collingwood to Cotton, 6 December 1809[1]

Admiral Cotton returned to Madingley within a week of leaving the *Hibernia*.[2] He likely met with Lord Mulgrave in London before proceeding home, but no evidence of such a meeting exists. The short duration of Cotton's stay in London implies that the government did not make an issue of his performance while stationed off Portugal. With the inquiry into the Convention of Cintra recently concluded and the government now concerned about the welfare of Sir John Moore's army, Cotton returned to his family and the management of his estate.

However, Madingley did not serve as a complete refuge from naval affairs; one unresolved matter in Portugal demanded Cotton's attention. The Russian ships *Yaroslav* and *Raphael*, left in the Tagus, had deteriorated significantly since Cotton's departure. Admiral Berkeley's letter of 1 March 1809 informed the Admiralty that after inspecting these ships "they were found so utterly unfit, and so very much decayed in every essential part of their frames as not to be seaworthy." This assessment of the vessels was inconsistent with Cotton's last report of their condition: "The caulking of the two Russian ships in the Tagus having been compleated [sic] on the 20th December, they were reported to be in a state to proceed to England in the spring of the year." Furthermore, Captain Halkett reported in late December 1808 that preparing the Russian ships for sea was an "easier task than [he] expected." Considering the disparity between the reports of Cotton, Halkett, and Berkeley, the Admiralty's main concern was about the British government's responsibility for the cost of maintaining the Russian ships. The Admiralty thus ordered Cotton to state the "grounds and conditions upon which the two Russian ships were left in the Tagus" and to confirm whether or not Seniavin was led to believe that the *Yaroslav* and *Raphael* had become the British government's responsibility, "their being delivered up with the others within six months after the conclusion of a peace" between Britain and Russia. Despite having never acceded to the additional article that stipulated maintenance of the Russian ships, the government nevertheless hoped that Cotton's reply would completely clear the British from any responsibility to spend money on the *Yaroslav* and *Raphael*.[3]

Although this inquiry was a nuisance, Cotton evidently sent a reply to London accompanied by copies of carpenter's reports. Regardless, the unsettled affair of the Russian vessels served only as a minor distraction to Cotton's business of managing the estate. Further Admiralty interruptions of Cotton's time at Madingley for the next year appear to have been few, if any. A letter from Admiral Collingwood in December 1809 suggests that Cotton had little concern for naval affairs during this period: "It is a good many weeks since I received your letter from Madingley and was glad to find you well, and enjoying yourself and the comfort of your family all round [sic] you. It is a scene I am a stranger to and almost give up the hope of ever seeing."[4] Ironically, Collingwood was the cause of Cotton's departure from this "scene," and Collingwood's intuition was right: He never did see his family again.

Essentially, Lord Mulgrave responded to Collingwood's request in 1808 for relief from the Mediterranean command by telling him that he was irreplaceable. Yet, the First Lord still gave Collingwood the authority to relinquish command and return to Britain. Mulgrave's appeal had the desired effect; Collingwood agreed to relinquish command of the Mediterranean Fleet "whenever it may be done with convenience."[5] Mulgrave's failure to realize the gravity of Collingwood's health and Collingwood's stubbornness and misguided sense of duty led to the admiral's premature death. Not until the progress of physical decline was irreversible did Collingwood put self-preservation above duty to king and country. On 3 March 1810 at Port Mahón, Minorca, Collingwood yielded control of the Mediterranean Fleet to rear admirals Sir George Martin and Sir Samuel Hood before proceeding to England aboard the *Ville de Paris*. He died at sea on the 7th.[6]

A few days after Collingwood's death, Lord Mulgrave received a letter from him that gave "so unfavourable an account of [Collingwood's] state of health" that the First Lord could no longer delay appointing a new commander in the Mediterranean. Unaware of Collingwood's death, Mulgrave ordered him home and nominated Cotton as his successor. On 10 March, the First Lord's application to the king stated:

Lord Mulgrave cannot hope in the person of any successor to supply the long experience and peculiar qualification of Lord Collingwood for that command; but in humbly submitting for your Majesty's decision the appointment of Admiral Sir Charles Cotton, Lord Mulgrave feels confident that the most unremitting attention and the most anxious zeal for your Majesty's service would be exerted by that officer if it should be your Majesty's pleasure that the command in the Mediterranean should be entrusted to him.[7]

The king approved Mulgrave's recommendation; this news soon reached an unsuspecting Cotton at Madingley.[8]

Cotton's memoir claimed that "many candidates high in family connections and powerful political interest" had sought the Mediterranean command, but that it was conferred on Cotton "unsought for and unasked."[9] Honored by the appointment to succeed Collingwood, Cotton must have known that he was the leading candidate for the Mediterranean command. Unknown are those who allegedly petitioned for the command, but only a few admirals on the active list ranked as high as Cotton in 1810. Of those with Cotton's same date of rank to vice admiral of the blue, only one, Charles Edmund Nugent, had a career judged distinguished enough to receive a memoir in James Ralfe's *Naval Biography of Great Britain*; however, Nugent refused to accept further professional employment after the promotion. Therefore, seniority, reputation, and patronage from the First Lord were the forces that propelled Cotton to the Mediterranean.[10]

Cotton's departure from Madingley must have been emotionally traumatic for his wife and four children because Admiralty policy specified a three-year duration for commanders of foreign stations. Nevertheless, he was again willing to sacrifice domestic life for the sake of naval service. He reported to London and acknowledged receipt on 10 April of his orders to relieve Lord Collingwood in the Mediterranean and assume command on that station. Two days later Cotton arrived at Portsmouth and hoisted his flag aboard the *Lively* frigate for passage to the Mediterranean.[11]

The scope and complexity of the Mediterranean command greatly exceeded that of any other offered by the Admiralty. Even Cotton's command of the squadron stationed off Lisbon seemed small and uncomplicated by comparison. The boundaries of the Mediterranean command extended 2,000 miles from the Dardanelles in the east to Cape St. Vincent in the west, including Cadiz. It encompassed the entire Mediterranean Sea, which could be divided conveniently into three major areas: the eastern basin from Sicily to Syria, the Adriatic Sea, and the western basin from Gibraltar to the strait between Sicily and Tunisia. Not only was the Mediterranean further away from London than from Portugal, it was bordered by several regions and states engaged in multiple disputes. Hence, the Mediterranean Fleet commander needed the skills and savvy of a diplomat as well as those of the naval profession; he needed to anticipate decisions made in London, several weeks away by packet ship. Collingwood remained in the Mediterranean for four years because he possessed these skills. Cotton had demonstrated an aptitude for diplomatic savvy and independent thinking in 1808, but only experience would determine if his abilities were adequate to replace Collingwood.[12]

Before Cotton sailed from Spithead, the British government had decided on a shift to the strategic defensive in the Mediterranean. This was prompted by the change in 1809 from Portland's to Spencer Perceval's ministry, as well as several other factors. Recently, the British army had suffered severe setbacks in Europe. The Walcheren expedition ended in September 1809 with 4,000 British soldiers dead from the fever and an erroneous claim as a successful strategic diversion from Napoleon's attack against Austria; Wellington's construction of the Lines of Torres Vedras and Marshal André Masséna's preparation for the third invasion of Portugal boded poorly for British fortunes in the Peninsula. Governing all of the ministry's military decisions was the issue of finance—the shortage of specie compelled Perceval to consider reductions in all theaters of war. However, by 1810, the Peninsular War had clearly become Britain's main effort against French hegemony in Europe. Though threats to British interests still existed in the Mediterranean, the government considered the naval and military forces present there sufficient to prevent a crisis from developing. It did not expect Cotton to implement major strategic initiatives in the Mediterranean but rather to maintain the status quo without diverting resources unnecessarily from military operations in Spain and Portugal.[13]

Nevertheless, the Mediterranean region remained a powder keg that required proactive measures and thoughtful leadership to prevent an explosion of instability. French troops on the Italian Peninsula threatened Sicily, where the king and queen of Naples ruled in exile from their court at Palermo. Marshal Joachim Murat, appointed King of Naples in July 1808 by Napoleon, was mobilizing to invade the island. Content that French troops in Naples diverted British attention from Portugal, Spain, and the Ionian Islands, Napoleon never fully supported Murat's invasion plan. The emperor's strategic diversion and Murat's tactical threat kept British attention focused on defending Sicily. Bound by treaty, the British had nearly 16,000 troops, commanded by Lieutenant General Sir John Stuart, garrisoned on the island for its defense in the spring of 1810. Less threatening were French schemes in the Levant. With defeat of Russia in 1807 and Austria in 1809, Napoleon acquired the Ionian Islands and the entire eastern coast of the Adriatic. However, British naval supremacy thwarted French efforts to gain a significant strategic advantage from these acquisitions. Despite abandoning plans for a large-scale operation in the Levant after 1808, Napoleon maintained several small troop detachments in the Ionian Islands. In October 1809, a British force led by Brigadier General Sir John Oswald captured the islands of Cephalonia, Zante, Ithaca, and Cerigo. British military offensives in the Ionians ended with Oswald's capture of Santa

Maura on 16 April 1810. Yet, a French garrison remained on Corfu to threaten Turkey, a British ally since January 1809.[14]

Russian naval activity in the Mediterranean ended on 10 March 1810, when Russian seamen marched out of Trieste after handing their vessels over to the French. Thereafter, naval conflict between Russia and Turkey was confined to the Danube and Black Sea. Meanwhile, French military advances into southern and eastern Spain attracted more of the Mediterranean Fleet's attention. On 5 February 1810, Marshal Claude Perrin Victor's corps laid siege to Cadiz, from where the Regency would attempt to exert its authority over Spain. In Catalonia, the French were marshaling their resources at Barcelona in preparation for a campaign to seize Tortosa and Tarragona. In addition, French and Algerian privateering along the Barbary coast presented an array of challenges for the Royal Navy.[15] Yet, Cotton's greatest concern would be at Toulon, where Vice Admiral Zacherie Jacques Allemand superseded Admiral Ganteaume as commander on 9 June 1810. The Toulon fleet was Napoleon's best means of advancing French schemes in the Mediterranean, whether in support of Murat's invasion of Sicily, as a convoy escort to Spain, or to attack British bases in the Balearic Islands, Malta, or elsewhere. Despite repeated failures at sea, Napoleon's resolve to use naval power to support French strategy remained firm. He told the Minister of War in July 1810: "I am going to have strong squadrons everywhere, in the Escaut, the Meuse, at the Texel, at Cherbourg, Brest, Lorient, in the roadsted of the Island of Aix, at Toulon, la Speizzia."[16] Though the Perceval ministry's emphasis on matters in the Mediterranean had decreased and enemy naval activity there had peaked during Collingwood's command, Cotton was entering a theater of war that still remained very active and was connected to Wellington's operations in Portugal and Spain.

At 11:00 a.m. on 28 April 1810, the 98-gun *Temeraire* fired a seventeen-gun salute as Cotton entered Cadiz harbor aboard the *Lively*.[17] He was greeted by Vice Admiral John Child Purvis and Rear Admiral Sir Francis Pickmore. Cotton brought Admiralty orders for Purvis' relief by Pickmore, who became one of three rear admirals under Cotton's command. While awaiting Cotton's arrival, Sir Samuel Hood commanded the squadron blockading Toulon, and Sir George Martin led the squadron based at Palermo. Pickmore wasted no time acquainting Cotton with the state of affairs. In addition to Britain's ten ships-of-the-line, a frigate, a sloop, a gun-brig, and four bomb vessels stationed at Cadiz, the Spaniards maintained ten ships-of-the-line and two frigates in the harbor.[18] The French establishment of new fortifications at Catalina and seizure of Fort Matagorda on 22 April placed the city within cannon range and forced the British and Spanish anchorage further into the harbor. In addition, the British believed that the French were about to capture the Spanish naval stores and ships-of-the-line at Carthagena. Consequently, Colonel Philip Roche, a British officer in the Spanish service, and Captain William Hargood of the *Northumberland* persuaded the authorities at Carthagena to send the 94-gun

San Carlos and 114-gun *Ferdinand VII* to Gibraltar. Although the French never seized Carthagena, Cotton received a report from Henry Wellesley, Minister Plenipotentiary to the Regency since 6 April, that Carthagena had probably fallen.[19]

As urgent as matters seemed at Cadiz, Cotton would have little direct influence over them. Cadiz was west of Gibraltar and maintained a closer administrative and logistical link to Admiral Berkeley's squadron at Lisbon than with the Mediterranean Fleet based at Port Mahón.[20] Furthermore, dependence on Cotton's judgment concerning politically sensitive issues was unnecessary with the presence of Henry Wellesley and Lieutenant General Thomas Graham, commander of British military forces at Cadiz. In addition, Pickmore's communication with the Admiralty would experience delays of several additional weeks if processed through Cotton in the Mediterranean. He thus instructed Pickmore: "You must be guided by such events as they occur, in concert with His Majesty's Minister and the Commanding British Military Officer at Cadiz, with whom I depend upon your most cordial co-operation in every incidental circumstance. . . . And you will make frequent communications to me on the Rendezvous of the squadron in the Mediterranean, and also to the Secretary of the Admiralty."[21]

After perusing dispatches that related to events in the Mediterranean, Cotton found "nothing very material to make known to Their Lordships" except extracts of letters from Rear Admiral Martin that addressed "the apprehension of attacks being made on Sardinia and Sicily."[22] Intelligence received by Captain William Hoste of the *Amphion* suggested that the combined French naval forces at Ancona and Venice—four frigates, nine brigs, and a schooner—were preparing to sail to Tarentum for an attack on Sicily; 45,000 French troops were reported assembling in Naples. Another matter that Cotton found "material" for the Admiralty was the condition of his fleet. Many vessels were in a defective state, and he perceived a shortage of ships-of-the-line and frigates. Consequently, Cotton sent Purvis to Spithead in the frigate *Leda* instead of the *Atlas*, which was in dire need of repair and had some crew to whom four or five years of pay were due. Cotton also ordered the *Hibernia*, his flagship in 1808, and the *Northumberland* to Spithead because of their defects. The size and condition of his fleet was a constant source of concern for the next year.[23]

As directed by the Admiralty, on 30 April Cotton moved from the *Lively* to the *San Josef*, which had been his flagship from 1803 to 1806 while serving in the Channel Fleet.[24] Administrative affairs kept Cotton occupied for the next few days at Cadiz. Among other matters, he reported to Admiral Berkeley at Lisbon the presence at sea of three frigates and a brig, believed to be Algerian; in response to a request from Henry Wellesley, Cotton promised the squadron's support for a *dos de mayo* celebration in Cadiz; and by the passage of the *Black Joke* lugger, Cotton took the opportunity to acquaint Robert Adair, the British ambassador to Constantinople, of his arrival in the Mediterranean. In conjunction with the *dos de mayo* celebration, Cotton met with the Junta of Cadiz on 2 May. The junta wanted the *San Carlos* and *Ferdinand VII* to proceed from Gibraltar to Mahón for greater security. The ships were not wanted in Cadiz because the city was over-populated and a sufficient naval force already existed.[25]

Upon concluding his affairs at Cadiz, Cotton proceeded on 3 May to join the squadron blockading Toulon. The next morning he stopped briefly at Gibraltar and found the *San Carlos* and *Ferdinand VII* at anchor. Cotton informed Commodore Manuel de Posada, whose flag flew on *Ferdinand VII*, of the Junta of Cadiz's intentions and authorized him to draw on British stores at Gibraltar. Cotton then received more disconcerting news about the condition of his fleet. In addition to physical defects, his ships were reported short of young boys, who usually amounted to between six and ten percent of a ship's company. They served primarily as officer's servants, but some were needed to work aloft on the topgallant and royal yards. With an unfavorable first impression of his fleet's condition, Cotton wanted, before rushing to conclusions, to examine its latest returns. These he would see upon arrival at Cape St. Sebastian off Catalonia, the winter rendezvous for the squadron blockading Toulon.[26]

Before leaving Gibraltar, Cotton received a request from the governor, Major General Colin Campbell, to establish a permanent light squadron for protection of the local sea ports and the garrisons at Gibraltar and Cueta. Campbell was anxious because the French controlled most of the Andalusian coast. Cotton agreed to commit the brig-sloop *Roman* to this service and directed Pickmore to send whatever vessels he could spare to Gibraltar. Finally, Cotton surveyed the nature of different services at Gibraltar. Consequently, he established a few new regulations for guidance of the port's senior naval officer and confirmed Collingwood's instructions to the resident agent of transports. Finally, the *San Josef* weighed anchor from Gibraltar on 6 May for the last leg of Cotton's passage to the Mediterranean.[27]

Instead of Cape St. Sebastian off the Catalonian coast, Cotton arrived on 14 May at the summer rendezvous, Cape Sicie near Toulon. After the traditional cannon salute, the *San Josef* joined Admiral Hood and the fleet, comprised of nine ships-of-the-line, a frigate, and a brig.[28] Assumption of command required a considerable period of time for a new commander to establish his authority and become familiar with everything within his sphere of responsibility. This process required several weeks for Cotton as information trickled to the rendezvous from Spain, Sicily, Sardinia, the Barbary coast, the Ionian Islands, Turkey, and Egypt. For instance, the latest report from Captain George Eyre in the Ionian Islands indicated that the Santa Maura expedition failed, when it in fact had succeeded a month earlier.

Meanwhile, the squadron off Toulon required Cotton's immediate attention. After conferring with Hood, he wrote to the victualling agent at Mahón about the urgency of immediately sending bread, flour, lemon juice, water, and wine to the fleet. If these items were not available at Minorca or Malta, Cotton authorized the agent to acquire them through unofficial channels at Sicily, as suggested by Admiral Martin.[29] An examination of additional reports provided by Hood confirmed the presumption Cotton formed at Cadiz. He informed the Admiralty in a secret dispatch on 21 May:

> I beg leave to call the attention of Their Lordships to the want of vessels of all descriptions, no less for the purpose of strengthening the different detachments of the fleet than for relieving others which Their Lordships will see require the same from their defective state. An increase of small vessels is particularly desirable at this time, more effectually to prevent the coasting trade which the enemy must necessarily establish in this quarter for supplying their forces on the coast, and which appears to be carried on to no small extent in every direction occupied by the French Army.[30]

Although the Mediterranean fleet enjoyed naval supremacy, it could not eliminate the French coastal trade. Convoys were able to shelter beneath a protective network of coastal batteries located along the shorelines of France and her allies. About 4,000 gun carriages were included in this network around Europe, with an excess of 110 cannon around Toulon.[31] Napoleon wanted to secure the coastal trade because it provided succor for his armies and facilitated his naval buildup. It was especially critical for French military operations in Catalonia, where the rugged terrain rendered overland supply very difficult and susceptible to guerrilla attacks. Before Cotton's arrival, the French and British were already deeply engaged in maritime maneuvers between Toulon and Catalonia. After allowing a French convoy of twenty-one vessels to reach Barcelona in April 1809, Collingwood set a trap for the next effort. In October 1809, a reduced British naval presence off Toulon enticed a convoy with at least twenty-seven vessels to depart Toulon, while the bulk of Collingwood's fleet waited off the southeast coast of France. After the British fleet dispersed the convoy, eleven French vessels were either captured or destroyed. Following this debacle, the French scaled down their coastal supply efforts to Spain. However, the coastal trade remained as important for Cotton's fleet to interdict as it did for the Toulon Fleet to protect. On 21 May, Cotton received information that the French at Toulon were again preparing to send a supply convoy to Barcelona.[32]

Intelligence gathered on 2 June by the frigate *Repulse* estimated twelve ships-of-the-line and eight frigates in the port of Toulon. Foregoing any losses, the size of the Toulon Fleet was expected to increase because of the shipyard there. Within Napoleon's empire, only Antwerp built more ships than Toulon, with construction peaking in 1811.[33] Cotton's anxiety about the size and condition of his fleet was no doubt increased by the growing size of the Toulon Fleet and Admiral Allemand's perceived willingness to use it. Considered "one of the most disagreeable men of his generation," he kept his fleet as active as the British blockade would allow by exercising it within and just beyond the harbor.[34] Allemand remained ever ready for strong gales to open the blockade, thus allowing the Toulon Fleet to escape unmolested.

Cotton learned from several reports that French naval activity in the Mediterranean went well beyond the port of Toulon. From the coast of Naples came Captain Jahleel Brenton's account of an engagement with a French squadron. Having chased the *Ceres* frigate, *Fame* corvette, *Le Sparviene* brig, and *Achilles* cutter into the mole of Naples on 2 May, Brenton's *Spartan* and Captain George Ayscough's *Success* patiently waited in the outer harbor. Uncharacteristically aggressive the next morning, the French squadron, reinforced by eight gunboats, headed in a close line directly for the British frigates. The battle lasted for two hours, with the frigates "exchanging broadsides when within pistol shot." Fortunately for the French, all their vessels except *Le Sparviene* avoided capture because they reached the protection of shore batteries.[35] Later, boats from Ayscough's *Success* and the *Espoir* sloop destroyed three small vessels and a battery near Castiglione, Calabria; Brenton subsequently led these warships in the capture of four vessels from under French batteries at Terracina.[36] Additional accounts reached Cotton from Sir William Hoste in the Adriatic. During the months of April, May, and June, Hoste's *Amphion*, the *Active*, and the *Cerberus*, all frigates, captured or destroyed forty-six vessels. Hoste claimed that the capture of one prize made the French commandant at Fiume "shed tears of rage at our impudence."[37]

These rousing exploits, and several others, contrasted sharply with the tedious blockade that Cotton supervised after the *San Josef* arrived at Cape Sicie in May until docking at Port Mahón in October. Because of the weather, however, the tedium was occasionally interrupted by periods of anxiety regarding the Toulon Fleet's whereabouts. After strong northwesterly gales began on 15 July, the main body of the British fleet was eventually blown east of Villafranca while the inshore squadron clung tenuously to the blockade. Upon returning to the rendezvous, Cotton learned that a division of the Toulon Fleet had come out of port on the 20th. These six ships-of-the-line and four frigates apparently intended to secure the safety of a convoy sailing from Bandol to Toulon. Though the convoy reached Toulon unmolested, the French warships sought an engagement with the frigate *Euryalus* and brig *Shearwater*, which had become isolated from the ships-of-the-line *Warspite*, *Conqueror*, and *Ajax*. The British ships-of-the-line, however, arrived in time to engage the French division and save their frigate and brig. An anxious commander-in-chief returned to Cape Sicie on the 24th to find the Toulon Fleet still in port. This experience reminded Cotton that the Royal Navy could not indefinitely contain the Toulon Fleet and that, inevitably, Allemand could exploit such opportunities in the future. Moreover, the heavy gales emphasized the importance of having a nearby anchorage, such as Port Mahón.[38]

Port Mahón was only 220 miles from Toulon, a third the distance to Gibraltar or Malta, and was centrally located in the western basin of the Mediterranean. From this port sailed vessels with bullocks, sheep, water casks, and other essentials needed to sustain Cotton's blockade of Toulon. Reliance on the distant facilities at Gibraltar or Malta would have increased the Mediterranean Fleet's vulnerability. Since the Anglo-Spanish transition from enemies to allies in June 1808, the Royal Navy enjoyed the use of Port Mahón's facilities and resources. Unfortunately, this privilege appeared threatened when Cotton arrived in the Mediterranean. On 1 and 2 March, an "immense number" of Minorquins at Mahón rebelled by forcing the Spanish authority to suspend the election of deputies for the Cortes.[39] They also suppressed the royal duties of the custom-house. In letters to his brother, Viscount Wellington, Henry Wellesley described the "dreadful state" of the Balearic Islands because of the "perpetual insurrections."[40] Admiral Pickmore recommended to Henry Wellesley on 15 May: "The island of Minorca should be immediately garrisoned by two or three regiments of Spanish troops. This measure would cause the port of Mahon to be most desirable for the fleet, and would probably remove one of the strong temptations which attract the French to the siege of Cadiz."[41]

Cotton already understood the tension between Spanish authority and the people when he received a letter from Major General Luis de Villava, the Spanish governor of Minorca. Villava welcomed Cotton to the Mediterranean and was pleased that "so glorious and famous an admiral should be the strong shield of these seas."[42] In addition, Cotton received a letter from the Jurat of Mahón apologizing for the behavior of "a blind multitude of people" during the March insurrection. The jurat had heard that a body of Spanish troops would soon arrive at Minorca to "inflict the most severe punishment" on those guilty of insurrection.[43] To prevent Spanish retribution, the jurat sought Cotton's intervention. However, the admiral refused to interfere with civil affairs on Minorca. He did mollify the jurat, however, by stating that their fear of retribution was groundless; Spanish troops destined for Minorca were for the purpose of protecting them "from the tyranny and persecution so fatally experienced by their countrymen on the Continent."[44]

No assurance of domestic tranquillity by the jurat, however, could relieve Cotton's concern about political instability at Mahón. With the *San Carlos* and *Ferdinand VII* from Gibraltar and the 74-gun *San Paobla* and *Solidad* frigate from Carthagena expected to arrive soon in the Balearics, Cotton anticipated further cause for unrest. He believed that Villava would have to levy additional taxes to support the crews of these ships, which would exacerbate the ongoing grain shortage in the islands. Even if remotely possible, Cotton wanted to minimize the chance of losing the British anchorage at Mahón. He explained in a private letter to the First Lord:

> The Spanish government have no disposable troops to secure the possession of the islands and enforce their authority. The harbour is of the greatest consequence to us. The stores and provisions there, the facility with which two or three ships refit and compleat occasioning for the service off Toulon, or the whole squadron when driven

from their station by bad weather finding shelter and completing at once, are objects that can only be secured by a British garrison occupying the island for war, with the consent of the Spanish government.[45]

Considering historical Spanish reluctance to allow British troops on their soil and the British government's attempts to transfer its troops out of the Mediterranean, fulfillment of Cotton's request seemed unlikely. In addition, Lord Mulgrave resigned from the Admiralty Board in April because of poor health and was replaced by Charles Philip Yorke. Though Mulgrave remained in the cabinet as Master General of Ordnance, Cotton had lost his greatest patron on the Admiralty Board. In a July letter to Cotton, Mulgrave expressed satisfaction that he had been an "instrument of your being placed in a situation to do so much service to your country, and I even hereby assure you that though I shall no longer have to share officially in your glories if the enemy should afford you an opportunity of meeting him, I shall nevertheless equally rejoice in any event which may be gratifying to you."[46] Cotton hoped that he would receive the quality of support from Yorke that he did from Mulgrave.

Factors other than political strife in the Balearics seemed to menace the security of Port Mahón. After departing Carthagena on 21 May under escort of Captain Charles Adam's 74-gun *Invincible*, the *San Paobla* and *Solidad* disembarked at Palma 300 Spanish troops commanded by General Gregorio Garcia de La Cuesta, infamous among the British for his performance with Arthur Wellesley at the Battle of Talavera in July 1809. The aged general was retiring to a post of little relative significance. The Spanish warships then proceeded to Mahón. Besides upsetting the Minorquins, Cotton worried that the Spanish warships would make Mahón a more alluring objective for the French. The presence of French naval forces at Toulon and Corsica made a *coup de main* in the Balearics possible. In fact, Napoleon authorized an expedition to rescue French prisoners on the island of Cabrera, about seven miles south of Majorca.[47]

The island of Cabrera, small and inhospitable, provided no sustenance for survival; the French prisoners were completely dependent on their jailers for the essentials of life. It was estimated that only 3,389 of 16,000 Frenchmen imprisoned at Cabrera during the war survived, yet only about 4,000 were on the island in 1810.[48] Cotton commented in a letter to the Admiralty that many of the prisoners had not a "vestige of clothing to cover their nakedness."[49] Though they were prisoners of the Spanish, Cotton ordered the collection of extra clothing from the ships off Toulon for distribution on the island. The fleet contributed 1,733 trousers, 780 shirts, 199 kersey and guernsey jackets, and nine kersey waistcoats valued at £622. Captain Nisbet Palmer of the sloop *Alacrity* delivered the clothing on 7 June and also collected mail for delivery to France. Perhaps because of Cotton's insistence to the Junta of Majorca, about 900 prisoners left Cabrera in August and sailed for Gibraltar. Admiral

Pickmore ordered several British transports there to receive them for a passage to Britain under escort of the *Hydra* frigate.[50]

Aware of the deplorable conditions at Cabrera and that it was guarded by only a couple Spanish gunboats and a British sloop, the French general Charles Antoine Morand appealed to Napoleon for a rescue attempt. Napoleon considered sending from Corsica three fast frigates, a landing force of 600 troops, and transports with a capacity for 2,000 prisoners. However, the expedition was canceled. It demonstrated the French willingness, yet inability, to launch an attack in the western basin of the Mediterranean.[51]

As the *San Josef* cruised off Toulon for the third straight month, Cotton became more suspicious of a French expedition to Majorca than to Cabrera. He wrote to the First Lord on 19 August: "In Majorca I have every reason to believe there is a strong French interest. The Minorquins are certainly more attached to us than either the French or Spaniards, but there is no force in either island to prevent their being carried by a coup de main, and with a very small force. Their situation is pretty well known to the French. There is a constant and regular intercourse between Marseille and the islands, under Algerine colours."[52]

Intelligence received from Spain in September reinforced Cotton's concern about Majorca. A "trusty" person from Brussels informed General Henry O'Donnell, commander of Spanish troops in Catalonia, that twelve ships-of-the-line at Rotterdam and Hamburg were destined for an attack on Majorca.[53] Although this report was specious, increased naval activity at Toulon hinted strongly at an expedition and kept Cotton guessing about French intentions. The number of enemy ships reported ready for sea on 1 August from the ports of Toulon, Genoa & Leghorn, Naples & Gaeta, Ancona, Venice, Trieste, and Corfu had been nine ships-of-the-line, fourteen frigates, thirteen corvettes, brigs, or schooners, and 142 gunboats, not including vessels fitting for sea or in dock.[54] Nine ships-of-the-line and four frigates were reported in the outer roads of Toulon, while the rest remained at the inner harbor fitting to sail. Cotton predicted that fifteen French ships-of-the-line would be ready in Toulon by October. With the gales of autumn and winter, he expected that "opportunities must be afforded them to come out and move either east or west as they wish."[55] Consequently, Cotton decided that the fleet would not move to the winter rendezvous at Cape St. Sebastian, but "preserve a station as near Cape Sicie as circumstances of wind and weather will admit."[56]

In the midst of controlling naval operations in the Mediterranean theater, Cotton's authority extended to several diplomatic affairs as well. Most intriguing of them all was a plot to rescue Pope Pius VII, held captive at Savona by the French. When informed on 3 June by Admiral Martin of the plot, Cotton considered it a "politic measure" and allowed it to progress unimpeded. Yet, when informed of the mission's failure on 26 July, he announced to the Admiralty that failure "had been foreseen and predicted." Why, then, did Cotton not oppose the mission from the beginning? The

Spanish minister at Palermo applied to William Pitt, Lord Amherst, British minister at court of Palermo, for a British warship to accompany a Spanish corvette to Savona, where the pope was unguarded and allegedly seeking to escape. Amherst agreed to support the Spaniards without his government's approval because George Canning had favored a similar plot in June 1808. The Spanish minister wanted to bring the pope to Alicante or any other secure part of Spain, where his presence "might rouse the inhabitants to make fresh exertions" against the French. Minorca and Sicily were other destinations if Pius refused to land in Spain.[57]

On 2 May, Lord Amherst ordered Admiral Martin to cooperate with the Spaniards. Martin immediately instructed Captain Charles Kempthorne Quash of the sloop *Eclair* to proceed with the Spanish corvette to the Maddalena Islands off Sardinia, where the person favoring the pope's escape would join the warships. Once off Savona, Quash would then "use every means in [his] power" to help the agent affect the pope's escape. The *Eclair* and Spanish corvette sailed from Palermo on 6 May, but after arriving off Savona, the person entrusted with the mission decided not to land. This was a wise decision because the pope would have refused to flee, as he did in 1809. He did not want to give Napoleon a pretext to provoke a schism in the Church. Cotton's reaction to this affair provides a subtle glimpse of his character. Remonstration against Amherst's decision would have accomplished nothing positive since Quash was already underway. Besides, Cotton's lack of familiarity with diplomatic affairs in the Mediterranean at the time was a logical reason to rely on the judgment of Amherst and Martin. As June progressed into July, Cotton probably learned of earlier attempts to rescue the pope and came to understand the pope's logic for not fleeing from captivity. Cotton emerges from this affair as an officer not prone to react to an urgent situation without first considering its consequences in detail.[58]

Cotton's most perplexing diplomatic challenge came from Algiers. It provided the fleet with fresh beef and grain and maintained a substantial naval presence in the Mediterranean. For pragmatic reasons, Cotton needed to maintain cordial relations with Algiers. Not surprisingly, the Dey, Sedi Hay Aly Bascia, had remained neutral in the war against France and allowed French privateers to carry British prizes into his ports. However, Henry Blanckley, British proconsul at Algiers, reported on 20 May to Rear Admiral Hood that the Dey was "inclined to favor" the British, but was prevented from ousting French privateers from his ports while his own vessels and subjects were in French ports.[59] Meanwhile, John Bennett, Master of Lloyds, had notified Lord Liverpool, Secretary for War and the Colonies, of the problem in Algiers. The King's Advocates determined that the Dey's practice of allowing French privateers with British prizes into his ports was in violation of the Treaty of Tripoli of 1762. Liverpool then sent instructions to Blanckley and Cotton to "make due remonstrance against the continuance of such a practice."[60]

Cotton received subsequent instructions from the Admiralty to help Blanckley persuade the Dey to sign a truce with Portugal and to inquire about British fishing rights upon the banks of the Algerine coast. The state of war existing between Portugal and Algiers had resulted in the captivity of many Portuguese seamen, whose miserable plight was well-known in Lisbon. Charles Stuart, the British ambassador to Portugal, also noted that most Portuguese ships were insured in London. The Regency of Portugal finally responded to the crisis by sending an envoy, Admiral Searnischia.[61] On 6 July, the Dey and Searnischia negotiated a two-year truce and arranged for the gradual redemption of 615 Portuguese captives, whose ransom was set at 642,857 Spanish dollars.[62] Before receiving confirmation of the truce, Cotton dispatched Captain George Dundas to Algiers in compliance with the Admiralty's dispatches regarding French privateers, Portuguese captives, and British fishing rights. Furthermore, Cotton instructed Dundas to conclude with the Dey "any treaty . . . to establish firmly the procuring of supplies for the service of His Majesty's fleet in the Mediterranean free of duties."[63] Dundas' frigate *Euryalus* departed the fleet off Toulon on 5 August.

Underscoring the urgency of Dundas' mission was the capture of the *Black Joke* lugger by two French privateers on 1 July. The privateers subsequently had taken the lugger into the port of Algiers. This event proved the inaccuracy of a report sent to Cotton by Captain Murray Maxwell that the Dey had declared war against France on 29 May. Cotton was particularly concerned about the *Black Joke* because its capture further delayed his communication with the Admiralty—his dispatches had missed the June packet from Malta.[64] The lugger also contained dispatches from Adair in Constantinople. Upon arrival at Algiers on 13 August, Dundas learned of the Algerine-Portuguese truce and that a state of war did not exist between Algiers and France. He immediately joined Blanckley, and they submitted their grievances to the Dey. Regarding French privateers, the Dey disagreed with the British interpretation of the treaty of 1762 but agreed to eject all French privateers and the French vice-consul from Oran. Furthermore, he issued an order that no privateer from any Christian nation could sail out of his ports to capture prizes. But if a capture were made before entering his ports, then he must accede to the treaties that he had made with the French. This was not a perfect solution for the British, but it would significantly hamper French privateering along the African coast.[65]

Dundas learned that Blanckley had arranged a contract for the coral fishery in 1806, but that no boats had resorted to this trade in 1810 because of enemy privateers and the alleged enslavement of a crew by the Bey of Tunis. Dundas recommended that a small armed vessel attend the fishery as protection against privateers and to prevent vessels from fishing on the banks without licenses. Finally, Dundas resolved the issue regarding procurement of supplies for the fleet, but not entirely to his satisfaction. He returned to the fleet off Toulon on 3 September. After reviewing Dundas' report, Cotton exclaimed to the

Admiralty: "I have much satisfaction in saying that the professions of the Dey of Algiers in favor of England appear to be in every respect consistent with the ancient alliance between the two nations."[66] Cotton then dispatched the sloop *Nautilus* to cruise the coast of Africa. Despite the apparent success of Dundas' mission, the Dey continued to distract Cotton. He refused to supply the *Nautilus* with livestock, claiming that only Oran or Bona could furnish them; Algerine warships captured a British merchant schooner and transport in the Atlantic because they did not carry Mediterranean passes; and an Algerine frigate hoisted English colors in the port of Pantelleria before capturing several men and bringing them in slavery to Algiers.[67]

While diplomatic relations with the Dey of Algiers appeared muddled, those with the Sublime Porte at Constantinople were more coherent. On 23 August, Cotton received aboard the *San Josef* Sir Robert Adair, who was on his way to England after closing the British embassy in Constantinople. Recently, French diplomatic and military interest in the region had waned as Napoleon focused more on affairs in central Europe and Spain. Adair considered "our peace with the Turks to be as secure as the uncertain state of Europe will admit." He had "no fear whatsoever from French artifice, intrigue, or menace so long as Spain [held] out and Austria [kept] aloof from a more strict alliance with Bonaparte."[68] Though believing that the current Anglo-Ottoman relationship obviated the need for a British ambassador in Constantinople, Adair nevertheless left Stratford Canning "in the character" of Minister Plenipotentiary to the Ottoman government.

Yet, Adair brought to Cotton's attention the Ottoman government's refusal to recognize the right claimed by Britain to search neutral vessels. The French were conducting an "immense trade" under the Ottoman flag in the Levant, which compelled searches of all Ottoman vessels by the Royal Navy. These searches injured Ottoman pride; the Ottoman government retaliated by threatening to declare the archipelago, drawing a line from the Morea to Egypt, a closed sea. Adair dealt with the threat by reminding the Turks that they had allowed, without opposition, French privateers to violate their neutrality by fitting out and commissioning in the harbor of Constantinople.[69] Adair's tactic diverted the Turks but did not resolve the issue of British searches. Before departing the *San Josef*, Adair suggested that Cotton issue special instructions for the officers stationed at Corfu and Smyrna "to be as forbearing as possible to the Ottoman flag."[70]

Cotton concluded that nothing appeared necessary to do on his part except issue special instructions according to Adair's guidance. In a general order, Cotton directed that "great moderation be observed in the exercise of our maritime rights in the seas and coasts adjacent to the Turkish empire; and that as much forbearance as possible be used towards vessels under the Ottoman flag that may be met with and suspected of carrying on a trade injurious to the rights and interests of the British nation, as it may affect commerce for the benefit of the common enemy."[71] This order did not completely stabilize affairs in the Levant. The viceroy of Egypt's refusal to admit any European vessels into the western harbor of Alexandria hindered British commerce and eliminated the sea port as a place of refuge during inclement weather. By direction of the Admiralty, Cotton ordered Admiral Martin on 28 July to send a competent frigate captain to Egypt to resolve the crisis. Before the frigate captain's arrival, however, the crisis had abated when the viceroy agreed to allow two ships of war and two merchantmen to enter the western harbor simultaneously. The British proconsul, Peter Schutz, considered the viceroy's decision "contrary to the spirit . . . of amity with the Sublime Porte" and would only accept it with Cotton's consent.[72]

Of affairs to the eastward, the situation at Alexandria probably seemed of minor consequence to Cotton when compared to naval operations in the Ionian Islands. On 2 September, Cotton prescribed new instructions for the senior officer off Corfu and its vicinity. Captain George Eyre had led British naval forces during the combined operation against Santa Maura the previous April and had since been blockading Corfu, which was garrisoned by "between 4 & 5,000 regulars, chiefly Italian, and between 2 & 3,000 Albanians"; a smaller British force commanded by General Oswald garrisoned Santa Maura.[73] In addition to the naval force off Corfu, Cotton ordered Eyre to assume command of Captain Hoste's squadron in the Adriatic. This consolidation simplified control of naval forces east of Sicily and had no material effect on Hoste's operations against French commerce in the Adriatic. Cotton's instructions further emphasized the importance of blockading Corfu and directed Eyre to station a sloop off the island of Lissa. Considering the vacuum of British influence in the Levant created by the British embassy's termination in Constantinople, Cotton wanted Eyre to assist the Vizier Ali Pacha of Janine's efforts to oppose French aggression on Ottoman territory and dependencies. Finally, Cotton advised Eyre to be prepared for an expedition by the Toulon Fleet to the eastward that fall or winter.[74] With the exception of this possibility, British naval dominance east of Sicily seemed assured for the remainder of Cotton's Mediterranean command. Consequently, the eastern basin and Adriatic increasingly became strategically irrelevant as Murat postured for his attack on Sicily and the Mediterranean Fleet's contribution to the Peninsular War became more urgent.

Meanwhile, the Admiralty had restructured subordinate commands within the Mediterranean Fleet. Rear Admiral Sir Richard Keats had arrived at Cadiz on 27 July to relieve Pickmore after only three months in command. The Admiralty apparently believed that Keats could be more effective than Pickmore in negotiating with the Spaniards. The relief affronted Pickmore, who voiced his disappointment to the First Lord. As a formality, Yorke later expressed his approval of Pickmore's performance. Nonetheless, after his relief, Pickmore proceeded in the *Temeraire* to replace Sir Samuel Hood in the Mediterranean; the Admiralty finally honored Hood's request to return to England because of poor health. Other appointments included Commodore

Charles Vinicombe Penrose and rear admirals Charles Boyles and Thomas Francis Fremantle. Penrose fulfilled a need recognized by Cotton and the Admiralty for greater naval security at Gibraltar; he arrived at Gibraltar in September to command the flotilla gathering there. The Admiralty ordered Boyles to assume duty as port admiral at Malta and place himself under Cotton's orders. He proceeded from Britain aboard McKinley's *Lively*, which wrecked at Malta on 10 September upon a reef of rocks dividing the bays of St. Pauls and Saline.[75] Leaving command of the royal yacht *William and Mary* because of his recent promotion, Rear Admiral Fremantle joined the fleet off Toulon in September and hoisted his flag aboard the *Ville de Paris*. He assumed command of the fleet's lee division while Hood remained commander of the weather division.[76]

The first five months of Cotton's command presented an array of problems, made more complicated by the vast jurisdiction of the Mediterranean Fleet. As during Collingwood's tenure, the blockade of Toulon remained the focal point of deterrence. Though Cotton inherited Collingwood's system of blockade, he deserves credit for maintaining its strength during a period when the Admiralty's attention was diverted to Wellington's defense of Portugal at the Lines of Torres Vedras. Cotton's continual presence with the fleet for five months off Toulon encouraged his subordinate commanders and left no doubt among the French that the blockade was his foremost concern. His management of the Toulon blockade, however, proved less challenging than management of the entire fleet. The incumbent administrative duties of courts-martial, promotions, fleet maintenance and supply, and reports to the Admiralty were more excessive than those Cotton experienced in 1808. Unlike the Tagus command, Cotton had three subordinate admirals in the Mediterranean, each of whom believed that his requests deserved highest priority. Warships were needed not only at Toulon, Cadiz, and Palermo but also for service in the Adriatic, at Gibraltar, and off Corfu, Sardinia, Catalonia, the Barbary coast, and Cabrera, not to mention as protection for trade convoys against the numerous privateers lurking in the Mediterranean.

Administrative challenges and the perceived shortage of warships did not prove detrimental to the Mediterranean Fleet's ability to execute Cotton's orders. The occasional capture of allied vessels by privateers and the French continuance of the coastal trade were unavoidable, but they were acceptable as long as the French did not embark on a major expedition in the Mediterranean. Viewed in context of the entire European theater, Cotton's first five months in command appeared unremarkable because of the defensive strategic posture assumed by the British in the Mediterranean. Cotton's job was to win by not losing, which attracts neither attention nor praise. Fortunately, little promise of recognition did not deter the efforts of Cotton or his subordinates. Cotton's fleet continued enforcing British policy in the Mediterranean, albeit without causing as much anxiety in London as in the recent past.

NOTES

1. Collingwood to Cotton, 6 December 1809, Cambridgeshire County Record Office, Cotton Naval Papers, 588/042.

2. Ibid., 588/c75. In a letter written on 17 January from London, Lord St. Vincent expressed regret that he missed Cotton before his return to Madingley. St. Vincent also advised Cotton to visit a spa to relieve his "rheumatics." St. Vincent to Cotton, 17 January 1809.

3. W.W. Pole to Cotton, 31 March 1809, PRO ADM 2/1368; Halkett to W.W. Pole, 27 December 1808, Cotton to W.W. Pole, 9 January 1809, PRO ADM 7/41; the *Raphael* caught fire and sank in the Tagus on 16 October 1809. See Brian DeToy, "Wellington's Admiral: The Life and Career of George Berkeley, 1753–1818," Ph.D. dissertation, Florida State University, 1997, note 13, 410.

4. Collingwood to Cotton, 6 December 1809, Cambridgeshire County Record Office, Cotton Naval Papers, 588/042.

5. Collingwood to Mulgrave, 10 January 1809, G.L. Newnham Collingwood, ed., *Selection from the Public and Private Correspondence of Vice-Admiral Lord Collingwood* (New York, 1829), 355.

6. Collingwood to his brother, 3 March 1810, Collingwood to Vice Admiral John Child Purvis, 3 March 1810, Edward Hughes, ed., *The Private Correspondence of Admiral Lord Collingwood* (London, 1957), 313–14.

7. Lord Mulgrave to the King, 10 March 1810, Arthur Aspinall, ed., *The Later Correspondence of George III* (Cambridge, 1962–1970), 5: 540–41.

8. John Wilson Croker to Collingwood, 9 April 1810, PRO ADM 2/924; Croker to Cotton, 10 April 1810, PRO ADM 7/41.

9. "Memoir of Cotton," *Naval Chronicle* 27 (1812): 387.

10. "List of British flag-officers on the active list at the outbreak of the war with France," in William Laird Clowes, *The Royal Navy: A History from the Earliest Times to the Present* (London, 1897–1903), 4: 193–94; James Ralfe, *The Naval Biography of Great Britain* (London, 1828; reprint, Boston, 1972), 2: 136–40.

11. Cotton to Croker, 10, 12 April 1810, PRO ADM 7/41. The Admiralty remained ignorant of Collingwood's death for over one month.

12. Piers Mackesy, *The War in the Mediterranean, 1803–1810* (London, 1957), 5.

13. Ibid., 356.

14. Ibid., 348-55, 364-67; Desmond Gregory, *Sicily, The Insecure Base: A History of the British Occupation of Sicily, 1806–1815* (Rutherford, 1988), 71–78; Roger Charles Anderson, *Naval Wars in the Levant, 1559–1853* (Princeton, 1952), 461–65; Captain George Eyre to Rear Admiral Sir George Martin, 18 April 1810, PRO ADM 1/416.

15. D. Fedotoff White, "The Russian Navy in Trieste during the Wars of the Revolution and the Empire," *American Slavic and East European Review* 6 (1947): 40; John William Fortescue, *A History of the British Army* (London, 1910–1930), 7: 362-65.

16. Napoleon to General Henri Clarke, 19 July 1810, Napoleon Bonaparte, *Unpublished Correspondence of Napoleon I* (New York, 1913), 3: 656–57.

17. Logbook of HMS *Temeraire*, 1807–1810, kept by Midshipman J. Harris, 28 April 1810, vol. 6, New York Public Library, Great Britain/Navy Box collection.

18. British warships at Cadiz were the *Caledonia* (120), *San Josef* (112), *Temeraire* (98), *Tonnant* (80), *Achille* (74), *Eagle* (74), *Triumph* (74), *Zealous* (74), *Bulwark* (74), *Invincible* (74), *Resistance* (38), *Delight* (18), *Basilik* (12), and the bomb vessels

Thunder, *Hound*, *Devastation*, and *Etna*. Spanish vessels included the *Principe de Asturias* (114), *Santa Ana* (114), *Neptuno* (84), *Pluton* (80), *San Lorenzo* (76), *San Fulgencio* (68), *Gloriosa* (76), San *Justo* (76), *San Paula* (76), *San Julian* (76), *Atocha* (40), and *Prueba* (40). Cotton to Croker, 28 April 1810, Purvis to Croker with a list of Spanish ships remaining in Cadiz harbor, 27 April 1810, PRO ADM 1/416.

19. Cotton to Croker, 29 April 1810, Extract of a letter from Captain Hargood to Purvis, 28 April 1810, PRO ADM 1/416. A useful reference for the Spanish navy is John D. Harbron, *Trafalgar and the Spanish Navy* (Annapolis, 1988). According to Captain Charles Adams of the *Invincible*, General Horace François Sebastiani's French troops entered Murcia to levy contributions of money and grain. The force was too small to seize Carthagena or Alicante; it retired from Murcia on 26 April. Adams to Cotton, 31 May 1810, PRO ADM 1/416.

20. After Berkeley's insistence for three years, the Admiralty placed the squadron at Cadiz under command of the admiral at Lisbon in June 1812. DeToy, "Life and Career of George Berkeley," note 3, 406.

21. Cotton to Pickmore, 29 April 1810, PRO ADM 1/416.

22. Hoste to Martin, 5 April 1810, PRO ADM 1/417.

23. Ibid., Cotton to Croker, 30 April 1810, 2, 6 May 1810; it was not uncommon for British naval commanders during the Napoleonic period to request from the Admiralty more vessels, especially frigates. See Paul Webb, "The Frigate Situation of the Royal Navy, 1793–1815," *Mariner's Mirror* 82 (1996): 28–40.

24. Log of HMS *San Josef*, 30 April 1810, Yale University, Sterling Memorial Library, Robert Nesser Collection, MSS 366 (Box 9).

25. Cotton to Berkeley, 29 April 1810, Cotton to Henry Wellesley, 30 April 1810, Cotton to Adair, 1 May 1810, Cotton to Manuel de Posada, commodore aboard the *Ferdinand VII*, 4 May 1810, PRO ADM 7/43.

26. Cotton to Croker, 6 May 1810, PRO ADM 1/416; N.A.M. Rodger, *The Wooden World: An Anatomy of the Georgian Navy* (Annapolis, 1986), 26–28.

27. Campbell to Cotton, 5 May 1810, PRO ADM 7/42; Cotton to Pickmore, 6 May 1810, Cotton to Lieutenant Nichols, Resident Agent of Transports at Gibraltar, 6 May 1810, PRO ADM 7/43.

28. The squadron off Toulon consisted of the *Centaur* (74), *Ville de Paris* (110), *Royal Sovereign* (100), *Warspite* (76), *Fame* (74), *Victorious* (74), *York* (74), *Sultan* (74), *Topaze* (38), and *Nautilus* (18). The name of one ship-of-the-line was illegible in the log. Log of *San Josef*, 14 May 1810.

29. Cotton to James Lavers, Agent Victualler at Mahón, 14 May 1810, Cotton to Hood, 15 May 1810, Cotton to Patrick Wilkie, Agent Victualler at Malta, 15 May 1810, PRO ADM 7/43.

30. Cotton to Croker, 21 May 1810, PRO ADM 7/41.

31. Napoleon to Clarke, 19 July 1810, Bonaparte, *Unpublished Correspondence*, 3: 656–57.

32. Collingwood to the Admiralty, 1 November 1809, *Naval Chronicle* 22 (1809): 502-503; Collingwood to his sister, 1 November 1809, Hughes, *Private Correspondence of Collingwood*, 301-302; Cotton to Captain Harvey of HMS *Leviathon*, 21 May 1810, PRO ADM 7/43.

33. Cotton to Croker, 3 June 1810, PRO ADM 7/41; Malcolm Crook, *Toulon in War and Revolution: From the Ancien Régime to the Restoration, 1750–1820* (Manchester, 1991), 211–12. According to Clowes, the *Wagram* (130) was launched in Toulon on 30

June, with the *Sceptre* (80) and *Trident* (74) still under construction. Clowes, *Royal Navy*, 5: 288.

34. Etienne Taillemite, *Dictionnaire des Marin Français* (Paris, 1982), 12–13.

35. Captain Jahleel Brenton to Rear Admiral George Martin, 3 May 1810, PRO ADM 1/416; Cotton to Brenton, 3 June 1810, PRO ADM 7/43. The *Spartan* suffered ten men killed and twenty-two wounded in this engagement.

36. Cotton to Croker, 4 June 1810, PRO ADM 7/41.

37. Ibid.; excerpt of letter from Hoste to his mother, 23 April 1810, in William Hoste, *Service Afloat, or The Naval Career of Sir William Hoste* (London, 1887), 148–51.

38. Captain Sir Henry Blackwood to Cotton, 20 July 1810, Cotton to Blackwood, 25 July 1810, Perkins Library, Duke University, North Carolina, Blackwood Papers; Cotton to Croker, 24 July 1810, PRO ADM 7/41; V. Brun, *Guerres Maritimes de la France: Port de Toulon ses armements,son administration, depuis son origine jusqu'a nos jours* (Paris, 1861), 2: 528–29.

39. Jurat of Mahón to Cotton, 8 June 1810, PRO ADM 7/42.

40. Henry Wellesley to Viscount Wellington, 2, 23 April 1810, 12 June 1810, Arthur Wellesley, Duke of Wellington, *Supplementary Despatches, Correspondence, and Memoranda of Field Marshal Arthur Duke of Wellington, K.G.* [hereafter cited as *Wellington's Supplementary Despatches*], ed. by his son (London, 1858–1872), 6: 502, 503, 513, 534, 535.

41. Pickmore to Henry Wellesley, 15 May 1810, PRO ADM 1/416.

42. Ibid., Luis de Villava to Cotton, 22 May 1810.

43. Jurat of Mahón to Cotton, PRO ADM 7/42.

44. Cotton to Villava, 16 June 1810, PRO ADM 1/416.

45. Cotton to Lord Mulgrave, 24 May 1810, PRO ADM 7/41.

46. Mulgrave to Cotton, undated, July 1810, Cambridgeshire County Record Office, Cotton Naval Papers, 588/042.

47. Adams to Cotton, 31 May 1810, PRO ADM 1/416.

48. Gabriel H. Lovett, *Napoleon and the Birth of Modern Spain II: The Struggle, Without and Within* (New York, 1965), 732–33. A condemned bread-stealer was either stoned to death or tied to a pine tree naked and without food for up to twenty-four hours. For more on life at Cabrera as a French prisoner, see Charles Ogé Barbaroux, *Adventures of a French Serjeant, during His Campaigns in Italy, Spain, Germany, Russia, &c. from 1805 to 1823* (Philadelphia, 1827), 94–118. In 1923, a rough monumental stone, surmounted by an iron cross, marked the burial place at Cabrera for 2,200 French prisoners. See Thorvald Solberg, "Some Notes on the Balearic Islands with Special Reference to Their Bibliography," *The Papers of the Bibliographical Society of America* 21 (1927): 83–84.

49. Cotton to Croker, 16 July 1810, PRO ADM 7/41.

50. Cotton to Palmer, 16 June 1810, Cotton to Pickmore, 10 July 1810, Cotton to Palmer, 10 July 1810, Cotton to the Principal Officers and Commissioners of His Majesty's Navy, 16 July 1810, Cotton to Captain Smith, 12 March 1811, PRO ADM 7/43; Captain Nisbet Palmer to Cotton, 27 May 1810, Pickmore to Keats, 11 August 1810, Keats to Croker, 14 August 1810, PRO ADM 1/417. Some French prisoners apparently escaped from Cabrera by presenting themselves as Italians or Germans for service in the Sardinian and Sicilian armies. On 12 March 1811, Cotton ordered Captain Smith of the *Sheerwater* to put an immediate stop to this practice.

51. Decision, 12 July 1810, Napoleon Bonaparte, *Correspondence de Napoléon Ier, publiée par order de l'Empereur Napoléon III* (Paris, 1858–1869), no. 16638, 20: 462–63. Had the expedition launched, it might have succeeded because of Cabrera's isolation and the questionable abilities of Captain Palmer, commander of the *Alacrity*. Palmer displayed ability on 14 October 1810, when his ship captured the French privateer *Three Brothers* near Sardinia. However, on 26 May 1811 off the coast of Corsica, the French corvette *Abeille* captured the *Alacrity* after a heavy engagement. Palmer's performance bordered on cowardice. See David J. Hepper, *British Warship Losses in the Age of Sail, 1650–1859* (East Sussex, 1994), 136–37; Cotton to Palmer, 20 October 1811, PRO ADM 7/43.

52. Cotton to Yorke, 19 August 1810, PRO ADM 7/41.

53. General Henry O'Donnell to Cotton, 29 August 1810, PRO ADM 1/417.

54. "Monthly Disposition of the State of the Enemy's Ships and Preparations in the different parts of the Coast comprehended within the Station of the Mediterranean," 1 August 1810, PRO ADM 1/416.

55. Cotton to Yorke, 12 August 1810, PRO ADM 7/41.

56. Cotton to Martin, 11 August 1810, Cotton to Rear Admiral Boyles, 11 August 1810, PRO ADM 7/43.

57. Ibid., Cotton to Croker, 3 June 1810, 26 July 1810; Martin to Quash, 3 May 1810, PRO ADM 1/416.

58. Martin to Quash, 3 May 1810, Martin to Purvis, 12 May 1810, PRO ADM 1/416; Gregory, *Sicily*, 141–46.

59. Blanckley to Sir Samuel Hood, 20 May 1810, PRO ADM 7/42.

60. Lieutenant Colonel Henry Bunbury to John Barrow, 19 April 1810, King's advocates' opinion, 16 April 1810, Barrow to Cotton, 24 April 1810, PRO ADM 7/41.

61. Charles Stuart to Richard Colley, Marquis Wellesley, 6 May 1810, Barrow to Cotton 21 May 1810, Barrow to Cotton, 7 June 1810, PRO ADM 7/41; Cotton to Croker, 26 July 1810, 5 August 1810, PRO ADM 1/417; Louis Casamajor to Cotton, PRO ADM 7/42.

62. "Declaration of the Voluntary and Charitable Subscription towards the Ransom of the Portuguese Captives at Algiers," undated, National Maritime Museum, Sir Samuel Hood Papers, MKH/116; The Mediterranean Fleet contributed $351 towards the ransom. See Cotton to Charles Stuart, 3 January 1811, PRO ADM 7/42.

63. Cotton to Croker, 4 September 1810, PRO ADM 7/41.

64. The Mediterranean packet service went between Gibraltar and Malta. Cotton requested the addition of Mahón to the packet route. The Admiralty denied the request because it would delay communication with Sicily. Cotton to Croker, 21 May 1810, PRO ADM 7/41; Barrow to Cotton, 23 August 1810, PRO ADM 2/925.

65. Copy of statement by Lieutenant Moses Cannadey of the *Black Joke*, undated, Dundas to Cotton, 27 August 1810, Cotton to Croker, 4 September 1810, PRO ADM 1/417; Maxwell to Cotton, 27 June 1810, PRO ADM 1/416; Blanckley to Cotton, 24 August 1810, PRO ADM 7/42; Cotton to Yorke, 12 August 1810, PRO ADM 7/41. According to a letter received by Peter Motta from Blanckley, the Dey followed through on his promise to eject French privateers and the French vice-consul at Oran. Motta to Cotton, 13 September 1810, PRO ADM 7/42.

66. Cotton to Croker, 4 September 1810, PRO ADM 1/417.

67. Ibid., Blanckley to Cotton, 17 September 1810.

68. Adair to Cotton, 7 June 1810, PRO ADM 7/42; Cotton to Croker, 24 August, PRO ADM 1/417.

69. Adair to Richard Wellesley, 3 July 1810, PRO ADM 7/42.

70. Ibid., Adair to Cotton, 7 June 1810.

71. General Order to the respective Captains, Commanders, and Commanding Officers of His Majesty's Ships and Vessels to the Eastward, 25 August 1810, PRO ADM 1/417.

72. Ibid., Peter Schutz to Cotton, 27 July 1810; Croker to Cotton, 22 May 1810, PRO ADM 7/41; Cotton to Martin, 28 July 1810, PRO ADM 7/43.

73. Extract of letter from Eyre to Cotton, 17 May 1810, PRO ADM 1/416.

74. Cotton to Eyre, 2 September 1810, PRO ADM 1/417.

75. Boyles to Cotton, 11 August 1810, Cotton to Croker, 12 September 1810, PRO ADM 1/417; "Disposal of *Lively*'s Ships Company" attached to Cotton to Martin, 11 September 1810, PRO ADM 7/43. For a detailed account of the wreck, see Lieutenant General Sir George Cockburn, *A Voyage to Cadiz and Gibraltar up the Mediterranean to Sicily and Malta in 1810, & 1811* (London, 1815), 1: 35–47.

76. Cotton to Croker, 26 July 1810, Pickmore to Yorke, 30 July 1810, PRO ADM 1/417; Cotton to Keats, 16 August 1810, Cotton to Boyles, 28 July 1810, PRO ADM 7/43; Boyles to Croker, 25 June 1810, PRO ADM 1/416; Yorke to Cotton, 12, 15 July 1810, Croker to Keats, 12 July 1810, PRO ADM 7/41; Yorke to Pickmore, 30 September 1810, British Library, Hardwicke Papers, ADD MSS 45044; Ann Parry, ed., *The Admirals Fremantle* (London, 1971), 82–89.

9

Rising Tide in the West: The Peninsular War and the Mediterranean Fleet, September 1810–July 1811

> I believe Cotton is quite aware that he is not likely to retain command here in the event of a change of government; and I am quite sure that if any minister was to see him only one week here, he would pronounce his incapacity for governing so large a fleet.
>
> —Rear Admiral Fremantle to the Marquis of Buckingham, 1 March 1811[1]

> The Board have decided upon appointing Sir Charles Cotton to their most honourable and important station: The Channel Fleet.
>
> —Charles Yorke, First Lord of the Admiralty, to Lady Cotton, 3 April 1811[2]

The report of Murat's ill-conceived attempt to invade Sicily across the two-mile Strait of Messina likely reaffirmed in Napoleon's mind his decision to cancel the invasion of Britain across the twenty-mile Strait of Dover in 1805. On the night of 17 September 1810, heavy winds forced Admiral Martin's squadron from its station in the Strait of Messina. Subsequently, about 3,500 Corsicans and Neapolitans under the leadership of General Jean-Baptiste Cavaignac embarked from Reggio and landed six miles south of Messina. This force, intended to seize a mountain ridge as a diversion for Murat's main effort to the north, was quickly attacked by British troops under the leadership of Major General James Campbell, adjutant-general for Sir John Stuart's army of 14,000 troops. While Campbell fought in the early morning light of the 18th, French troops embarked in boats along the Calabrian shore and waited impatiently for some sign of success from Cavaignac's force. Seeing none along the heavily defended Sicilian shore, General Paul Grenier, commander of the French main body, refused to send his divisions across the strait. Cavaignac's force hastily retreated, but not before the British captured 700 of his soldiers and four boats of the flotilla. Hence, Murat's 400 unarmed boats, sixty gunboats, and 25,000 troops mobilized between Scilla and Reggio failed to capture Sicily. Having proved that the straits could be crossed, however, Murat declared victory and ordered the withdrawal of his army and flotilla to Naples. Martin concluded that "the prospect of any immediate attack upon Sicily is at an end."[3] Napoleon, of course, was angered by Murat's initiative and poor judgment. Because of Murat's failure, the French army in Italy lost its legitimacy as a strategic diversion for the allied campaigns in Iberia.[4]

Thereafter, British naval operations from Sicily eastward had diminishing strategic relevance. An injunction in the fall of 1810 against taking unwarranted risks represented the Admiralty's desire to conserve resources in operational theaters on the periphery of the Iberian Peninsula. Raids conducted by seamen and marines in boats belonging to His Majesty's ships earned great admiration, but the Admiralty held the opinion that "this kind of warfare has in many instances been carried too far."[5] The Admiralty did not want these operations conducted when the odds were not in British favor and "when the object to be gained is not of sufficient importance to justify the risk of lives to be incurred in the attainment of it." Yet, privateers, the coastal trade, and minor enemy expeditions kept the Mediterranean Fleet active to the east of Sicily well after the Admiralty's injunction. Captain Eyre maintained the blockade of Corfu; Captain Hoste still lead a squadron in the Adriatic; Captain Beauford of the frigate *Frederickstein* commanded a small detachment in the archipelago; and Rear Admiral Boyles safeguarded trade at Malta. A naval engagement by Hoste's squadron illustrates how the French continued challenging British naval dominance in the eastern Mediterranean as late as March 1811. On the 11th, a French squadron of five frigates, a corvette, a brig, two schooners, a gunboat, and a xebec sailed from Ancona for the island of Lissa to establish a garrison of 500 troops. Two days later, the French squadron attacked Hoste's force, consisting of the frigates *Amphion*, *Active*, *Volage*, and *Cerberus*. The British suffered fifty killed and 150 wounded, but managed to win the battle by capturing the 44-gun *Corona* and 32-gun *Bellona* and causing the 44-gun *Favorite* to "[blow] up with a dreadful explosion." Some 200 French troops landed at Lissa, but they surrendered to the British on the 15th.[6]

This action was another tactical masterpiece by Hoste that earned praise from Cotton and admiration in England. However, by then the strategic stakes were low in the eastern Mediterranean compared to those in the west. While the Toulon blockade prevailed as Cotton's main concern, the growing sense of crisis in eastern Spain drew more of his attention towards the provinces of Andalusia, Murcia, Valencia, and Catalonia. In addition, French advances against ports in these provinces and the arrival of additional Spanish ships-of-the-line at Mahón heightened apprehension about the security of the Balearics.

Since the beginning of the Peninsular War, the Mediterranean Fleet had kept a squadron actively employed along the east coast of Spain. It adhered to the spirit of Collingwood's discretionary order to Captain Thomas Cochrane to "render every possible assistance to the Spaniards against the French."[7] Cochrane's frigate *Imperieuse* conducted numerous operations in 1808 along the Catalonian coast, establishing a precedent of Anglo-Spanish cooperation that was followed by other frigate captains for the next couple of years as the French and Spanish grappled for control of the region. After the occupation of Barcelona in February 1808, a succession of generals and marshals led the French war effort in Catalonia: Philibert Guillaume Duhesme, Honoré Charles Reille, Gouvion St. Cyr, Pierre François Augereau, and finally, in May 1810, Jacques Étienne Macdonald. Napoleon ordered Marshal Macdonald to seize Tortosa and Tarragona in conjunction with General Louis Gabriel Suchet's 3rd Corps from Aragon. After the fall of these Catalonian fortresses, Suchet's corps would advance on Valencia. In August 1810, the 3rd Corps invested Tortosa while Macdonald's 7th Corps established defensive positions near Lerida to oppose Spanish reinforcements—Major General Henry O'Donnell commanded 22,000 Spanish troops in Catalonia.[8]

Meanwhile, Marshal Victor's 1st Corps pressed the siege of Cadiz and controlled most of the Andalusian coast with support from Marshal Adolphe Édouard Mortier's 5th Corps and General Horace François Sebastiani's 4th Corps. By September 1810, Victor had amassed nearly 300 guns and mortars in fortifications around Cadiz harbor and was constructing a gunboat flotilla. Unfortunately for the French, Keats lived up to his reputation by dramatically improving the Anglo-Spanish naval situation at Cadiz. Henry Wellesley was so impressed that he believed Keats could have prevented French occupation of the Trocadero if he "had been here at the commencement of the siege."[9] Keats reduced the number of vessels anchored within the harbor and strengthened the British naval presence with additional gunboats. The Admiralty authorized him to reinforce Cadiz with half of Commodore Penrose's gunboat force at Gibraltar. Despite remarkable results, Keats felt constrained by his subordination to Cotton and wanted an independent command. Without doubt, Keats knew the situation at Cadiz far better than Cotton and probably considered Cotton's inquiries an annoyance. By an order dated 30 August, the Admiralty "suggested" to Cotton that Keats "be not interfered with in the execution of his duties." Having essentially been granted an independent command by this suggestion, Keats nevertheless continued reporting faithfully to his commander-in-chief.[10]

Though not yet occupied by French troops, the provinces of Murcia and Valencia were strategically significant. This was made clear to Cotton by Colonel Philip Roche. Henry Wellesley had sent the colonel to the Balearics in May 1810 to learn as much as possible about the islands. Roche's 26 June letter to Cotton comprehensively described the condition of the Balearics, as well as the eastern Spanish provinces. Roche believed that the French would inevitably occupy Valencia and use the promontory of Denia to embark an expedition to Ibiza, the "stepping stone" to invade Majorca and Minorca. He had no faith in the Spanish army's ability to defend the islands and proposed their "immediate and absolute" British occupation. Roche overstated to Cotton: "This is the precious moment we should seize to avoid all those inevitable evils. Therefore now while probably we can effect it we shall make a point of having [the Balearics] placed altogether under our protection, subject to any conditions of restitution hereafter. If you don't do this, you do nothing effectual, but however any thing is better than leaving them in the state of abandonment they are now."[11] Captain Charles Rowley of the *Eagle* later told Cotton: "Colonel Roche seems to possess activity and zeal, but like all young men considers the salvation or downfall of the cause depending immediately on the success of his mission, and the immediate spot he is at."[12] Regardless, Roche's report made Cotton cast a wary eye toward Spain, while the other continued its vigil over the Toulon Fleet.

Within the province of Murcia, the subject of naval stores at Carthagena also distracted Cotton's attention from Toulon. The naval stores were valued by both the French and British, especially since the Spanish navy was nearly defunct as a viable fighting force. In June, Captain Adam of the *Invincible* notified Cotton about the stores, claiming that enough oak timber existed in the arsenal for the frames of a ship-of-the-line and two frigates, including a variety of masts, bowsprits, spars, and anchors. Cotton forwarded Adam's information to the Admiralty and ordered the *Invincible* back to Carthagena. He also sent Colonel Roche with Adam to "aid in the object of removing the remaining Spanish ships and stores from thence" to Mahón.[13] Meanwhile, Rear Admiral Pickmore had dispatched Rowley's *Eagle* to Carthagena with a similar mission. The *Eagle* arrived on 3 August at Carthagena, where Rowley, Cotton's brother-in-law, assessed the arsenal's contents. In a report to his sister's husband, Rowley recommended the removal of the ships-of-the-line and an estimated 3,134 oak timbers and 1,212 spars. Removal of the frigates and anchors could wait for a more opportune time and circumstance. In addition, Rowley reported Roche's attempt to convince the 700 artificers at Carthagena to serve the British government at either Malta or Gibraltar. To their credit, Cotton and Pickmore acted on the situation at Carthagena before receiving authorization from the Admiralty, which was granted on 2 August.[14]

A couple of problems obstructed the immediate removal of the stores from Carthagena. First, not enough transport tonnage was available in the Mediterranean. Cotton did dispatch 600 transport tonnage to Carthagena, but it was initially intended for the conveyance to Gibraltar of 700 German deserters from the French army. Rowley would send the naval stores to Mahón with any remaining transport tonnage. Complicating the process of evacuating the stores, Keats delayed sending transports from Cadiz and Gibraltar because the Spanish government had already ordered the governor of Carthagena to remove the stores to Mahón. He waited for Rowley's report to determine if further British support was necessary. When Keats later ordered the preparation of transports at Gibraltar, their departure for Carthagena was delayed further by a fever-induced quarantine imposed by the lieutenant governor. The fever also broke out at Carthagena sometime in September or October, which prompted Eusebio de Bardaxi, Minister for Foreign Affairs, to close all communication with that port. Despite these setbacks, Rowley arrived at Mahón on 8 October with the 74-gun *Guerrero* and an undisclosed amount of naval stores. Cotton estimated that six large transports were needed to remove the remaining naval stores from Carthagena. He asked Keats to provide them because transports in the Mediterranean were committed to supplying the fleet.[15]

However, British possession of the naval stores did not imply ownership, nor would Henry Wellesley consider their purchase. Bardaxi made clear that sale of the stores to Britain was at the moment unacceptable: "Such a proposal if it were to reach the Cortes . . . will not fail to make an unfavorable impression upon that assembly."[16] Until British use of the spars and oak timbers was authorized through diplomatic channels, Cotton and Keats would have to be satisfied that their efforts kept the stores at Carthagena away from the French.

The fleet's contribution to the war in Spain pleased Cotton, who told his wife in August 1810: "My dealings with [the Spaniards] has been chiefly by deputy, and all I have employed hitherto have been popular with them."[17] While Cotton's decisions related to Murcia anticipated a French attack, his fleet had been decisively engaged against the French in Catalonia since his arrival as commander-in-chief. Cotton's deputy that summer was Captain Charles Bullen, senior captain of the squadron stationed off Catalonia. Naval support for the Spanish had become more critical as the French siege of Tortosa progressed and investment of Tarragona appeared imminent. On 20 July, Captain Francis William Fane's frigate *Cambrian* joined Cotton at sea with a Spanish colonel, who possessed an urgent message from General O'Donnell for more powder and muskets for distribution among the peasants, "who ask with the greatest enthusiasm and ardour for arms to repel the infamous enemy."[18] The general's letter concluded by making clear the defensibility by sea of Tarragona at various points and urged Cotton to "succour me if necessary with some maritime forces to preserve the only port which at present serves for the commerce of this principality with the allied nations and other free ports of the Peninsula." Cotton immediately sent the *Cambrian* back to Tarragona with eighty barrels of gunpowder collected from the fleet. In addition, he directed the ordnance storekeeper at Malta to send any available ammunition to Catalonia.[19]

In his memoir, Suchet summarized General O'Donnell's operations during the investment of Tortosa. O'Donnell concentrated his army at Tarragona and then conducted sorties as circumstances required. Whenever Macdonald's corps advanced towards Tarragona, O'Donnell divided his army to escape. For want of provisions, the French would soon be forced to withdraw towards Barcelona.[20] This strategy prevented the corps of Suchet and Macdonald from effectively coordinating their efforts and consequently prolonged the siege of Tortosa. Soon after the *Cambrian*'s return to Catalonia, its firepower contributed to O'Donnell's campaign against Macdonald. In late August 1810, the French drove O'Donnell's army within the walls of Tarragona. While a general engagement between French and Spanish troops commenced near the fortress on the morning of the 21st, Captain Bullen's *Volontaire* fired broadsides against a detachment of French cavalry, "with a view to dislodge them." Meanwhile, Bullen had sent the *Cambrian* to nearby Cambrils and Salou in the event that the French would send a force to levy contributions from the inhabitants. A detachment of French cavalry and infantry arrived there as Bullen had anticipated. Consequently, Fane's frigate fired broadsides, which dispersed the French "with considerable loss."[21] Colonel Charles W. Doyle, British commissioner in Catalonia, estimated that the *Cambrian*'s fire killed or wounded about forty men, while the *Volontaire* accounted for above 100 French casualties, including a general officer.[22] Following the battle, Macdonald's force withdrew north to Mont Blanc.

Doyle's account of the battle, including the contributions of Bullen and Fane, alleviated some of Cotton's apprehension about affairs in Catalonia. On 4 September, Cotton read Doyle's letter to General Stuart in Sicily: "Tortosa is for the present free of access and large supplies of every kind are on the road to it. The fruitful plain of Tarragona is again under Spanish protection." In addition, all French convoys and detachments in Catalonia had been "cut off," including the French garrison at the border fortress of Figueras; "a corps of 5,000 armed peasants were about to enter France"; and favorable situations existed for Spanish armies in Valencia and Aragon.[23] During September, Cotton's "deputies" contributed more to the "common cause." They helped the Spaniards gain possession of the entire coastline between Rosas and Palamos, with the exception of the Medas Islands.

General O'Donnell decided on another operation to divert attention away from the siege of Tortosa by attacking isolated French units north of Barcelona. While a Spanish division marched north from Tarragona, an Anglo-Spanish naval force sailed north to attack the Castle of Las Medas. O'Donnell wanted to attack the Medas Islands because they facilitated French coastal communication with Barcelona. Captain Fane's *Cambrian*, with Colonel Doyle aboard, departed Tarragona on 5 September, accompanied by two Spanish xebecs containing sixty soldiers and two cannons. The Spanish frigate *Diana* joined them the next day. Finding an attack upon the castle at Medas impracticable, plans were changed for an attack against an enemy battery at Bagur. On 10 September at 12:30 p.m., the boats of the *Cambrian* and *Diana* launched, with forty-seven and seventy-six marines respectively. About 130 French troops, divided between the castle of Bagur and a battery of five guns, opposed the landing force. In only one hour, the Anglo-Spanish force dispersed the enemy garrison, destroyed the battery, and captured thirty prisoners.[24]

Men from the *Cambrian* and *Diana* executed another raid on 14 September at Palamos, while O'Donnell attacked General François-Xavier Schwarz's force at nearby Bisbal. As Spanish soldiers attacked an estimated 290 French troops at Palamos, launches from the *Cambrian* provided support with two howitzers and a carronade. A French shot sunk a launch before the combined effect of naval gunfire from the frigates and the Spanish troops forced a surrender. The *Cambrian* returned to Tarragona on the 19th with O'Donnell, who was badly wounded in the leg. As a result of O'Donnell's diversion, augmented by the raids at Bagur and Palamos, the allies captured over 1,000 prisoners, including General Schwarz. However, Macdonald did not learn of the diversion until two weeks later. By then, he decided to remain in the vicinity of Tortosa.[25]

On 1 October, Captain Colin Campbell's *Minstrel* sloop delivered Bullen's account of the latest affairs in Catalonia to Cotton off Toulon. Though pleased by the news, Cotton's thoughts were preoccupied by the difficulty of maintaining the fleet's blockade. Heavy gales compounded the inconvenience created by the fleet's supply shortage. On 11 September, the fleet was at two-thirds rations and needed an estimated 673,079 pounds of bread, 85,296 gallons of wine, 171,680 pounds of flour, 66,707 gallons of lemon juice, and many other items. The depot at Mahón, where Cotton wanted a three-month stock for 10,000 men, had none or few of these items. Problems requisitioning supplies from Algiers and Turkey, a poor wheat crop in Sardinia, lack of transport tonnage, and a dispute between the commissioner and victualling agent at Malta led a frustrated Cotton to assert that "the only source of supplies for the fleet in the Mediterranean to be relied upon is the same being forwarded from England."[26]

The fleet's supply problem exacerbated the difficulty of supporting O'Donnell in Catalonia, a province that lately had begun to attract more of Wellington's attention. He suggested to Lord Liverpool in August: "It would be very desirable to have a squadron of men of war, with a few victuallers and store ships, on the East coast of the Peninsula, and in communication with the General Officer commanding the troops in Catalonia and Valencia, in order to assist these places, to encourage their resistance to the enemy, and eventually, if necessary and practicable, to carry off their garrisons."[27] On 4 October, Cotton received a copy of Wellington's dispatch with the Admiralty's endorsement. Obviously, the Mediterranean Fleet could not provide the support desired on the Spanish coast while the Toulon blockade was inadequately maintained. Therefore, Cotton decided to leave the inshore squadron off Toulon while the fleet proceeded to Mahón for provisions and water. The inshore squadron left at Toulon consisted of the *Warspite*, *Euryalus*, and *Blossom*. Cotton notified the squadron commander that the fleet would return to the rendezvous immediately after replenishment.[28]

The fleet arrived off Mahón on the morning of 5 October and, to Cotton's relief, was joined by victuallers from Gibraltar and two transports from Palermo with "ample supplies for the fleet." For the moment, Cotton could ignore the vexatious matter of supply and focus on other problems demanding his attention. The status of Rear Admiral Pickmore had become a concern. Upon relief at Cadiz, the Admiralty had ordered Pickmore to join Cotton's fleet to relieve Sir Samuel Hood. Pickmore proceeded in the *Temeraire* to Gibraltar; there he took the *San Carlos* and *Ferdinand VII* under escort and arrived at Mahón on 12 September. He then made arrangements to escort several supply vessels to the fleet. Departing on 1 October, Pickmore's convoy bypassed the fleet on its passage to Mahón. However, Pickmore soon recognized what had happened and returned to Mahón with his convoy on the 12th.[29]

Meanwhile, Admiral Hood, whose health had been steadily declining, was anxiously awaiting Pickmore's arrival. Hood requested to depart the fleet on 26 September, but Cotton considered Hood's services indispensable until Pickmore's arrival. The rear admiral thus reluctantly continued commanding the fleet's weather division while Fremantle continued with the lee division. Inexplicably, on 4 August, the Admiralty reneged on Hood's relief and appointed Pickmore First Captain of the Fleet.[30] The First Captain was usually the senior captain in the fleet, but he could also be a rear admiral. He served as the commander-in-chief's advisor and chief-of-staff. The position was not always popular with ambitious officers because it restricted their independence and opportunities. Captain Benjamin Hallowel, one of Nelson's "band of brothers" and well respected in the Royal Navy, had turned down an appointment to serve as Cotton's First Captain that summer.

Cotton notified Pickmore of the appointment on 12 October. He refused it, but suggested that Cotton accept him aboard the *San Josef* until circumstances allowed a return to the *Temeraire*. Like many naval officers, Pickmore did not want his opportunities for independent command constrained by serving as First Captain. Cotton accepted the offer, stipulating that Pickmore would assist in administrative duties and further guidance would be sought from the Admiralty. Pickmore, in essence, became an acting First Captain with the flexibility to leave the position when convenient. The Admiralty later acknowledged Pickmore's unique position and authorized Cotton to chose his own First Captain from forty available senior captains.[31]

Many other issues occupied Cotton's attention during the fleet's ten days at Mahón. The *San Carlos*, *Ferdinand VII*, *Guerrero*, *Glorioso*, *Justo*, *Paulo*, and *Neptuno*, all anchored at Port Mahón, raised both British and Spanish consciousness about security against a French expedition, which the weak garrison at Minorca could not hope to repel. With this in mind, the Admiralty issued Cotton "most secret" instructions pertaining to the Spanish ships. They were to be burned and destroyed if threatened by the French, without consent of the Spanish commodore, Manuel de Posada. Cotton hence ordered Captain William Cummings of the 74-gun *Bombay* to comply with these instructions and draw a barrel of pitch and one of tar from the *San Josef* to fire the Spanish ships. Later, Cotton expressed doubt about the wisdom of the plan: "The Spanish officers . . . with the force now here would prevent as much as they possibly could the destruction of their ships, and the force that I can ever leave here (two sail of the line) hardly competent to compleat it effectually and provide for their own security."[32] Authorization for destruction of allied property, without the ally's consent, demonstrated the Admiralty's belief in the French navy's ability to elude the Mediterranean Fleet as the gales of winter approached. It also demonstrated the arrogant attitude of the British to protect their own interests at the expense of an ally.

Treaties may bind nations, but they often do not forge the bond of mutual trust necessary for individuals to cooperate in the best interest of the alliance. Though Cotton and Villava had a much better relationship than Junot and Seniavin, mutual trust and tranquil relations between the British and Spanish at Minorca was yet to be achieved. Villava petitioned Cotton with a variety of grievances that, if collectively ignored, could possibly disrupt the Royal Navy's use of Port Mahón. First, Villava believed that Peter Motta, British Vice Consul at Mahón, was "weak and without character" because of an unwillingness or inability to address problems.[33] For instance, several deserters from the French army, while awaiting transport for British service in Sicily, were quartered at Mahón's Royal Lazaretto. They proceeded to deface the property, for which Villava sought restitution from the British government. Motta would not pay without first consulting a higher British authority. The Frenchmen had also caused public disturbances, which, according to Villava, Motta essentially ignored. To combat this lawlessness, Villava applied to Cotton for a British guard because he was "in want of troops to garrison the island, which is so far unprotected that justice, police, and even the Spanish sovereignty are overthrown and disobeyed."[34]

Cotton and Villava met on 8 October to discuss many urgent issues. The agenda of their conference likely included Port Mahón's security, quarantine procedures, depredations by the French deserters, and the island's ability to supply the fleet—issues discussed in recent correspondence. The frivolous matter of a disrespectful British merchant stomping his feet in anger at Villava was also a matter of concern at the time! Having vowed not to meddle in civil affairs, but realizing Motta's unpopularity, Cotton probably placated Villava with words of reassurance and minor concessions. Notwithstanding the occasional trivial complaint, Cotton and Villava established a mutually beneficial relationship that facilitated the Royal Navy's use of the port facilities at Mahón.[35]

A few days after Villava met with Cotton, the *Blossom* arrived at Mahón with three Spanish officers and a Monsieur Charabot, allegedly a captain in the old French navy. The four men had departed Marseille in a boat and succeeded in joining the *Warspite*. The Spaniards had no motive except to escape from France, but they might have been used to legitimize the presence of Charabot, who claimed to carry intelligence from General Emmanuel-Maximilien Guidal at Marseille. As a similar mission had occurred a year earlier with Collingwood, Cotton was suspicious of Charabot's motives. After interrogating the Frenchman, Cotton decided to send him back to Marseille with only an acknowledgment of Guidal's communication. However, Cotton ordered Captain

Stewart to remain off Marseille in the *Blossom* to receive further communication. Villava vouched for the Spaniards, who then returned to their homes.[36]

With provisioning completed a few days later than Cotton intended, the fleet sailed from Mahón on 15 October. Three days later, Cotton found the French fleet still at Toulon, having come out in his absence only for its usual exercise during the day before returning to its anchorage in the evening. The next two weeks exacted a heavy toll on the Mediterranean fleet. From his experience off Brest while in the Channel Fleet, Cotton knew the high cost of maintaining a winter blockade. Yet, St. Vincent and Cornwallis were determined to keep a squadron continuously off the French coast, despite the weather. As their student, Cotton took the same kind of determination to the Mediterranean, but he learned that the conditions off Brest in 1805 and Toulon in 1810 were very different. The sense of urgency in 1805 was greater, and the winter weather off Brest, though difficult, paled in comparison to Toulon. Collingwood had learned that it was best to leave only a few small warships off Toulon, preserving the rest of the fleet at Mahón or Malta for the spring. Despite Cotton's determination, experience would teach him the same lesson. Admiral Fremantle believed that Cotton's successor, Sir Edward Pellew, would also learn the same lesson the hard way: "I perceive that [Pellew] like all other commanders who have been before him must buy his experience, he thinks he will be enabled to keep his station during the winter months, which I know he cannot."[37] Fremantle believed himself qualified to make such an assessment because of his previous service in the Mediterranean Fleet: 1793–1797 under Lord Hood and Sir John Jervis and 1805–1806 under Nelson and Collingwood.

In addition, Fremantle believed that Cotton's blockade was overzealous and detrimental to the fleet's long-term strength. On 29 October, Cotton denied Fremantle's request to refit his ship, claiming that "the state of the enemy in Toulon renders it impossible that the services of the *Ville de Paris* can be dispensed with at the present moment."[38] However, as returns from the fleet arrived over the next few days, Cotton realized the sensibility of Fremantle's request. The *Resistance* and *Seahorse* were "disabled in tempestuous weather"; the head of the *Temeraire*'s mainmast was rotten; and the *Leviathan* had sprung its mainmast. On 2 November, after just fifteen days off Toulon, Cotton decided to take the fleet back to Mahón "to refit the ships in general."[39] No doubt, Fremantle felt smug as the fleet sailed for Mahón.

If the British had possessed the Îles d'Hyères, twelve miles east of Cape Sicie, then the fleet might have been spared the passage back to Mahón. Understanding that these islands had the potential to provide a superb winter anchorage, offer "refreshments," and allow the fleet to "more effectually check the plans of the enemy at Toulon," the Admiralty ordered Cotton to examine the expediency of capturing them.[40] However, the French established several batteries and garrisoned hundreds of troops on the islands to protect their coastal trade. Based on his observations, Cotton concluded that a considerable force was needed to permanently secure the islands and that mobilization of such a force would be difficult. The British generals at Malta, Sicily, and Gibraltar could not spare any troops, and Cotton believed that any additional troops sent to the Mediterranean should proceed to Minorca, an object of unquestionable strategic value. British occupation of the Hyères, a good idea to the Admiralty in London, was considered impracticable by Cotton.[41]

The fleet arrived on 4 November off Mahón, where it remained until 22 March 1811, after three unsuccessful attempts to gain the rendezvous off Toulon. As explained to the First Lord on 17 November, Cotton intended to conduct the winter blockade differently from what actually transpired: "I intend to run for this port or shelter among the islands whenever the weather is such as to justify the quitting the coast, occasionally stretching as far to the westward as Cape St. Sebastian."[42] The fleet's first attempt to leave Mahón was on 11 December, after intelligence brought by the *Euryalus* reported the Toulon Fleet at sea on the 8th. The report proved false, and "strong adverse gales" forced the fleet to take shelter back at Minorca.[43] During the ensuing week, gales prevented two more attempts to depart. Cotton finally realized that the Mediterranean Fleet could not function like the Channel Fleet during the winter months. In early January 1811, he changed the winter rendezvous from Cape Sicie to the original site, Cape St. Sebastian. Bowing to the reality of adverse weather, he finally settled on wintering the fleet at Mahón.[44]

While the fleet anchored at Mahón during the winter, a squadron of three or four frigates maintained vigil over the Toulon Fleet, and command of the squadron off Catalonia passed from Charles Bullen to Thomas Rogers and then to Sir Edward Codrington. Although the fleet was not subjected to the drudgery of blockade or winter gales, for some, these conditions might have been more preferable than those at Mahón in December, January, February, and March. Upon arriving off Catalonia in February 1811, Codrington remarked: "The coming upon this sort of quiet cruise from the bustle of Mahon is like leaving town for a country life."[45] The fleet developed a busy routine in port. It had to be kept in a constant state of readiness to intercept the Toulon Fleet; officers and men were employed in caulking and refitting each vessel; the marines went on shore every Tuesday and Friday for training exercises; and accommodations had to be made for the seven Spanish ships-of-the-line, transports, merchantmen, and various other vessels that used the port's facilities.[46] Supervision of these tasks was the least of Cotton's concerns, compared to improving the island's political stability and state of defense.

Ironically, improvement of Minorca's security decreased its political stability. Since arriving in the Mediterranean, Cotton had petitioned his government to provide a sufficient garrison to protect the Balearics. However, the Spanish government refused to admit a British garrison; besides, Wellington refused to spare British troops from the peninsula. According to Cotton, the Minorquins would react unfavorably to the introduction of any troops except British. The Spanish government compromised by allowing a

British officer, Major General Sir Samuel Whittingham, to command the 10,000 Spanish troops planned for the defense of the Balearics.[47] Before his arrival in the islands in June 1811, about 250 troops of the Walloon Regiment from Tarragona arrived at Mahón on 26 December 1810. They were comprised mostly of French deserters and were commanded by an officer with well-publicized anti-British views. Cotton doubted that the Walloons would improve security and was apprehensive of how Villava would react to their presence. Already the governor levied contributions with a hard hand and acted "most impolitically by threats." A troubled Cotton wrote to Henry Wellesley: "At present the troops sent only increase the danger by irritating the natives who must and ought to support them. They must be left to forage at discretion, and there will be a convulsion in the islands in which we must materially suffer, as our provisions will be too great a bait to be resisted."[48] When the Walloons arrived, Minorca was experiencing a grain shortage to an extent that the Jurat of Mahón had requested Cotton's intercession in their effort to acquire wheat from Sicily. Fortunately, the grain supply at Mahón improved to the extent that in February Cotton no longer needed to rely on large supplies of bread and flour from England. As the food crisis subsided, so too did the probability of insurrection by the Minorquins and depredations by the Walloons. Yet, Cotton continued to worry about the security of his base and the "suspicious character" of the Walloon Regiment.[49]

Cotton encountered a few other annoyances while the fleet anchored at Mahón. British honor was insulted when a sentinel at Fort St. Philips, which protected the mouth of the harbor, presented his musket with the purpose of impeding Admiral Fremantle and two captains, each in uniform. A promise by the Spanish commander to prevent such a recurrence satisfied Cotton.[50] Of a more sensitive nature was a misunderstanding with Commodore Posada. He vehemently asserted that three Spanish anchors were taken from the arsenal by officers from Cotton's fleet. The accusation proved false, and Cotton wanted an official apology from Posada because it was "an occasion which so much involves the honor and credit of the English nation."[51] Finally, selection of a First Captain of the Fleet proved more difficult than anticipated. To replace Admiral Pickmore, Cotton chose Captain Neave, but poor health soon required his return to England. Cotton then applied for Captain George McKinley's assignment to the *San Josef*, but he was presently in England. Meanwhile, Captain Ferrier succeeded Neave, but after two weeks was reassigned to a frigate. Cotton settled on Captain Sir Richard King, whom Fremantle believed would not "be of much service" as First Captain.[52]

In the wake of Captain King's selection, Fremantle privately expressed his disdain for Cotton to his patron, the Marquis of Buckingham. Fremantle claimed that Cotton consulted none of his subordinate admirals during the selection process. He then severely attacked Cotton's ability as commander-in-chief: "Indeed, nothing can stand lower than our chief in the estimation of us all, and the total want of energy and decision becomes more apparent every day." He continued: "We are all perfectly at our ease, and live well together; and if the squadron is in high order, it is to the captains and officers we are indebted; for the commander-in-chief troubles himself very little about such matters, and does not, I believe, listen to a single person except his secretary, who deceives him."[53] Where do reality and perception collide? Cotton appeared at fault for not consulting his subordinates during the search for a First Captain, but consistent isolation from his admirals cannot be deduced from this incident. Fremantle's correlation between leadership style and professional competence was likely influenced by the flamboyance and aggressiveness of Nelson. Since these were not Cotton's strongest traits, Fremantle probably interpreted his unassuming character and deliberativeness as signs of incompetence. However, Fremantle was known for his quick temper and negative criticism of senior officers. Even Collingwood was not spared his invective after Trafalgar.[54] Granting some legitimacy to Fremantle's comments, a more animated style of leadership might have raised Cotton's esteem in the minds of his subordinates. For all his criticism, curiously, Fremantle concluded after the fleet departed Mahón in March: "There is as much good will and good sense in [Cotton's] fleet as any that ever were in the Mediterranean."[55]

Perhaps Cotton troubled "himself very little about such matters" at Mahón, as Fremantle lamented, because events at Carthagena, Catalonia, and Toulon demanded more attention. The fever at Carthagena had delayed removal of the naval stores during the final months of 1810. With the quarantine lifted, Cotton ordered seven transports under escort of the *Cossack* from Gibraltar to Carthagena, where they arrived on 25 January 1811. He also sent Captain Adam in the *Invincible* to provide assistance. Colonel Roche, at the insistence of Henry Wellesley, superintended the operation at Carthagena and was extremely appreciative of Cotton's support: "The entire salvation of all the Spanish squadron and valuable naval stores from this arsenal is solely due to your extreme readiness in affording, upon every occasion, the necessary assistance for their removal."[56] Roche employed about 400 soldiers to drag the timber and spars, which he estimated worth £90,000, out of the holding ponds and on to the transports. Needing at least twelve additional large transports for the remaining stores, Roche asked Cotton to spare what he could from Mahón. Cotton could spare none and had already ordered Keats and Penrose to send any available transports to Carthagena.[57]

Nevertheless, most, if not all, of the stores were sent to Mahón, including about 300 artificers. Through the conscientious exertions of Roche, Cotton, and Henry Wellesley, the valuable naval resources at Carthagena were kept from the French, but the Spanish government still refused to sell them to the British. In May 1811, however, the destitute state of the Spanish navy at Mahón forced Commodore Posada to offer a portion of the stores evacuated from Carthagena for sale. To Cotton's dismay, Fremantle accepted Posada's offer. The Spanish government at Cadiz still had not authorized the British purchase of these stores, despite Posada's initiative.[58]

While the evacuation at Carthagena concluded favorably, allied fortunes in Catalonia had declined during the winter. In December, Suchet's investment of Tortosa entered its final stage before the collapse of Spanish resistance. In addition, Cotton's squadron suffered a severe setback at Palamos on 13 December. Pursuant to his own sense of the situation and Admiralty guidance, Cotton sent Captain Rogers' 74-gun *Kent* and the 74-gun *Ajax* from Mahón on 21 November to reinforce the squadron off Catalonia. Not long after Rogers' arrival, eleven French vessels laden with supplies for Barcelona took shelter beneath protective batteries at Palamos. Unable to attack the convoy, Rogers ordered Captain Fane of the *Cambrian* to destroy the French batteries with a landing party consisting of 350 seamen and 250 marines. Fane accomplished his objective, which enabled Rogers' squadron to close on and destroy the unprotected convoy. Unfortunately, Fane's force failed to withdraw before the arrival of French reinforcements. In addition to 122 British casualties, the French captured Fane and eighty-six others from the landing party. Cotton estimated that making up this loss would reduce the complement of each ship in the fleet by twenty to thirty men.[59] Rather than strongly reprimanding Rogers for the disaster at Palamos, Cotton stated: "I am by no means dissatisfied with any part of your conduct on the occasion in question, lamenting only that a proper degree of caution was not observed in the retreat of the men."[60]

Suchet captured Tortosa on 2 January 1811; consequently, Tarragona became the next French objective in Catalonia. With General O'Donnell convalescing at Majorca, the Marquis de Campoverde assumed command of Spanish troops in Catalonia. Campoverde, Macdonald, and Suchet spent the ensuing months preparing for the inevitable campaign for Tarragona. In the midst of preparation, Campoverde asked Commodore Posada to send all available powder and gun carriages from Mahón to Tarragona. At Campoverde's request, Cotton provided the *Cambrian* to assist a Spanish frigate in transporting 300 quintals of powder and several carriages. He later sent to Tarragona the *Minorca* and a transport with additional powder and shot. Cotton reassured the Spanish commander: "The keeping a squadron on the coast of Catalonia has ever been an object of my attention consistently with the important service of keeping in check the enemy's naval force at Toulon and other ports in these seas."[61]

Meanwhile, the French persisted in their efforts to slip convoys into and out of Barcelona. On the night of 10 January, a Captain Meynard eluded the British frigates off Toulon and proceeded to Barcelona with three frigates and a convoy laden with grain. The convoy safely arrived at its destination, and the frigates returned to Toulon on the 16th. Meynard received the *Légion d'honneur* for this exploit. However, the vessels of Meynard's convoy were not so fortunate on their return journey; nearly all of them were captured by Codrington's squadron in mid-February. Aboard one of the vessels were 120 French invalids. Because of the difficulty of caring for prisoners, especially invalids, Cotton ordered their return to Barcelona. Also taken on one of the vessels was an aide-de-camp carrying papers destined for Napoleon. From them it appeared that Tarragona was indeed the next French objective in Catalonia and that a reinforcement of 18,000 French troops was required. Cotton duly forwarded this information to London.[62]

Despite capturing the French convoy, Codrington experienced frustration while he helplessly witnessed French army operations along the coast during March and April. His squadron occasionally fired a few rounds but could not prevent the French from exacting contributions from the coastal villages. Codrington believed that a few gunboats and extra small vessels "might do wonders" to increase Catalan morale. Yet, Cotton did not increase the squadron off Spain beyond a few frigates and sloops. His attention was fixated predominantly on the Toulon Fleet, where Admiral Allemand had intentions other than sending supply convoys to Barcelona.[63]

On 12 December 1810, the frigates *Pauline* and *Thémis* embarked for Corfu with munitions; with the same destination, the *Pomone* and *Persane* left Toulon on 12 February. Both expeditions disembarked troops at Elba and both arrived at Corfu without pursuit, thus proving the vulnerability of Cotton's winter blockade. Napoleon hoped to exploit this vulnerability in March 1811 by sending an expedition to either Sicily or Sardinia with 15,000 troops, fifteen ships-of-the-line, six frigates, and various other vessels. Preparations were underway at Toulon while the Mediterranean Fleet anchored at Mahón.[64]

Cotton received indications of Allemand's preparation by intelligence from Captain Charabot and General Guidal. They claimed in February that between 8,000 and 10,000 troops at Toulon were preparing for a maritime expedition to either Sardinia or Sicily. By then, Cotton was convinced of the Frenchmen's sincerity. Most of their intelligence had already been confirmed by British observations. Furthermore, Charabot was apparently motivated to gain the release of his son from an British prison, for which Cotton made an application. Guidal went so far to gain Cotton's confidence that he requested an interview; Cotton respectfully declined for obvious security reasons. The Admiralty later granted him an expense account between £500 and £1,000 to maintain communication with the Frenchmen. Because of increased suspicion of a French expedition to the eastward, Cotton dispatched *Ajax* and *Unité* from Mahón to cruise between Corsica and Genoa. They preceded the fleet's departure for Toulon by only three days.[65]

The fleet hastened from Mahón on 22 March to deter the expected French sortie from Toulon. However, recent French setbacks in the Peninsula further distracted Napoleon's attention from the Mediterranean; the expedition from Toulon was postponed until circumstances were more favorable, perhaps in 1812.[66] Wellington had already repulsed the third French invasion of Portugal at the Lines of Torres Vedras, and Marshal Masséna officially abandoned his offensive on 5 March 1811, the same day that an Anglo-Spanish force fought the Battle of Barrosa. In January, Marshal Soult ordered Victor to send part of his corps north to support a diversion in favor of Masséna's campaign. General Graham and General Joachim Blake of the Regency seized this as an opportunity to end the siege of Cadiz and drive the French from Andalusia. Keats' squadron supported the Barrosa campaign by transporting British and Spanish troops to Algeciras and Tarifa and by conducting amphibious demonstrations as circumstances required. Graham's force soundly defeated Victor's troops on the 5th, but without assistance from General Thomás La Peña's Spaniards. Because of La Peña's reticence, Graham's tactical victory was devoid of strategic value—the siege of Cadiz lasted for seventeen more months. According to Henry Wellesley: "The expedition [had] thus terminated gloriously for the British troops engaged in it, but most deplorably for the objects proposed by it."[67]

Upon the fleet's arrival off Cape Sicie on 24 March, Cotton learned that the frigates *Apollo* and *Imperieuse* had proceeded eastward in pursuit of two French frigates that had left Toulon three days earlier. Inclement weather then forced the fleet southward on the 27th, which provided an opportunity for the French to dispatch three more frigates and a storeship to the east. After quickly returning to Cape Sicie, Cotton now believed that the French troops collecting at Corsica were intended for an invasion of Sardinia. Subsequent strong gales forced the fleet back to Minorca for a week in mid-April before it returned to the rendezvous on the 19th. Thereafter, the drudgery of blockade duty resumed for the summer. Its nature for the next few months was best summarized by a marine sergeant aboard the *Temeraire*: "We employed ourselves to watch the motions of the French fleet. They often left the harbour, when the wind was right for them to get back again; and so soon as our fleet gave them chase, they would run in directly."[68]

Convinced of Allemand's intention to embark his fleet on an expedition, Cotton ordered the withdrawal of his ships-of-the-line on the coast of Catalonia. With more ships-of-the-line off Toulon, he would "be enabled to make further detachments with a view of counteracting any operations the enemy may meditate."[69] Cotton ordered the withdrawal without realizing the critical need for British warships off the coast of Catalonia as Suchet advanced toward the investment of Tarragona. Fortunately, Cotton countermanded the order. He directed Codrington to proceed to Barcelona in the 74-gun *Blake*; take under his command the *Cambrian*, *Volontaire*, *Termagant*, and *Sparrowhawk*; and continue active operations along the coast. Codrington's squadron made many valuable contributions during the seven-week siege of Tarragona, which commenced on 8 May.[70]

On 3 April, the Admiralty appointed Cotton to command of the Channel Fleet. The First Lord of the Admiralty appeared determined to enforce the system of relieving admirals from their stations after three years—Lord Gambier had succeeded to command of the Channel Fleet in May 1808. Cotton received Yorke's announcement of the appointment on 24 April and immediately addressed a letter to his wife: "I . . . bless kind Providence that has guarded and led me to the top of my profession. I should think that my successor Sir Edward Pellew would be out in the next month or June when I shall return homewards in my dear old ship with all my people about me, another proof of friendly attention that I shall never forget."[71] The wait for Pellew lasted until 15 July, when he arrived off Toulon in HMS *Caledonia* of 120 guns, the largest ship ever built in a British dockyard. Meanwhile, the campaign for Catalonia progressed without regard to Cotton's scheduled departure.[72]

Codrington supported Campoverde's defense of Tarragona by delivering reinforcements and supplies, withdrawing the wounded and noncombatants, and conducting naval bombardments against the French lines. In addition, his squadron conducted diversions in cooperation with the Spanish navy. For instance, Captain Adam's *Invincible* led a naval detachment of two frigates and ten xebecs to support the attack by a Valencian unit upon the French post at La Rapita, fifty miles south of Tarragona. On 9 May, Adam began a naval bombardment of the stronghold after the French commander refused to surrender. Moreover, he landed five guns for use by a detachment of Valencian artillerymen. The operation went awry when a French relief column of 800 troops from Tortosa negated the initial success of the Anglo-Spanish effort. Because of Suchet's focus, the defenders of Tarragona benefited little from the attack upon La Rapita. He remarked: "The commander-in-chief found himself . . . at the risk of seeing the English repeat their landings and attacks on the coast. He wished not to disperse his forces, but, on the contrary, to concentrate them still more, if possible, on the single point of Tarragona."[73]

Construction of batteries to drive Codrington's squadron to an anchorage beyond the range of naval gunfire was the first object of Suchet's siege. An exchange of cannon fire commenced on 13 May between the French and the *Blake*, *Cambrian*, and *Termagant*. On the 14th, some French deserters reported that British gunfire had caused nearly 400 French casualties. Because of damage to his ships, their rapid expenditure of ammunition, and progress of the French works, Codrington extended his anchorage further from the shore. Furthermore, he criticized the Spaniards for not aggressively attacking the French lines. A lack of offensive zeal was demonstrated during a failed attempt to destroy the French seaside batteries—the Spanish assault force of 1,200 troops suffered only about fourteen casualties. Codrington believed that preparation of the defense was not proceeding well because of "apathy and indifference" from those who should set the example.[74] Nevertheless, he continued supporting Campoverde wholeheartedly.

After permanent establishment of the French seaside batteries, Codrington sent the heavily damaged *Termagant* to Mahón with a Spanish representative who sought to procure more supplies. Having anticipated the shortage at Tarragona, Cotton had already sent from Mahón the *Bombay* and *Bustard* sloops with two transports full of "all the succours it is in my power to grant from our naval resources in this quarter."[75] Meanwhile, Campoverde directed

Codrington to collect reinforcements, supplies, and ammunition from Valencia. With the assistance of the 74-gun *Centaur*, *Invincible*, *Sparrowhawk*, and several British transports, Codrington landed a considerable amount of supplies and ammunition at Tarragona by 7 June, including about 6,300 infantry and 300 artillery soldiers. Cotton applauded the effort of Codrington's squadron but sensed its futility as long as Campoverde led the Spanish effort.[76]

Campoverde sailed from Tarragona on 31 May to recruit and lead a relief force, leaving General Juan Contreras to command the garrison. He collected an army of 11,000 troops in Catalonia, but conducted only distant diversions, without an attempt to decisively engage Suchet's force. On 21 June, the French army captured the Lower City, thereby forcing Codrington's squadron to the Milagro roadstead off the Upper City, where its naval gunfire was useless. Despite continued exertions, Codrington and his squadron could now do little to prevent the tragedy about to unfold. The situation was so desperate that he would not allow the disembarkation of 1,100 British reinforcements from Cadiz after their arrival off Taragona on the 26th. Two days later, Suchet's army captured the Upper City. Codrington's grim final task off Tarragona was to rescue some 600 survivors from the waters off the Upper City. Suchet had gained a decisive victory, and the Catalans lost over one-half their regular army and their last sea port. With a marshal's baton destined for Suchet, his attention then turned south to Valencia.[77]

With nothing further to do in the waters off Tarragona, Codrington moved his squadron north off Villaneuva and intended to "remain upon the coast until the crisis has passed . . . and to show the suffering people that with the fall of their principal fortress, they have not lost the assistance of England." Cotton received Codrington's account of Tarragona's fall on 5 July, ten days before Pellew arrived off Toulon. He fully approved of Codrington's performance, only regretting that his exertions "had not the effect of inspiring [the Spaniards] with energy correspondent to the true spirit of patriotism and bravery which the Catalans might have maintained under more experienced officers."[78] Though intended to complement the Catalans, Cotton's comments could be interpreted as yet another example of British arrogance. The British had less than 100 casualties during the battle for Tarragona, while the Spanish defenders lost 15,000 in the process of causing nearly 5,000 French casualties. The fall of Tarragona marked the last significant milestone of Cotton's command in the Mediterranean. Cotton had probably become impatient waiting for Pellew, who did not embark from Spithead until 14 June because of an extended leave of absence. Assumption of command in the Mediterranean proved easier for Pellew than it did for Cotton, who did not have the benefit of conferring with his predecessor. Cotton relinquished command and sailed from Toulon on 18 July, after briefing Pellew for three days about his experiences as commander-in-chief. After a port call at Portsmouth, the *San Josef* arrived at Plymouth on 18 August. It was stripped and went into dock for refitting. Cotton hoisted his flag temporarily aboard the *Venerable* at Portsmouth before proceeding to Madingley, where he arrived at the end of the month.[79]

Cotton had several weeks during the passage home to reflect on his performance in the Mediterranean. He certainly felt little of the apprehension associated with the return voyage from Portugal in December 1808. None of his decisions in the Mediterranean had produced a potentially career-ending controversy. For fifteen months, he had prevented the Toulon Fleet's escape, the only event in the Mediterranean at the time that could have sent shock waves to London. This was what the Admiralty Board noticed, and why Cotton received the Channel Fleet command, notwithstanding seniority. The Board might not have been impressed by Cotton's day-to-day handling of the fleet, as Fremantle suggested, but rarely does an introspective analysis of a large, diversified organization reveal flawless administration.

Cotton deserves some criticism for uninspiring leadership in the Mediterranean, but it must be mitigated by circumstances of the time. Fremantle might have wished Cotton were charismatic in the likeness of Nelson. Apparently, Nelson was the only senior officer that Fremantle respected. However, Fremantle, a malcontent himself, was not supported by the comments of others of equal rank. Cotton was not a risk-taker by nature, and Admiralty guidance explicitly directed commanders in the Mediterranean not to risk engagements unless certain of favorable results. Because the French fleet never made an appearance in force beyond the immediate waters off Toulon, by default, Cotton deferred heroic action to the likes of captains Eyre, Hoste, Codrington, and Adam. If Cotton's spirit was not aggressive, it did not dampen the efforts of his subordinates in the Adriatic, off Sicily, Catalonia, and elsewhere. Furthermore, considering the Mediterranean Fleet commander's scope of responsibility, a certain amount of detachment and selective listening prevented mental paralysis from too many details. Despite Cotton's relatively uninspiring leadership style, he achieved the desired end state: strategic stability in the Mediterranean while the British government focused on the Peninsular War.

NOTES

1. Admiral Fremantle to the Marquis of Buckingham, 1 March 1811, Duke of Buckingham and Chandos, K.G., *Memoirs of the Court of England, during the Regency, 1811–1820* (London, 1856), 1: 54, 55.

2. Charles Yorke to Lady Cotton, 3 April 1811, Cambridgeshire County Record Office, Cotton Naval Papers, 588/c96.

3. Martin to Cotton, 1 October 1810, Amherst to Cotton, 20 September 1810, PRO ADM 1/417; Lieutenant General Sir Henry Edward Bunbury, *Narratives of Some Passages in the Great War with France, from 1799 to 1810* (London, 1854), 399–403;

George Cockburn, *A Voyage to Cadiz and Gibraltar up the Mediterranean to Sicily and Malta in 1810, & 1811* (London, 1815), 1: 80–87, 96–102.

4. Napoleon to Clarke, 13 October 1810, Napoleon Bonaparte, *Correspondence de Napoléon Ier, publée par order de l'Empereur Napoléon III* (Paris, 1858–69), no. 17042, 20: 215–16; Desmond Gregory, *Sicily, The Insecure Base: A History of the British Occupation of Sicily, 1806–1815* (Rutherford, 1988), 86–87; A. Hilliard Atteridge, *Joachim Murat: Marshal of France and King of Spain* (New York, 1911), 216–17.

5. Cotton to Keats, 20 November 1810, National Maritime Museum, Keats Papers, KEA 12/7.

6. Hoste to Eyre, 14, 15 March 1811, Eyre to Cotton, 24 March 1811, Cotton to Croker, 17 April 1811, PRO ADM 1/416.

7. Thomas Cochrane, *Autobiography of a Seaman* (London, 1908), 142.

8. Marshal Louis Suchet, Duke d'Albufera, *Memoirs of the War in Spain, from 1808 to 1814* (London, 1829), 1: 180–85.

9. Henry Wellesley to Richard Wellesley, 23 August 1810, Arthur Wellesley, Duke of Wellington, *Supplementary Despatches, Correspondence, and Memoranda of Field Marshal Arthur Duke of Wellington, K.G.* [hereafter cited as *Wellington's Supplementary Despatches*], ed. by his son, the Duke of Wellington (London, 1858–1872), 6: 579–80.

10. Cotton to Keats, 11 September 1810, PRO ADM 7/43; Keats to Croker, 25 September 1810, Acknowledgement of letters received by Cotton from the Admiralty, 4 October 1810, PRO ADM 1/417; Edward Pelham Brenton, *The Naval History of Great Britain from the Year 1783 to 1822* (London, 1825), 4: 442–43; Antony Brett-James, *General Graham, Lord Lynedoch* (New York, 1959), 197–98; Edward Fraser and L.G. Carr-Laughton, *The Royal Marine Artillery, 1804–1923* (London, 1930), 1: 138.

11. Roche to Cotton, 26 June 1810, PRO ADM 7/42.

12. Rowley to Cotton, 5 August 1810, Cambridgeshire County Record Office, Cotton Naval Papers, 588/c76(b).

13. Roche to Cotton, 26 June 1810, PRO ADM 7/42.

14. Cotton to Croker, 17 June 1810, Croker to Cotton, 2 August 1810, PRO ADM 7/41; Rowley to Cotton, 5 August 1810, Cambridgeshire County Record Office, Cotton Naval Papers, 588/c76(b); Cotton to Rowley, 12 August 1810, Cotton to Pickmore, 12 August 1810, Cotton to Keats, 12 October 1810, PRO ADM 7/43; Croker to Cotton, 2 August 1810, PRO ADM 2/294. A report on 23 August, included in Cotton's letter to Keats on 12 October 1810, calculated 3,134 pieces of oak timber and 1,212 spars at Carthagena.

15. Henry Wellesley to Keats, 28 August 1810, 15 October 1810, Keats to Croker, 30 August 1810, 9 November 1810, Keats to Henry Wellesley, 16 October 1810, PRO ADM 1/417; Cotton to Keats, 8, 12 October 1810, Cotton to Penrose, 18 October 1810, PRO ADM 7/43. The *Guerrero* was constructed in 1735 and broken up in 1844, perhaps the longest continuous service of any ship-of-the-line. See John D. Harbron, *Trafalgar and the Spanish Navy* (Annapolis, 1988), 17.

16. Henry Wellesley to Keats, 8 November 1810, PRO ADM 1/417.

17. Cotton to his wife, 27 August 1810, Cambridgeshire County Record Office, Cotton Naval Papers, 588/c95.

18. O'Donnell to Cotton, 12 July 1810, PRO ADM 7/42.

19. Cotton to Croker, 20 July 1810, PRO ADM 7/41.

20. Suchet, *Memoirs*, 1: 181–82.

21. Bullen to Cotton, 28 August 1810, PRO ADM 1/417.

22. Ibid., Doyle to Sir John Stuart, 28 August 1810.

23. Ibid., Cotton to Croker, 12 September 1810.

24. Ibid., Bullen to Cotton, 28 September 1810, Fane to Bullen, 29 September 1810; O'Donnell to Fane, undated, September 1810, PRO ADM 7/42. Extracts from "Diary of Royal Marine Colonel Daniel Robinson," in possession of Dr. Robin N.W. Thomas, University of Southampton; Robin N.W. Thomas, "British Operations on the Coast of Catalonia, 1808–1811," in *New Lights on the Peninsular War*, ed. Alice Berkeley (Almada, Portugal, 1991), 51–52.

25. Thomas, "British Operations," 52; Charles William Chadwick Oman, *A History of the Peninsular War* (Oxford, 1902–1930), 3: 497–99.

26. Cotton to the Commissioners for Victualling His Majesty's Navy, 12 September 1810; Cotton to Hugh McGraith, Agent Victualler, Palermo, 10 September 1810; Cotton to Fraser, Commissioner at Malta, 11 September 1810; Cotton to Bullen, 2 October 1810, PRO ADM 7/43.

27. Wellington to Liverpool, 8 August 1810, Admiralty to Cotton, 31 August 1810, PRO ADM 7/41.

28. Cotton to Blackwood, 6 October 1810, PRO ADM 7/43; Cotton to Croker, 7 October 1810, PRO ADM 1/417.

29. Cotton to Pickmore, 18 September 1810, PRO ADM 7/43; Cotton to Croker, 7, 12 October 1810, "Disposition of the Ships of His Most Catholic Majesty," undated, PRO ADM 1/417.

30. Brian Lavery, *Nelson's Navy: The Ships, Men and Organisation, 1793–1815* (London, 1989), 252.

31. Cotton to Hood, 26 September 1810, Cotton to Pickmore, 4, 12, 14 October 1810, PRO ADM 7/43; Pickmore to Cotton, 13 October 1810, Cotton to Pickmore, 14 October 1810, PRO ADM 1/417; Croker to Cotton, 12 December 1810, PRO ADM 2/925.

32. Cotton to Yorke, 7 January 1811, British Library, Wellesley Papers, ADD MSS 37292; Yorke to Cotton, 30 August 1810, Cotton to Cummings, 12 October 1810, Cotton to Captain Sir Henry Blackwood, undated, December 1810, PRO ADM 7/41.

33. Villava to Cotton, 4 October 1810, PRO ADM 7/42.

34. Ibid., Villava to Cotton, 5, 8 September 1810.

35. Ibid., Villava to Cotton, 4, 8 October 1810.

36. Ibid., Villava to Cotton, 11 October 1810; Cotton to Croker, 12 October 1810, 26 December 1810, PRO ADM 7/41.

37. Thomas Fremantle to William Fremantle, 16 July 1811, Ann Parry, ed., *The Admirals Fremantle* (London, 1971), 87–88; Cotton to Croker, 22 October 1810, PRO ADM 1/417; Piers Mackesy, *The War in the Mediterranean, 1803–1810* (London, 1957), 298.

38. Cotton to Fremantle, 29 October 1810, PRO ADM 7/43. With an impression formed after nine months' service with Cotton, Fremantle concluded: "If Cotton had common sense he would change them about, and give all an opportunity of refitting, but he cannot make up his mind to let a line of battle ship leave the fleet." Thomas Fremantle to William Fremantle, 29 June 1811, Parry, *Admirals Fremantle*, 86–87.

39. Cotton to Croker, 1, 2 November 1810, PRO ADM 7/41.

40. Ibid., Barrow to Cotton, 30 August 1810.

41. Ibid., Cotton to Croker, 4 October 1810.

42. Ibid., Cotton to Yorke, 17 November 1810.

43. Ibid., Cotton to Croker, 15 December 1810.

44. Cotton to Penrose, 5 January 1811, PRO ADM 7/43.

45. Codrington to his wife, 11 February 1811, Lady Jane Bourchier, ed., *Memoir of the Life of Admiral Sir Edward Codrington* (London, 1873), 1: 198–99.

46. Thomas Rees, *A Journal of Voyages and Travels, by the late Thomas Rees, Serjeant of Marines* (London, 1822), 40–41.

47. Whittingham arrived at Palma as an inspector-general of division. He raised a cavalry corps of 2,000 and in February 1812, established an academy at Palma to train officers and cadets for his division. See Major-General Ferdinand Whittingham, ed., *A Memoir of the Services of Lieutenant-General Sir Samuel Ford Whittingham* (London, 1868), 148–72.

48. Cotton to Henry Wellesley, 28 December 1810, Cotton to Yorke, 17 November 1810, 26 December 1810, PRO ADM 7/41; Henry Wellesley to Cotton, 6 November 1810, PRO ADM 7/42; Admiral Fremantle claimed that "not more than 600 Spanish troops" protected Minorca, one-half of whom were former French prisoners. Thomas Fremantle to William Fremantle, 5 January 1811, Parry, *Admirals Fremantle*, 83.

49. Yorke to Liverpool with extracts, 13 March 1811, British Library, Liverpool Papers, ADD MSS 38246; Jurats of Mahón to Cotton, 5 November 1810, PRO ADM 7/42; Cotton to the Commissioners for Victualling His Majesty's Navy, 9 February 1811, PRO ADM 7/43.

50. Cotton to Villava, 5 January 1811, Villava to Cotton, 6 January 1811, Cotton to Colonel de la Loy, 9 January 1811, PRO ADM 7/42.

51. Ibid., Posada to Cotton, 24 January 1811, Cotton to Posada, 25 January 1811, Cotton to Posada, 12 February 1811.

52. Fremantle to the Marquis of Buckingham, 1 March 1811, Buckingham, *Memoirs of the Court of England*, 1: 54–55; Cotton to Croker, 1, 24 February 1811, PRO ADM 7/41.

53. Fremantle to the Marquis of Buckingham, 1 March 1811, Buckingham, *Memoirs of the Court of England*, 1: 54–55.

54. David Horwarth, *Trafalgar: The Nelson Touch* (New York, 1969), 60–62.

55. Ibid., Fremantle to Buckingham, 25 March 1811; Parry, *Admirals Fremantle*, 84. Fremantle persuaded Cotton to leave him in charge of Mahón while the fleet removed to Toulon. He preferred a semi-independent command in a smaller ship, HMS *Rodney*(74), than sailing as fourth in command in the *Ville de Paris*.

56. Roche to Cotton, 13 February 1811, in "Memoir of Cotton," *Naval Chronicle* 27 (1812): 387–88; Cotton to Henry Wellesley, 2 February 1811, PRO ADM 7/42; Cotton to Yorke, 17 November 1810, Cotton to Croker, 24 February 1811, PRO ADM 7/41.

57. Cotton to Keats, 2 February 1811, Cotton to Adams, 16 February 1811, PRO ADM 7/43.

58. Cotton to Croker, 12 April 1811, PRO ADM 7/41; Fremantle to Cotton, 10 May 1811, Parry, *Admirals Fremantle*, 84–85.

59. Barrow to Cotton, 14 September 1810, Cotton to Croker, 21, 26 November 1810, 19 December 1810, Cotton to Yorke, 26 December 1810, Cotton to Croker, 2 February 1811, PRO ADM 7/41; Cotton to Rogers, 19 December 1810, PRO ADM 7/43; Edward Pelham Brenton, *The Naval History of Great Britain from the Year 1783 to 1822* (London, 1823–1825), 4: 431-32; Robin Thomas, "Palamos Revisited: December 13,

1810," *Journal of the Napoleonic Association* (Spring, 1987): 7, 8. General David-Maurice-Joseph Mathieu, governor of Barcelona, requested Cotton's permission to allow an ill general to embark from Barcelona for a French port. Cotton denied the request because of the mistreatment of Captain Fane at Perpignan.

60. Cotton to Rogers, 22 December 1810, PRO ADM 7/43.

61. Cotton to Campoverde, 29 January 1811, Campoverde to Cotton, 21 January 1811, PRO ADM 7/42; Cotton to Codrington, 23 February 1811, PRO ADM 7/43.

62. Cotton to Croker, 24 February 1811, PRO ADM 7/41; Cotton to Codrington, 23 February 1811, PRO ADM 7/43; V. Brun, *Guerres Maritimes de la France: Port de Toulon ses armements, son administration, depuis son origine jusqu'a nos jours* (Paris, 1861), 2: 534–35.

63. Codrington to his wife, 27 February 1811, 5 March 1811, *Memoir of Codrington*, 1: 201–02.

64. Brun, *Guerres Maritimes de la France*, 2: 539–40; Cotton to Croker, 8, 24 February 1811, PRO ADM 7/41; Cotton to Eyre, 8 February 1811, Cotton to Captain Campbell, 23 February 1811, Cotton to Rowley, 24 February 1811, PRO ADM 7/43.

65. Cotton to Guidal, 12 December 1810, Cotton to Croker with three intelligence extracts, 26 December 1810, 19 March 1811, Cotton to Yorke, 26 December 1810, Cotton to Wellesley, 28 December 1810, Croker to Cotton, 8 February 1811, PRO ADM 7/41; Cotton to Boyles, 15 March 1811, PRO ADM 7/43. In August, Charabot was identified in Marseille as a spy by two deserters from the fleet. He was arrested, sent to Paris, and executed on 23 October 1812 before a firing-squad at l'Ecole militaire. See C. Northcote Parkinson, *Edward Pellew, Viscount Exmouth, Admiral of the Red* (London, 1934), 397; and Georges Six, *Dictionnaire Biographique des Généraux and Amiraux Français de la Révolution et de L'Empire, 1792–1814* (Paris, 1934), 1: 541.

66. Napoleon to Decrès, 8 March 1811, *Correspondence de Napoléon Ier*, no. 17434, 21: 446–48; Brun, *Guerres Maritimes de la France*, 2: 540–41.

67. Henry Wellesley to Wellington, 11 March 1811, *Wellington's Supplementary Despatches*, 7: 80; Keats to Cotton, 7 March 1811, *Naval Chronicle* 25 (1811): 339–40.

68. Rees, *Journal of Voyages and Travels*, 41; Cotton to Croker, 31 March 1811, PRO ADM 7/41.

69. Cotton to Croker, 31 March 1811, PRO ADM 7/41; Vice Admiral Maurice Julien Émeriau assumed command of the Toulon Fleet on 8 March 1811. See Brun, *Guerres Maritimes de la France*, 2: 540.

70. Cotton to Codrington, 18 April 1811, *Memoir of Codrington*, 1: 206.

71. Cotton to his wife, 24 April 1811, Cambridgeshire County Record Office, Cotton Naval Papers, 588/036; Yorke to Cotton, 3 April 1808, National Maritime Museum, Charles P. Yorke Papers, YOR/3.

72. Sir Samuel Hood also received orders to return to England, thus leaving Fremantle at Mahón, Pickmore with the fleet, and Boyles at Sicily when Pellew arrived. That summer, Keats replaced Hood as second-in-command; Pickmore replaced Fremantle at Mahón; and Fremantle replaced Boyles at Palermo. Cotton to Hood, 14 June 1811, National Maritime Museum, Hood Papers, MKH/116.

73. Suchet, *Memoirs*, 2: 32.

74. Codrington to Cotton, 15 May 1811, Charles Doyle to Sir John Stuart, 15 May 1811, British Library, Liverpool Papers, ADD MSS 38246.

75. Ibid., Cotton to Croker, 22 May 1811.

76. Ibid., Codrington to Cotton, 15 May 1811, Cotton to Croker, 4 June 1811; Codrington to Cotton, 15 June 1811, *Naval Chronicle* 26 (1811): 170–71; John William Fortescue, *A History of the British Army* (London, 1910–1930), 8: 245–46.

77. Codrington to his wife, 28 June 1811, Bourchier, *Memoir of Codrington*, 1: 224; Codrington to Cotton, 29 June 1811, *Naval Chronicle* 26 (1811): 172–74.

78. Codrington to Cotton, 1 July 1811, Cotton to Codrington, undated, Bourchier, *Memoir of Codrington*, 1: 230, 238; Oman, *Peninsular War*, 4: 525–26.

79. *The Times* of London, 21, 23, 26 August 1811; Parkinson, *Edward Pellew*, 389.

10

Channel Fleet Command: The Peninsula Encircled, August 1811–February 1812

> The only stations in which the French have any fleet from which danger could be apprehended to any quarter are the Scheldt and Toulon. . . . As to the other French ports in the Channel and Bay of Biscay, they have only one ship-of-the-line at Brest, one at Rochefort, not ready for sea, and four at L'Orient, of which, two only can be said to be ready for sea, and those wretchedly manned.
>
> —Liverpool to Wellington, 3 October 1811[1]

Lord Liverpool underestimated the French navy's strength in the Channel and Bay of Biscay in October 1811. Instead of six ships-of-the-line in these ports, the Channel Fleet's September return accounted for thirteen, including eleven frigates. Regardless, Liverpool correctly apprised Wellington of the enemy's threat to Admiral Berkeley's naval force off the Tagus. As long as the Royal Navy contained French naval forces in the Scheldt and Mediterranean, Wellington had no reason to fear an interruption of the sea lanes between Lisbon and Britain that supported his army. Though French naval forces in the Channel were larger than Liverpool estimated, they posed no credible threat to British operations in Spain and Portugal.[2]

Despite the inability of French warships at Brest, L'Orient, the Loire, Sables-d'Olonne, Rochefort, Île d'Aix, and San Sebastián to affect military operations in the Peninsula, they managed to menace British commercial interests. The aggressive spirit of the French navy and numerous French privateers had not completely dissipated by 1811. One example, among many others, occurred on 15 July, when three armed pinnaces captured and carried into Sable-d'Olonne the becalmed British schooner *Snapper*.[3]

When Cotton assumed command of the Channel Fleet during the last week of August 1811, no question existed about its ability to protect Britain against an invasion. The occasional French naval victory in the Channel or Bay of Biscay proved bothersome, but had little material effect upon the Royal Navy's dominance of these waters. The Channel Fleet appeared a relatively quiet station for Cotton to spend this three-year assignment and finish his active naval career. However, as the British government's interest in eastern Spain increased during Cotton's command in the Mediterranean, so too did its interest in northern Spain while he commanded in the Channel.[4] With jurisdiction over the Spanish coast extending to El Ferrol, the Channel Fleet's role in the Peninsular War became more significant as Wellington's army pressed towards the northern Spanish provinces in 1811 and 1812. In his final command, Cotton's influence on the war in Spain and Portugal extended completely around the Peninsula.

Soon after assuming command of the Channel Fleet, Cotton departed Plymouth on furlough to return to Madingley after a seventeen-month absence. He found his wife and four children "perfectly well" and remained at home through September until departing for Plymouth on 7 October.[5] Estate management was a priority because, apparently, it had not been a prosperous year. The wheat crop was "complained of," and the overall harvest was inferior to the year before. Because of a recently implemented "potato system for sheep," however, Madingley produced an abundance of wool. Unfortunately, Cotton could not find buyers.

The most crucial personal business that Cotton conducted was the enclosure of Madingley's fields. Prior to 1811, the medieval open-field strip system was used by the tenants who farmed there. Being permanently assigned relatively close to home, Cotton could now give more detailed attention to the transformation from the old system to the new. Enclosure in the eighteenth and nineteenth centuries meant transforming the local landscape, replacing the scattered allotment-like strips in the arable common fields by larger rectangular fields held in severalty. In most communities in which there were several owners, this change required an Act of Parliament and produced a wealth of documents. In Madingley, of which Cotton was in effect the sole owner, no such procedure was necessary—the landlord could make what changes he liked when he wanted. An estate map from 1811 reveals that Cotton leased the newly enclosed fields to six tenants.[6]

Notwithstanding personal business while at home, Cotton maintained an active correspondence with the Admiralty and his command at Plymouth. Consequently, he became more familiar with the Channel Fleet's organization and disposition before his departure from Cambridgeshire County. His second-in-command was Rear Admiral Sir Harry Neale, who led the fleet's main squadron along the coast, usually near L'Orient or Quiberon Bay. In addition, the fleet had permanent detachments off Brest, Rochefort, and the north coast of Spain. Recently, Captain Hood Hanway Christian of the *Iris* frigate completed a special mission to Spain and had written an extensive report for Cotton and Lord Liverpool.[7]

On 11 April 1811, Lord Liverpool addressed a letter to Wellington that sought the objectives of his upcoming campaign plan and the means necessary to accomplish them. The war secretary also asked him to consider if advantages could be derived by assisting the Spaniards with offensive operations by a "small disposable corps" on the coast of Spain, either at Cadiz, Catalonia, or the Biscay provinces: "It may be worth considering, therefore, whether an effort of this description to assist them might not have the effect of instilling new energies into the people of those countries, and of materially embarrassing the operations of the enemy in the provinces contiguous to France."[8] Wellington had a different reason to encourage operations in these areas, especially in northern Spain, where Marshal Jean-Baptiste Bessières commanded the Army of the North. Wellington did not want Bessières' mobile force of 15,000 troops threatening the left flank of his Anglo-Portuguese army while it attempted to capture the frontier fortress of Badajoz that summer. Rather than use British troops to accomplish this diversion, Wellington encouraged the Spanish Army of Galicia to distract the Army of the North; General José Santocildes complied with the duke's request.[9]

Meanwhile, Lord Liverpool had dispatched Captain Christian to the north coast of Spain to assist the guerrillas and, apparently, to ascertain the utility of amphibious operations in the future. Captain Sir Home Popham had received similar instructions for his mission to Spain in 1810.[10] After conferring with British and Spanish agents at La Coruña, Christian sailed on 16 June; his *Iris* operated along the coast until departing for Plymouth on 20 August. He intended to land arms and ammunition at various ports for use by the partisan forces led by Francisco Mina, Juan Diaz Porlier, Francisco Longa, Don Gaspar Jaureque, and the guerrilla chief Campillo. However, French signal stations along the coast monitored the *Iris's* progress, which enabled the French to react quickly to British landings. Nonetheless, Christian made contact with the partisans on several occasions. Campillo received 200 muskets and a small quantity of ammunition at Laredo on 14 June; and Jaureque received 100 muskets, 30 pistols, 50 sabers, and 10,000 pounds of ammunition at Motrico on 4 July. After landing arms and ammunition for Mina at Motrico on 7 August, the *Iris* was joined by the frigates *Rhin* and *Princess Charlotte*. They then joined Captain Sir George Ralph Collier, who was preparing his frigate the *Surveillante* to cooperate with Porlier in an attempt to drive the French from Santander. Arriving too late to help, the *Iris* landed more supplies at Llanes on the 18th before leaving the coast for England. As a result of the naval support for the partisans in the Biscay provinces and the Army of Galicia's offensive, Bessières' Army of the North did not threaten Wellington's operation against Badajoz.[11]

In his report, Christian made several recommendations. Regarding cooperation and moral support for the partisans, he noted their sensitivity towards British control. The British should avoid hurting their "feelings" lest proclamations and letters distributed by the French draw them over to the enemy's cause. Furthermore,

It would be advisable to attend to the request of the guerrilla leaders to a certain extent in regard to the nature of supplies. They want ammunition more than arms, for the nature of their warfare does not admit of their making any depots. The general feature of the country, mountainous and rugged, renders artillery useless, and when acting offensively can never follow up their success as the enemy invariably retreat to entrench themselves in the nearest village from whence they cannot be dislodged by musketry.[12]

Christian then addressed the subject of naval cooperation. He understood the commercial and military advantages the French gained by controlling San Sebastián, Guetaria, Bermeo, Bilbao, and Santoña. Destruction of all the region's small craft was the best means of hindering the French, but this measure would alienate the lower classes from the British. Therefore, Christian suggested: "The enemy's garrisons may be harassed by feints and those between San Sebastián and Santoña would fall easily if attacked by the guerrillas and a small squadron." In fact, the French garrisons at Lequito and Santander were overrun the next summer by partisans in cooperation with Popham's squadron.

Christian's report did not provide any startling new insight into how the British should conduct operations on the north coast of Spain, but rather contributed to a developing framework of ideas. Another report regarding northern Spain, this one from Captain Collier, reached Cotton at Madingley. It contained a series of questions seeking to establish the boundaries within which he could support the guerrillas.

1st. May I supply General Porlier or any other patriot general with a proportion of ammunition on urgent occasions, taking his receipt for my voucher?

2nd. May I supply him with a proportion of biscuit in case of exigency, when about to undertake a march or on a conjunct attack upon an enemies [sic] post, where expedition and secrecy are necessary?

3rd. On finding a man capable and willing to produce intelligence of the state of a particular town or garrison or of the movements of the enemy: May I employ him at a moderate rate and obtain payment on certificate from the British Commissary and Agent at Corunna?

4th. As there are instances where fishing boats being armed had surprized boats of some of the small cruizers and as the same description of boats are frequently made use of for conveying troops, ammunition, etc. . . . May I destroy a few belonging to such towns whence boats have been so employed?[13]

Collier's and Christian's reports served notice to Cotton of his fleet's involvement off the north coast of Spain. With Wellington's advance towards the Biscay provinces, Cotton realized that his fleet would have a more direct impact on the war than the naval operations off distant Catalonia.

Cotton's estate management and preparation for command were interrupted by a dispute that followed him to the grave. On 10 February 1811, Captain George Cockburn, best remembered for burning the White House in 1814, arrived at Cadiz with nearly 2,000,000 dollars of specie from Spanish America. The Spanish government paid Cockburn a two and one-half percent remuneration on the whole sum delivered. According to naval law and custom, he then paid a third of the remuneration to Admiral Keats' secretary for distribution among the admirals of the Mediterranean Fleet. However, the recent case of *Captain Janverine vs. Admiral Montagu* raised questions about the legality of this practice. Cockburn, with the assistance of two lawyers, then respectfully asked Cotton to return his portion of the freight money, an estimated 7,000 dollars.[14]

Cotton understood that cession to Cockburn's demand would establish a precedent harmful to all British admirals, who often relied on freight money to compensate them for service-related expenses. He refused to comply with Cockburn's request and notified his former subordinates of the case pending against them. Sir Samuel Hood's argument against Cockburn's demand best summarized the admiral's perspective:

> Why are the customs of the navy, when guided on many year's practice, to be broken through by opinions that seem to change the very foundation of the laws of England? If indeed these opinions have been given from an idea that the captain is the only one responsible for the security of the money so conveyed, they are formed to overturn the same constructive right of admirals sharing for captures at which they are not actually present. . . .[I]t certainly should be conceived that the commander-in-chief and other admirals of a fleet ought at least to be felt responsible both to the capture of ships and conveyance of money.[15]

In addition, admirals Keats, Pickmore, Pellew, Berkeley, and Thornbrough firmly supported Cotton's position. Pickmore accused Cockburn of greed; Berkeley believed that once freight money had been paid "without hesitation," a captain could not recover it; and Thornbrough concluded that "if both freight and head money should not be restored to [admirals] it will make many commands scarce worth accepting."[16]

As the case progressed, Cockburn regretted bringing it to litigation. He sought on several occasions to meet with Cotton and perhaps individually settle the dispute, thereby rescuing as much money as possible "from the clutches of lawyers." Cockburn proposed dividing the disputed money between them, but Cotton would not compromise. For both men, the case interfered with their naval duties, and Cockburn certainly had no taste for pressing the litigation upon Lady Cotton after her husband's death in February 1812. Cockburn wrote to her in June of that year: "I am sorry that I ever undertook the business and am most anxious to get rid of it. The lawyers as usual encourage both sides to proceed." The next month the matter was closed by consent of both parties with the legal opinion that money once paid, even if by mistake, could not be recovered. However, it took another year for the case to close completely.[17]

After six weeks' leave of absence, the time had arrived for Cotton to raise his flag once again in the Channel. His last departure from Madingley was not affected by the sadness that usually accompanied his previous extended absences. During Cotton's final months of life, his family lived with him at Stoke House near Plymouth.[18]

At 3:00 p.m. on 8 October, Cotton proceeded from the Plymouth dockyard stairs in his barge with an admiral's flag in the stern sheets. He boarded the *San Josef* and was greeted by its captain, his friend George McKinley, before hoisting his flag at the mizzen. Sir Robert Calder, the port admiral, then fired a seventeen-gun salute, which the *San Josef* returned with an equal number.[19] Sir Richard King, as he had been in the Mediterranean, was Cotton's First Captain of the Fleet. While his ship continued preparing for sea, Cotton reviewed his instructions from the Admiralty: "So soon as the *San Josef* shall be ready for sail, you are to proceed in her and join the blockading squadron either off Rochefort, L'Orient, or Brest, as you may judge most advisable, or make such a distribution of your force as shall enable you to visit all those stations for such time as you may deem necessary."[20] After inspecting the condition of his fleet and readiness of French naval forces at the various ports, Cotton could deploy to any part of his station at his own discretion. This order illustrated the tighter control exercised by the Admiralty over the Channel Fleet commander compared to commanders on more distant stations. Cotton no longer had the independence he enjoyed in the Mediterranean, but that was a matter of little consequence because of his unpretentious character.

On 12 November, the *San Josef* sailed from Plymouth for its first destination, Brest, where the detachment was commanded by Lord Colville, captain of the 74-gun *Queen.* His orders were based upon general and specific instructions that the Admiralty had developed with Admiral Gambier over the last few years and had passed on to Cotton. Cotton forwarded to Colville the standing orders for Brest and emphasized reconnaissance of that port as often as the weather would allow. Furthermore, he wanted Colville to destroy enemy vessels at every opportunity and to watch for French vessels reportedly about to leave L'Orient for Brest. As these were standard procedures that had been conducted by the detachment off Brest for several years, Cotton apparently was satisfied with what he had inherited from Gambier. The Admiralty directed the only significant changes, which were based on recent intelligence reports. If the French squadron escaped from Brest undetected, then Colville would lead his detachment to La Coruña, Cape St. Vincent, and Madeira before returning to Brest.[21] Another of the Admiralty's concerns was the presence of "fire balls" with every vessel in the French fleet at Antwerp. The "fire balls," as reported by a spy, were "most destructive" and "all the French officers affirm that bad as your Congreve's Rockettes are, these will be ten times more mischievous."[22] Having given Lord Colville his orders, Cotton then proceeded to join the squadron off L'Orient and Quiberon Bay, commanded by Rear Admiral Neale.

As Cotton's second-in-command, Neale was in charge of the fleet's operations from the Garonne River at Bayonne northward to the Isle of Ushant. Cotton told Neale to pay particular attention to prevent a French escape from Brest, the Charente River, and especially L'Orient, where Vice Admiral Allemand had recently arrived from Toulon. The 80-gun *Eylau*, three 74's, and a corvette were allegedly preparing to embark from L'Orient to Brest. In addition, Neale was to take advantage of any opportunity to conduct offensive operations that had a high "probability of success." Opportunities ranged from naval engagements between ships-of-the-line to the "general annoyance of the enemy" by intercepting privateers and the coastal trade with frigates and small vessels.[23]

Cotton remained at Quiberon Bay from mid-November until early December before proceeding further south to Basque Roads off Rochefort. While with Neale's squadron, he had prepared orders for Captain William Fahie off Rochefort and Captain George Tobin off the north coast of Spain. Fahie's instructions were very similar to those given to Colville and Neale, but Tobin's differed considerably because of the Peninsular War. Cotton ordered Tobin to relieve Collier, who had become more involved with operations along the coast and would continue to do so for the next two years.[24] In addition to other reports, Collier had recently requested "a few troops for the purpose of surprizing some of the enemy's small posts on the coast and keeping up an alarm." Consequently, the Admiralty directed Cotton to order Collier to communicate with Lieutenant Colonel Sir Howard Douglas, the British military commander at La Coruña, and "to undertake no service on shore" without first consulting that officer.[25] Tobin received the same instruction to guide his operations against the "depredations of the enemy": "You will employ the ships and vessels under your orders in cruizing from Corunna to the eastward along the north coast of Spain to Bayonne for the purpose of intercepting any supplies the French may attempt to throw in for the use of their armies in Spain, and of affording such assistance as may be required by the Spanish government."[26] With the exception of consulting Sir Howard Douglas, the senior officer along the north coast was restricted only by geographic boundaries. Despite having some knowledge of the situation in northern Spain, Cotton wisely refrained from the tendency of senior leaders to complicate operations by imposing well-intentioned, yet restrictive measures. He understood that Douglas and the senior naval officer off the coast were best qualified to make decisions that advanced the cause in Spain. As commander-in-chief, logistical support was his main responsibility for Tobin's squadron.

After visiting the stations "deemed necessary," Cotton returned to Plymouth on Christmas eve and shifted his flag to HMS *Bulwark* while the *San Josef* went to replenish at Spithead. The Admiralty had ordered all three-decked ships in the Channel Fleet to replenish there instead of Cawsand Bay. The Admiralty had also given Cotton the option of returning to Plymouth instead of remaining off the coast of France. Apparently satisfied with the condition of the fleet by his inspection, Cotton decided to exercise command of the fleet that winter from Plymouth while his subordinates maintained the blockade. Perhaps his experience in the Mediterranean had tempered his attitude about the necessity of the commander-in-chief to maintain a vigil off the coast during the winter. Moreover, ensuring that the fleet was properly manned, equipped, and supplied were tasks best accomplished in port, where communication with the Admiralty only took a matter of hours.[27]

Meanwhile, the French remained active in the Channel. Eleven British officers and eighty-two seamen and marines were captured in early January 1812 when boats from the *Colossus* and the *Conquistador*, two 74s, attacked a convoy going from Rochelle to Île d'Aix. On 9 January, the French frigates *Ariane* and *Andromaque* sailed from Nantes to conduct attacks against commerce in the Atlantic. Furthermore, the report of an expedition fitting out at Brest ensured that the winter would not pass away too quietly for Cotton at Plymouth with his family. A Captain Erskine had come to Britain as commissary of a cartel with the crew of the frigate *Nereide*, which the French had captured on 18 September 1810 in the Indian Ocean. He claimed that three ships-of-the-line, two of these coming from Cherbourg, and six frigates were preparing to embark from Brest with 5,000 troops. Heeding the report, the Admiralty hastened the refitting of the ships-of-the-line at the various Channel ports. Consequently, Cotton could grant no leave of absence for periods more than a week.[28]

Cotton continued commanding from the *Bulwark* in Cawsand Bay until February, when he ordered Captain King to proceed in that ship to relieve Neale off Quiberon Bay.[29] Before Neale's return to Plymouth, however, Cotton died on the morning of 23 February at Stoke House from what his *Naval Chronicle* memoir described as an "apoplectic" attack. He had retired that evening just before midnight, and at 1:30 a.m., Lady Cotton awoke to the movement of his getting out of bed. In the midst of seizure, Cotton sat in a bedside chair before slumping to his death. Lady Cotton failed in her attempt to revive him. Beyond earlier bouts of rheumatism, there were no previous indications that his health was impaired, so his death came as a shock to his family and associates.[30]

Most deaths are tragic, but Cotton's demise seemed more so because of the family left behind and the fact that he was struck down at the pinnacle of his career after such a brief occupation. A letter of condolence to Lady Cotton from the officers of the *San Josef* was but a small token to relieve her suffering.

> The officers of H.M.S. San Josef, deeply lamenting the loss of their highly esteemed commander and patron, beg leave to offer their most sincere sentiments of condolence to Lady Cotton, on an occasion so truly mournful and afflicting. After a long and uniform

experience of every indulgent favor, and the most humane and generous attention to their several comforts and wishes, they cannot but conceive it a duty peculiarly incumbent on them, at this melancholy crisis, to entreat, that Lady Cotton would condescend to accept this tribute of unfeigned respect, and affectionate regard, for the memory of their late exemplary and honorable Admiral.[31]

The deceased received full military honors on 6 March, when the body began its journey from Stoke House to the place of interment in Cambridgeshire. With the hearse led by a troop of horse artillery, the Field Officer's Guard of the Royal Chesire Militia, and a Marine Band, the procession proceeded to the Plymouth dockyard. On its way, a gun from one of the port batteries fired every minute, the band played its solemn music, and Fore Street was lined by local militia with their arms reversed and colors draped with crepe. The Chief Mourner was Reverend Alexander Cotton, one of Sir Charles's two surviving brothers. Also in the procession, among others, were Captain Rowley, the admiral's brother-in-law, and admirals Charles Boyles, Sir Harry Neale, and Sir Robert Calder. Upon the body's arrival at the dockyard, it was conveyed by a barge to Captain Rowley's *Pelorus* sloop, which fired a seventeen-gun salute before its departure to Sheerness. The body finally came to rest on 13 March in the family vault at the ancient church of Landwade. A memorial plaque that summarized his naval career was later placed "amidst the scenes which he most loved and cherished" at Madingley Church. Thus ended a naval career that began nearly forty years earlier when a nineteen-year-old midshipman joined the *Deal Castle*.[32]

Admiral Cotton did not live long enough to make a definitive impact on the Channel Fleet. Though the Admiralty greatly influenced the Channel Fleet's administration and operations, the commander's leadership nonetheless made a difference by establishing high standards and affecting morale. Cotton was present with the fleet for four months and at sea with it for only six weeks—enough time for him to determine its condition, but not enough to implement and enforce any needed changes. Had he lived, his term of command in the Channel would have expired in August 1814. Hence, Cotton would have been associated with Popham's raids along the north coast of Spain in 1812, Collier's blockade of San Sebastián in 1813, and Wellington's campaign in southern France in 1814. Instead, Admiral Lord Keith inherited these distinctions.[33]

Compared to his commands off Portugal and the Mediterranean, Cotton's service as Channel Fleet commander had little direct influence on the Peninsular War because the senior naval officer off the north coast of Spain received specific instructions from Sir Howard Douglas at La Coruña. Cotton certainly ensured that the squadron off Spain received needed logistical support, but his greatest contribution was by an act of omission. After giving very general discretionary orders to the senior naval officer, he made no attempt to interfere with Douglas's recommendations.

NOTES

1. Liverpool to Wellington, 3 October 1811, British Library, Liverpool Papers, ADD MSS 38246.

2. Cotton to Croker with monthly return of enemy's force, 1 September 1811, PRO ADM 1/147.

3. Ibid., Croker to Cotton, 3 September 1811.

4. In September 1810, the British government established General Walker as a special agent at Coruña to assist the guerrillas and provide intelligence for London. John William Fortescue, *A History of the British Army* (London, 1910–1930), 7: 239.

5. Cotton to Lord Hardwicke, 1 September 1811, British Library, Hardwicke Papers, ADD MSS 35649; On 14 September, Cotton requested an extended leave of absence for two weeks. Cotton to Croker, 14 September 1811, PRO ADM 1/147.

6. Lecture notes by Lionel Munby, archivist of Madingley Hall, undated; Copy of the "Plan of the Parish of Madingley, 1811," in possession of the author.

7. Cotton to Croker, 3 September 1811, PRO ADM 1/147; Captain Christian's mission from June-August 1811 was not mentioned in Fortescue's and Oman's accounts of the war, nor was it mentioned in Brenton's or Clowes' naval histories. However, these historians addressed in detail Captain Home Popham's operations off the north coast of Spain in 1810 and 1812.

8. Liverpool to Wellington, 11 April 1811, Arthur Wellesley, Duke of Wellington, *Supplementary Despatches of Field Marshal Arthur Duke of Wellington, K.G.* [hereafter cited as *Wellington's Supplementary Despatches*], ed. by his son (London, 1858–1872), 7: 104–05.

9. Charles William Chadwick Oman, *A History of the Peninsular War* (Oxford, 1902–1930), 4: 460–65; Fortescue, *British Army*, 8: 239.

10. Popham to Keith, 30 May 1812, Christopher Lloyd, ed., *The Keith Papers*, (London, 1955), 3: 267–68; Hugh Popham, *A Damned Cunning Fellow: The Eventful Life of Rear-Admiral Sir Home Popham, KCB, KCH, KM, FRS, 1762–1820* (Tywardreath, Cornwall, 1991), 193–94.

11. Christian to Cotton, 26 August 1811, Christian to Liverpool, 26[?] August 1811, British Library, Liverpool Papers, ADD MSS 38246.

12. Christian to Cotton, 26 August 1811, British Library, Liverpool Papers, ADD MSS 38246.

13. Collier to Gambier, undated, 2 August 1811, 7 September 1811, Cotton to Croker, 18 September 1811, PRO ADM 1/147.

14. Copy Case and Opinions by William Garrow and Serjeant Best, 20 August 1811, 5 September 1811, Cockburn to Cotton, 6, 10 September 1811, Cambridgeshire County Record Office, Cotton Naval Papers, 588/044. In Cockburn's biography, the author makes no mention of the freight case against Cotton. See James Pack, *The Man Who Burned the White House: Admiral Sir George Cockburn, 1772–1853* (Emsworth, Hampshire, 1987), 132–36.

15. Observations of Sir Samuel Hood, undated. Cambridgeshire County Record Office, Cotton Naval Papers, 588/044.

16. Ibid., Vice Admiral Edward Thornbrough to Cotton, 4 January 1812, Berkeley to Cotton, 23 November 1811, Keats to Cotton, 13 December 1811, Pellew to Cotton, 14 December 1811, Pickmore to Cotton, 23 December 1812.

17. Ibid., Cockburn to Cotton, 1 January 1812, and one undated letter, Cockburn to Lady Cotton, 2 June 1812, and one undated letter, Judgment of John Lens, Lincolns Inn, 4 July 1812, Joseph Blandford to Lady Cotton, 9 July 1813.

18. "Memoir of Cotton," *Naval Chronicle* 27 (1812): 390.

19. *The Times* of London, 9, 21 October 1811.

20. Croker to Cotton, 7 October 1811, PRO ADM 2/966.

21. Cotton to Captain, the Honorable John, Lord Colville, 11 November 1811, National Maritime Museum, Keith Papers, KEI/35/1; *The Times* of London, 15 November 1811.

22. Extract of a letter received from Antwerp 19 September 1811, Croker to Cotton, 30 September 1811, National Maritime Museum, Keith Papers, KEI/35/1.

23. Ibid., Barrow to Cotton, 18 September 1811, Cotton to Neale, 30 November 1811.

24. Tobin embarked from Plymouth after receiving his orders. Strong eastern winds kept him bound to Coruña into January. Collier had not yet returnd to Coruña from his cruise, which included a raid in conjunction with the guerrillas on Bermeo in October. Collier to Croker, 20 October 1811, *Naval Chronicle* 26 (1811): 430; Tobin to Cotton, 10 January 1812, National Maritime Museum, Keith Papers, KEI/35/1.

25. Barrow to Cotton, 27 September 1811, National Maritime Museum, Keith Papers, KEI/35/1.

26. Ibid., Cotton to Tobin, 2 December 1811.

27. Ibid., Barrow to Cotton, 28 September 1811, 1 November 1811, Barrow to Cotton, 28 December 1808; *The Times* of London, 27 December 1811.

28. Unsigned report from the Foreign Office, 4 January 1812, Calder to Cotton, 6 January 1812, Barrow to Cotton, 11 January 1812, National Maritime Museum, Keith Papers, KEI/35/1; J.J Colledge, *Ships of the Royal Navy* (London, 1987), 381; Barrow to Cotton, 7 January 1812, PRO ADM 2/966; William Laird Clowes, *The Royal Navy: A History from the Earliest Times to the Present* (London, 1897–1903), 5: 499.

29. Cotton to King, 6 February 1812, National Maritime Museum, Keith Papers, KEI/35/1; Barrow to King, 24 February 1812, PRO ADM 2/966.

30. "Memoir of Cotton," *Naval Chronicle* 27 (1812): 390.

31. The Officers of HMS *San Josef* to Lady Cotton, 5 March 1812, Cambridgeshire County Record Office, Cotton Naval Papers, 588/c97.

32. "Memoir of Cotton," *Naval Chronicle* 27 (1812): 390–93.

33. Admiralty to Keith, 24 February 1812, *The Keith Papers*, 3: 224.

Epilogue

> If Fortune denied him opportunities of shining amongst the more illustrious naval heroes and conquerors of his time, Fame must, in justice to his memory, consign his steady perseverance, constant employment in the service of his country, uniform rectitude and integrity of conduct, and his generally useful, if not brilliant services, to the reverence of posterity; while there can scarcely be occasion to remark, that every British admiral cannot attain the envied distinction of a Nelson.
>
> —Dr. Thomas Morgan[1]

If James Ralfe intended to develop his own assessment of Cotton's naval career, he either failed or agreed entirely with the description offered by Cotton's secretary in 1812. Morgan's words were repeated verbatim in Ralfe's *Naval Biography*, without elaboration. But it seems that Ralfe refrained from comment because Morgan summarized the essence of Cotton's career so well. Even if the admiral's "picture" was looked at "in the most favourable point of view" with some defects omitted, Morgan's and Ralfe's final assessment was well-balanced.

Cotton lived during one of those rare periods in history when war was nearly a constant for a generation of officers. The professional benefits are obvious because experience usually is the best teacher and war opens doors of opportunity for glory and promotion not possible during peacetime. Attaining the rank of post-captain in 1779, the same year as Nelson and a year before Collingwood and Berkeley, Cotton was one among many senior British naval officers during the Napoleonic period whose formative years were shaped by participation in the war for American independence. Serving under admirals the likes of Rodney, Howe, and St. Vincent, Cotton and his contemporaries learned that successful naval operations depended on careful planning and centralized authority, combined with decentralized responsibility and bold execution. Every officer needed the skill and confidence to operate independently. No doubt, Cotton understood the nature of naval warfare as well as any of his peers. No notable example during his entire career cast doubt upon his technical mastery of the naval profession. However, two questions about Cotton beg an answer: Did "Fortune" deny him "opportunities of shining amongst the more illustrious naval heroes?" Did he fail to grasp the opportunities that were presented? The answer to both is yes.

Misunderstood communications and the *Boyne*'s fragile condition kept Cotton out of the fight at the Battle of Martinique on 17 April 1780. Condemnation of the Boyne a month after the battle suggests that the ship might not have been as responsive as Cotton had wished. Unfortunate positioning of the *Majestic* near the rear of the line appeared the main reason that Cotton did not have a more decisive ship-to-ship engagement on "The Glorious First of June" in 1794. Admiral Lord Howe's self-admitted bungling of the awards process left an emotionally distraught Cotton without this battle's gold medal and chain. His rendezvous with destiny continued on hold. Apparently Cotton missed commanding the lee division at Trafalgar because he was unavailable when Cornwallis needed an officer to lead a squadron to El Ferrol. The First Lord ordered Cotton to El Ferrol with twenty ships-of-the-line three days after Cornwallis, upon his own initiative, had sent Sir Robert Calder there with a squadron. That squadron subsequently proceeded to Cadiz, where, had Cotton gone, he was senior to Collingwood and presumably would have become second-in-command at Trafalgar. It thus seems that bad luck plagued Cotton throughout his career. Yet leaders often create their own luck, a talent that Cotton lacked to a certain extent. If Cotton had had a more aggressive instinct, for example, then the *Boyne* and *Majestic* might have been in better positions for decisive engagements. And it will forever be left to speculation how Cotton's fifteen ships-of-the-line would have fared against Admiral Ganteaume's twenty-one ships-of-the-line when they temporarily anchored off the entrance to Brest on 27 March 1805.

It is not suggested that Cotton was timid in the face of battle. He had ample opportunities to prove his physical courage. The best example was in June 1795 during the withdrawal of Admiral Cornwallis' small detachment from a French force of nearly thirty sail. His handling of the *Mars* in a rearguard action was crucial to the British escape. Nevertheless, while Cotton proved steady and courageous in the face of physical danger, his career offers no evidence that he could be expected to make the morally courageous decisions that placed Nelson in the pantheon of heroes. Cotton's consistent reliability and sound judgment compensated, however, for a risk-averse instinct concerning decisions with profound strategic consequences. Still, the nature of his command responsibilities required him to make important operational and strategic decisions on a routine basis. Fleet administration, blockade duty, and diplomacy rarely required brilliance or aggressiveness. These missions were best accomplished by the application of an admiral's expertise, patience, and strategic awareness. Cotton, as shown in the previous chapters, consistently displayed these traits during his various commands around the Iberian Peninsula. Carl von Clausewitz's definition of character aptly explains the foundation of Cotton's naval proficiency: "Strength of character does not consist solely in having powerful feelings, but in maintaining one's balance in spite of them. Even with the violence of emotion, judgment and principle must still function like a ship's compass, which records the slightest variations however rough the sea."[2]

Two of Cotton's contemporaries, Thomas Grenville and Thomas Francis Fremantle, were extremely critical of his professional ability. Cotton probably deserved some of their criticism, but it was too narrowly focused to conclude that he was incompetent or unprofessional. In addition, the credibility of Grenville's and Fremantle's criticism was highly suspect. Grenville was First Lord for only six months; Fremantle did not limit his harsh criticism to Cotton alone. Their criticism does suggest, however, that Cotton's ability to inspire confidence in seniors and subordinates needed improvement. Senior leaders in any field of endeavor need a degree of presentation and charisma, not only to inspire but also to discourage negative criticism. To further balance the opinions of Grenville and Fremantle, several respected British leaders held Cotton in high regard and relied on his abilities.[3] Admirals Cornwallis and St. Vincent trusted him as an able lieutenant in the Channel Fleet for several consecutive years; Collingwood considered him a good friend and professional equal; and Lord Mulgrave and Charles Yorke, First Lords of the Admiralty, also demonstrated their trust and confidence by appointing him to the commands off the Tagus, in the Mediterranean, and in the Channel.

Having held three distinct commands that encompassed the Iberian perimeter, Cotton had a unique influence on the Royal Navy's contribution to the Peninsular War. He made an important impact in 1808 by his assistance to the Portuguese and support of Wellesley's campaign. Cotton's cooperation with the Portuguese as they prepared for war against the French serves as a useful case study for leaders in today's strategic environment, where the integration of military and civil operations is the cornerstone for success in an increasing number of international stability operations; the nearly seamless integration of naval and land power by Cotton and Wellesley when the British army arrived in Portugal remains one of the best historical examples of the right way to conduct an amphibious campaign. Though Cotton fulfilled his original mission off Portugal by capturing Admiral Seniavin's Russian squadron in the wake of Wellesley's campaign, it was not accomplished in the manner by which "Fame" designates heroes for "the reverence of posterity"—there was a conspicuous, albeit admirable, absence of violence and bloodshed, and some considered the provisions of the settlement a stain upon British honor. The question of Cotton's influence upon the unpopular Convention of Cintra discouraged public recognition for his overall contribution to the Portuguese cause in 1808 and will forever be a subject for debate.

The First Lord nonetheless perceived the value of Cotton's service off the Tagus and trusted him with command of the Mediterranean Fleet, where the scope of responsibilities was exponentially greater, spanning the entire Mediterranean. Hence, Cotton's involvement with the Peninsular War while at Mahón or off Toulon was much less focused than it had been in 1808. Yet his emphasis on securing the naval stores at Carthagena and interest in the squadron off Catalonia provided notable moral and material support for the beleaguered Spaniards in 1810 and 1811, a time when Wellington called for more intensive military efforts on the Iberian perimeter to serve as diversions in support of his Anglo-Portuguese army based in Lisbon. Unfortunately, death prevented Cotton from making an assessable impact on the war along the north coast of Spain in 1812. Had he lived, his name would have been linked to Admiral Popham's and Captain Collier's naval operations, which more directly supported Wellington's army as it advanced toward the Pyrenees and shifted its base of operations from Lisbon to the Biscay ports. No other naval officer at the time of Cotton's death had his breadth of experience with the Peninsular War, and, with the exception of Admiral Berkeley who succeeded him in the Tagus, perhaps no other had a better comprehensive understanding of how naval power contributed to the war's prosecution.

If "Fortune and Fame" are not the standards of measurement, then Admiral Sir Charles Cotton had a successful naval career worthy of emulation. He reached the pinnacle of rank and held prestigious, important commands. Most of his peers, some cloaked with the glory of naval combat, could not claim these distinctions. Cotton earned these honors through hard work, resolute character, and life-long devotion to the service whose "wooden walls" protected his beloved country. Without doubt a conspicuous battle death at the height of his career would have resulted in innumerable leadership studies of him. Yet, there has been only one Nelson, whose "cult" has dominated the way succeeding generations have perceived naval leadership during the age of Napoleon. In this shadow, there were many officers like Sir Charles Cotton without whom the Royal Navy would have failed miserably in its attempt to neutralize French naval power and establish conditions for allied military success on the Continent. These overlooked officers rise from obscurity as testimonies to the enduring value of leadership, which history has shown to be the deciding factor in warfare when all other factors are equal.

NOTES

1. "Memoir of Cotton," *The Naval Chronicle* 27 (1812): 395; James Ralfe, *The Naval Biography of Great Britain* (London, 1828), 2: 223.

2. Carl von Clausewitz, *On War*, ed. and trans. Michael Howard and Peter Paret (Princeton, 1989), 107.

3. Though he was an experienced politician, Thomas Grenville's military experience was limited. In 1779 he was gazetted a lieutenant in the 80th Foot, but he was soon forced to resign this appointment. His service as First Lord of the Admiralty lasted from 29 September 1806 to March 1807. Nelson significantly influenced Thomas Fremantle's naval career. Fremantle was with Nelson at Bastia in 1794, Copenhagen in 1801, and Trafalgar in 1805. See Leslie Stephen and Sydney Lee, eds., *Dictionary of National Biography* (London, 1885–1901), 7: 688, 689, 8: 575, 576; Chris Cook and John Stevenson, *British Historical Facts, 1760–1830* (New York, 1980), 17.

Bibliography

MANUSCRIPTS

The Cambridgeshire County Record Office contains the Cotton Naval Papers, one of the most valuable collections used in this work. In addition to many private and official letters related to Cotton's career, several personal letters to and from his family and a log book of the *Prince* are held in this collection.

The British Library, in London, contains pertinent correspondence in the following ADD MSS: 23207, 35201, 35649, 35755, 35684, 37292, 38246, 49487, and 49489 in the papers of Hardwicke, Wellesley, Bridport, Liverpool, and John Willoughby Gordon. Of particular significance were the Liverpool MSS, which provided letters related to the north coast of Spain in 1811, and the Hardwicke MSS, which provided a few letters related to Cotton's personal life.

The Public Record Office, in Kew, London, provided the bulk of manuscripts used in this work. Most substantial was the Admiralty correspondence found in ADM 1/339, 1/340, 1/416, and 1/417 (letters to the Admiralty) and ADM 7/41, 7/42, and 7/43 (letters to and from the Admiralty; to and from subordinates). In addition, several ADM 2 letters from the Admiralty proved useful.

The National Maritime Museum, in Greenwich, contained several useful letters and documents, including: AGC/36, KEA/12, KEI/35, MKH/116, and YOR/3. The Sir Samuel Hood and Charles Philip Yorke papers provided much relevant information for the years 1810–1812.

The University of Southampton's Hartley Library holds the Duke of Wellington Collection. Though most letters from Wellington have been published, many to him have not. The collection contains several valuable unpublished letters from Cotton to Wellesley in 1808.

The Duke University's William R. Perkins Library contains two letters from Cotton to Blackwood in July 1810.

The Huntington Library, in San Marino, California, provided a letter from the Stowe-Grenville Collection.

The Library of Congress, in Washington, D.C., proved of limited value. The Mary

Edith Powell Collection in the Special Collections contains only an appointment certificate and a letter related to Cotton from 1781.

The New York Public Library contains numerous log books, but I used only that of HMS *Temeraire*, 1807–1810.

The Yale University's Sterling Memorial Library contained the log book of Cotton's flagship, HMS *San Josef*, 13 May 1809–14 May 1813.

PUBLISHED CORRESPONDENCE, MEMOIRS, DIARIES

Aspinall, Arthur, ed. *The Later Correspondence of George III*. 5 vols. Cambridge: Cambridge University Press, 1962–1970.

Barbaroux, Charle Ogé. *Adventures of a French Serjeant, during his campaigns in Italy, Spain, Germany, Russia, &c. from 1805 to 1823*. Philadelphia: J.J. Woodward, 1827.

Barrow, John. *The Life and Correspondence of Admiral Sir William Sidney Smith*. 2 vols. London: Richard Bentley, 1848.

Bathurst, Henry. *Report on the Manuscripts of the Earl Bathurst preserved at Cirencester Park*. Historical Manuscripts Commission. London: His Majesty's Stationery Office, 1923.

Bonaparte, Napoleon. *Correspondance de Napoléon Ier, publiée par order de l'Empereur Napoléon III*. 32 vols. Paris: Imprimerie Impériale, 1858–1869.

———. *Napoleon's Letters*. Translated by J.M. Thompson. London: J.M. Dent & Sons, 1934.

———. *Unpublished Correspondence of Napoleon I preserved in the War Archives*. Published by Ernest Picard and Louis Tuetey. Translated by Louise Houghton. 3 vols. New York: Duffield, 1913.

Bourchier, Lady Jane, ed. *Memoir of the Life of Admiral Sir Edward Codrington*. 2 vols. London: Longmans, Green, and Company, 1873.

Brenton, Edward Pelham, ed. *Life and Correspondence of John Earl of St. Vincent*. 2 vols. London: Henry Colburn, 1838.

———. *The Naval History of Great Britain from the Year 1783 to 1822*. 5 vols. London: C. Rice, 1823–25.

Buckingham and Chandos, K.G., Duke of, ed. *Memoirs of the Court and Cabinets of George the Third*. 4 vols. London: Hurst and Blackett, 1855.

———, ed. *Memoirs of the Court of England, during the Regency, 1811–1820*. 2 vols. London: Hurst and Blackett, 1856.

Bunbury, Lieutenant General Sir Henry Edward. *Narratives of Some Passages in the Great War with France, from 1799 to 1810*. London: Richard Bentley, 1854.

Castlereagh, Robert Stewart, Viscount. *Memoirs and Correspondence of Viscount Castlereagh, second Marquess of Londonderry*. 12 vols. Edited by his brother, Charles Vane, Marquess of Londonderry. London: H. Colburn, 1848–1853.

Cochrane, Thomas, Earl of Dundonald. *Autobiography of a Seaman*. London: Maclaren and Comapany, 1908.

Cockburn, Lieutenant General Sir George. *A Voyage to Cadiz and Gibraltar up the Mediterranean to Sicily and Malta in 1810, & 1811*. 2 vols. London: J. Harding, 1815.

Collingwood, G.L. Newnham, ed. *Selection from the Public and Private Correspondence of Vice-Admiral Lord Collingwood.* New York: G. & C. & H. Carvill, 1829.

Corbett, Julian, ed. *Fighting Instructions: 1530–1816.* 1905. Reprint, New York: Burt Franklin, 1967.

Cornwallis-West, G., ed. *Life and Letters of Admiral Cornwallis.* London: Robert Holden, 1927.

Dalrymple, Lieutenant General Sir Hew. *Memoir of His Proceedings as Connected with the Affairs of Spain and the Commencement of the Peninsular War.* London: Thomas and William Boone, Strand, 1830.

Fortescue, J.B. *Report on the Manuscripts of J.B. Fortescue, Esq., preserved at Dropmore.* 10 vols. Historical Manuscripts Commission. London: Her Majesty's Stationary Office, 1892–1927.

Foy, Maximilien Sébastian. *History of the War in the Peninsula.* 2 vols. Translated from the French. London: Treuttel and Würtz, 1827.

Gavin, William. *The Diary of William Gavin, Ensign and Quarter-master, 71st Highland Regiment, 1806–1815.* Privately printed, 1921.

Graham, Gerald S., and R.A. Humphreys, eds. *The Navy and South America.* London: Navy Records Society, 1962.

Hoste, William. *Service Afloat, or The Naval Career of Sir William Hoste.* London: W.H. Allen & Co., 1887.

Huges, Edward, ed. *The Private Correspondence of Admiral Lord Collingwood.* London: Navy Records Society, 1957.

Jackson, Thomas Sturges, ed. *Logs of the Great Sea Fights, 1794–1805.* 2 vols. London: Navy Records Society, 1899–1900.

King-Hall, Louise, ed. *Sea Saga, being the diaries of four generations of the King-Hall family.* London: Victor Gollancz, 1935.

Laughton, John Knox, ed. *Letters and Papers of Charles, Lord Barham, Admiral of the Red Squadron, 1758–1813.* 3 vols. London: Navy Records Society, 1907–1911.

Leach, Jonathan. *Rough Sketches of the Life of an Old Soldier.* London: Longmans, Rees, Orme, Brown, and Green, 1831.

Lewis, W.S., and A. Dayle Wallace, eds. *Horace Walpole's Correspondence with the Reverend William Cole.* 48 vols. New Haven: Yale University Press, 1937-1983.

Leyland, John, ed. *Dispatches and Letters Relating to the Blockade of Brest, 1803–1805.* 2 vols. London: Navy Records Society, 1902.

Lloyd, Christopher, ed. *The Keith Papers.* Vol. 3. London: Navy Records Society, 1955.

Molyneux, Thomas More. *Conjunct Expeditions; Or Expeditions that have been carried on jointly by the Fleet and Army; with a Commentary on a Littoral War.* London: R. and J. Dodsley, 1759.

Mundy, Godfrey B. *The Life and Correspondence of the Late Admiral Lord Rodney.* 2 vols. 1848. Reprint, Boston: Gregg Press, 1972.

Narrative of the Proceedings of His Majesty's Fleet under the Command of Earl Howe, from the Second of May to the Second of June. London: privately printed, 1796.

Nicolas, Nicholas Harris, ed. *The Dispatches and Letters of Vice Admiral Lord Viscount Nelson.* 7 vols. London: Henry Colburn, 1844–1846.

Paget, Arthur, Lord Hylton, ed. *The Paget Brothers, 1790–1840.* London: John Murray, 1918.

Papers, Presented to the House of Commons, Relative to the Russian Fleet in the Tagus, and to the Convention concluded with the Russian Admiral. 2 parts. London: House of Commons, 9 February 1809.

Parry, Ann, ed. *The Admirals Fremantle.* London: Chatto & Windus, 1971.

Perrin, W.G., ed. *The Keith Papers.* Vol. 1. London: Navy Records Society, 1927.

Proceedings upon the Inquiry relative to The Armistice and Convention, &c. made and concluded in Portugal, in August 1808, between The Commanders of the British and French Armies. London: House of Commons, 1809.

Rees, Thomas. *A Journal of Voyages and Travels, by the late Thomas Rees, Serjeant of Marines.* London: Harvey and Darton, 1822.

Richmond, Rear Admiral Sir Herbert W., ed. *Private Papers of George, Second Earl of Spencer, First Lord of the Admiralty, 1794–1801.* 3 vols. London: Navy Records Society, 1913–1924.

Robinson, Daniel. "Diary of Royal Marine Colonel Daniel Robinson." In possession of Dr. Robin N.W. Thomas, University of Southhampton, United Kingdom.

Rodney, George. *Letter-Books and Order-Book of George, Lord Rodney, Admiral of the White Squadron, 1780–1782.* 2 vols. New York: New York Historical Society, 1932.

Russell of Liverpool, Lord. *Knight of the Sword: The Life and Letters of Admiral Sir William Sidney Smith G.C.B.* London: Victor Gollancz, 1964.

Smith, David Bonner, ed. *Letters of Admiral of the Fleet The Earl of St. Vincent, whilst First Lord of the Admiralty, 1801–1804.* 2 vols. London: Navy Records Society, 1927.

Suchet, Marshal Louis Gabriel. *Memoirs of the War in Spain, from 1808 to 1814.* 1829. Reprint, Felling, England: Worley, 1986.

Thiébault, Baron Paul Charles. *The Memoirs of Baron Thiébault.* 2 vols. Translated by Arthur John Butler. London: Smith, Elder & Co., 1896.

———. *Relation de l'expédition du Portugal, faite en 1807 et 1808, par le 1er corps d'observation de la Gironde, devenu armée de Portugal.* Paris: Magimel, Anselin, et Pochard, 1817.

Warre, Lieutenant General Sir William. *Letters from the Peninsula, 1808–1812.* Edited by his nephew, The Reverend Edmond Warre. London: John Murray, 1909.

Wellington, Arthur Wellesley, Duke of. *The Dispatches of Field Marshal the Duke of Wellington, during His Various Campaigns in India, Denmark, Portugal, Spain, the Low Countries, and France, from 1799 to 1818.* 8 vols. Edited by John Gurwood. London: John Murray, 1852.

———. *Supplementary Despatches, Correspondence, and Memoranda of Field Marshal Arthur Duke of Wellington, K.G.* 15 vols. Edited by his son, The Duke of Wellington, K.G. London: John Murray, 1858–1872.

Whittingham, Major General Ferdinand, ed. *A Memoir of the Services of Lieutenant-General Sir Samuel Ford Whittingham.* London: Longmans, Green, and Co., 1868.

NEWSPAPERS, JOURNALS

The Naval Chronicle. 40 vols. London: Joyce Gold, 1799–1818.

The Times of London. 1800, 1808–1812.

SECONDARY SOURCES

Allardyce, Alexander. *Memoir of the Honourable George Keith Elphinstone, K.B., Viscount Keith, Admiral of the Red.* London: William Blackwood, 1882.

Anderson, M.S. "Great Britain and the Growth of the Russian Navy in the Eighteenth Century." *Mariner's Mirror* 42 (1956): 132–46.

Anderson, Roger Charles. *Naval Wars in the Levant, 1559–1853*. Princeton: Princeton University Press, 1952.

Arthur, Charles. *The Remaking of the English Navy by Admiral St. Vincent: Key to the Victory over Napoleon*. New York: Lanham, 1986.

Atteridge, Andrew Hilliard. *Joachim Murat: Marshal of France and King of Naples*. New York: Bretano's, 1911.

Barrow, John. *The Life of Richard Earl Howe, K.G., Admiral of the Fleet, and General of Marines*. London: John Murray, 1838.

Beatson, Robert. *Naval and Military Memoirs of Great Britain from 1727 to 1783*. 1804. Reprint, Boston: Gregg Press, 1972.

Bennett, Geoffrey. *Battle of Trafalgar*. Annapolis: Naval Institute Press, 1977.

Blanning, T.C.W. *The French Revolutionary Wars, 1787–1802*. London: Arnold, 1996.

Brett-James, Antony. *General Graham, Lord Lynedoch*. New York: St. Martin's Press, 1959.

Brun, V. *Guerres Maritimes de la France: Port de Toulon ses armements, son administration, depuis son origine jusqu'a nos jours*. 2 vols. Paris: Henri Plon, imprimeur-éditeur, 1861.

Cambridge American Cemetery and Memorial. American Battle Monuments Commission. 1975.

Chevalier, Édouard. *Histoire de la Marine Français sous la Première République*. Paris: L. Hachett, 1886.

Clausewitz, Carl von. *On War*. Edited and translated by Michael Howard and Peter Paret. Princeton: Princeton University Press, 1989.

Clowes, William Laird. *The Royal Navy: A History from the Earliest Times to the Present*. 7 vols. London: Sampson Low, Marston, and Company, Ltd., 1897–1903.

Colledge, J.J. *Ships of the Royal Navy: An Historical Index*. London: Greenhill Books, 1987.

Colley, Linda. *Britons: Forging the Nation, 1707–1837*. New Haven: Yale University Press, 1992.

Come, Donald R. "French Threat to British Shores, 1793–1798." *Military Affairs* 16 (1952): 174-88.

Cook, Chris, and John Stevenson. *British Historical Facts, 1760–1830*. New York: Macmillan, 1980.

Cooper, Guy E. "The Methods of Blockade and Observation Employed during the Revolutionary and Napoleonic Wars." *Journal of the Royal United Service Institution* 61 (1916): 523–50.

Corbett, Julian S. *Some Principles of Maritime Strategy*. London: Longmans, Green, and Co., 1911. Reprint, Annapolis: Naval Institute Press, 1988.

Cormack, William. *Revolution and Political Conflict in the French Navy, 1789–1794*. Cambridge: Cambridge University Press, 1995.

Creswell, John. *British Admirals of the Eighteenth Century: Tactics in Battle*. London: Archon Books, 1972.

———. *Generals and Admirals: The Story of Amphibious Command.* Westport, Conn.: Greenwood Press, 1976.

Crook, Malcolm. *Toulon in War and Revolution: From the Ancien Régime to the Restoration, 1750–1820*. Manchester: Manchester University Press, 1991.

Crowhurst, Patrick. *French War on Trade: Privateering, 1793–1815*. Aldershot: Gower Publishing Company, 1989.

Daly, Robert W. "Operations of the Russian Navy during the Reign of Napoleon I." *Mariner's Mirror* 34 (1948): 169–83.

Davydov, I.U. *Seniavin*. Moscow: Molodaia Gvardiia, 1972.

Delaporte, André. "Combats de Prairial et Convoi de Vanstabel: le point de vue français." *Revue historique des armées* 4 (1995): 13–22.

Desbrière, Édouard. *Projets et Tentatives de Débarquement aux Iles Britanniques, 1793–1805*. 4 vols. Paris: R. Chapelot, 1900–1902.

De Toy, Brian M. "Wellington's Admiral: The Life and Career of George Berkeley, 1753-1818." Ph.D. dissertation, Florida State University, 1997.

Deutsch, Harold C. *The Genesis of Napoleonic Imperialism*. Cambridge: Harvard University Press, 1938.

Douin, Georges. *La Campagne de Bruix en Méditerranée, Mars-Août 1799*. Paris: Société d'Éditions Géographiques, Maritimes et Coloniales, 1923.

DuPont, Maurice. *L'Amiral Decrès et Napoleon, ou la fidélité orageuse d'un ministre*. Paris: Economica, 1991.

Emmott, N.W., and J.N. Portney. "The Seniavin Saga." *Litton Avionics Newsletter*, United States Air Force Academy Library (undated): 66–96.

Field Manual 100-5: Operations. Headquarters, Department of the Army. 1993.

Fortescue, Sir John William. *A History of the British Army*. 20 vols. London: Macmillan, 1910–1930.

Fraser, Edward, and L.G. Carr-Laughton. *The Royal Marine Artillery, 1804–1923*. 2 vols. London: The Royal United Service Institution, 1930.

Fugier, André. *Napoléon et l'Espagne*. 2 vols. Paris: Librairie Félix Alcan, 1930.

Gill, Conrad. *Naval Mutinies of 1797*. Manchester: Manchester University Press, 1913.

Glover, Michael. *Britannia Sickens: Sir Arthur Wellesley and the Convention of Cintra*. London: Leo Cooper, 1970.

Grasset, Alphonse Louis. *La Guerre d'Espagne (1807–1813)*. 3 vols. Paris: Berger-Levrault, 1914.

Gregory, Desmond. *Sicily, The Insecure Base: A History of the British Occupation of Sicily, 1806–1815*. Rutherford: Fairleigh Dickinson University Press, 1988.

Gutridge, Tony. "Aspects of Naval Prize Agency, 1793–1815." *Mariner's Mirror* 80 (1994): 45–53.

Harbron, John D. *Trafalgar and the Spanish Navy*. Annapolis: Naval Institute Press, 1988.

Harding, Richard. "Sailors and Gentlemen of Parade: Some Professional and Technical Problems Concerning the Conduct of Combined Operations in the Eighteenth Century." *Historical Journal* 32 (1989): 35–55.

Hepper, David. *British Warship Losses in the Age of Sail, 1650–1859*. East Sussex: Jean Boudriot Publications, 1994.

Horsfield, John. *Art of Leadership in War: The Royal Navy from the Age of Nelson to the End of World War II*. Westport, Conn.: Greenwood Press, 1980.

Horward, Donald D. "British Seapower and Its Influence upon the Peninsular War, 1808–1814." *Naval War College Review* 31 (1978): 54–71.

———. "Portugal and the Anglo-Russian Naval Crisis, 1808." *Naval War College Review* 34 (1981): 48–74.

Howarth, David. *Trafalgar: The Nelson Touch*. New York: Atheneum, 1969.

Jenkins, Ernest. *A History of the French Navy*. London: Macdonald and Jane's, 1973.

Lavery, Brian. *Nelson's Navy: The Ships, Men and Organisation, 1793–1815*. London: Conway Maritime Press, 1989.

Lewis, Michael A. *The Navy in Transition, 1814–1864: A Social History*. London: Hodder and Stoughton, 1965.

Lovett, Gabriel H. *Napoleon and the Birth of Modern Spain II: The Struggle, Without and Within*. New York: New York University Press, 1965.

Low, Charles R. *Her Majesty's Navy, including its Deeds and Battles*. 3 vols. New York: J. Arnot Penman, 1892.

MacKay, Charles. "The Tempest: The Life and Career of Jean-Andoche Junot, 1771–1813." Ph.D. dissertation, Florida State University, 1995.

Mackesy, Piers. "Problems of an Amphibious Power: Britain against France, 1793–1815." *Naval War College Review* 30 (Spring, 1978): 16–25.

———. *The War for America, 1775–1783*. Cambridge: Harvard University Press, 1964.

———. *The War in the Mediterranean, 1803–1810*. London: Longmans, 1957.

Madingley Hall: A guide to the interior and exterior of the house. Cambridge: University of Cambridge Board of Continuing Education, 1986.

Marcus, Geoffrey Jules. *The Age of Nelson; the Royal Navy, 1793–1815*. New York: Viking Press, 1971.

Marshall, John. *Royal Navy Biography*. London: Longman, Hurst, Orme, and Brown, 1823–1835.

Maurer, Maurer. "Coppered Bottoms for the Royal Navy: A Factor in the Maritime War of 1775–1783." *Military Affairs* 14 (1950): 57–61.

Munby, Lionel. "Lecture Notes on Sir Charles Cotton." In possession of the author, undated.

Oman, Sir Charles William Chadwick. *A History of the Peninsular War*. 7 vols. Oxford: Clarendon Press, 1902–1930.

Pack, James. *The Man Who Burned the White House: Admiral Sir George Cockburn, 1772–1853*. Emsworth, Hampshire: Kenneth Mason, 1987.

Parkinson, C. Northcote. *Britannia Rules: The Classic Age of Naval History, 1793–1815*. London: Weidenfield and Nicolson, 1977.

———. *Edward Pellew, Viscount Exmouth, Admiral of the Red*. London: Methuen & Co., 1934.

Penrose, John. *Lives of Vice-Admiral Sir Charles Vinicombe Penrose, K.C.B., and Captain James Trevenen*. London: John Murray, 1850.

Popham, Hugh. *A Damned Cunning Fellow: The Eventful Life of Rear-Admiral Sir Home Popham, KCB, KCH, KM, FRS, 1762–1820*. Tywardreath, Cornwall: Old Ferry Press, 1991.

Ralfe, James. *The Naval Biography of Great Britain: Consisting of Historical Memoirs of Those Officers of the British Navy Who Distinguished Themselves during the Reign of His Majesty George III*. 1828. Reprint, Boston: Gregg Press, 1972.

Rodger, N.A.M. *The Wooden World: An Anatomy of the Georgian Navy*. Annapolis: Naval Institute Press, 1986.

———. "Patronage and Competence." In *Les Marines de Guerre Européennes XVII–XVIIIe siècles,* ed. Martine Acerra. Paris: Presses de l'Université de Paris-Sorbonne, 1985.

Rose, John M. "Landing of Expeditionary Forces." *Journal of the Royal United Service Institution* 39 (1895): 672–720.

Ross, R.D. "The Naval Officer, 1793–1815: His Efficiency, Conditions of Service, Prospects and Handicaps." *Army Quarterly and Defence Journal* 78 (1959): 71–95.

Ryan, A.N. "The Causes of the British Attack upon Copenhagen in 1807." *English Historical Review* 68 (1953): 37–55.

———. "The Royal Navy and the Blockade of Brest, 1689–1805: Theory and Practice." In *Les Marines de Guerre Européennes XVII-XVIIIe siècles,* ed. Martine Acerra. Paris: Presses de l'Université de Paris-Sorbonne, 1985.

Saxby, Richard. "Lord Bridport and the Spithead Mutiny." *Mariner's Mirror* 79 (1993): 170–78.

Schneer, Richard M. "Arthur Wellesley and the Cintra Convention: A New Look at an Old Puzzle." *Journal of British Studies* 19 (1980): 93–119.

Shapiro, A. *Admiral Dmitri N. Seniavin*. Moscow: Voennoe izdatel'stvo, 1958.

Shore, Henry N. "The Navy in the Peninsular War." *United Service Magazine* (June 1912–March 1914, in thirteen parts).

Six, Georges. *Dictionnaire Biographique des Généraux and Amiraux Français de la Révolution et de L'Empire, 1792–1814*. 2 vols. Paris: Librairie Historique et Nobiliaire, 1934.

Solberg, Thorvald. "Some Notes on the Balearic Islands with Special Reference to their Bibliography." *The Papers of the Bibliographical Society of America* 21 (1927): 69–146.

Spinney, David. *Rodney*. Annapolis: Naval Institute Press, 1969.

Stephen, Leslie, and Sydney Lee, eds. *Dictionary of National Biography*. 22 vols. 1885–1901. Reprint, London: Oxford University Press, 1949–1950.

Syrett, David. "The Role of the Royal Navy in the Napoleonic Wars after Trafalgar, 1805–1814." *Naval War College Review* 32 (1979): 71–84.

Taillemite, Etienne. *Dictionnaire des Marin Français*. Paris: Editions Maritimes, 1982.

Thomas, Robin. "British Operations on the Coast of Catalonia, 1808–1811." In *New Lights on the Peninsular War*, ed. Alice D. Berkeley. Almada, Portugal: British Historical Society of Portugal, 1991.

———. "Palamos Revisited, December 13, 1810." *Journal of the Napoleonic Association* 2d ser., no. 1 (1987): 7–12.

Thomazi, A. *Napoléon et ses Marins*. Paris: Editions Berger-Levrault, 1950.

Thornton, Percy M. *Foreign Secretaries of the XIX Century to 1834*. 2 vols. London: W.H. Allen and Co., 1881.

Warner, Oliver. *The Glorious First of June*. New York: Macmillan, 1961.

———. *Nelson's Battles*. New York: Macmillan, 1965.

Webb, Paul. "The Frigate Situation of the Royal Navy, 1793–1815." *Mariner's Mirror* 82 (1996): 28–40.

Wheeler, H.F.B., and A.M. Broadley. *Napoleon and the Invasion of England: The Story of the Great Terror.* London: John Lane, 1908.

White, D. Fedotoff. "The Russian Navy in Trieste during the Wars of the Revolution and the Empire." *American Slavic and East European Review* 6 (1947): 25–41.

Wright, G.N. *Life and Campaigns of Arthur, Duke of Wellington, K.G.* 4 vols. London: Fisher, Son, & Co., 1841.

Index

About the Author

PAUL C. KRAJESKI currently serves in an infantry battalion in Tennessee. He has taught in the Department of History at West Point.

Recent Titles in
Contributions in Military Studies

The Moroccan Goums: Tribal Warriors in a Modern War
Edward L. Bimberg

Military Assistance: An Operational Perspective
William H. Mott IV

Desert Storm at Sea: What the Navy Really Did
Marvin Pokrant

A Peripheral Weapon? The Production and Employment of British Tanks in the First World War
David J. Childs

Where a Man Can Go: Major General William Phillips, British Royal Artillery, 1731–1781
Robert P. Davis

Truman, MacArthur, and the Korean War
Dennis D. Wainstock

Secret Soldiers of the Revolution: Soviet Military Intelligence, 1918–1933
Raymond W. Leonard

The Writing of Official Military History
Robin Higham, editor

Reorganizing the Joint Chiefs of Staff: The Goldwater-Nichols Act of 1986
Gordon Nathaniel Lederman

Bullies and Cowards: The West Point Hazing Scandal, 1898–1901
Philip W. Leon

The Bradley and How It Got That Way: Technology, Institutions, and the Problem of Mechanized Infantry in the United States Army
W. Blair Haworth, Jr.

Soldier and Warrior: French Attitudes Toward the Army and War on the Eve of the First World War
H. L. Wesseling

ISBN 0-313-31039-4
90000>
EAN
9 780313 310393
HARDCOVER BAR CODE